THE ILLUSTRATED
Rise & fall
OF THE
British Empire

On the Shores of Lake Albert Edward Nyanza

ley at Bay. Mount Rowenzora in the distance.

of Major Barttelot.

Slaves on the March.

Meeting of Emin and Stanley.

Tippoo Tib

THE ILLUSTRATED
Rise & fall
OF THE
British Empire

Lawrence James

Abridged by Helen Lownie

TED SMART

A Little, Brown Book

This edition produced for The Book People Ltd,
Hall Wood Avenue, Haydock, St Helens WA11 9UL

First published in Great Britain by Little, Brown and Company 1994
First published in paperback by Abacus 1995
Reprinted 1995, 1996 (twice), 1997, 1998

This illustrated edition abridged and published in Great Britain by
Little, Brown and Company 1999

A CIP catalogue record for this book
is available from the British Library.

ISBN 0 316 85147 7

Designer: Caroline Hill
Editor: Arianne Burnette
Maps: Neil Hislop

Printed and bound in Italy

Little, Brown and Company (UK)
Brettenham House
Lancaster Place
London WC2E 7EN

To the memory of Vivian and Tim Williams

I would like to thank my wife, Mary, for her encouragement
and forbearance during the preparation of this book and my sons, Edward
and Henry, for their assistance. Suggestions, advice and assistance in the
procurement of pictures were also provided by Geordie Burdett-Stuart,
Arianne Burnette, Julia Charles, Gregory Gifford, Gordon Hector, CMG,
CBE, Colin Lindsey-Macdougal, Andrew Lownie, Katherine MacDonald-
Keir, Richard Demarco, Alan Samson, Linda Silverman, Michael Staniforth,
Andrew Williams and Percy Wood. I am also indebted to the staffs of the
Imperial War and National Army Museums, the India Office Library,
the National Library of Scotland and, in particular, St Andrews University
and the university's photographic department.

Special thanks must be given to Helen Lownie
for the patience and flair she exercised in producing the abridgement and to
Caroline Hill for the same qualities in preparing text and pictures.

PICTURE PAGE 1

HM the Queen and Prince Philip visiting Fiji:
these visits were an excuse for festivities and strengthened the emotional bonds
within the Commonwealth.

PICTURE PAGE 3

Pathfinder:
Henry Morton Stanley, the Welsh journalist and explorer who
'found' Livingstone, surrounded by others who penetrated the Dark Continent
in the name of civilisation and progress.

CONTENTS

Introduction   8

PART ONE
EXCELLENT OPPORTUNITIES
1600-1689

1 My New-Found-Land: NORTH AMERICA   11
2 Baubles for the Souls of Men: THE WEST AND EAST INDIES   18
3 The Necessary Union of Plantations: CROWN AND COLONIES   24
4 Dispositions of Providence: THE COLONISTS   26

PART TWO
PERSIST & CONQUER
1689-1815

1 Rule of the Main: THE MAKING OF BRITISH SEAPOWER 1689–1748   31
2 'Tis to Glory We Steer: GAINS AND LOSSES 1749–1783   37

3 The Empire of America: SETTLEMENT AND WAR 1689–1775   42
4 The Descendants of Britons: NORTH AMERICA REBELS 1765–1775   49
5 The World Turned Upside Down: THE AMERICAN WAR OF INDEPENDENCE 1775–1783   53
6 The Terror of Our Arms: CONQUEST AND TRADE IN INDIA 1689–1815   60
7 The Desert of Waters: THE PACIFIC AND AUSTRALASIA   70
8 Wealth and Victory: THE STRUGGLE AGAINST FRANCE 1793–1815   76

PART THREE
WIDER STILL & WIDER
1815-1914

1 Power and Greatness: COMMERCE, SEAPOWER AND STRATEGY 1815–1870   85
2 We are Going as Civilisers: EMPIRE AND PUBLIC OPINION 1815–1880   90
3 The Mission of Our Race: BRITAIN AND THE 'NEW IMPERIALISM' 1880–1902   104
4 The Miracle of the World: INDIA 1815–1905   118
5 They Little Know Our Strength: THE FAR EAST AND THE PACIFIC   136
6 A Great English-Speaking Country: SOUTH AFRICA   149
7 That Heroic Soul: THE STRUGGLE FOR THE NILE   165
8 The Greatest Blessing that Africa has Known: EAST AND WEST AFRICA   178

9 Ye Sons of the Southern Cross: THE WHITE DOMINIONS 192

10 Be Brave, Be Bold, Do Right!: THE EDWARDIAN EMPIRE AND THE PEOPLE 202

11 To Join the Khaki Line: THE EMPIRE AND THE COMING OF WAR 214

PART FOUR
THE AGE OF IMPERIALISM IS ENDED
1914-1945

1 E is for Empire for which We Would Die *1914–1918* 223

2 Clear Out or Govern: TROUBLES, MAINLY IRISH *1919–1939* 233

3 Their Country's Dignity: EGYPT *1919–1942* 238

4 The Haughty Governess: THE MIDDLE EAST *1919–1942* 242

5 A New Force and New Power: INDIA *1919–1942* 250

6 For the Benefit of Everyone: CONCEPTS OF EMPIRE *1919–1939* 260

7 The Bond of One Spirit: THE PUBLIC FACE OF EMPIRE *1919–1939* 266

8 Finest Hour: THE EMPIRE AT WAR *1939–1941* 275

9 Steadfast Comrades: THE STRESSES OF WAR 283

10 The Defence of Archaic Privilege: THE EMPIRE RESTORED *1942–1945* 287

PART FIVE
THE SETTING SUN
1945-1993

1 The Colonialists are on the Rampage: THE EMPIRE IN THE POST-WAR WORLD 293

2 Friendly Relations: INDIA AND THE LIQUIDATION OF EMPIRE *1945–1947* 299

3 The World as It Is: MIDDLE EASTERN MISADVENTURES *1945–1956* 308

4 Kick Their Backsides: THE SUEZ WAR AND BEYOND 315

5 The Old Red, White and Blue: REACTIONS TO A DYING EMPIRE 320

6 Uhuru: TYING UP LOOSE ENDS *1959–1980* 325

7 Unfinished Business 336

Photographic Acknowledgements 342

Index 343

LIST OF MAPS

1 Seventeenth-Century Settlement in North America 13

2 The Caribbean and West Indies in the Eighteenth Century 19

3 The British Empire *1713* 33

4 North America *1755–1775* 43

5 American War of Independence *1776–1783* 54

6 Eighteenth-Century India 61

7 The British Empire *1850* 89

8 Nineteenth-Century India 120

9 China *1839–1900* 138

10 Nineteenth-Century Malaya 145

11 Southern Africa *1815–1902* 150

12 The Nile Valley *1882–1898* 169

13 East Africa in the Nineteenth Century 179

14 West Africa in the Nineteenth Century 185

15 Africa Partitioned *1914* 189

16 The British Empire *1914* 224

INTRODUCTION

Some time early in the 1980s I undertook a brief tour of what had once been the commercial powerhouse of the British empire. By then, that complex of wharves and solid brick warehouses which stood along the north shore of the Thames was derelict. Nonetheless, the overall effect was impressive, and the cast-iron street signs (Jamaica Street, Ceylon Street) advertised the sources of past prosperity. The abandoned docks of London and Liverpool and Bristol are among the grander monuments to Britain's moment of empire and world power.

There are others: the shells of Lancashire cotton mills which spun yarns for India; the shipyards of the Clyde and the Tyne which built steamers to carry Britain's trade and the men-o'-war which protected it; and the country houses of the merchants and nabobs-turned-country-squires who raked in the profits. One of the latter, Sir Charles Cockerell, having made a fortune in India at the end of the eighteenth century, had his mansion, Sezincote, built in a style which combines the novelties of the Prince Regent's Brighton Pavilion with Indian motifs, including a dome of the sort which would have been set over a mosque (see page 89). The Cotswold landscape around the house is enhanced with ornamental gardens with an Indian shrine and a bridge decorated with Brahmin bulls. Bringing India to Gloucestershire was a nice reminder that imperialism was a two-way process.

Human memorials of the empire are abundant. David Livingstone, one hand resting on his revolver and the other clasping a Bible, overlooks Prince's Street, Edinburgh. Walk up towards the castle and one is confronted by embattled, and, thanks to weathering, gaunt stone Highlanders, who form their countrymen's monument to the Boer War. Churches and cathedrals are draped with dusty, threadbare regimental ensigns embroidered with exotic names such as 'Chillianwala' and 'Tel-el-Kebir', and the men who died in these and other battles are often commemorated nearby in marble and brass. Pub signs celebrate imperial heroes, and street names conquests and conquerors. In the northern suburbs of Southampton I once saw a Khartoum Road and an Omdurman Road, and in the small West Riding town of Crosshills, a Rhodesia Road. All, to judge by the houses built along them, date from the beginning of the century.

The physical impact of the empire on Britain is easy to see, the mental is less obvious. Readers may detect in my chapters on the empire and the people the origins of codes of behaviour and outlook which still hold some sway, though less so than thirty or forty years ago when the empire was still in existence. I have tried to show that possession of an empire profoundly influenced the ways in which the British thought of themselves and the rest of the world. The British character was changed by the empire, and this is important. It encouraged a sense of superiority, which is also a feature of another former imperial power, France, that frequently bordered on downright xenophobia. It also fostered racial arrogance. And yet at the same time, deeply rooted liberal and evangelical ideals produced a powerful sense of imperial duty and mission. The empire existed to civilise and uplift its subjects, or so its champions claimed.

They had to, for the British were never entirely easy with the idea of territorial empire. From the seventeenth century, and with considerable official encouragement, the British were taught to be proud of their laws, individual freedoms and elected government. But, many asked, were the rights of the British exclusive, or could they be exported and shared by everyone under Britain's rule? This question dogged the empire throughout its history and, given that at crucial moments the answer was 'yes', proved to be its eventual undoing. In looking at the eighty years, roughly from the mid-1880s to the mid-1960s, when the empire reached its zenith and then declined, I have endeavoured to examine a related issue, how the

British saw their empire. During this period, Britain became a democracy and so the empire could not have been sustained without the general approval of the British people. This is vital both in explaining imperial growth and imperial decline.

Ideas alone did not make the empire. Its story is the sum of the lives of the men and women who built and ruled it. Some achieved greatness, making headlines and in time finding themselves heroes whose deeds became schoolroom reading. Their characters, carefully sifted of all baser qualities, became models for future generations. The superheroes of empire were a mixed bag. There were the conventional but brilliant commanders and statesmen such as Pitt, Wolfe, Rodney, Nelson and Wellington who did their duty according to lofty principles, and were respected accordingly. There were also the wayward who, shipped to a foreign land, discovered hidden energies and vision. Clive was the first, and then Gordon, who, like so many empire-builders, imagined himself the agent of a Divine Providence which had singled out Britain as the maker of a better world. Britain's imperial destiny was also Rhodes's lodestar, but it was clouded by ambition and ruthlessness. Lastly, for the twentieth century there was Lawrence of Arabia, meretricious but fundamentally decent, adding a dash of lustre to the imperial sunset.

Making an empire and setting one's personal stamp on it were more glamorous activities than dismantling it. No one emerged from imperial disengagement with the romantic allure of a Clive or a Lawrence. Mountbatten came close, but he was a shallow figure who owed more to his royal attachments (between the death of William IV and the late 1980s the royal family enjoyed unprecedented reverence) than any outstanding talent. Rather, it was Attlee, Macleod and Macmillan who were, I believe, the real heroes of imperial retreat, which they supervised with considerable political adroitness. Unlike France's, Portugal's or Russia's, Britain's empire did not dissolve in tears.

At every stage in this survey, I have looked at the thoughts and actions of many lesser figures. Most important perhaps are the millions who took part in the British diaspora, that process which took colonists to North America, Australasia and South Africa. On this subject, I have been as careful as possible to sidestep the quagmire of post-imperial guilt, that peculiar *angst* which has troubled the British and American intelligentsia for the past thirty or so years. Wherever possible, I have avoided joining in those battles between armies of the night who contend over the rights and wrongs of empires. History cannot be unwritten or written in the subjunctive, and the wholesale application of late twentieth-century values distorts the past and makes it less comprehensible. I have, therefore, left conquerors and colonists to speak for themselves, aware that their authentic voices may sometimes grate on today's sensibilities.

What matters most today is that the British empire transformed the world. What it has now become is in considerable part the consequence of three hundred years of British overseas expansion. The present-day demography, economy and political life of North America and much of Asia, the Middle East, Africa and the Pacific owes much to former British rule and influence. English is the most widely spoken global language, and the governance, everyday lives and habits of mind of hundreds of millions of men and women have been shaped by prolonged contact with Britain and its values. For better or worse, the modern, post-imperial world is the product of that age of empires which extended from the early sixteenth to the early twentieth centuries. Britain got most, in every sense, from this surge of European expansion.

I have tried to explain how, why and with what result, and I hope that I have done so with a certain degree of dispassion. I have written in the knowledge that the complex legacy of the British empire remains. Its physical and psychological impact was enormous everywhere, including in Britain. That this country is now a multi-racial nation is a direct consequence of its having once been an imperial one. For this reason alone, it is worth looking closely at the making and nature of the empire, the more so since its history and that of its creators is being excised from school syllabuses. What I have written will, I hope, make its past more understandable to all those who are its inheritors.

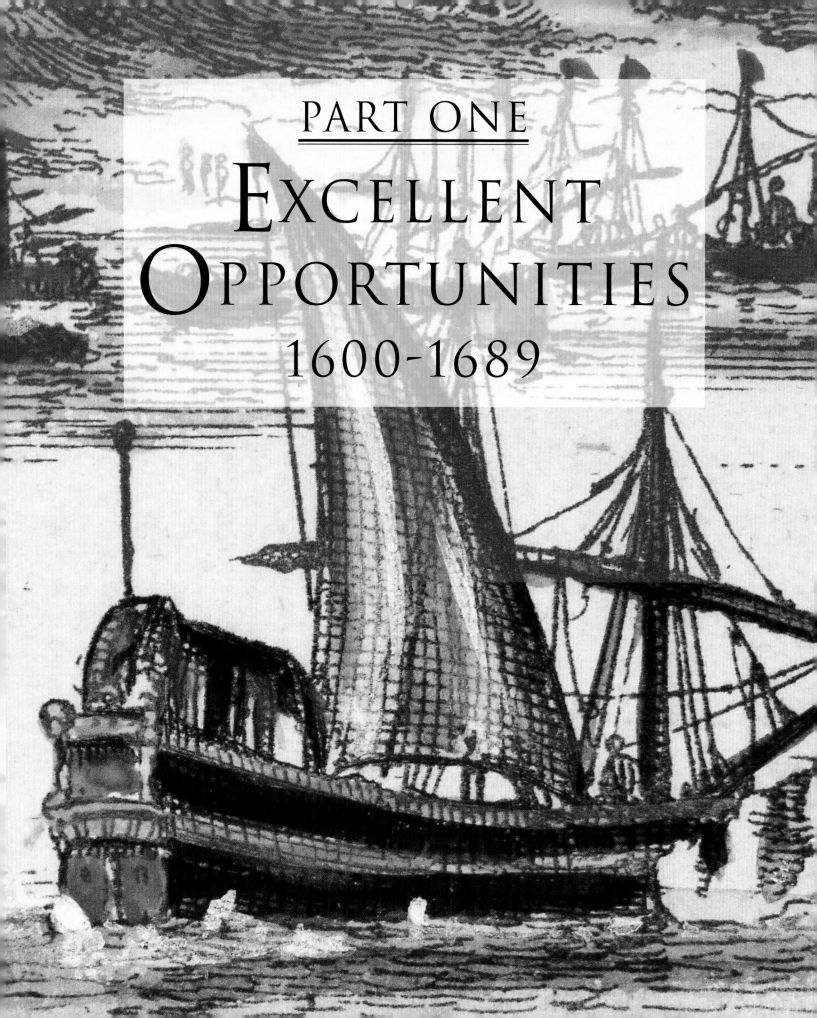

PART ONE

EXCELLENT OPPORTUNITIES

1600-1689

I

MY NEW-FOUND-LAND:

NORTH AMERICA

During the summer of 1605 London's theatregoers were diverted by a new play, *Eastwood Ho*, performed in Blackfriars by a troop of boy actors calling themselves the Children of Her Majesty's Revels. It had been written in some haste by George Chapman, Ben Jonson and John Marston and was a satire rich in topical allusions, some of which were directed against the Scots and earned Jonson the displeasure of the new King, James I. The speed of the play's creation owed much, if not everything, to the authors' desire to exploit the current public excitement generated by the Virginia venture. This project to found a North American colony was a source of intense speculation, both intellectual and financial.

Three of the central characters, Sir Petronel Flash, an impoverished and witless gentleman, Quicksilver, an idle apprentice, and Security, a devious moneylender, have conspired to collect funds for an expedition to Virginia where they expect to find gold. Security, on hearing from Quicksilver that the money has been secreted aboard Flash's ship, is beside himself with excitement:

> *Now a frank gale of wind go with him, Master Frank, we have too few such knight adventurers. Who would not sell away competent certainties, to purchase, with any danger, excellent uncertainties? Your true knight venturer ever does it.*

Later, when the would-be adventurers gather for a pre-embarkation drinking bout, they are entranced by Captain Seagull's description of the wealth of the Virginian Indians:

> *Why, man, all their dripping pans and their chamber pots are pure gold: and all the chains, with which they chain up their streets, are massy gold; all the prisoners they take are fettered in gold; and for rubies and diamonds, they go forth on holidays and gather 'em by the seashore, to hang on their children's coats . . .*

This was a parody of the extravagant claims made by Sir Walter Raleigh, who had promised England riches and power far in excess of those enjoyed by Spain in return for investment in an expedition to uncover El Dorado, a treasure-house of precious metals somewhere deep in the Guianan jungle. Seagull's hyperbole echoed Raleigh's, and there may have been laughter at Security's praise of 'knight adventurers', bold spirits who were prepared to take high risks. Crossing the seas in search of fortune was a fitting activity for a gentleman and equal in virtue to the pursuit of honour on the battlefield.

Such sentiments, in various forms, had been the staple of colonial propagandists for the past thirty years. The most persuasive had been Richard Hakluyt, an Oxford graduate, whose purpose had been to awaken his countrymen to what he considered their divinely ordained national duty as colonisers. His *Principal Navigations*, first published in 1598, was an extensive recital of all the voyages undertaken by Englishmen and was intended to demonstrate the existence of a long and noble tradition of overseas enterprise. By revealing what had been achieved in the past, Hakluyt hoped to evoke in his contemporaries a sense of destiny which would impel them to found colonies and penetrate distant oceans in search of trade.

Hakluyt's vision of an expansionist England accorded with the aggressive policies of an influential group of courtiers and councillors, including the Earl of Leicester, Sir Francis Walsingham and Raleigh, all Hispanophobes and passionate anti-Catholics. They were willing to support colonisation projects as a means of damaging Spain and, in the case of a 1580 scheme for a settlement of Newfoundland, as a way of removing potentially subversive Catholics from England. None of these plans came to anything; the minute and under-funded settlements placed on Roanoke Island and Newfoundland during the 1580s soon withered.

One reason for the collapse of these enterprises was the concentration of national energies and resources on the conflict with Spain. Moreover, the largely private-enterprise seaborne war against Spain satisfied those with a taste for glory and quick profits. It attracted sharks like Sir Francis Drake and plenty of minnows who also fared well. Consider George White, a Dorset mariner and owner of the thirty-five-ton *Catherine of Weymouth* that was valued at £89 and armed with two falcons (three-pounder cannon) and two falconets (two pounders). In 1590–1, the *Catherine* captured three Portuguese Brazilmen which with their cargoes were worth £3,600. Encouraged by his success, White sold the *Catherine* and invested in a larger vessel with which he took another Brazilman valued at £4,200 and an East Indiaman crammed with Chinese silk, gems and cochineal.

White and the other Elizabethan sea dogs had turned a public emergency to private advantage. They belonged to a well-established English tradition that stretched back to the Hundred Years War against France during which aristocratic commanders had fought for royal wages and profits from ransoms and plunder. Soldiers and sailors who went overseas to fight did so in the expectation that they might return richer. A popular life of Drake, published in 1628, urged the youth of 'this Dull or Effeminate Age to follow his noble steps for Gold and Silver'. Many did for the next two hundred or so years; a strong cord whose fibres were greed and fearlessness linked the Elizabethan sea rover, the eighteenth-century naval captain hungry for prize money and the early Victorian soldier, for whom the storming of an Indian city offered the chance of loot.

Many thought that there were riches to be gained in the new Virginia Company which was licensed by James I in 1607 and enthusiastically backed by Parliament. A prospectus issued in 1620 promised that the expanding settlements on the Chesapeake Bay would, in time, give Britain a self-sufficiency in materials which had hitherto been imported at a great cost to the country. The North American plantations would replace Scandinavia as a source of tar and timber for ship-building. The colony would also provide the mother country with 'The Wines, Fruit and Salt of France and Spain' and 'the silks of Persia and Italy'. Persuaded by such arguments investors, who included noblemen, courtiers, civil servants, country squires (details of the company's activities were broadcast in the shires by London newssheets) and merchants, subscribed £200,000 in thirteen years.

The Virginia Company's promoters and the early settlers had imagined that the entire coastline of North America from Newfoundland south to the Carolinas lay in a temperate zone that enjoyed 'a moderate equality of heat and cold'. At the same time, since the Chesapeake Bay colony shared a common latitude with Spain it was assumed that it would provide an abundance of Mediterranean crops. Vine dressers were among the first ashore and even as late as 1620 plans were in hand for planting olive

PREVIOUS PAGES
Seaborne trade:
shipping off New York,
late seventeenth century.
(© Boston Public Library)

groves. By then everyone involved should have known better. It was soon discovered that the region lay within a malarial belt and that new arrivals required 'seasoning' during the hot summer months when, like timber, they sweated profusely. Winters were bitterly cold and during that of 1609–10 the disheartened wished themselves 'in England without their limbs' and begging on the streets rather than in Virginia. Within a dozen years the company was near to bankruptcy and in 1624 its settlements were taken over by the Crown.

Tobacco rescued Virginia and made it thrive in a manner that astonished the colonists and the government. The first tentative planting of imported South American tobacco plants had been undertaken in 1617. It was a success and began a revolution that transformed the infant colony and the British economy. At the time, tobacco was still a luxury and smoking the indulgence of the rich, some of whom would pay as much as £2 a pound for the prized Guianan leaf. Mass imports from the Virginian plantations changed this and by mid-century the retail price had plummeted to one shilling (5p) a pound. Smoking became a universal habit embraced by every class in Europe. The opening up of what proved to be an unlimited market for a drug which both calmed and stimulated was the chance result of overproduction in the 1630s. By 1700, Britain imported 13 million pounds of Virginian tobacco for domestic consumption and a further 25 million for re-export to Europe, figures that rose steadily throughout the next century.

The Virginian tobacco boom had a profound impact on Britain and its economy. Viewing the colony's prosperity during the 1620s, one commentator perceptively observed that 'Spain is more

Seventeenth-Century Settlement in North America

damaged by the King's peace than by the Queen's war'. His logic was simple and would be repeated by later advocates of colonial expansion. The wealth which flowed from Virginia contributed to that of Britain and its power grew accordingly.

In terms of the generation of wealth, Virginia overshadowed the smaller colonies of Newfoundland, established in 1610, and those under the control of the Massachusetts Bay Company, founded in 1620. In all there was a gap between expectation and reality. A 1611 report of one early settler in Newfoundland, written to drum up further investment, described the tiny colony as 'very honest, peaceful and hopeful, and very likely to be profitable'. A visitor the previous year wrote home that 'this savage country of Newfoundland gives men little content but only cruel hard labour hoping to make the best content they can have with small profit.' The attraction of this bleak land lay in the cod fishing banks offshore which had drawn English fishing fleets since the 1520s. The cod were caught (at first with hook and line) then salted, dried and smoked and, with barrels of their oil, were shipped to the ports of the Iberian Peninsula to be traded for local products. By 1620, 300 ships visited the region annually and, according to a petition for naval protection, employed 10,000 sailors 'thereby relieving 20,000 more people of the western parts of England, who are wholly dependent on them for their existence'.

Further south, the Puritan settlers of the fledgling New England colonies faced an equally unkind land. They had crossed the Atlantic ignorant of the local climate which they imagined to be the same as England's. They were soon disabused and in 1629 one wrote mournfully that 'from the middest of October to the middest of May there is a sad face of winter upon all this land' and noted that many were dying from the 'intolerable cold'.

The death rate was high, but the Puritans were psychologically prepared for it, and for the grinding work of clearing woodlands, ploughing and sowing crops. They were men and women with a profound sense of the working of God's will who had voluntarily withdrawn from England where their Calvinist creed attracted official mistrust and, during the 1620s and 1630s, systematic persecution by the state-sponsored Church of England.

By 1660 the largely Puritan New England settlements had a population of about 30,000, many of whom were refugees who had challenged and then fled from the rigid orthodoxy of the first, coastal colonies. Theological wrangling was endemic among Puritans and it caused fragmentation as deviant preachers left communities which found their opinions intolerable. Roger Williams, a young divine who like John Milton had learned his Puritanism at Cambridge, arrived in New England in 1631. His doctrinal radicalism, which led him to deny the legal right of James I and Charles I to give away Indian lands to his fellow settlers, caused his voluntary exile in 1636. With a handful of his adherents he founded a new colony, Rhode Island, where he was later joined by other banished heretics.

Plans to rid England of another body of religious dissidents, Catholics, had been considered since the early 1570s. Excluded from Virginia, English Catholics finally gained a colony when Lord Baltimore persuaded a sympathetic Charles I to issue him a charter in 1634. The new settlement was named Maryland, in honour of Charles's queen, Henrietta Maria, and its colonists were officially cautioned to hold their masses discreetly for fear that they might antagonise their Protestant neighbours.

But why were those who were not persecuted for their faith willing to leave Britain for what was, even by the standards of the age, a hard and uncertain existence? Perhaps the strongest impulse lay in habit: there was an old and deeply rooted tradition for craftsmen, labourers and domestic servants to move around the countryside looking for employment. It was therefore not a difficult step for, say, a Devonshire tiler accustomed to wandering from town to town for work to accept passage from Bristol to Jamestown, Virginia. Specialist skills were keenly sought by the Virginia Company, which in 1620 was advertising for 'choice men, born and bred up to labour and industry', especially Sussex ironworkers.

Nearly all those who went to North America went as indentured servants, legally bound to labour on the plantations, or practising their own craft for fixed periods of between four and ten years in return for wages. When their terms of service had expired they were free to enter the local labour market or return home. Between 1654 and 1660 just over 3,000 of these indentured servants were shipped from Bristol, more than half destined for the tobacco colonies of Virginia and Maryland. Former yeomen farmers and farmhands were the biggest group but there was a scattering of skilled artisans such as blacksmiths and coopers. Most came from the counties adjacent to Bristol and South Wales and were between eighteen and twenty-five.

Such young men (and women too) were the sinews of the new colonies. All hoped to flourish in a society where the domestic obstructions to advancement did not exist. In time it was widely imagined that those with talent, application and an injection of good luck would flourish irrespective of birth or connections. In the next century, Daniel Defoe used the fictional career of Moll Flanders to illustrate this principle. Moll, born in Newgate gaol, returns there after a sequence of picaresque adventures in which she displays resource and intelligence. Transported as a felon to Virginia, she and her highwayman husband eventually overcome their backgrounds and become respected and wealthy planters.

Moll Flanders was not pure fantasy, nor a tract by a writer who believed that a person's place in the world should be determined by ability. In 1755 an officer serving with General Edward Braddock's army in Virginia recalled having supper with a 'rich planter'. His wife, he discovered, 'had passed through the education of the college of Newgate as great numbers from thence arrive here yearly; most being cunning jades, some pick up foolish planters.' But this man was no fool, he had married his wife for her charms and her 'art and skill' in managing his business.

The pursuit of profit remained the most powerful driving force behind Britain's bid for North American colonies. But from the start it was closely linked to a moral imperative founded upon contemporary conceptions of Divine Providence and the nature of the world and its inhabitants.

In a sermon compiled in 1609 by a clerical apologist for the Virginia Company, America was described as a land which had been 'wrongly usurped by wild beasts and unreasonable creatures' (i.e. native Americans, or Indians as they were then known); according to the author, God intended the land

*License my
roaving hands, and
let them go
Before, behind,
between, above,
below.
O my America! my
new-found-land . . .*

JOHN DONNE

to be redeemed by English settlement. In 1625, Simon Purchas, a churchman and disciple of Hakluyt, insisted that what he called the 'Virgin Portion' of North America had been divinely allocated to his countrymen, 'God in wisdom having enriched the savage countries, that those riches be attractive for Christian suitors'.

The conceit that the American continent was a richly endowed virgin bride awaiting a husband enjoyed considerable usage at this time. It was not just a courtier's knack for flattery that had inspired Raleigh to name the eastern seaboard of North America 'Virginia' in honour of Elizabeth I. A deeper meaning was intended since Raleigh, in his plea for the occupation of Guiana, had described it as 'a country that hath yet her Maidenhead, never sacked, turned, nor wrought, the face of earth hath not been torn, nor the virtue and the salt of the soil spent by manurance'. In coarser vein, Captain Seagull rallied the settlers in *Eastward Ho* with the cry, 'Come boys, Virginia longs till we share the rest of her maiden-head.' Most famously this likeness of America to an unblemished maiden is employed by John Donne (among other things a chaplain to the Virginia Company) in his 'To his Mistris Going to Bed', in which the seducer is both explorer and planter.

*Safeguarding an
infant empire:
fort on the Piscataqua
River, New
Hampshire, 1699.
(© PRO)*

The moral question faced by Englishmen was: by what authority could they claim the fertile, untilled lands of North America? A broad and infallible answer was provided by the prevailing view of the divine ordering of the world and man's place in it. 'God', wrote John Milton in a defence of colonisation, 'having made the world for use of men … ordained them to replenish it.' The newly revealed American continent was favoured with abundant natural resources by a benevolent God, but it was peopled by races who had never recognised nor acted upon their good fortune. Their wilful inertia, combined with other moral shortcomings, debarred them from their inheritance, which passed to more industrious outsiders. Similar arguments, with variations, would later be applied to Australasia and Africa.

One hundred years of detailed reports from European explorers had created a literature in which, almost without exception, the Amerindians were represented as a degenerate and inferior species of mankind. Sir Martin Frobisher, encountering the Inuits of Northern Canada in the 1580s, described

them as 'brute beasts' who 'neither use table, stool or tablecloth for cleanliness' and lived in caves. Fifty years later a French Jesuit missionary, horrified by the cannibalism and public torture of prisoners among the Indians of the St Lawrence basin, called them 'ferocious beasts having nothing human about them save the exterior formation of body'. The standards of Renaissance European civilisation were absolute and, judged by them, the native Americans were found wanting.

The natives of America, when first confronted with Europeans, believed they were in the presence of supernatural beings. In Mexico, the Aztec Emperor Moctezuma imagined that his people's conqueror, Hernán Cortés, was a reincarnation of the god Quetzalcoatl. Sixty years later, in 1569,

Exotic imports:
colonial flora and fauna
were widely imported into
Britain by the curious
and the status conscious.
The Newfoundland dog
was an indigenous breed
kept by native Americans.
It became a fashionable
pet during the Regency:
one was owned by
Lord Byron.

when Drake landed in California, the Miwok Indians identified him and his party as gods. Sacrifices were immediately offered and, much to their visitors' distress, some Miwoks mutilated themselves, as they did when they fancied themselves in the presence of ghosts. Everywhere Amerindians regarded Europeans as gods whose ships were floating islands, their sails white clouds and their cannon the makers of thunder and lightning. Such naïveté was easily exploited; in 1633 a French sea captain entranced Indians by using a magnetised sword blade to pick up a knife so that, in his words, they would 'imagine some great power in us and for that love and fear us'.

In the beginning the promoters of the Virginia Company had made much of plans for the conversion and education of Indians, and during the colony's early years relations between settlers and natives had been harmonious. But as the colony grew the settlers clamoured for fresh land which could only be gained at the Indians' expense. War broke out in 1622 and after a massacre in which over 300 colonists were killed, a new and understandably fierce mood prevailed. 'The way of conquering them is more easy than civilising them by fair means,' ran a pamphlet issued by the company, 'for they are a rude, barbarous, and naked people, scattered in small communities, which are helps to Victory, but hindrances to Civility.' In future the native Americans would be brought to heel by the destruction of their camps and crops and 'by pursuing them with our horses, and Blood-Hounds to draw after them, and Mastiffs to tear them, which take these naked, tanned deformed Savages, for no other than wild beasts.'

This mandate for extermination anticipated similar calls for ruthless wars against a dehumanised enemy that would be heard from land-hungry colonists in southern Africa, New Zealand and Australia.

It was also a reminder that the first colonisation of North America was contemporaneous with the far larger settlement of Ireland, mainly by Presbyterian Scottish immigrants. Between 1620 and 1642 120,000 colonists arrived to help undertake what Sir Francis Bacon revealingly called 'the reduction to civility' of the Gaelic-speaking, Catholic Irish. On both sides of the Atlantic the settlers faced sporadic but determined resistance and their response was the same, a resort to counter-massacre and the most extreme forms of repression. Half a century of land wars against the Indians calloused the New England settlers' consciences. In 1703, soon after the slaughter of Pequot Indians, a soldier wrote, prompted by a clergyman, 'Sometimes the scripture declareth women and children must perish with their parents.'

Native Americans were not the only people who advanced territorial claims in North America. In 1494, Spain and Portugal had signed the Treaty of Tordesillas by which the New World was divided between them, and their agreement was endorsed by a papal bull. This accord was naturally disregarded by Protestant Englishmen who undermined its legality with counter-claims based on John Cabot's 1497 voyage. He had, at Henry VII's bidding, crossed the Atlantic and made landfall at either Nova Scotia or Newfoundland, no one is sure which, and formally annexed the region in the King's name. Furthermore, there was the legendary transatlantic expedition made by the twelfth-century Welsh prince, Madoc. This insubstantial tale assumed, in the hands of Elizabethan expansionists, the force of historical truth and was cited to override Spanish and Portuguese claims.

Such antiquarian nonsense was superfluous since, by 1600, it was obvious that the Iberian nations lacked the seapower to defend their New World monopoly. The limitations of their control had been repeatedly and dramatically exposed by French, Dutch and English privateers from 1560 onwards. Nevertheless, Spain did expel the French from their settlement at San Augustin in 1565 and for a few years the Virginians feared similar treatment. It was not meted out by a state which had been at peace with Britain from 1604 and, after 1609, needed all its resources for a renewed war with the Netherlands. For the first thirty years or so of their existence, the North American settlements enjoyed a vital immunity from foreign interference.

With God on their side: New England settlers over Pequot Indians, c.1636–7. (© Mary Evans Picture Library)

2

BAUBLES FOR THE SOULS OF MEN:

THE WEST
AND EAST INDIES

Englishmen had first been drawn to the Caribbean, often known as the Spanish Main, in the middle of the sixteenth century. Sir John Hawkins, a Devon shipowner and entrepreneur, led the way having heard, according to Hakluyt, that 'Negroes were very good merchandise in Hispaniola [the Spanish colony of Española, now Haiti], and that the store of negroes might easily be had upon the coast of Guinea'. The Spanish settlers were grateful for Hawkins's cargoes of West African slaves, but their government objected to his infraction of the official monopoly that gave Spaniards alone the right to trade with Spanish possessions. In 1568, Hawkins's tiny flotilla of trading vessels was ambushed at San Juan de Ulúa and driven off with heavy losses. He soon returned with others, including Drake, as a privateer preying on Spanish shipping.

This was a holy war for Protestantism as well as a trawl for profit in ill-defended waters. Drake recited passages from Foxe's *Book of Martyrs* to captive Spanish seamen, and one of his captains, John Oxenham, turned the tables on a captured official of the Inquisition by placing a chamber pot on his head and striking him 'many fisticuffs'. Oxenham himself was later taken and burned by the Inquisition for his combination of heresy and temerity. Piracy may not have done much for the Protestant cause, but many pirates prospered. Memories of their more spectacular coups against treasure ships remained evergreen and in 1621, when Anglo-Spanish relations were deteriorating, the Puritan Earl of Warwick proposed the despatch of a massive armada to the Caribbean whose costs, estimated at £364,000, would be met by public subscription.

This scheme for a profit-making, maritime crusade came to nothing, but a preliminary reconnaissance of the Caribbean revealed the existence of Barbados, a fertile, well-watered and uninhabited island that was said to be highly suitable for tobacco-growing. The vision of a second Virginia lured investors and in 1627 Charles I granted a charter to the newly formed Barbados Company. Its settlers were soon in difficulties; Barbadian tobacco failed to compete with the Virginian product and a hurried switch to cotton did nothing to revive the island's fortunes.

Sugar saved Barbados. It was first planted in 1643 and within fifty years sugar plantations covered four-fifths of the island and refined sugar, molasses and rum made up nine-tenths of its exports. What later historians called the 'sugar revolution' transformed the economy of the West Indies, opened the way for a subsidiary but equally profitable commerce in negro slaves and, incidentally, made the region into a war zone where, until 1815, Britain, France and Spain struggled for control of the islands and mastery of the seaways. Sugar enabled some plantation owners to become millionaires. In 1681 it was calculated, perhaps optimistically, that £5,000 invested in a sugar estate would within a few years yield £1,000 annually. By this date a mass domestic and European market for cheap sugar was emerging and British producers were getting the upper hand in a price war with competitors in Portuguese Brazil. The boom benefited Britain and its government, which levied duties on sugar imports which, between 1699 and 1701, were valued at £280,000.

Barbados's success story accelerated the occupation of other islands by settlers. By 1660, St Kitts, Antigua, Nevis, Montserrat and Jamaica (seized from Spain in 1655) had been occupied and planted with sugar cane. In 1638 a small party attempted to settle St Lucia but were soon driven out by the native Caribs who ingeniously 'smoked out' the colonists from their forts with bonfires of dried peppers.

Day-to-day existence in the Caribbean was always precarious. Soldiers and sailors, whose diet was sparse and unhealthy, suffered the worst and a West Indian posting was always dreaded. During a brief campaign on the Nicaraguan coast in 1778–9, three-quarters of an 1,800-strong force died from fevers, and most of the survivors, including Captain Horatio Nelson, were infected with malaria. The value of the chinchona bark, from which quinine was extracted, as a prophylactic against malaria had been discovered from the Amerindians, but it was not used generally until the mid-nineteenth century.

Endurance of infections and extremes of heat and humidity was the common lot of the men and women who emigrated to the West Indies to make their fortunes from sugar. But the drive to make money alone could not compensate for physical suffering and, by the end of the century, it was customary for the richer planters to place their estates in the hands of managers and return to Britain and live, often in high style, from the profits.

The early planters were not so fortunately placed, nor were the indentured servants they hired in Britain. Initially the sugar estates followed the precedent established in Virginia and imported their labour, but it was soon apparent that British labourers were not up to the physical demands of sugar cultivation in the tropics. Knowledge of the conditions they would encounter and the planters' habit of working new arrivals hard to recoup the cost of their transport deterred men and women from freely committing themselves to indentured service in the West Indies. Various measures were adopted to overcome what, by the 1650s, was a permanent labour shortage. These included using captured rebels from Cromwell's Irish and Scottish campaigns of 1650–2 and buying convicts from English gaols.

The prospects for those who found themselves compelled to undertake indentured service were not entirely bleak. If they survived until the end of their term they received £10 or 400 pounds of sugar with which to better themselves. Some became overseers, earning as much as £50 a year, and those with such skills as carpentry could make twice as much. Nevertheless, work on the plantations remained intensely unpopular and for many it was a gruelling alternative to the gallows, prison or starvation.

Given the insoluble problem of finding a willing and hardy workforce, it was inevitable that British plantation owners would adopt the Spanish colonial system of using imported African slave labour. The Spaniards, having through forced labour, overwork, the spread of alien germs and viruses, and systematic massacre exterminated most of the Caribbean Amerindians by the mid-sixteenth century, turned to negro slaves. They were the only means by which the highly labour-intensive Spanish latifundia and mines could be sustained. For economic rather than demographic reasons, British planters followed the Spanish example and, from 1650 onwards, slaves gradually replaced indentured labourers on the plantations. At the same time slave labour was introduced to the Chesapeake basin tobacco estates and, soon after, slaves were imported into Carolina.

Economic necessity was always the first and, for its supporters, the strongest justification for slavery. Their reasoning was simply outlined in a report prepared in 1663 to procure royal backing for the occupation of the Dutch colony of Surinam on the Guianan coast. 'Were the planters supplied with negroes, the sinews and strength of this western world,' it was claimed, 'they would advance their fortunes and His Majesty's customs.' Slavery underpinned the expanding West Indian economy and enriched both planters and the home government which, it went without saying, would direct additional revenues towards the protection and enlargement of this new source of national wealth.

There was, and few would have denied this in a country where much store was set on individual freedom, a moral issue involved in the sale and exploitation of slaves. In his *Reform of Manners* (1702) Daniel Defoe, usually a fervent upholder of British overseas enterprise, expressed doubts about 'the barter of baubles for the *souls of men*', but overcame them by reference to what he imagined to be the 'Natural Temper' of the negro, that is awe of and thraldom to the white man. This view was widely and uncritically held throughout Europe during the late seventeenth and eighteenth centuries. As with the Native Americans, the negro was measured against the standards of contemporary European civilisation and judged unfavourably. He was, asserted the eighteenth-century philosopher, David Hume, 'naturally inferior' because his race possessed 'No ingenious manufactures . . . no arts, no sciences'. Those who travelled to Africa, often in connection with the slave trade, endorsed such conclusions with lurid tales of a dark and chaotic land whose people indulged in fetish cults, cannibalism, massacres and tribal wars.

Although burdened by moral and intellectual disabilities, the negro was part of a divinely ordered world in which the prime justification for a man's existence was his productive usefulness. This principle of the utility of all humankind impelled British governments to deport idlers, vagrants and criminals to the colonies where they would redeem themselves through work, and the French to condemn miscreants to perpetual labour rowing war galleys. Plantation slavery was the means by which negroes could fulfil the role for which God had intended them and add to the general well-being of the world. 'I was shock'd at the first appearance of human flesh exposed for sale,' wrote John Pinney, an absentee Nevis planter in 1764. 'But surely God ordain'd 'em for the use and benefit of us: other his Divine Will would have been manifest by some sign or token.'

Enslavement was not without its advantages. With breathtaking smugness Gilbert Burnet, Bishop of Salisbury, argued in the early 1700s that since the slaves had given so much to Britain it was only proper that they should receive Christianity in return. This exchange was unwelcome to planters who imagined, with good reason as it turned out, that conversion would make their slaves 'more perverse and intractable'. Addressing the Barbadian plantocracy, assembled in the island's parliament in 1681, the governor, Sir Richard Dutton, remarked that slaves deserved the 'good usage of Christian servants, but as to make negroes Christians, their savage brutishness renders them wholly incapable'. Slave-owning was compatible with the Christian life, at least in the form it was taught by Catholic and Church of England divines. In 1711 Bishop Fleetwood preached that 'The laws of God did not forbid the keeping of Christian slaves, nor do the laws of the land'. The following year his church's missionary organisation, the Society for the Propagation of the Christian Gospel, was bequeathed a plantation in Barbados. Each of its slaves was branded on the chest with the word 'Society' to denote his new owner; not surprisingly the rate of conversion was disappointing.

Nevertheless, the admission that slaves could be converted opened a debate, which intensified as the eighteenth century progressed, as to how, if at all, a religion that claimed the equality of souls before God could reconcile itself to a system founded upon the hereditary inferiority of one part of mankind. Moreover, as the planters predicted, a knowledge of Christian doctrines led many slaves to interpret their own circumstances unfavourably.

The brandmark that identified the Society for the Propagation of the Christian Gospel's slave was an unmistakable reminder that he or she was, in the eyes of the law, the property of a master. According to the constitution of Carolina that was framed by the philosopher John Locke in 1669 'every free man' was 'to have absolute authority over his negro slaves', a principle which, in different forms, obtained throughout much of North America and the West Indies. Its everyday application gave plantation life a peculiar and often grotesque brutality. Much has been written about this, so one incident set down in the diary of the manager of a Jamaican estate may stand for many others: '(25 May 1756) Derby caught by Port Royal [both slaves] eating canes. Had him well flogged and pickled, then made Henry [another slave] shit in his mouth.'

Some play:
Jamaican slaves
enjoying a carnival.
(© Fotomas Index)

Eating the young cane shoots was the inevitable outcome of having to undertake heavy physical labour on a sparse diet. A recent forensic examination of 101 skeletons of slaves exhumed from a Barbadian graveyard, in use between 1660 and 1820, revealed an average life expectancy of twenty-nine and a high death rate for children under ten. Evidence of nutrition indicated a diet that was inadequate for the tasks demanded of the slaves, who commonly assuaged their hunger by smoking tobacco in pipes. This high wastage rate was not offset by the slaves' ability to reproduce themselves, despite the active encouragement of concubinage. This phenomenon was explained with some percipience by one planter who noted in his journal that, 'Negresses can produce children at pleasure, and when they are barren, it is just as hens will frequently not lay eggs on shipboard, because they do not like their situation.' Low birth rates and high death rates meant that planters had continually to replenish their stock of slaves and so the slave trade was perpetuated.

The mechanics of the transatlantic slave trade were simple. Negroes were obtained by barter with the tribal rulers of the West African seaboard states, confined in compounds attached to trading posts and then shipped for sale in the West Indies. During its early stages, returns from the slave trade were very high. A slave could be exchanged for goods worth between £4 and £5 and the cost of passage was a further £5, including his food and the attendance of a doctor. On a West Indian quayside the slave would be sold for between £15 and £17 or 2,400 pounds of sugar depending on his or her age and health. The high profit margin was in great part a reflection of the losses of slaves during the voyage, for as many as one in four perished from sickness or despair, or a mixture of the two.

During the 1650s the trade was already flourishing, with an average of 3,000 slaves being sold annually in Barbados, some for re-export to other islands or Virginia and Maryland. The scope of the trade, with markets in Dutch as well as British colonies, attracted the intervention of the government which hoped to secure a share of the profits. In 1660 a monopoly was granted to the Company of Royal Adventurers (in which Charles II invested £5,000) which gave it the right to sell licences to British slave traders who did business on the West African coast. Reorganised as the Royal African Company in 1672, the corporation controlled a string of fortified and garrisoned trading stations on the shores of what today

And all work:
slaves labouring on
a sugar plantation.
(© Peter Newark's
American Pictures)

are Gambia, Senegal, Ghana and Nigeria. The company never enjoyed a total monopoly – enterprising slavers operating out of Boston and New York ignored it and traded with Madagascar. In 1698 it was abolished, allowing hundreds of traders to stake a claim in the commerce.

Among the commodities bartered for slaves were cheap textiles imported from India by the East India Company. Indian and Far Eastern markets had first been penetrated by the Portuguese at the beginning of the sixteenth century. The arrival of their heavily gunned caravels was unwelcome, but proved unstoppable. In 1501 Vasco da Gama's men-o'-war bombarded Calicut to show its inhabitants the power of European cannon, and a year later his outnumbered flotilla decisively defeated an Arab fleet off the Malabar coast. These victories gave the Portuguese a local supremacy that lasted for nearly a hundred years.

The challenge to Portugal's domination of the trade in spices and textiles came from English and Dutch merchants and shipowners. After a number of preliminary reconnaissances, the London-based East India Company was formed in 1600, the brainchild of Levant Company merchants who were keen to by-pass middlemen in the eastern Mediterranean and deal direct with spice suppliers in the East Indies (modern Indonesia). The company was small, with a capital of £68,000, and at first confined itself to annual expeditions by small fleets. The risks, not least of the journey around the Cape of Good Hope, were great. When the *Globe* and the *Peppercorn* returned in 1617 with full holds and the prospect of a good return, the governor led the stockholders in prayer for 'all ought to lift up their hearts unto God to be thankful . . . and to be more thankful for the same; not doubting that the more thankful we be, the more His blessings will increase.'

The blessings and the profits did increase, satisfying the business acumen and piety of investors in an age which believed that God never failed to reward His elect. Those who put their money on the early voyages received, on average, a return of twenty per cent. Moreover, in 1614 two company ships had engaged and driven off four Portuguese vessels by the mouth of the River Tapti, a demonstration of British fighting skill which was watched by the Mughal army on shore. In India at least the company had secured a toehold and, within twenty years, the Portuguese had conceded the East India Company the right to set up factories, as trading posts were known, wherever it chose on the Indian coast.

And yet as the company's name indicated, its founders had pinned their hopes on gaining a share in the spice trade at its source: Malaya, Java and the Molucca Islands. Here the rival Dutch Compagnie van Verre (Company of Far Distant Lands) was already strongly entrenched and ready to resist interlopers. Founded in 1602 with capital of £500,000, the Dutch company quickly established fortified trading posts at Batavia (Jakarta), Amboina Island and Malacca on the Malay coast which they took from the Portuguese in 1641. Tolerance of British intruders was thin and, in 1623, eighteen British merchants were tortured to death in an exercise of brutality designed to frighten off others. It did not wholly succeed but it helped turn the minds of British traders towards India where their presence was not opposed.

The Mughal emperors, India's overlords, and their provincial nawabs (governors) were willing to come to terms with the East India Company and allow them to secure a string of trading posts along the western and eastern shores of the subcontinent. A continual flow of ships replaced the earlier annual sailings and by the mid-century a profitable trade was developing. In 1674–5 the company exported £155,000 worth of British manufactured goods and £410,000 in silver bullion, and imported £860,000 worth of Indian goods, largely textiles. Between 1699 and 1701 imports of textiles totalled £522,000 and two-thirds were re-exported to Europe and West Africa where they were exchanged for slaves. At the same time, and in imitation of the Portuguese and Dutch, the company was entering the shipping business, carrying goods between India and ports in southern Arabia and the Far East. In 1664 a minute amount of tea, still an exotic luxury, was obtained from China solely for the use of the directors. As the company's interests expanded and diversified, its establishments became larger, although the directors insisted that it had no political or territorial ambitions in a country that was enjoying a period of stability under Mughal government.

Some corner of a foreign field: the gravestone of Charles Bacchus, 'an African' who 'gave hopes of Proving a faithful Servant and a Good Man' before his death in 1762, aged sixteen (Culworth churchyard, Northants).

3

THE NECESSARY
UNION OF
PLANTATIONS:
CROWN AND COLONIES

I n 1645 the trading vessel *Dolphin* left London with a cargo of manufactured goods that included glass, castors, shoes, hats, bales of canvas, and pewter, iron and brass utensils, all for sale to the New England colonists. These wares were unloaded at Boston where the hold was filled with local products: wheat and rye, barrels of preserved beef, pork, herrings and mackerel, and 7,000 pounds of tobacco, presumably shipped from Virginia and Maryland. The *Dolphin* then sailed southwards to Barbados where some of its cargo was discharged and replaced with sugar. It then began the haul across the Atlantic, pausing at the Canaries where the pickled fish was removed for sale to those pious Catholics who obeyed the Church's rules concerning meatless Fridays.

This round voyage and hundreds like it marked a significant change in the pattern of British trade. Fine woollen cloth, so long Britain's main export, was steadily losing ground to tobacco, sugar, fish and, during the last quarter of the century, Canadian beaver pelts for hat-making. By 1700 the re-export of these commodities made up 30 per cent of Britain's foreign trade. Cloth's share of the export market had fallen dramatically from 90 per cent in 1640 to 47 per cent at the end of the century and continued to decline. At the same time new markets were emerging. Between 1630 and 1700 half a million men and women had emigrated to the colonies, two-thirds of them to North America, and all were dependent on home-manufactured goods; during the 1650s 20,000 pairs of boots and shoes and 1,500 horses were imported into Barbados.

The early stages of this economic revolution coincided with a period of domestic political instability which culminated in the outbreak of the Civil War between Charles I and Parliament in 1642. The principle source of contention was control over the making of policy, particularly in matters concerning religion and taxation. The waves stirred by the war in Britain sent ripples across the Atlantic. From 1640 onwards, many New England Puritans returned home to fight for Parliament and in Virginia its governor, Sir William Berkeley, a former courtier and playwright, welcomed royalist refugees after the collapse of their cause in 1649.

The establishment of the Commonwealth in 1649 may be reckoned as marking a major turning point in the history of the empire. The next eleven years witnessed continuous and dynamic government activity to preserve and enlarge Britain's overseas possessions and their trade. There was legislation to assert the total dominance of Britain over all aspects of colonial commerce; an ambitious programme of naval rearmament; a challenge to Dutch seapower; and a partially successful offensive against Spain in the Caribbean. In 1664 Charles II's Treasurer, the Earl of Danby, argued that it was a matter of urgency that arrangements were made to 'bring about the Necessary Union of all Plantations in America which will make the King great and extend his royal empire in those parts.'

One thing was clear to the ministers and civil servants who framed these policies: Britain's colonies and the new transatlantic commerce they were generating were a vital national asset to be coveted, protected and extended, if necessary by aggression. At every turn, the government was influenced by the prevailing economic dogma, mercantilism. This assumed that a limit existed to global trade and measured a nation's wealth in terms of its self-sufficiency. Autarky, especially in raw materials, was also an indicator of a country's international status since it released it from dependence on other powers and allowed it to accumulate a surplus of treasure. For this among other reasons James I and Charles I had been willing to charter colonies which, their promoters hoped, would provide alternative sources for commodities previously imported from Europe. They were largely mistaken, but, unexpectedly, the American and Caribbean settlements offered products for which there appeared a growing but finite continental market. If trends already detectable during the 1640s continued, Britain would soon become the focus of a transatlantic commerce based upon tobacco, sugar, fish and the new traffic in slaves.

Until the mid-1670s measures for the safeguard of the settlements in North America and the Caribbean had been haphazard and amateurish. The need for garrisons of professional soldiers and closer royal supervision of government was evident. In 1676 Virginia was convulsed by an insurrection against the allegedly feeble Indian policy of Governor Berkeley, his corrupt and partial government, and an assembly where, according to the insurgents, 'all the power is got into the hands of the rich'. To restore order, the government in London had to despatch over a thousand troops, artillery and warships. While Virginia faced what was close to a class war, the New England colonies were engaged in interminable frontier wars against the Indians who were getting stronger thanks to French assistance. Indians captured in New York in 1689 carried French muskets, bayonets and cutlasses.

The colonists could not face these perils without outside assistance, and this uncomfortable fact of life made them acquiesce to a series of measures which reduced the powers of local assemblies and great landlords. Administrative adjustments were conceded, sometimes grudgingly as in New England, but colonial parliaments still retained considerable law-making powers. These bodies, it must be added, were representative rather than democratic. Like their English and Scottish counterparts, they were the exclusive preserve of men of wealth and property. The North American and West Indian legislatures were filled with planters, merchants, estate-owners and lawyers who were thought to have the best interests of their colony at heart. These men accepted the supremacy of the King's governors, judges and officials as the price for protection.

Stairway to wealth: American walnut, specially imported, was used for the stairwell at Dyrham Park, begun in 1692 by William Blathwayt, the Secretary of War who was responsible for the defence and administration of the colonies.
(© Country Life)

4

DISPOSITIONS OF PROVIDENCE:
THE COLONISTS

Britain's overseas colonies would not have happened without large numbers of emigrants who were prepared to abandon their homes, undertake long and hazardous voyages and then submit themselves to a régime of hard labour in an unfamiliar and often unkind environment. Elizabethan expansionists had likened the process to a bodily evacuation, a spewing out of unwanted and harmful matter. This image was invoked by a visitor to Barbados in 1655: 'This island is the Dunghill whereon England doth cast forth its rubbish: Rogues and whores and such like people are those which are generally brought here.'

The temptation to escape must sometimes have been very great, but so were the dangers of recapture on the island colonies or falling into Indian hands in North America. These risks diminished as the colonial population rose and made it easier for the fugitive to find anonymity.

In 1704 there were 30,000 men and 7,000 women, 85 per cent of them indentured servants, in Maryland. Female servants were normally allocated domestic work indoors, although 'some wenches that are nasty and beastly' were ordered to labour in the fields. Those free to do so married young; the average age in Maryland was sixteen, twenty-one in Virginia, and brides were frequently pregnant. Indentured servants, who were usually twenty-four or twenty-five when their terms expired, married later. There was also a high illegitimacy rate despite the humiliating public punishments laid down for unmarried mothers by colonial legislators.

By 1700, a large proportion of colonists were native born. Population growth in the Chesapeake basin colonies had been slower than elsewhere thanks in part to the shortage of women and a high death rate. A twenty-year-old immigrant who survived seasoning might expect to live another twenty years, while a locally born Virginian or Marylander who picked up some immunities would survive a further ten years. Life expectancy in the more astringent climate of New England was sixty.

The lack of women was a handicap in the early phases of colonisation, but it was unavoidable. Clearing forests, breaking ground, tending crops and building houses required a male workforce, a fact of life that was reflected in the occupations of those emigrants who were in most demand by settlement companies and proprietors. The most urgent need was always for skilled artisans. On board the *Increase*, which sailed for New England in 1636, were 116 passengers including a butcher, carpenter, clothier, stonemason, ploughwright, sawyer, surgeon, tailor, two linen weavers, a joiner and a dozen farm labourers.

There were also twelve men without trades, twenty-four adult women, twenty-six girls under eighteen and thirty boys. This distribution of occupation, age and sex was typical, although there was no certainty as to whether it would be reproduced in the colony because of losses during the voyage and acclimatisation.

The ideal colonists were described by the Massachusetts Bay Company in the 1630s as 'endowed with grace and furnished with means'. The first quality was essential for the fulfilment of the Puritan vision of a settlement peopled with men and women who knew themselves to be chosen by God and therefore were glad to submit themselves to disciplined labour and regulations based on Old Testament texts.

At the same time an immigrant needed cash and a stock of tools. The transatlantic fare was about £5 a person, to which had to be added the price of food during the voyage, and freightage was £4 a ton. An English yeoman farmer with his family and their farming implements and domestic utensils would expect to pay at least £100 for transit to North America. Given that such a man's annual income might be between £40 and £60, if he wished to emigrate he would be forced to sell his land. In other words,

Boston: *imperial* entrepôt, *c.1750*: *this port supplied timber, victuals and fish for the slave colonies of the West Indies and imported tobacco, rum and cotton for the expanding New England colonies. (© Mary Evans Picture Library)*

his decision to leave would have to be final. Of course there were many cases where companies subsidised colonists who were, at least for the Massachusetts Bay Company, carefully screened beforehand to weed out the morally unsuitable, and there were direct inducements. In 1667 the potential colonist for the Cape Florida settlement was lured with the promise of a hundred acres for himself and a further hundred for each of his children and musket-armed servants (this was Indian country) at an annual rent of ten shillings for every thousand acres. A further fifty acres would be granted for every female servant or slave in his possession.

On the expiry of his contract, every indentured servant was to be given a hundred acres by his master, together with farming tools and two suits of clothing. This pledge was deliberately framed to attract men who already enjoyed considerable wealth in England, for they would have had to have provided the costs of shipping and sufficient stocks of food to see themselves and their households through the time it took to cultivate, harvest and market cash crops.

To a large extent the existing, but never inflexible, British social hierarchy was transported across the Atlantic and re-erected in North America and the Caribbean. In the colonies gentlemen commanded the same respect as they did in Britain. One gentleman, who died during the early days of Virginia, had a memorial brass imported for his gravestone which showed him in full armour, an anachronism on the battlefield but still the accepted public token of his social standing. It was set in the floor of Jamestown church from where it was later stolen. As in the home country, property was the ultimate measure of social position for, as one tobacco planter observed, 'If a [man] has Money, Negroes and Land enough he is a complete Gentleman.'

The dominance of the rich gave colonial society a cohesion and made it easy for public order to be maintained since humbler immigrants were already conditioned to accept the magistracy of men of substance and property. In the New England settlements public responsibility was confined to the senior and invariably more prosperous members of church congregations. The laws they framed in their assemblies and enforced from the bench combined the Common Law of England with the injunctions for a pure life extensively laid down in the Old Testament. Blasphemers and homosexuals faced execution, as did masturbators, in New Haven, and fornicators were whipped, a punishment from which, revealingly, gentlemen were excluded. Such laws and proscribed penalties poured from the small legislatures of the New England states and reflected, in an extreme manner, a mentality that prevailed in Britain. Wickedness in all its forms was endemic throughout society and was most concentrated among the lower classes, who required constant and often condign reminders of their duty to God and the civil authorities who upheld His and the King's laws.

This need for a harsh and vigorously enforced code of law was most obvious in the slave-owning colonies. There the élite was ultimately defined by the colour of its skin and, from the second half of the seventeenth century onwards, it stood in continual danger of being overwhelmed by the spiralling slave population. In 1628 Barbados contained 14,000 inhabitants, most of them white indentured labourers. There was a rapid influx of negroes after 1650 and by 1673 their total was 33,000 compared with 21,000 whites. As more and more manual work was undertaken by negroes the European population slumped; in 1712 it was 15,000 against 42,000 slaves.

Fears about security were inevitable. The governor of Barbados expressed misgivings in 1692 about the deployment of the local, all-white militia in the island's forts which might encourage a negro insurrection. Soon after, a suspected conspirator revealed, under torture, the existence of a plot to seize one of the island's arsenals in which, interestingly, several disaffected Irishmen were involved. The Barbadian demographic pattern was repeated in Jamaica and caused similar alarms about the racial imbalance in population. In 1690 there was an uprising by 500 slaves on a plantation in which several whites were killed. After its suppression, a relieved governor informed the royal council, 'The rebellion might have been very bloody considering the number of negroes and the scarcity of white men.' His apprehension was shared by members of the island's assembly which, in 1697, pleaded with the government to recruit 'poor craftsmen' in England for 'white men are so scarce that they will easily find employment'.

The reaction of the West Indian and North American legislatures to the presence in their societies of huge numbers of potentially rebellious slaves was paranoid. Deep fears expressed themselves in sheaves of laws which restricted the movements and activities of slaves and inflicted ferocious penalties, including castration and burning alive, for every form of insubordination. According to the 1696 Barbadian code, which was later imitated in South Carolina, the negroes' 'barbarous, wild, savage natures' placed them beyond the bounds of the laws by which white men lived. Instead they had their own regulations specially drafted to 'restrain the disorders, rapines and inhumanity to which they are naturally prone and inclined'. Special prominence was given to bans on sexual relations between negroes and white women. There was also a need to produce a legal definition of slavery, which had not existed in Britain since the early Middle Ages, and the powers exercised by the master over his slave.

The negro's place within colonial society was at the bottom of the pile. Like a pet dog he owed his name to his master. He also learned to speak and think in a new language, English. Writing in 1724, a

I have a large Family of my own, and my Doors are open to Every Body, yet I have no Bills to pay, and half-a-crown will rest undisturbed in my Pocket for many Moons together. Like one of the Patriarchs, I have my Flocks and my Herds, my Bond-men and Bond-women [indentured labourers], and every sort of trade amongst my own servants, so that I live in a kind of Independence on everyone but Providence.

PLANTER IN 1726

Virginian clergyman noted that 'the languages of the new Negroes are various harsh jargon', but those born in the colony 'talk good English, and affect our language, habits and customs'. Assimilation was limited; African traditions and mythology were perpetuated in what became the slaves' underground culture. A suspect interrogated after the discovery of a plot to seize Antigua in 1736 revealed that a magician or *obeah* man had used his supernatural powers to ensnare conspirators. Not surprisingly, colonial lawmakers saw the transmission of African customs as subversive and slaves were forbidden crepuscular drumming, blowing on conch shells and fetish ceremonies. The submission of the negro, and for that matter the native American, was the foundation of the colonial order.

A significant person in the community was the merchant who, if he possessed diligence and skill, could flourish in the new colonies. However, his life was hard and monotonous. The diary of Anthony Beale, governor of a Hudson's Bay trading post, is a record of what must often have been a tedious existence in an extremely remote region where a strong sense of duty was essential for men to survive. The highlight of the year, in terms of activity, was midsummer when the Company's ships arrived to unload supplies and collect the furs and beaver pelts which were brought to the post by local Indians and exchanged for manufactured goods. There followed the frozen winter of the tundra when the only occupations were fishing and shooting and trapping game which seems to have been plentiful. A tenuous and emotional link with home was the celebration on 23 April of Queen Anne's birthday when the Union flag was hoisted and every man was given 'a bottle of strong beer'.

The colonists persisted for many complex reasons, not least necessity, and nearly all attributed their success to the intervention of a just God who rewarded faith and industry. Those who exerted themselves – and not all did – had, by the end of the seventeenth century, created a thriving empire. This word was not in general usage until well into the eighteenth century, when it began to replace 'colonies' or 'plantations'. Psychologically, the change of title was important, carrying with it notions of grandeur and power on a world scale. And yet the period which witnessed the first growth of Britain's colonies also saw the first germination of that aggressive, self-confident patriotism which flowered during the next two hundred years and facilitated further imperial expansion. Seventeenth-century colonial expansion had taught the British how to make money overseas, given impetus to ideas about national destiny and God's mandate to colonists, and produced pioneers who demonstrated what could be accomplished by men of energy and dedication.

Charleston, Carolina, 1671: fortified against Indians from inland and rivals from the sea, this settlement exported cotton, rice and tobacco. (© Mary Evans Picture Library)

What was achieved fascinated subsequent generations who attempted both to romanticise the founders of empire and invest all of them with qualities they never possessed. During the late-Victorian surge of empire-building, the stories of the sixteenth- and seventeenth-century settlers and seafarers were retold in a form designed to inspire the young to follow their example. Drake, Morgan and the American pioneers were endowed with such contemporary virtues as manly courage, fortitude, comradeship and a love of adventure for its own sake, and the ruthless pursuit of profit was underplayed or left unmentioned. This was a distortion both of the men and their motives, but an attractive one which, during this century, has been given a new lease of life through Hollywood's popular, swashbuckling pirate movies.

In a more serious vein, American historians have minutely examined the world of the early colonists to find evidence in support of theories that today's social attitudes and political systems were rooted in the assumptions and behaviour of the Anglo-Saxon settlers rather than the later frontier experience or the ethnic multiplicity that followed mass immigration in the nineteenth century. What has been revealed is, not surprisingly, a rich diversity of outlook and motive among the settlers; if anything bound them together it was a common urge for self-improvement coupled with a determination to master their environment.

PART TWO
PERSIST & CONQUER
1689-1815

I
RULE
OF THE MAIN:
THE MAKING OF BRITISH SEAPOWER
1689–1748

etween 1689 and 1783 Britain was almost continuously at war with its arch rival, France. The Nine Years War (1689–97) was followed by the War of the Spanish Succession (1702–14), the War of the Austrian Succession (1739–48), the Seven Years War (1756–63) and the American War of Independence (1775–83) in which the French intervened in 1778. What added up to over forty years of fighting consisted of two parallel struggles, one fought to prevent France from establishing a hegemony in Europe, the other to enlarge Britain's overseas trade and colonies at the expense of France and Spain.

Although France had a larger population and greater foreign trade earnings, Britain was always the stronger power because, at times of crisis, she could raise huge amounts of money without resort to additional taxation. The British method of paying for wars was an emergency measure introduced in 1692–3 when it seemed that existing arrangements for obtaining credit were on the verge of collapse. Then, the government adopted the expedient of what became known as the national debt. Corporations and individuals were invited to loan money to the government in return for stock which paid an annual dividend. Investors received a reliable source of income and the government found the wherewithal to pay for armies and navies whenever they were needed. It also freed them from anxieties about public opinion, which would have inevitably reacted adversely to emergency taxation or extra customs duties that might easily have harmed trade and triggered inflation.

The deposition of James II in 1688 and the accession of the Dutch William of Orange and his wife Mary in 1689 had witnessed an irreversible shift in the balance of power between the Crown and Parliament. The legislation of what was called the Glorious Revolution of 1688–9 placed executive authority in the hands of the King's ministers, who in turn depended upon the support of a majority of members of, the House of Commons. The actual process by which ministers assumed their new responsibilities was gradual, and throughout the eighteenth century the Crown continued to exert often considerable influence over the shaping of policy.

What mattered was that neither kings nor ministers could ignore the voice of the Commons, an assembly whose members spoke up both for their own interests and what they saw as the country's. The largest sectional interest within the Commons and the Lords was land, but it never enjoyed a complete dominance. Aristocrats and country squires had to share power with merchants, shippers and financiers from the City of London which, since the 1690s, had developed rapidly as a centre for stock-dealing, banking and marine insurance. There was also a strong presence in both houses of men with direct and indirect colonial interests such as plantation owners, former Indian traders, directors of the East India Company and naval and army officers, of whom nearly three hundred served as MPs between 1754 and 1790. Commercial and colonial interests could and did exert a strong pressure on the King's ministers.

By and large, the commercial and colonial lobbies endorsed aggressive, acquisitive, anti-French and anti-Spanish policies because they regarded them as serving the national interest; wars that ended with annexations offered fresh opportunities for overseas trade and investment. Wars also stimulated domestic productivity, particularly ship-building and the expanding metallurgical industries of the Midlands; Birmingham-made muskets and swords armed the troops of the East India Company. Increased trade meant more revenue from customs that satisfied the dominant landed class which was spared increases in land taxes. During the eighteenth century, there emerged a significant concert of interests among the politically active classes, irrespective of individual attachment to Whig or Tory factions. They believed that it was necessary for Britain to go to war to become richer and to assert her mastery of the seas. No one ever objected to increases in the annual vote of funds for the navy. More importantly, the national debt meant that a belligerent foreign policy caused no undue distress to taxpayers or manufacturers.

France was less fortunately placed when it came to waging war. It was impossible for her governments to harness national resources effectively, thanks to a system of public finance which had become ossified and grossly inefficient. Wholesale tax exemptions were enjoyed by the clergy and aristocracy who resolutely defended their privileges, with the result that, whenever a national emergency occurred, the government had no choice but to borrow from the money markets and pay back loans and interest from increased imposts. These fell heavily on imports, exports and domestic commercial transactions and had the effect of strangling commerce.

The imbalance between French and British resources did not guarantee automatic British success; far from it. Throughout this period, France could field a formidable army and, when the occasion demanded, a powerful fleet, as well as large numbers of privateers who harassed British trade. Moreover, and this was a permanent headache for the élite of ministers who devised British strategy, if France allied with Spain then their combined fleets could overturn the maritime balance. In this situation, Britain could not be strong everywhere and the government would face uncomfortable choices as to where to concentrate its ships and where to allow its enemies superiority.

This dilemma was first encountered in 1689, when Louis XIV attempted to overthrow William III and restore the Catholic James II, thereby fracturing the Anglo-Dutch front which stood in the way of his expansionist policies in Europe. In terms of numbers of ships, France was capable of challenging both powers in the Channel for, since the early 1660s, Louis's minister, Jean-Baptiste Colbert, had masterminded an ambitious policy of naval rearmament. However, despite initial success, France's strategy was marked by missed opportunities and mismanagement. By 1692 the Anglo-Dutch fleet had secured the upper hand with twin victories at Barfleur and La Hogue, and the French wisely shunned fleet actions and turned instead to a war of commerce raiding intended to undermine Anglo-Dutch trade. Despite a handful of audacious commanders, like Jean Bart, this war of attrition in the end failed to produce the expected result. There was, however, one nasty shock for the Allies. Between 1689 and 1691, French pressure in home waters had forced the Royal Navy to withdraw its presence from the Mediterranean, which damaged Britain's trade with Italy and the Levant. An attempt to reassert British naval power in the Mediterranean was made in 1693 and ended in calamity when a heavily escorted convoy of 400 merchantmen was attacked in Lagos Bay in southern Portugal. A hundred ships were lost, but the French again chose not to exploit their success. During 1694–5, the French Mediterranean fleet remained bottled up in Toulon harbour and its adversaries resumed their command of that sea.

Outside Europe, naval operations were limited. At this time, French overseas trade was not great, although this did not stop hundreds of British privateers, including the infamous Captain Kidd, from

PREVIOUS PAGES

The cutting edge of conquest: *British dragoons capture a Mahratha standard, 1803–5.* (© NAM)

The British Empire, 1713

seeking official letters of marque to attack French merchant ships. Neither side gained a decisive advantage at sea between 1689 and 1697, although the Allies could claim some satisfaction at having seen off the French challenge in the Channel and the Mediterranean. On land the story was similar, and both sides, exhausted and war-weary, made peace. It was in fact only a truce since Louis, through diplomatic manipulation, secured, by 1700, what amounted to an amalgamation of France with Spain.

It was unthinkable that Britain could stand by and allow France to take possession of Spain, its Italian territories and, most importantly, its transatlantic empire. From the start, Louis was determined to engross all Spanish commerce, from which the British and Dutch were to be excluded. This was a disaster for Britain; markets would be lost and command of the seas pass to the Franco-Spanish fleet. War began in 1702 with Britain as the lynchpin and paymaster of the Grand Alliance whose other members included the Netherlands, Austria and Prussia, all of whom wanted to resist French domination in Europe.

The decisive battles of the War of the Spanish Succession were fought on land by the armies directed by John Churchill, the Duke of Marlborough. Most of the men he commanded, whether British, Dutch or German, were paid for by Britain which, in 1711, had 171,000 men on its payroll. British seapower alone played a peripheral part in this conflict which was marked by no decisive, full-scale fleet actions. Nevertheless, in terms of the future use of the navy, the war provided useful lessons and experience.

From the beginning, British strategy aimed at the elimination of Franco-Spanish power in the Mediterranean. This required the acquisition of a naval base in the region so that men-o'-war could be armed, victualled and overhauled without having to sail back to ports in Britain. To this end, Gibraltar was occupied and held in the teeth of a Franco-Spanish counter-attack (1702–4) and Minorca, with its deep-water harbour at Port Mahon, was seized in 1708. Both acquisitions were of tremendous importance, for British fleets could now be permanently stationed in the Mediterranean and British political influence exerted over its small maritime states.

As a token of Britain's new position in this area, Admiral Sir Clowdisley Shovell's fleet cruised in the western Mediterranean in 1703 to demonstrate to local rulers that Britain was now a force to be reckoned with. Such a show was hardly needed; in 1705 Barcelona was occupied after an amphibious landing, and three years later a similar attack on Toulon did severe damage to the French fleet anchored there.

These enterprises were part of a larger strategy, warmly endorsed by Marlborough, by which France was driven to split her land forces to counter threats in southern Europe, including an invasion of Spain itself by an army under Lord Peterborough. His campaign, like Wellington's a century later, could not have been sustained without the Royal Navy's domination of the Atlantic and Mediterranean.

Beyond European waters, the Royal Navy undertook a number of small-scale operations against French and Spanish shipping and colonies with mixed results. A small squadron, under the command of Vice-Admiral John Benbow, a determined and courageous officer, cruised in the West Indies and severely mauled a French flotilla in a six-day engagement off Santa Marta in April 1702.

By 1710 France, on the defensive and close to bankruptcy, had been fought to a standstill. In Britain a new, Tory ministry adopted a strategy which, it was imagined, would bring the country advantages in the form of French colonies. Successful amphibious attacks were made on French settlements in Newfoundland and Nova Scotia, but in 1711 the capture of Quebec failed because of careless planning and ignorance of the St Lawrence River.

In 1714 peace was made at Utrecht, where France recognised continued Spanish independence. Britain was rewarded with Gibraltar and Minorca, confirming her ascendancy in the Mediterranean, and Nova Scotia, and the grant of the *asiento*, an official licence that permitted one ship a year to trade with the Spanish American

Treasures of the Orient: guided by Mercury, the East offers its riches to Britannia. Seated below is 'Old Father Thames'. Painting by Spiridone Roma from the ceiling of East India House, 1778. (© British Library)

colonies. The war had marked Britain's coming of age as a European and a global power, a status which owed everything to her fleet of 124 ships, nearly twice the strength of the combined Franco-Spanish navies. While her adversaries and the Dutch had been debilitated by twelve years of conflict, British overseas trade had increased. This achievement had been in large part the result of the 1708 Cruisers and Convoys Act which bound the navy to allocate warships to protect merchantmen against privateers and commerce raiders, a duty which, by the close of the war, occupied two-thirds of the navy's strength.

From 1714 to 1739 Britain and its colonies enjoyed a period of peace, domestic tranquillity and economic growth. Relations with France were outwardly cordial, but many Frenchmen were deeply apprehensive about the scope of Britain's global ambitions. 'The financial power of the English … gets every day larger and more ambitious,' observed a French official in 1733. Commercial competition between the two nations was keen, in particular in North America, the Caribbean and on the east coast of India, where France was extending its network of trading posts, alarming the East India Company.

It was Spanish high-handedness rather than fears of French enterprise which led to war in November 1739. For the past five years, the Spanish authorities in America had been cracking down on what, with good reason, they considered abuses of the *asiento* contract by British merchants. The attempts of the *guarda-costas* (customs officers) to stem the flow of contraband led to violent incidents when British ships were boarded, searched and, in many cases, their captains and cargoes arrested. Most famously, one zealous *guarda-costa* sliced off the ear of Captain Jenkins of the *Rebecca* and suggested that he took the organ to George II in language that was too coarse to be repeated in the Commons. When MPs debated this and other outrages in March 1739, the mercantile interest clamoured for war. They claimed that

Naval heritage: *Captain John Bentinck and his son. (© NMM)*

In Greenland's icy waters: British whalers in the Arctic. Remoteness and unkind climates never deterred businessmen in pursuit of profit. (© NMM)

Britain's entire transatlantic commerce would be ruined unless Spain was taught a sharp lesson. The navy was the obvious means of bringing home to Spain the folly of meddling with British trade. The doctrine of the corrective use of seapower which later, and after many applications, would be known as gunboat diplomacy was born.

Almost immediately war had been formally declared, Admiral Edward Vernon took command of a fleet under orders to harry Spanish trade and colonies in the Caribbean. What was in effect a war of smash-and-grab raids opened on an encouraging note with the capture of Porto Bello. Further attacks were launched against Cartagena (on the coast of modern Colombia), Havana and Santiago de Cuba during the next two years, but were bloodily repelled. By the end of 1742 hopes of quick, profitable victories had evaporated. From the start, British strategy had been flawed. To have any chance of success, assaults on Spanish strongholds in the Americas required their isolation, which could only be achieved by a blockade of Spain's Atlantic ports. Operational difficulties, most notably the inadequate base facilities at Gibraltar, prevented the Mediterranean fleet from stopping the flow of reinforcements and munitions from Spain to its colonies.

By 1744 the war against Spain had become a general European conflict in which Britain, the Netherlands and Austria were fighting Spain, France and Prussia. The perilous military situation in Flanders and the need to defend George II's province of Hanover demanded a large commitment of British troops to the Continent. There was a further call on manpower in 1745, when Prince Charles Edward (the 'Young Pretender'), backed by French troops and cash, landed in Scotland. The last Jacobite insurrection was a desperate gamble from start to end; the Prince's only substantial support lay in the Highlands of Scotland, where, after an excursion as far south as Derby, his army was cornered and overcome at Culloden in April 1746. Throughout the campaign he had been denied further French assistance by the Royal Navy.

The Jacobite uprising, which caused some temporary and highly exaggerated alarm in England and the Lowlands of Scotland, was a distraction from a war where France was now identified as the main enemy. A methodical strategy was evolved, aimed at the extinction of her overseas trade and the occupation of her settlements in North America. A squadron of men-o'-war was also despatched to assist the East India Company in its miniature campaign against French enclaves on the Coromandel coast and to interrupt France's Asian commerce.

In America, the war opened with a successful attack on Cape Breton Island at the mouth of the St Lawrence and the capture of Fort Louisbourg in 1745 by a force which included a 4,000-strong New England volunteer contingent. Within a few months, preparations were in hand to establish a naval base at Fort Louisbourg which would serve as a springboard for amphibious operations against Quebec. These had to be abandoned when a French relief force arrived the following year.

1747 saw British maritime supremacy preserved, with Admiral Sir George Anson and Rear-Admiral Sir Edward Hawke emerging from the war as heroes. Elsewhere the war had become a stalemate for, while unable to defend their colonies, the French had occupied most of the Austrian Netherlands (modern Belgium). In 1748 the exhausted combatants agreed the Peace of Aix-la-Chapelle, which did little more than restore the pre-war *status quo*, although Britain had to sacrifice Louisbourg in order to secure the removal of French forces from the Low Countries. Aix-la-Chapelle was, in fact, an armistice.

Let the wise politicians of France *and of* Spain *Threat to take from* Great Britain *her rule of the main, Their plate ships shall pay for such arrogant talk If they come in sight of the* Lord Anson *and* Hawke.

PATRIOTIC BALLAD, 1770s

2

'TIS TO GLORY
WE STEER:
GAINS AND LOSSES
1749–1783

The peace of Aix-la-Chapelle settled nothing: Anglo-French commercial and colonial rivalry persisted and deepened after 1748. The French remained convinced that their antagonist's long-term aim was to stifle their trade and expropriate their colonies. Britain continued to fear a concert between the Bourbon Louis XV and his Spanish cousin which would bring their fleets into a dangerous conjunction. Despite the late war, Britain was becoming richer and more and more dependent on trade with her colonies. Exports to North America rose from a yearly average of £524,000 in the late 1720s to just over £1 million twenty years later. During the same period the annual total of exports to the West Indies increased from £473,000 to £732,000 and to India from £112,000 to £522,000.

And yet as exports to the colonies spiralled, Britain's economic future remained uncertain. The chief threat came from France and was most menacing in India and North America where fighting had hitherto been limited and inconclusive. The danger was greatest in North America where, by 1754, violent clashes had increased as the advance guards of British and French settlers collided in the Ohio valley. The French and their Indian allies had been penetrating the Ohio River for some years, moving southwards from Quebec. Far to the south, parties of Frenchmen were simultaneously edging north from their coastal settlements on the Gulf of Mexico along the Mississippi River. If uninterrupted, France would, in the near future, establish a title to the entire region around the Mississippi and its tributaries and so occupy a broad swathe of territory from New Orleans in the south to Quebec in the north, blocking the westwards expansion of Britain's colonies.

Skirmishes between French and Virginian frontiersmen along the upper Ohio set the alarm bells ringing in London during the summer of 1754. National prestige was at stake and possibly the future of British North America. Measures were immediately taken to draft regular troops to Virginia and additional warships to North American waters, and the French followed suit.

In 1756 Britain became engaged in a war on the Continent in order to protect George II's province of Hanover and was consequently obliged to dilute the forces she had originally intended to concentrate in America. With free use of the Austrian Netherlands with the creation of the Franco-Austrian-Russian axis, France could muster men along the Channel coast and force her opponent to divert men and material to counter an invasion threat. Moreover, subsidies to Prussia deprived Britain of cash that was needed elsewhere.

It was not the burden of Britain's Continental commitment, but unpreparedness, ill-luck and operational problems which led to a dismal sequence of reverse during 1756 and 1757. The worst was the loss of Minorca after Admiral John Byng refused to risk an engagement with the French Mediterranean fleet, and withdrew to Gibraltar. His prudence, based upon the fear that it was better to preserve his fleet rather than hazard a battle, was almost universally interpreted as cowardice by an indignant public. Byng was recalled in disgrace, court-martialled and executed in March 1757, in Voltaire's words, *'pour encourager les autres'*. He was as much a scapegoat for a discredited ministry as a warning to faltering admirals who failed to manifest the expected pugnacious spirit whenever the French appeared.

Elsewhere, the navy was in more difficulties. There had been a quick mobilisation, thanks to the direction of Anson, First Lord of the Admiralty, but it took time to build new ships and refit old ones. The navy also had to find and retain sailors to serve in its ships, many of which were forced to go to sea partially manned. The biggest problem was wastage; out of 70,000 men recruited between 1756 and 1759, 12,700 deserted and a slightly larger number died from disease. By contrast, 143 died as a result of enemy action between 1755 and 1757. The immediate solution was the widespread use of the press gang, which was unpopular with its victims, their kinsfolk and merchants and shipowners, who lost skilled seamen to the navy. In the long term, the answer to wastage lay in the preservation of sailors on ship and shore. In this field, and contrary to the commonplace historical view of everyday life in the Georgian navy, considerable and often highly successful efforts were made to keep sailors in good health. Whenever possible, crews were given rations of fresh meat, and vegetables as a preventative against scurvy, which decimated crews despite the knowledge that regular eating of lemons or marmalade reduced the chances of catching it. Naval pay in the 1750s compared well with that of sailors in the merchant service and was from time to time augmented with prize money, although ordinary seamen never received more than a few pounds. A sailor could, therefore, find some satisfaction in his lot compared with that of the soldier.

In retrospect, the years 1756 and 1757 were a period of slow, methodical mobilisation for later offensives. Contemporaries, dismayed by the retirement from the Mediterranean, fears of invasion, the temporary loss of control over the Atlantic, reverses in Canada and India, and the poor performance of the Prussians which opened the way for an invasion of Hanover, blamed a government which appeared confused and faltering. The war effort was subject to critical scrutiny inside Parliament and outside by journalists and pamphleteers on the look out for evidence of ministerial incompetence.

On the German front the tide was turning in Prussia's favour. In November 1757 a Franco-Austrian army was resoundingly beaten at Rossbach; a month later Frederick defeated an Austrian army at Leuthen and, the following spring, won a victory over the Russians at Zorndorf. There was also heartening news from India where, in June 1757, Robert Clive had routed Siraj-ud-Daula's army at Plassey and restored British power in Bengal.

At sea, the French suffered two dire misfortunes. An epidemic of typhus broke out among the crews of the squadron which had protected Louisbourg and was carried back to Brest when the ships returned at the close of the year. Early in 1758 the Toulon squadron, under orders to sail to the West Indies and North America, were driven back to port by a combination of operational muddles, bad weather and a brief engagement with a British force off eastern Spain. Morale throughout the French navy was sagging; low pay and thin rations drove men to desert in large numbers from ships which were unseaworthy thanks to inefficient dockyards. Meanwhile, the Royal Navy was steadily growing in strength. In 1757 there were ninety ships of the line in commission and a further 149 frigates, sloops and bomb ketches. Two years later the fleet had grown to 300 ships of all kinds.

Britain's naval supremacy made possible William Pitt's grand strategy of the piecemeal conquest of France's stranded colonies. In May and December 1758, the fortified slaving stations of Fort Louis and Gorée on the coast of Senegal were taken at little cost. The latter surrendered after a brief exchange of fire between warships and shore batteries in which the British casualties were 23 dead and 68 wounded.

The heaviest blow was delivered in North America. Louisbourg was captured in 1758, and the following year a three-pronged land and sea offensive was launched against Quebec, which was finally taken in September. In the West Indies, the reduction of the French sugar islands began with the capture of Guadeloupe in February 1759. As the year progressed and Pitt's strategy unfolded, it seemed only a matter of time before the whole of France's empire would be swallowed and her overseas trade extinguished. Unable to match the Royal Navy in North American, Indian and West Indian waters, France had no chance of reinforcing her outnumbered colonial garrisons. Her only hope lay in an invasion of Britain, a project advanced by Louis XV's chief minister, Etienne-François, Duc de Choiseul, who believed it would force Pitt to pull back men and ships to defend his country's shores.

The first prerequisite of the 1759 invasion scheme was the amalgamation of France's Brest and Toulon fleets. This was frustrated by Edward Boscawen who intercepted and scattered the Mediterranean fleet off Lagos Bay in June. The 21-strong Brest fleet was discovered off Quiberon Bay in November by Hawke who, in a dramatic chase, routed the French and, in so doing, became a national hero. The battle of Quiberon Bay was the last in a gratifying tally of victories on land and sea during 1759. It joined Lagos Bay, Quebec, the fall of Guadeloupe and Minden, in which an Anglo-Hanoverian army defeated the French and guaranteed Hanover's security. National self-esteem and self-assertion grew stronger, as did the deep-rooted sense that Britain was specially favoured by Providence.

In 1762 Martinique and a scattering of French sugar islands were taken by Admiral Sir George Rodney. Profit-seekers followed the landing parties for his victories and the admiral was struck by the speed with which planters from British islands flocked to Martinique to stake out claims to land.

Great prizes were now available, since Spain had taken the plunge and joined France. Almost immediately, she suffered two stunning blows. Manila surrendered to an expeditionary force from India, and Havana was surprised by a fleet commanded by Admiral Sir George Pocock which had, at considerable risk, approached its target by the Old Bahama Channel, a seaway normally shunned because of its reefs and cays. The gamble paid off; thirteen Spanish battleships were taken in Havana harbour and Pocock and Lord Albemarle, who commanded the landing force, each received £123,000 in prize money.

At the moment when optimistic patriots believed that the Spanish as well as the French empires might pass into Britain's hands, the government was negotiating a peace. Although both France and Spain were prostrate, there was a fear among some that what the Whig Duke of Bedford called Britain's 'monopoly' of seapower would 'excite all the naval powers of Europe to enter into a confederacy against us', a pusillanimous view which ignored the fact that these other nations did not possess enough ships to challenge the Royal Navy. In fact, it was the rising cost of the war and resort to additional taxation, including increased duties on beer, which encouraged the government to reach a settlement.

The Treaty of Paris, signed early in 1763, was controversial. Britain retained the slaving forts on the Senegal coast; the West Indian islands of Grenada, St Vincent, Dominica and Tobago; Canada and all the lands to the west of the Mississippi, Minorca and Florida, which the Spanish conceded in return for the evacuation of Havana. France withdrew its forces from Germany and was allowed to keep Gorée Island, St Lucia, Martinique, Guadeloupe, a share in the Newfoundland fisheries and all the possessions she had held in India before 1749, so long as they were de-militarised. Manila was returned to Spain in return for a ransom (which was never paid) and given title to land west of the Mississippi.

These terms excited much public indignation, on the grounds that too much had been surrendered merely to provide for the security of Hanover. Ineptitude of one kind or another marked the performance of all the ministries between 1763 and 1775, a period dominated by politicians of limited talents and narrow horizons. Matters were not helped by the frequent interventions of George III.

Politics after the Treaty of Paris revolved around relations with the North American colonies and these will be examined in a later chapter. Of equal importance, from the point of view of the overall development of the empire, was the massive programme of naval rearmament begun by the French in 1762. The impetus behind this attempt to rebuild the French fleet was Choiseul, who was determined to avenge the defeats of 1759–62 and restore his country's former position as an imperial, global power. Within eight years, the total of French battleships had risen from 40 to 64, and frigates from 10 to 50.

This development was closely watched by the Admiralty, which had a well-organised network of agents in France and Spain, managed, until his death in 1770, by Richard Wolters, the British consul in Rotterdam. During the Seven Years War, Wolters controlled spies in Versailles, Brest, Toulon, Le Havre, Rochefort and Madrid who reported to him on the movements of French warships. Although still little-known even today, the Admiralty's intelligence-gathering system was extremely valuable in giving advance warning of the deployment of the French navy, and was continued in peacetime. Additional details were given by British consuls elsewhere who regularly sent the Admiralty information they considered useful.

This excellent service enabled the Admiralty to keep an accurate and up-to-date breakdown of the numbers and condition of ships in the French and Spanish navies. By 1770, the picture emerging from intelligence sources indicated that the gap between the Royal Navy and the combined fleets of its former antagonists was narrowing. Between them, France and Spain had a total of 121 ships of the line against Britain's 126. Pitt had estimated that 125 of this type of vessel was the minimum needed for security everywhere, a figure that had been kept to in spite of a post-war reduction in the naval budget.

For the moment British naval paramountcy seemed unassailable. The threat of naval action alone had upheld British claims to the Turks Islands, defended British loggers' rights to cut mahogany on the Honduran coast and ensured the expulsion of the French from slaving posts in the Gambia. In 1769–70 the fleet had been mobilised in the Falkland Islands and, rather than risk war, the Spanish gave way.

These successful exercises in gunboat diplomacy may have encouraged official complacency, but they did not excuse the government's short-sightedness after the first outbreak of rebellion in North America in 1775. Lord North's administration assumed that the insurgents would be easily and swiftly

Come cheer up, my lads, 'tis to Glory we steer,

To add something new to this wonderful year;

To honour we call you, not press you like slaves,

For who are so free as we sons of the waves?

DAVID GARRICK, 1759

overcome, and that no other power would consider intervention. Both judgements were mistaken; after two years of fighting it was clear that the Americans would survive and the surrender of General Burgoyne's army at Saratoga in 1777 finally convinced the French that the moment had come to launch a war of revenge against Britain. France entered the war in February 1778, followed by Spain in June 1779 and then the Netherlands. The remaining powers of Europe were malevolent neutrals.

Between 1778 and 1783 the British empire faced a crisis which remained without equal in seriousness until the summer of 1940. Britain had no allies in Europe; her main line of defence, the navy, was outnumbered; and no outstanding statesman or commander came forward to match the time. Fortunately, as it turned out, there was a similar lack of imaginative leadership among Britain's enemies and, while the French navy had been physically transformed, it had yet to produce a breed of aggressive commanders prepared to adopt bold, if risky, tactics. Time and time again, when presented with a tactical advantage, French admirals allowed it to slip from their grasp.

France had three major strategic objectives. The first was to transfer troops to North America and assist the rebels there; the second was to attack and occupy British sugar islands in the West Indies, and the third, and most ambitious, was an invasion of the southern coast of England. The early phases of each campaign were disappointing. The Comte d'Estaing's North American squadron disembarked troops on the shores of Delaware Bay, but discovered that a smaller British squadron had escaped. Unable to establish local superiority in North American waters, d'Estaing sailed southwards to begin the conquest of the British West Indies. This required complete dominance of the Caribbean, which eluded him after he allowed a badly mauled British force to withdraw after an engagement off Grenada in July 1779.

The French record in home waters looked more promising and, by August 1779, Britain faced the ominous prospect of losing control of the Channel. The combined Franco-Spanish fleet mustered 63 battleships and 16 frigates in comparison to a mere 42 ships which could be raised by the British. However, weak leadership, half-hearted commitment by the Spanish, rough weather, delays in the deliveries of rations and an outbreak of scurvy all bedevilled the Franco-Spanish armada and in mid-September Admiralty agents reported that the invasion had been postponed. Instead, France shifted her resources to the West Indies and North America and to increase a blockade on Gibraltar. Released from the threat of invasion, the British were able to divert more ships to other fronts.

However, the British failed to re-establish dominance in the Caribbean, and the French fleet continued to sail unchallenged in West Indian and American waters. Meanwhile, the tide of war swung irreversibly against Britain in North America after the surrender of Major-General Sir Charles Cornwallis's army at Yorktown in October 1781. The following spring the French and Spanish decided to launch a seaborne attack on Jamaica. The British encountered the French off Les Saintes between Guadeloupe and Dominica. The battle was long, bloody and decisive, and the British were victorious.

In October 1782 the siege of Gibraltar ended and a war-weary France and Spain agreed to the Peace of Versailles a few months later. The North American colonies apart, Britain's losses were confined to Minorca and Florida which were delivered to Spain; Senegal, St Lucia and Tobago which were returned to France; and Ceylon which was handed over to the Netherlands. Britain had come out of the war relatively well, thanks largely to the government's ability to borrow huge sums, but the vulnerability of the empire had been exposed. Maritime supremacy had been preserved but only just.

The architect of victory: a Rococo celebration of empire and seapower on the monument to William Pitt, Earl of Chatham in Westminster Abbey. Neptune crouches beneath Britannia's trident and the inscription praises the Prime Minister who with the aid of 'Divine Providence exalted Great Britain to an height of Prosperity and Glory unknown in any former age'. (© Warburg Institute)

3

THE EMPIRE OF AMERICA:
SETTLEMENT AND WAR
1689–1775

Throughout the first half of the eighteenth century pioneers in North America moved inland along the banks of the Hudson, Delaware and Potomac rivers and their tributaries. Woodlands were razed, land ploughed and small settlements appeared in the wilderness. Between 1710 and 1730 the population of Pennsylvania alone grew from 24,500 to 85,700, an increase largely made up of incomers.

A new phase in the development of the North American colonies was underway, with expansion westwards across the Appalachians and northwards towards the St Lawrence basin. The new migration aroused misgivings among the Indian tribes, whose lands lay in its path, and alarm among the French, whose underpopulated colony of New France seemed in danger of being overwhelmed. Both reacted with defensive measures, but neither the Indians nor the French possessed resources adequate for the task. They could temporarily deflect, but never stem the advance of the colonists who, when the going got tough, could summon up assistance from Britain.

The Indian tribes were sadly ill-equipped to understand, let alone take action to prevent what was happening to them. They could never wholly grasp the alien, European principle of land-ownership and all the legal paraphernalia of deeds of sale and titles that went with it. Nor could Europeans appreciate the Indian concept of the land, which was simply expressed many years later by a Sauk chieftain: 'The Great Spirit gave it to his children to live upon, and cultivate, as far as is necessary for their subsistence; and so long as they cultivate it, they have a right to the soil.'

It was therefore possible for a tribe to sell large tracts of land in the belief that they retained the right to cultivate it or hunt its game. When they discovered that this was not so, and were excluded by settlers from what they still considered their property, Indians were puzzled and angry. Often tribes were unclear as to what they had relinquished since they knew nothing of European measurements, delineating boundaries by reference to natural features rather than lines drawn on maps. The agents of the land speculators, who were the forerunners of the colonists, commonly used every form of chicanery to dupe a people only dimly aware of what was being asked of them. Alcohol was the lubricant which eased many Indians off their lands. Ever since the arrival of the first settlers, Indians had been tempted and undermined by spirits, which were made freely available by unscrupulous traders.

The frontier tribes had long ago abandoned a culture based upon stone, animal skins and bone, and become dependent on the goods offered by the colonists. In return, the Indians could offer beaver pelts and furs. The pelt, carefully trimmed to leave a thin covering of fur, was a tough, waterproof material that had been used for hat-making in Europe since the mid-seventeenth century. The familiar tricorn hat, a mark of social respectability and universally worn throughout most of the eighteenth century, had its origins in the rivers and streams of North America. Europe's millinery fashions provided the staple trade of the North American frontier: by the 1750s, the annual value of beaver pelts exported from New York and the Hudson's Bay Company posts in northern Canada was £250,000.

From the mid-seventeenth century, the commerce in furs and beaver skins had been intensely competitive. The French had tried, vainly, to evict the Hudson's Bay Company traders from their bases and had taken steps to secure a monopoly of fur and beaver-pelt trading with all the tribes along the St Lawrence basin and the shores of the Great Lakes. In the last quarter of the century, French governors in Quebec had negotiated treaties with the Indians that allowed them to build a chain of fortified posts which ran west from Montreal to the northern tip of Lake Michigan. Each was strategically sited to seal the narrow waterways between the lakes and so control the routes taken by fur-traders. Forts Frontenac, Niagara, Detroit and Mackinac were more than guardposts: they marked the southern limits of New France and laid a tenuous claim to a wilderness that would shortly be entered by British settlers.

North America 1755-75

French domination of this area was challenged in 1727, when New York established a fort at Oswego on the south-eastern shore of Lake Ontario. Four years later, the French countered by erecting a stronghold at Crown Point on the southern extremity of Lake Champlain. It served both to defend the approaches to Montreal and as a barrier against New York colonists advancing along the Hudson.

Fort-building and efforts to win over the six tribes of the Iroquois Confederacy, who occupied the region south of Lake Ontario, were part of a cold war between the British colonists and the French. The strengths and weaknesses of both sides were exposed in 1744 when Britain and France declared war. There was a series of minor actions at various points along the frontier, the most serious of which were a sequence of Franco-Indian raids which devastated isolated settlements on the upper Hudson and Mohawk rivers. In the struggle for the hearts and minds of the Indians, the French had the upper hand, largely because both parties were apprehensive about the scope of British expansion.

The British colonists' war effort was fragmented and therefore ineffectual. The colonies were disunited and without an apparatus to prepare and execute a common defensive strategy. Nevertheless, in 1745, the New Englanders had responded enthusiastically to a summons to send volunteers to the siege of Louisbourg. There were widespread festivities when the fort was taken and many who celebrated were already looking ahead to the collapse of New France and, with it, opportunities to move into and settle the empty lands of Lower Canada. The land-hungry were disappointed; the peace of 1748 restored the situation in North America to what it had been at the start of the war.

There was no peace in the disputed territory between New France and British North America. After 1748, the focus for contention shifted to the upper Ohio, where the Ohio Company was in the process of buying 200,000 acres from the local Indians. The French reaction was swift and designed to stem the inevitable flow of pioneers into the region. The Marquis Duquesne, governor of Quebec, ordered an armed reconnaissance of the Ohio valley in 1749. This expedition was followed by further shows of force and, by the end of 1752, a string of outposts had been constructed which linked the southern shores of Lake Erie with Fort Duquesne, placed at the confluence of the Ohio, Monongahela and Allegheny rivers. British settlers and fur-traders who ventured too close to the new centres of French power were warned off.

Duquesne's bold move in the frontier chess game stunned the British colonists. Pennsylvania, the colony immediately threatened, was in a state of disarray since the Quaker minority, which dominated political life, had refused to contemplate any measures to defend the colony. Without any machinery with which to plan and coordinate a common defence policy, the response of the other colonies was fumbling. An attempt by a detachment of the Virginia militia, commanded by a young landowner, George Washington, to keep a toehold in Ohio came unstuck in April 1754 when he had to abandon Fort Necessity.

This setback panicked the colonies into action. Representatives assembled at Albany, New York in the spring of 1755 in an effort to create a common front against the French and the Iroquois. The colonists' position appeared extremely perilous. They were confronted by what seemed the overwhelming strength of New France, an offshoot of Europe's greatest military power. Recent events indicated that France was now intent on pursuing an aggressive frontier policy which, if it succeeded, would confine the British to a coastal strip of North America. Moreover, France was a Catholic nation, which aroused deep fears among the colonists, a large proportion of whom were Presbyterians. Their anxiety was not solely based upon an ancestral loathing of Popery; Catholic priests and missionaries were abroad among the Iroquois and, with official approval, were warning them that the British intended to seize all Indian lands.

The outcome of the Albany assembly was an appeal to the British government for help. Britain would not allow the colonies and their wealth to slip from her grasp, even if this meant a war with France, although the government hoped that the conflict would remain localised. The eventual decision to send troops to North America had far-reaching consequences. It was a recognition of how vital the colonies were for Britain and it transformed North America into a war zone in which British forces were fighting for dominance. Furthermore, and this was not fully appreciated by all those involved, the colonists had been placed under an obligation to the home government which would have to be redeemed. For their part, the colonists had for the first time found the will to shed their particularism and join together.

A priority in 1754 was the reassertion of British authority in the Ohio valley. In September, General Edward Braddock was sent to Virginia with two regiments of foot, an artillery battery and orders to expel the French from Fort Duquesne. He was a competent officer who had learned his trade on the battlefields of Europe where warfare had become an exact art. Firepower – that is concentrated, synchronised, close-range musketry – was the key to victory. Therefore soldiers, elegantly uniformed and drilled, manoeuvred in rigid lines to take positions from where they could fire the volleys which won battles. It would be very different in the backwoods of North America, as Braddock soon discovered.

In May 1755, Braddock set up his forward base at Fort Cumberland, a hundred or so miles from Fort Duquesne. His regulars had been augmented by some Virginian militiamen, who were rated by Braddock 'very indifferent men'. Equally unpromising in the eyes of a professional soldier were the droves of Indians who congregated around the fort and offered their services. All these men, and in many cases their wives and children, needed rations and these were carried by packhorses and horse-drawn wagons which were obtained, with much difficulty, from colonial governors.

'Deal with your Quaking Friends': a playing card advertising the sale of lands in Pennsylvania, c.1690.
(© Worcester College, Oxford)

Transport problems had to be put aside after Braddock received intelligence that 3,000 French regulars, under Johann Herman von Dieskau, were expected in Quebec by midsummer. Von Dieskau was a specialist in the then novel art of partisan warfare in rough country, a subject about which Braddock knew next to nothing. Nevertheless, he had with him men like Washington who knew the rudiments of a type of fighting in which concealment, ambushes and rapid withdrawals were all important.

If Braddock received any advice on this subject it was ill-heeded, since he took no precautions against sudden attack nor sent men ahead to spy out the land. His column, with its cumbersome tail of horses and wagons, trundled through the forests, watched at every turn by unseen Indian scouts in the French service. Soon after it forded the Monongahela River, the vanguard was ambushed by a Franco-Indian detachment who drove it in confusion back into the centre of the column. Panic followed; a third of Braddock's army was lost and he was fatally wounded. Prisoners were tortured to death by the Indians, a practice which was tolerated by the French, and for which the British would later take condign revenge. The detritus of Braddock's army retired to Fort Cumberland, leaving the French masters of the region.

The disaster on the Monongahela shook the colonists and bruised British prestige, but it did not alter the balance of power in North America. The French army there was scattered across the mid-west in penny packets and was nowhere strong enough to deliver a sustained offensive. It did, however, give its opponents some nasty surprises; in August 1756 Fort Oswego was captured and, during the following year, there were raids against settlements in the Mohawk valley.

In the meantime, the colonial authorities and the British army took stock of the situation. The Quakers were ousted in Pennsylvania and the colony placed on a proper war footing. Most significantly Braddock's successor, John Campbell, Earl of Loudoun began a programme of training soldiers to fight a bush war. Loudoun was well-qualified for the task since he had had experience of guerrilla fighting during and after the 1745–6 Jacobite rebellion. Undistinguished as a field-commander, he had the good sense to realise that a new form of warfare required a new type of soldier. They were the Ranger, an American huntsman or trapper, and the light infantryman, a British regular chosen for his stamina, agility and quick-wittedness. They were given practical uniforms, often dark green or dun-coloured, which allowed them to pass unnoticed through woodland and bush.

The Ranger and light infantryman learned the arts of woodcraft, marksmanship and rapid move-ment across rough terrain, accomplishments which enabled the British army to fight a partisan war on equal terms with the French and Indians. Such troops, deployed as scouts and skirmishers ahead of a column, were also an insurance against the sort of disaster that had overtaken Braddock.

Flexible and imaginative commanders were needed if soldiers adept in frontier warfare were to be used to the best effect. These were provided by Pitt, who sent to North America two outstanding and energetic officers in their thirties, Major-General Jeffrey Amherst and Brigadier James Wolfe. This new high command in North America in 1758 was the instrument of Pitt's grand strategy for the invasion and conquest of Canada. The cabinet was convinced that nothing short of the complete extinction of French power in North America would guarantee the future security of Britain's colonies there. Such an ambitious undertaking required a massive concentration of sea and land forces and, it went without saying, a tight sea blockade that would deny succour and reinforcements to the French.

Three armies invaded New France in 1758. General Lord Abercromby, the commander-in-chief, with 11,000 regulars, advanced on Forts William, Henry and Ticonderoga. Brigadier John Forbes, with nearly 7,000, mostly colonial militia, followed in Braddock's tracks to take Fort Duquesne. The third and largest army of 30,000 was led by Amherst, who was directed to make a seaborne attack on Louisbourg and then, if time permitted, proceed down the St Lawrence to assault Quebec. His transports were escorted by a squadron of twenty-three battleships and nineteen frigates commanded by Boscawen.

The largest imperial campaign yet undertaken met with mixed fortunes. Abercromby was thrown back from Ticonderoga by the French commander, Louis-Joseph, Marquis de Montcalm, and Forbes occupied Fort Duquesne unopposed. In the Louisbourg operation a fearless Wolfe led the first wave of light infantry which landed on the Cape Breton Island beaches and cleared the way for the disembarkation of the rest of the army and its siege-train. The siege dragged on through June and July before the French surrendered. Many, Wolfe among them, were keen to press on to Quebec, but Boscawen was uneasy about taking his ships into the hazardous waters of the St Lawrence. Furthermore, if operations extended into November, the armada would be stranded when the river froze.

Pitt's masterplan had whittled down, not destroyed, French power in North America. The following year it was the chance of new generals. The dud Abercromby was replaced by Amherst, who conducted a renewed offensive against Ticonderoga. Wolfe was chosen by Pitt to command the St Lawrence expedition, on the recommendation of those officers who had served with him at Louisbourg, and because the war minister had been deeply impressed by his commitment to the campaign's objective. He nearly had second thoughts after a private dinner during which Wolfe delivered a histrionic exhibition of his martial ardour. Newcastle, on hearing of the incident, is alleged to have warned George II that Wolfe was mad. 'Mad is he?' remarked the King. 'Then I hope he will bite some of my other generals.'

The Quebec campaign, begun in June 1759, proceeded smoothly at first. Wolfe's transports were protected by a squadron of twenty-two battleships under an able and brave officer, Admiral Sir Charles Saunders, whose valuable contribution to the operation has often been overlooked. Much depended on him; his light craft sailed ahead of the main force with officers skilled in navigation aboard, including the future explorer James Cook, who charted a course through what was still a little-known waterway.

Progress was methodical and slow in a campaign where time mattered. Outnumbered, and unlikely to get assistance from France, Montcalm's only chance of avoiding defeat lay in delaying his adversary until the beginning of winter. For a time it appeared that he might succeed. After occupying the Ile d'Orléans at the beginning of July, Wolfe found his way impeded by the French batteries on the bluffs downstream from Quebec. A landing by the Montmorency Falls, intended to dislodge these cannon, went awry when the assault force of grenadiers and light infantrymen from the recently raised Royal American Regiment were driven back to their boats by the volleys of French-Canadian militiamen.

Wolfe was disheartened by this reverse, which was made more galling by the fact that his finest troops had been routed by amateurs. He considered colonial militiamen as no more than an armed rabble, and described them as: 'the dirtiest, most contemptible cowardly dogs that you can conceive.' As the war progressed, it revealed a deep social gulf between aristocratic British officers and colonials, whom they believed to be without moral fibre. This disdain was shared by French officers, one of whom observed that French-Canadian militiamen were 'very brave behind a tree and very timid when not covered'.

Other tensions emerged during Britain's first large-scale imperial war of conquest. British officers were appalled to discover that European laws of war, devised to restrain its worst excesses, went unrecognised on the frontier. Wolfe, like many of his fellow officers, was shocked by the promiscuous brutality of colonial warfare, in particular the murder of prisoners and civilians by Indians. Wolfe blamed Montcalm personally for the Indian outrages and pledged himself to repay in kind. A year before he set off for Quebec, he had given notice of the sort of punishment he had in mind in a letter to his friend, Lord George Germain. 'I am neither inhuman or rapacious yet I own it would give me pleasure to see the Canadian vermin sack'd and pillaged.' He kept his word; during the summer of 1759, parties of Rangers and other light troops harried the villages along the shores of the St Lawrence, burning houses and crops and carrying off what they could. Those French-Canadians who refused to swear allegiance to George II were evicted from their homesteads. A pattern was set for future colonial wars. Ideals of humanity held by often highly urbane and well-read officers were very soon shed when they were confronted by the primitive struggle for survival which lay at the heart of frontier conflicts.

The deadlock at Quebec ended early in September. Wolfe, faced with the onset of winter, agreed to a plan proposed by some of his senior officers. It involved a risky nocturnal dash past Quebec and a

Death of a hero:
Benjamin West's painting
of the death of Wolfe at
Quebec in 1759 became
an icon of self-sacrifice
in the name of empire.
(The Royal Collection
© Her Majesty
The Queen)

dawn landing upstream from the city. With British troops between Montcalm and his supply base, Montreal, he would be forced to emerge and offer battle on the Plains of Abraham. Everything went as predicted; the British were able to disembark undetected and form up in time to meet Montcalm's attack.

The battle for the control of North America was fought in an orthodox manner with columns and lines marching to the beat of the drum. The French manoeuvred clumsily, partly because the militiamen misunderstood what was expected of them in an unfamiliar kind of battle, and the entire French line crumpled under British volley fire. Montcalm was killed in the confusion as was Wolfe. Both had a reputation for gallantry and their deaths gave the campaign the quality of an epic contest between two worthy adversaries. Wolfe was quickly transformed into an imperial hero, the first of a breed that would proliferate over the next century and a half, whose patriotism, courage, attachment to duty and perseverance were set up as examples to be followed by their countrymen.

The fall of Quebec did not mark the end of the campaign. Disturbed by Amherst's presence at Ticonderoga, Montcalm had detached a substantial force, under the Chevalier de Lévis, to protect Montreal. These troops tried to retake Quebec in the spring of 1760 and were beaten in a hard-fought battle at Sainte-Foy, in which both sides suffered casualties four times as great as on the Plains of Abraham. The capture of Quebec and its less well-known sequel at Sainte-Foy marked the end of French power in Canada. There were suggestions during the peace negotiations in 1762–3 that part of New France might be restored to France in return for keeping Guadeloupe, but in the end the long-term security of British North America counted for more than quick profits from sugar.

The British government, having acquired complete control over North America, was immediately faced with a dilemma. Stability, which had been the war's principle objective, proved elusive. Having removed the external threat to the colonies' security, the government had to cope with new, unexpected threats to local tranquillity, all indirect consequences of the fall of Quebec. First, policies had to be devised to satisfy the aspirations of 70,000 French Canadians, and to reassure an unknown but larger number of Indians, who were scattered across Britain's new territories in America's mid-west. At the same time as attending to the needs of its new subjects, the government had to heed the demands of the old; thousands of colonists were impatient to exploit the fruits of victory and move westwards.

Land speculation boomed between 1763 and 1774. A new empire was in the offing, which would be carved from the territories now open beyond the Appalachians, and speculators swarmed into the region to stake their claims. On both sides of the Atlantic investors were quick to respond, and land companies found no difficulty in attracting capital. Greed, and a faith in the ability of the new lands to pay their way, bound together American men of substance, such as the scientist and political philosopher Benjamin Franklin, and British aristocrats, such as his future antagonist, Lord Dartmouth. The land fever also infected men of humbler means; in 1771–2, Clydesdale farmers and artisans combined to form their own company which, they hoped, would purchase land in America for settlement by Scots.

Immigrants poured into North America at an unprecedented rate to people the vast tracts of wilderness being purchased by the speculators' agents. Between 1760 and 1775, 30,000 English, 55,000 Irish and 40,000 Scots crossed the Atlantic; many, perhaps the biggest proportion, hoped to settle on the frontier. Two thousand pioneers passed annually down the Shenandoah Valley in western Virginia on the way towards the backlands of Carolina. The appeal of the West was always the strongest; during the early 1770s plans were in hand to create two new inland colonies, named, in a wonderful flight of fancy, Transylvania, roughly modern Kentucky, and Vandalia, which lay between the Ohio and Allegheny rivers.

'To Fool away a Sporting Sum in North America': a late seventeenth-century playing card satirizing colonial settlement. (© Worcester College, Oxford)

Reports of abundant and cheap land in America were naturally most enticing to those who faced a bleak future in Britain. A recession during 1773–4 in the woollen, cotton and silk-weaving industries forced men and women to leave the West Country, Yorkshire, Spitalfields in London and Paisley. There were also plenty of others discontented with their lot. In the Scottish Highlands and Western Isles there was a mass flight from grinding lairds who demanded high rents for poor land. It was the same in Ireland, where rack-renting had reached a peak in the early 1770s. Crofters and smallholders were joined by indentured servants, who were naturally in demand to undertake the donkey work of breaking new lands. By 1770, the old underworld of kidnappers and cozeners of indentured servants was back in action.

The government, landlords and employers were dismayed by the scale of emigration and in Scotland, where it was believed that three per cent of the population had shifted to America in less than ten years, an attempt was made to stem the flow. This was legally impossible since no authority could remove a British subject's traditional liberty to go where he or she wished. Some pondered where it would all end and foretold that Britain, like Greece and Rome, would eventually lose the sources of its wealth and power which would pass to America.

Britain was not the only loser from this wave of immigration. Many were destined for lands which had been appropriated from Indian tribes who, during the early 1760s, fought a number of unsuccessful campaigns to expel the intruders. The familiar pattern of frontier warfare repeated itself with neither side showing pity. And yet, in the eyes of the British government, the Indians were subjects of George III and, as long as they kept his laws, had the right to expect his protection. From 1763 onwards, the King's ministers and their officials in North America endeavoured to fulfil this obligation, in particular protecting the Indians from the legal chicanery practised by speculators. However, every solution to the problem proved unsatisfactory or created new difficulties. Bans on settlement, which pleased the Indians, were unenforceable, and reverence for the rights of property was so strong that ministers were reluctant to take too firm a line with speculators who, for all their underhand methods, often possessed legally defensible claims to Indian lands.

A means to cut through the tangle of conflicting rights and claims was finally devised in the summer of 1774. The Quebec Act defined the frontiers of Canada, which were extended as far south as the Ohio and Allegheny basins. This region would be detached from the North American colonies and governed from Quebec according to a peculiar mixture of old French and English laws. The Quebec Act ended over fifty years of expansion by the North American colonists and barred them from those western lands to which they had long believed themselves entitled. It was widely and bitterly resented, but the British government soon found itself faced with an infinitely greater problem, a colonial rebellion.

4

THE DESCENDANTS OF BRITONS:
NORTH AMERICA REBELS
1765–1775

The influx of immigrants into North America coincided with an intense and increasingly passionate debate about the nature of the empire and the identity of its inhabitants. These issues were first raised in the summer of 1765 when Lord Grenville's ministry passed the Stamp Act, a measure which imposed a levy on all legal documents throughout the empire. It provoked an outcry in the West Indies and North America, where the colonists resurrected the precedent of the 1754 crisis and called a Continental Congress, which agreed to place an embargo on British imports. Simultaneously, and throughout the colonies, there were rowdy demonstrations in which gruesome threats were uttered against those officials whose job it was to collect the stamp duty.

This spontaneous and violent reaction took the government completely by surprise. Grenville's successor, the Marquess of Rockingham, decided to temporise and withdraw what was obviously a detested and, given the mood of the colonists, an unenforceable law. The parliamentary exchanges which marked the repeal of the Stamp Act revealed two conflicting views about the relationship between Britain and its colonies and the political rights of the colonists.

George III, Grenville and defenders of the Stamp Act asserted that the British Parliament had an unquestioned right to make laws for the colonies. They clung to the old orthodoxy that the colonies were economic satellites of Britain, and existed solely to generate wealth for the mother country. This dogma was deeply rooted in official thinking and was expressed, no doubt with an eye to his minister's approval, by Governor Patterson of Prince Edward Island in his annual report for 1770. 'This island,' he wrote, 'with proper Encouragement in its infantile state, may be made extremely plentiful and useful to the Mother-Country.' The use of the word 'infantile' is instructive, since it reflected the widely held contemporary view that the colonies were Britain's offspring and needed firm but kindly guidance from their parent.

The patriarchal view of empire was explained during the Stamp Act debate by Grenville who likened the Americans to children, placed in their lands by a generous father, who had subsequently made every provision for their welfare. Implicit in this statement was the assumption that the colonists would continue to look to their parent for assistance and security. Evidence for this lay easily to hand; in the recent war British troops and warships had removed the threat posed by France, and redcoats continued to man the forts which held the frontier against Indians. These benefits were expensive and it was reasonable that part of the bill should be paid by the grateful colonists.

Dissident Americans and their supporters in Britain agreed that the empire was an extended family, but differed in their interpretation of the ties of kinship. Rhode Islanders, who assembled in 1765 to burn the effigies of revenue officers, declared themselves the heirs in spirit of those Englishmen whose defiance of the Stuarts in the last century had secured the constitution and liberty of the subject. Their claims were echoed in Parliament during the Stamp Act debate, when William Pitt, now Earl of Chatham, argued that 'The Americans are the sons, not the bastards of England.' It was therefore proper that they should share all the legal and political rights of their siblings in Britain.

This concept of a common inheritance of freedom was the mainstay of the American argument against governments which asserted parliamentary supremacy over all colonists and offered no representation in return. In 1775, Governor Jonathan Trumbull of Connecticut demanded to know why Americans were disbarred from 'the constitutional rights and liberties delivered to us as men and Englishmen, as the descendants of Britons and members of an empire whose fundamental principle is liberty and security of the subject'. The question had been continually asked by Americans over the past ten years and they had been given no answer. Instead, they had been told to accept that they were unequal members of a family and that their individual rights had been suspended or diluted for no other reason than that they or their ancestors had crossed the Atlantic.

What was perhaps most perplexing to Americans, faced with an arbitrary view of their status, was that they were excessively proud of their Britishness. Benjamin Franklin assured readers of the *London Chronicle* in November 1770 that Americans 'love and honour the name of Englishmen; they are fond of English manners, fashions and manufactures; they have no desire of breaking the connection.' It was, he said, a measure of their patriotism that they insisted that 'the Parliament of Britain hath no right to raise revenue from them without their consent'.

There was much truth in Franklin's view of the pervasive Britishness of America. Over nine-tenths of the colonists were of British descent and many lived in towns and villages which had been deliberately given British names; in southern New York there were a Stamford, Rye, Gravesend and two Bedfords. The settlers had built homes in the vernacular style of the British countryside and had preserved the popular culture of their homeland by passing down folk tales and folk songs. Educated Americans saw themselves not as provincials, but as part of the mainstream of British intellectual and political life. Later, when a political break with Britain seemed unavoidable, Franklin was distressed by its possible cultural repercussions for him and his countrymen. Would they be cut off for ever from Shakespeare?

In general, the American temperament was egalitarian and obstreperous and men from all backgrounds did not submit unquestioningly to authority as a matter of habit. In April 1775, Sir James Wright, the governor of Georgia, detected 'a levelling spirit and contempt for government' abroad in his colony. The cure was a permanent garrison because British troops would 'keep up some little show of dignity and command respect, and the officers mixing in with the gentlemen of the towns, the young people would hear the King and government spoken of with that veneration which is proper and due.'

By this time, the government was becoming exasperated by the waves of protests and demonstrations which had greeted each of its attempts to raise money from America. After the repeal of the Stamp Act early in 1766, ministerial face had been saved by a Declaratory Act which insisted that Parliament had full powers to make laws for the North American colonies. This gesture had had little impact since the colonists, having discovered their political muscle and encouraged by the overturning of the Stamp Act, continued to resist new taxes and soon scored further successes.

The 1767 Townshend duties on tea and manufactured imports proved uncollectable because of a campaign of mass intimidation, and were withdrawn after two years. The chief problem was that the day-to-day administration of the colonies, like that of Britain, depended upon the goodwill of unpaid officials

Those blessings our Fathers obtain'd by their blood, We are justly oblig'd as their sons to make good: All internal Taxes let us then nobly spurn, These effigies first — next the Stamp Paper burn.

POPULAR SONG, 1767

drawn from the ranks of property-owners and, in the towns, the richer merchants. By 1770, this group had become divided, and many of its members were no longer willing to cooperate with a government whose policies they disagreed with. Royal governors and excisemen therefore found themselves isolated figures without the wherewithal to enforce the King's laws.

Faced with continual assaults on its authority, the government turned in 1770 to that most foolhardy of all policies, selective and limited coercion. A small garrison was stationed in Boston to uphold a hard-pressed administration, and keep the peace in the most intractable town in America. The force deployed proved not enough to cow the Bostonians, but more than enough to stiffen their resolve and swell the numbers of the rest of the dissident colonists. The shooting of some civilians after a scuffle at the end of December, known as the 'Boston Massacre', gave the Americans their first martyrs and a propaganda coup. There was further violence in 1772 when a revenue cutter, the *Gaspée*, was set alight after it had been beached on Rhode Island. The Tea Act of 1773, contrived to assist the monopoly of the East India Company, was challenged by a party of Bostonians who, masquerading as Indians, came aboard a merchantman and tipped its cargo of tea into the harbour. Boston had clearly not been overawed, and fresh astringents were applied in the form of regulations devised to stifle its commerce.

NODDLE-ISLAND or HOW are we decieved.

This new stern line on America was taken by Frederick North who had become Prime Minister in 1770. Lord North's strength lay in his skills as a parliamentary manipulator and dispenser of patronage rather than his vision or intellect. He remained in power until early 1782, relying on the steadfast support of a parliamentary mountain of Tory backbenchers who were happy to let ministers do their thinking for them. What bound North's adherents together was common hostility towards anyone who rocked the boat, whether in Britain or America.

There existed within the inner recesses of the contemporary Tory mind a suspicion that a democratic spirit was infecting Britain and America. At home, it was fomented by John Wilkes who, having survived prosecution for criticising the government in 1763, had emerged as a focus for popular, extra-parliamentary opposition to the King and his ministers. The demonstrations which followed his election as an MP in 1768, and ham-fisted government attempts to unseat him, ran parallel to and mirrored the current unrest in America. Furthermore, and this thoroughly alarmed the Tories, Wilkes and the colonists were willing to fight their political battles in concert with the mob. Disturbed by what seemed to be an upsurge in disloyalty and popular insolence,

Military overheads: a cartoon of 1776 mocks both the current fashions in ladies' hairstyles and the burdens of war in America. (© British Museum)

both at home and in North America, North's supporters reacted by closing ranks and minds against any form of censure of the King and his ministers.

What might otherwise have appeared bone-headed reaction could be defended, up to a point, on the grounds that concessions to American opinion threatened the integrity of the empire. Firmness, always commendable in a father, would quickly silence the tumult that had been stirred up by a minority of Americans, who had been allowed to become intoxicated by libertarian ideas. Once the government's resolution had been demonstrated, their countrymen would return to their senses and allegiance.

This simple diagnosis of complaint and remedy was rejected by a small group within Parliament who pressed for a compromise. Chatham, Rockingham and, later, Edmund Burke passionately believed that British and American subjects were morally and legally entitled to the same rights and freedoms. Moreover, the sixteenth-century precedent of returning MPs from Calais and Tournai was cited as evidence that Britain's overseas possessions had the right to a voice in Parliament. If this was withheld, and their judgement of the mood of the Americans correct, North's opponents argued that his uncompromising line would create the rupture he was striving to avoid. The King, his ministers and the mass of backbenchers were unmoved and pointed out that the Americans, by the very recklessness of their actions, showed themselves strangers to reasoned compromise.

In the end, it was the Quebec Act of 1774 that impelled Americans to adopt a course of action which transformed civil protests into an armed rebellion. There was much anger against those provisions which closed the frontier and attached to Canada a great swathe of territory south and west of the Great Lakes which Americans had hitherto believed would be open to them for settlement. The official recognition of Catholicism in Canada provoked an outburst of Protestant hysteria. The lurid imagery of ancient sectarian nightmares was revived among a population which was overwhelmingly Protestant, and among whom memories of the persecutions and wars of the past century were evergreen. Early in 1775, the New England backwoods buzzed with rumours that Popery was about to be imposed and that the King was sending Anglican bishops to harass American Presbyterians.

New England farmers, already fearful of the imminent arrival of Popery, were further agitated by tales that the government intended to reduce them to abject tenantry under English lords. Apprehensions of this kind, skilfully manipulated by the anti-government press and individual agitators, helped convince many waverers that American freedoms were in danger of being swept away by a ruthless king, whose government would stop at nothing in its efforts to assert its authority over the colonies. As paranoia gripped much of America, it was easy for propagandists to convince the credulous that they would soon find themselves enslaved. This American dread of slavery struck Samuel Johnson as ironic; 'How is it', he asked, 'that we hear the loudest *yelps* for liberty among the drivers of slaves?'

The American political response to the Quebec Act and the measures taken against Boston was rapid, and followed a pattern which had proved efficacious during previous crises. A Continental Congress was convened at Philadelphia in September 1774 to devise a programme of retaliatory measures which, it was hoped, would make the British government think again. The delegates proceeded cautiously for, while they were united in their rejection of parliamentary sovereignty, they did not want to precipitate a complete break with Britain. First, they repeated their legal position as subjects of a government which denied the existence of what they knew to be their inalienable rights. Then, they brandished the sword of American economic power with a call for a boycott of all trade with Britain and its other colonies.

Representatives at the Congress were careful not to discuss military preparations publicly even though, while they debated, the British government banned the import of arms and gunpowder into North America. In response, many Congress supporters began to stockpile weapons and make arrangements for the swift mobilisation of militiamen in case the government used force to disarm them. The headstrong went further and seized colonial arsenals and forts; in December a body of men, in which the 'Sons of Liberty' were prominent, occupied Fort William and Mary at Portsmouth.

5

THE WORLD TURNED UPSIDE DOWN:

THE AMERICAN WAR OF INDEPENDENCE

1775–1783

At the close of 1774 the British empire faced a crisis of unprecedented seriousness. During the past six months British power in North America had evaporated. Colonial governors had become stranded symbols of an authority they lacked the means to assert. Real power was passing into the hands of hard-line supporters of Congress. By April 1775, local committees of these men had superseded the governors of New Jersey, Pennsylvania, Maryland, Virginia and South Carolina. There was nothing which the government could have done to halt this process, beyond issuing minatory proclamations which were largely ignored. Americans in 1774 enjoyed considerable political freedom; their press was unfettered so ideas could be freely expressed and circulated; they could travel where they wished, and hold public meetings whenever and wherever they chose. It was therefore easy for the agents of Congress to consolidate and organise the committed, convert the lukewarm and bully the Loyalists.

It took time for the reality of the situation in America to be fully understood in London. Here, George III and his ministers vacillated between policies of concession and coercion. By the new year, the King was convinced that parliamentary sovereignty could only be restored in America by condign measures. North and Dartmouth concurred, but clung to the hope that the Americans would ultimately back down rather than risk war, and that a negotiated settlement could be arranged. The policy which evolved during the early months of 1775 was therefore both placatory and threatening. On the one hand, North offered conciliation with promises of fiscal concessions in return for American acknowledgement of Parliament's supremacy, and on the other, he prepared for war.

The prospect of a war with the Americans was greeted with dismay inside Britain. Many agreed with the poet William Cowper, who thought that Britain and America were 'one country', which made the imminent conflict a civil war. There was a strong feeling among military men that the Americans were bluffing and that, when put to the test of arms, they and their cause would quickly fall apart. In a report to Lord Sandwich, the First Lord of the Admiralty, in March 1775, Major John Pitcairn was confident that 'one active campaign, a smart action, and burning two or three of their towns, will set everything to rights.' His commanding officer, Lieutenant-General Thomas Gage, was less sanguine and feared that precipitate action would provoke resistance, which might prove too much for the troops at his disposal.'

His misgivings were confirmed on 19 April when, acting on Dartmouth's instructions, he sent a column of his best men to secure the arsenals at Worcester and Concord. Alerted by spies inside Boston, the Massachusetts militia mobilised. A small section was scattered after a brief exchange of fire at Lexington, but a larger body forced the British column to abandon Concord. As it retreated to Boston, it endured a sequence of guerrilla attacks in which it suffered 300 casualties, nearly three times as many as its adversaries. Within a few days, an American force, under the impetuous and highly talented Benedict Arnold, occupied Forts Ticonderoga and Crown Point, opening the way for an invasion of Canada.

The slide to war was now irreversible. News of the skirmishes in Massachusetts left the cabinet with no choice but to apply *force majeure* to all the colonies. This move was welcomed by George III, who had always been impatient with appeasement, and by those amateur and professional strategists who imagined that well-trained soldiers would easily disperse what was commonly seen as a rabble in arms.

Foremost among the advocates of a short, sharp war was Lord George Germain, who, in August, replaced the more flexible Dartmouth as Secretary for the Colonies with a mandate to mastermind operations throughout North America. Germain's formula for victory was based upon a variety of American intelligence sources which agreed that the colonists' will to fight was fragile and would never survive a major defeat. He therefore proposed to deploy a large force in America which would seek out, engage and overcome the rebel army in a single, decisive action. It was confidently imagined that a victory of this nature would not only destroy the rebels, but would also give encouragement to Loyalists and those who had remained aloof from the contest. Again, intelligence reports from America had described the existence of a substantial Loyalist element, temporarily driven underground by the intimidation of Congress supporters, which would reveal its sympathies when it was safe to do so. The forthcoming war would be a struggle for hearts and minds, and the British generals knew that one of their most important tasks was to assure the Loyalists that they would be protected for, as Major-General Sir Henry Clinton later observed, they would never declare themselves 'before there is the strongest certainty of his army being in a condition to support them'.

Initial derision of the Americans' fighting stamina quickly gave way to grudging respect. A year's campaigning taught Clinton that 'the Americans were trained to stratagem and enterprise' and 'they knew every trick of chicane'. They were also capable of fighting in the conventional manner, which was proved in June 1775 during the struggles for Breed's and Bunker's Hills overlooking Boston. Further north, Benedict Arnold and General Richard Montgomery had taken the initiative and launched an invasion of Canada which they advertised as a war of liberation.

American War of Independence, 1776–83

Loyalist Areas

As the Americans advanced towards Quebec, they called on the French-Canadians to free themselves from tyranny, and for a time it was expected they might. In fact, most Canadians remained prudently neutral and waited to see what, if any, success the Americans would achieve. The arrival of winter, Montgomery's foolish decision to besiege Quebec with an outnumbered force and Carleton's brilliantly improvised defence combined to frustrate the Americans. The city was relieved in May 1776 by a British flotilla, by which time Arnold had withdrawn with the remnants of his army.

It was impossible to hold Boston. Relations between townsfolk and soldiers were sulphurous and the Americans controlled the immediate hinterland. In March 1776, the commander-in-chief, Sir William Howe, ordered the city's evacuation. 'It is not possible to describe to you the confusion everything is in here,' Lieutenant Charles Cochrane of the King's Regiment told his uncle. 'To embark (under the guns of those Rascals) the above remaining stores with the heavy baggage of Women and Children, friends of the Government, which last, I believe, might be put in a canoe, is such an operation as probably never happened before.' It was the climax to a year of humiliation. Nevertheless, Cochrane believed that the army's fortunes would soon revive once Germain's grand strategy was implemented.

Cochrane's confidence was misplaced. The North American battlefield encompassed a million square miles, most of them covered with mountains, woodland and scrub. Armies were easily swallowed up in this wilderness, through which they often marched blindly; Clinton, traversing New Jersey in 1778, had only the vaguest idea of Washington's whereabouts until he was attacked at Monmouth. The possession of major towns counted for less than it did in Europe because economic resources, such as iron foundries, were scattered. Boston, New York, Philadelphia and Charleston were all under British control at various times, but their occupation did little to hamper the American war effort.

Bold and imaginative generals might have overcome these difficulties, but the thinking of the British high command was uninventive and often timid. Moreover, and this became painfully apparent as the war proceeded, the British command structure was shaky. Germain in London retained overall direction of strategy, but his instructions to the commanders in America were often delayed by as much as eight to ten weeks because the ships carrying them faced contrary winds. Misunderstandings between him and his subordinates remained uncorrected, and in some instances the generals in the field had no choice but to follow their own judgement. There was also, at least in 1775–6, confusion over objectives. Germain favoured an all-out effort while North still held out hope for a negotiated settlement.

It took time for these flaws to reveal themselves. Howe's operations in the summer of 1776 had started slowly, thanks to delayed reinforcements, but they showed every sign of prospering. He had decided to concentrate his forces on New York in the centre of an area where Loyalism was believed to be strong. The landing on Staten Island went off smoothly and, in mid-August, Howe launched his 23,000-strong army against the outer defences of New York City. A solid, painstaking commander, Howe proceeded cautiously and in doing so missed the opportunity to fight a decisive engagement. For a time, Washington had been prepared to risk the bulk of the rebel army to save the city, but Howe did not offer

The long arm of King George:
Royal Navy warships and transports carrying troops arrive off Boston, 1768, in the first stage of the confrontation with the American colonists. (© Mary Evans Picture Library)

battle. Instead he attacked the enemy's earthworks piecemeal and, when it was clear that New York would fall, shrank from a pursuit of the badly mauled and demoralised American army.

There now seemed no need for the hammer-blow which Germain had imagined would end the war. Howe's successes around New York during the autumn of 1776 indicated that the British army was unbeatable, and at the end of November he felt strong enough to issue a proclamation which offered an unconditional pardon to all rebels who surrendered and reaffirmed their allegiance to George III. Many Americans, well aware of the pitiful state of Washington's army, were glad to accept Howe's clemency. The temper of the colonists seemed to be changing and Howe, several victories to his credit and with a base at New York, felt he could safely alter his strategy. Henceforward he would aim to occupy territory rather than coaxing Washington into a full-scale engagement. This shift offered tempting political dividends; wavering rebels would be further disheartened and the presence of British troops in an area would rally the local Loyalists.

This was not to be. At the end of the year Washington's troops were victorious at the battles of Trenton and Princeton. Although militarily they were small-scale affairs, they had a disproportionate effect on American opinion. In July 1776, the radicals inside Congress had pushed for and obtained a Declaration of Independence which severed all links with Britain, and ruled out any future compromise based on British sovereignty over America. It is impossible to assess precisely how many Americans supported this move; John Adams, one of the signatories to the Declaration, calculated that about a third of the colonists were wholeheartedly behind independence and that the rest were either Loyalists or neutral. To judge by the numbers who took advantage of Howe's amnesty, the balance was in danger of swinging against supporters of independence. Trenton and Princeton reversed this trend by demonstrating that the British army was not invincible and that there was plenty of fight left in the Americans.

The year 1777 marked the turning point of the war. After over a year's fighting, the British army had made little headway; there had been no signal victory over the Americans, inroads into territory held by Congress had been limited and Loyalist support had proved disappointing. Germain's strategy for 1777 was an invasion of Pennsylvania by units of Howe's army. Simultaneously, a mixed force of 8,000 British, Hessians, Canadians and Indians, commanded by Burgoyne, would advance southwards along the Hudson towards Albany, where he would be joined by reinforcements sent by Howe from New York. If everything went to plan, a wedge would have been driven between the militant New England colonies and the rest of America. Howe, however, refused to assist Burgoyne, deciding that his attack on Pennsylvania needed most of his resources, and a totally inadequate force was left behind in New York under Clinton, who was ordered to do what he could to support Burgoyne.

What followed was a débâcle. Burgoyne's lines of communication were cut and his path was blocked by superior forces. Rather than squander the lives of his men in a battle he had no chance of winning, Burgoyne surrendered his army to General Horatio Gates at Saratoga on 16 October. There were no compensations in Pennsylvania where Howe had nothing but bad luck. Philadelphia was taken, but it could not be held since the British had failed to secure control of the Delaware River.

The events of the autumn of 1777 confirmed the Declaration of Independence and the survival of the American republic. Germain's grand strategy was in ruins and hopes of restoring British sovereignty over all the colonies had been shattered. France, hitherto a benevolent neutral, threw in its lot with the colonists in February 1778 and the American struggle became part of the global war.

Outright victory was beyond the grasp of the British army so all efforts were directed towards a salvage operation to conquer and retain Georgia and the Carolinas, where Loyalism was reportedly still strong. The campaign of conquest and conciliation was directed by Clinton, who had replaced Howe as commander-in-chief, and it opened promisingly. Savannah was captured in December 1778 and Charleston in May 1780. The mood of the army was now buoyant, and some sensed that a swift and triumphant end to the war was imminent. On hearing the news of Charleston's fall, General James

Underpaid, underfed and under fire:
in return for sixpence (3p) a day the redcoat was expected to retrieve America for Britain, 1778.
(© British Museum)

Robertson wrote to Germain that, 'Britain will recover her former grandeur and the Question you will leave posterity to discuss will be, whether bravery or humanity had the greatest share in reducing America to obedience.' As the campaign in the Carolinas progressed, the old problem of Loyalism re-emerged. There were, as predicted, plenty of Loyalists, but they would only cooperate if their safety was guaranteed by the British army. Some of those who did found themselves embroiled in a subsidiary war of terror and counter-terror that was waged with enormous ferocity in remoter parts of South Carolina.

There was also, in 1779, an attempt by the British to enlist the help of the slaves. An appeal to them had been made in November 1775 by Lord Dunmore, the fire-eating and energetic governor of Virginia, who eventually mustered 300 runaways in his 'Ethiopian Regiment', whose uniforms carried the slogan 'Liberty to Slaves'. The local plantocracy had been horrified and Dunmore's daring move was ultimately self-defeating since it drove scared whites into the arms of Congress.

Between 1779 and 1781 thousands of negroes made their way to the British army, drawn by Clinton's offer of freedom to any slave of a rebel. Most found themselves employed as labourers, digging earthworks or looking after the army's massive transport train. By the end of the war, large numbers had been carried to New York from where some were sold back into servitude.

Neither the white Loyalists nor black slaves who flocked to the British army as it proceeded through the Carolinas made any impact on the campaign. General Sir Charles Cornwallis, who had charge of the operations, won two victories, at Camden in August 1780 and Guilford Court House the following March, but lacked the men to maintain a permanent occupation of the territory which fell into his hands.

The end of the war in the South came, unexpectedly, in October 1781 at Yorktown. The events which led up to this battle were in many respects a rerun of those of 1777. The British high command was again beset by misfortune and muddle, which were made worse by ill-feeling between Clinton and Cornwallis, who later accused his commander-in-chief of starving him of men. This was debatable, but what was certain early in 1781 was that neither general had any clear idea of how best to deploy their forces.

Cornwallis favoured an attack on Virginia, launched a half-hearted invasion and then settled down at Williamsburg to await Clinton's instructions. Clinton, who had built up a formidable intelligence network, feared an attack on New York, but hoped that he might forestall it by diversionary operations undertaken in Pennsylvania or Rhode Island in conjunction with Cornwallis. Much to his annoyance, Cornwallis was therefore ordered to hold himself in readiness for a seaborne evacuation, and to this end he placed his army within a fortified encampment at Yorktown on the estuary of the York River in southern Virginia. In the meantime, the Franco-American attack on New York had materialised.

At this point the key to the campaign was seapower. So long as supplies and reinforcements could pass by sea between Yorktown and New York, Cornwallis and Clinton were relatively secure. This was not the case after late August when Admiral de Grasse's fleet arrived from the West Indies and took up positions in the Chesapeake Bay. After a brief, inconclusive action the British North American squadron retired to New York, and with it went Cornwallis's chances of reinforcement or escape. As the balance of naval power swung against Britain, Washington, forewarned of de Grasse's intentions, broke camp and began a 450-mile dash from New York to Yorktown. The upshot was that Cornwallis, outnumbered, isolated and under bombardment, surrendered his army on 17 October. As his men marched out and laid down their arms, the band played a popular song, 'The World Turned Upside Down'.

The disaster at Yorktown was a profound shock for the British. An army had been lost and hopes of holding on to the southern colonies had evaporated. For a time both sides had been showing signs of war-weariness: there had been serious mutinies by American troops, dissatisfied with their pay and conditions, in 1780–1, and there were signs that the discipline of some British regiments was cracking.

For six months George III had pig-headedly refused to acknowledge the verdict of Yorktown, and a few other diehards, including Cornwallis, wished to fight on. North was not one of them, and in March 1782 the King finally accepted his resignation. The new Prime Minister, Rockingham, was a moderate who opened negotiations with the Americans. The successful defence of Gibraltar and the restoration of British seapower in the Caribbean strengthened the hand of British diplomats and the Americans proved willing to forgo claims to Canada on the grounds that a British presence in North America was an insurance against possible French and Spanish expansion in the region. Nevertheless, Britain was obliged to cede those lands to the west of the Mississippi which had been incorporated in Canada under the terms of the Quebec Act.

Pre-war predictions that the British empire would not survive the loss of the American colonies proved false. Naturally there were alarms about the commercial consequences of a break between Britain and America, and in January 1781 a frantic attempt was made to retain the American market with the American Intercourse Bill. But this measure, designed to give American traders exemptions from the navigation laws, was unnecessary for, as the bill's critics pointed out, the new republic could not survive economically without Britain.

This was true; the volume of Anglo-American trade actually increased after 1783, in particular exports of raw cotton, which rose from an annual average of 15.5 million pounds in the late 1780s to 28.6 million by 1800. Only the American, slave-worked and partly mechanised cotton plantations could provide the output needed to satisfy the demands of the new, machine-operated Lancashire mills. By 1840, 80 per cent of Lancashire's supplies of raw cotton came from America. The harvest failures of 1799–1800 led British grain importers to buy up American surpluses which, between 1810 and 1812, helped feed the British army in Spain and Portugal.

The post-war pattern of British trade undermined the economic arguments which had hitherto justified the empire. Moreover, the events of the American War strongly suggested that Britain, having enlarged its territories by the victories of 1759–62, had overstretched its naval and military resources to a point where contraction was inevitable, even desirable. French operational difficulties and not the strength of the home fleet had prevented the invasion attempt of 1779. The strain had been too great and it only needed a temporary loss of seapower in North American waters during the autumn of 1781 to demonstrate that the defence of a global empire required Britain to be equally strong everywhere. Cornwallis's capitulation at Yorktown may have been a psychological shock, but it was not a surprise.

No distinctly imperialist political ideology had emerged after the spectacular conquests of the Seven Years War. Then and later, the ownership of a vast overseas empire was generally seen as a source of wealth and a monument to national virtues, in particular those displayed on the battlefield. In 1778, a despairing American Loyalist wrote from England: 'I fear this nation has sunk into too selfish, degenerate, luxurious a sloth, to rise into such manly, noble exertions as her critical situation seems to demand.' The question as to whether moral decadence contributed appreciably to slipshod planning and poor generalship was left unasked. The crisis in 1774–6 had, however, prompted some examination of the political nature of the empire and a discussion about its future. Some British Whigs and Radicals accepted that there were no moral or political reasons to prevent the Americans from choosing to go their own way, even if this meant independence. In practical terms, it was ridiculous to spend large sums of money in holding down the colonies and, at the same time, allege that they were a vital source of national wealth. The abandonment of rigid control by London and its replacement by some form of American self-government would not automatically dissolve the economic connection between Britain and North America. If there were any imperial bonds between Britain and the colonists they were, as many Americans pointed out, those of shared beliefs in personal liberty and representative institutions.

Thinking along these lines influenced post-war official policy towards the Canadian provinces. After 1783 their population had been swelled by thousands of Loyalist refugees and former soldiers in the Loyalist corps who had been rewarded with land grants. There were also schemes to give financial help to the new settlers who ended the demographic imbalance between French and British colonists. The political future of Canada was given consideration with plans for representative assemblies which would enjoy powers and rights similar to those of the British Parliament. In taking such a line, the British government showed that it had learned something from the recent upheavals in America, but it was hoped that an 'aristocracy' of wealth and talent would emerge in Canada which would naturally attach itself to the British Crown rather than lead a movement for complete self-government.

Liberty victorious: an allegory of American independence, 1783. (© Boston Public Library)

6

THE TERROR
OF OUR ARMS:
CONQUEST AND
TRADE IN INDIA
1689–1815

The East India Company was founded purely as a commercial enterprise, and during the seventeenth and early eighteenth centuries it imported and exported goods from its factories in Bombay, Madras and Calcutta, unconcerned with the internal politics of India. By 1815, the Company owned the most powerful army in India and governed, directly and indirectly, Bengal, much of the upper Ganges basin and extensive areas of eastern and southern India. Independent native princes feared its power and many sought its friendship and protection. Most important of all, the Company was flexing its muscles as a major Asian power; during the past twenty years its army and navy had seen action in Arabia, Mauritius, Malacca and Java.

Trade still mattered, but less than before. Since 1793 the Company's monopoly had been whittled away by the British government, which was falling under the spell of Adam Smith's economic theories of free trade. The Company lost out; by 1810 interlopers had captured a quarter of the Indian market and were selling goods worth £2 million a year. Changing patterns of trade rescued the Company, in particular the mass importation of cheap Lancashire cottonware which was underway by the early 1800s and which, incidentally, swamped and extinguished India's village-based cotton industry. There was also a burgeoning and lucrative two-way trade with China which imported Bengali opium and exported tea for the British market. Opium exports were worth a million rupees in 1802–3 (about £250,000), a total which rose by 20 per cent in the next ten years. And yet, despite new opportunities for trade, the Company was, by 1800, principally dependent on land taxes collected from the provinces it ruled.

The metamorphosis of the Company was accomplished without any plan and according to no general principle. It was largely undertaken by a handful of ambitious officials and generals, who sincerely believed that they could enrich themselves while at the same time advancing the interests of their country and their employer. Their predatory and private-enterprise imperialism was ideally suited to conditions in eighteenth-century India where the central authority of the Mughal emperors was dissolving. Of course, opportunism and greed were already endemic among the Company's servants, all of whom were in India to accumulate enough capital to return to Britain and a life of ease. 'I may be made Governor, if not that I may make a fortune which will make me live like a gentleman,' Stair Dalrymple told his elder brother in 1752. He was seeking a Company post and needed £500 to cover a bond for his good behaviour and a further £200 for his kit and passage out. This investment would soon be recovered once Dalrymple exercised his right to trade on his own account, although, like other fortune-seekers, he faced exposure to diseases and a climate which reduced his chances of returning home.

At the time when Dalrymple was importuning his brother, new and unlooked for ways of self-enrichment were presenting themselves to the Company's employees. In 1742 Joseph-François, Marquis Dupleix, had taken up the post of governor of the French Compagnie des Indes. In many ways he was very similar to the belligerent, greedy and overreaching British proconsuls with whom he and his successors contended for the next twenty years. During the final year of the War of the Austrian Succession, the principal French trading port of Pondicherry had been threatened by a Company army operating from Madras. Worried about its safety and knowing that a further Anglo-French war was extremely likely, Dupleix decided that Pondicherry needed a defensive *glacis*. To this end, he set about making the Compagnie des Indes the power-broker of the Carnatic.

Dupleix excused this meddling in local affairs by promising his employers rich returns from the land taxes levied on those areas which passed into French control. There were also, although this was omitted from his despatches to Paris, vast opportunities for him and his staff to divert some of these revenues into their own pockets, along with gifts from Indian princes who sought France's friendship. Dupleix began his excursion into the complex, uncertain and violent world of Indian dynastic politics in 1749 when he engineered the installation of his stooge, Chandra Sahib, as nawab (governor) of the Carnatic.

The East India Company's governor and council at Madras could not stand by and allow the Carnatic to slip into French hands and they were soon sponsoring a rival nawab, Muhammad Ali Khan. Both companies supported their puppets with troops, and a proxy war for control of the region was underway by 1750.

Among the British officers engaged was Robert Clive. He had come to India, aged nineteen, in 1744 as a clerk and had drifted into soldiering four years later. In England he had been an idle misfit whose despairing family (Shropshire gentry) arranged his shipment to India. There he might have remained in obscurity, but for a French sally against Madras in 1748 which released in him remarkable talents. He swiftly absorbed all that was needed to master the art of war as it was waged in India, and revealed a knack for commanding the Company's Indian troops, or sepoys. He was physically brave at a time when, like their British counterparts, Indian soldiers responded to daring and courageous officers. Clive was also highly ambitious: he craved what his age called 'glory', that public lustre which attached

Eighteenth-Century India

Areas under direct British rule, or whose rulers were under British protection to victorious generals, and once his career was underway he used his fortune to propel himself into the British ruling class. As a soldier and later as an administrator, Clive came in close contact with Indians and he later believed himself the possessor of that arcane branch of human knowledge, an understanding of the inner working of the Indian mind. All Indians, he imagined, were accustomed to that form of arbitrary government which his liberal-minded countrymen called 'despotism', were mesmerised by temerity and awed by 'prestige', an abstraction which blended military prowess and moral authority in roughly equal proportions.

The siege of Arcot in 1751 gave Clive the chance to display his flair as a commander. He held off a superior Franco-Indian detachment and his leadership was, allegedly, so charismatic that a battalion of French-trained sepoys later deserted and demanded to serve under him. The small-scale operations which characterised the struggle for the Carnatic dragged on for three more years, by when it was clear that Dupleix had bitten off more than he could chew. Nonetheless, he had every reason to persevere and so did the British; Robert Orme, an officer serving with the Company's army, heard that in 1753 the Compagnie des Indes had extracted £535,000 in land tax from the territory it occupied.

The stakes were high and, as Orme observed, winning presented few difficulties for Europeans or European-armed and trained troops. The key to victory lay in what he called the 'superiority of European arms' and Clive agreed, writing later that 'the terror of our arms' was so great that Indian armies were often psychologically defeated before they even offered battle.

The French too were learning the lessons of Indian warfare, and Dupleix, faced with a stalemate in 1753, resolved to end it by an infusion of French professional troops. To even the local balance of power, the East India Company asked the British government for reinforcements, and received the 39th Regiment and four warships.

The French and British governments' decision to intervene in what hitherto had been a contest between rival commercial interests had momentous consequences for India. Backed by the military and naval resources of Britain and France, the two companies were now a formidable political force in India.

European power in India was tested in Bengal, in an unexpected war which broke out in June 1756. Siraj-ud-Daula, the local nawab, was nervous about the spread of the Company's power in Bengal and the abuse of its commercial privileges at the expense of his revenues. He attacked and occupied Calcutta in a surprisingly easy operation which astonished the Bengalis, who afterwards mocked the British as 'banchots' (cowards). Calcutta was retaken in January 1757 by Clive and Admiral Charles Watson and war was declared against Siraj-ud-Daula. It was masterminded by Clive who proceeded by diplomatic stealth and cunning against an adversary whose weak character, capriciousness and predatory sexuality made him an Indian Caligula. Like the Roman emperor, Siraj was encircled by courtiers and soldiers of brittle loyalty who were easily seduced into a conspiracy against him. Mir Jafir, the commander of Siraj's army, needed little coaxing to accept Clive's bribes and the promise of the Bengal throne, and Siraj's financial props, the Seth banking clan, were also enticed into Clive's web. Politically undermined by Company cash, Siraj was finally destroyed by the Company's firepower at Plassey on 23 June 1757.

Plassey was a spectacular demonstration of the Company's military muscle and one which made a deep and lasting impression on the Indian mind. Outwardly, the two armies were unequally matched: Clive commanded 1,000 European troops, 2,000 sepoys and eight small-calibre cannon and a howitzer, while Siraj mustered a host of at least 50,000 cavalry and infantry and a large train of massive, bullock-drawn cannon. This vast, sprawling and loosely commanded horde was driven by internal dissension. (Mir Jafir's contingent deliberately stayed aloof from the fighting) and was soon unnerved by the unfamiliar tactics of its adversaries. Those who retained some will to fight soon lost it when faced with volleys of musketry and close-range bombardment. Clive's gunners knew from experience how to create havoc by aiming at artillery bullocks and the elephants which carried Indian commanders. The wounded beasts stampeded and careered wildly through the ranks of infantry and cavalry. What tipped the balance was

Clive's overwhelming self-confidence and offensive spirit which made his army like a tiger, who 'never charges if he can scatter his enemies with a roar'. The roar proved too much for Siraj's army; it fell apart and fled. Shortly after, he was taken and murdered by Mir Jafir's servants. The Company's losses were seventy-three killed and wounded.

Plassey proved, crudely but effectively, that the Company was a force to be reckoned with in India. For the next fifty years, the rulers of Mysore, Hyderabad, the Mahratha states and the Punjab scrambled to acquire the new military technology and the specialists, usually Europeans, who would train their soldiers to use it. Other Indian princes chose to preserve their independence by seeking an accommodation with the Company through unequal treaties, in which they agreed to surrender revenues and some of their authority in return for the Company's protection in the form of a permanent garrison.

The pattern of expansion by coercion and treaty was first seen after Plassey when Clive played kingmaker and installed Mir Jafir as nawab of Bengal, Orissa and Bihar. All the customary land taxes of these provinces passed to the Company and Mir Jafir was left responsible for justice and policing, functions that were taken over by the Company in 1772. The revenue from Bengal subsidised the campaign against the French and by 1762 the Company held the upperhand and French pretensions in southern India were in shreds.

Bengal gave the Company the wherewithal to sustain its new position as a major military power within India. The circumstances of its acquisition gave impetus to further wars of conquest and

Paternal concern:
the sons of Tipu Sultan are delivered as hostages to Lord Cornwallis who is reported to have received them like a father, making them presents of watches. This scene from the 1791 Mysore War symbolised the new paternal and protective image of the British rule in India.
(© British Library)

pacification as civilians and soldiers discovered that the profits of war far exceeded those of trade. Looking back on twenty years of intermittent campaigns, Edmund Burke told the Commons in 1785 that, 'The great fortunes made in India at the beginnings of the conquest, naturally excited emulation in all parts, and through the whole succession of the Company's servants.'

This was true. Those who played the game of high politics and war in India found themselves tantalisingly close to huge sources of wealth which could be easily tapped. It was, Clive correctly stated, 'the known and usual custom of Eastern Princes' to make generous gifts to those who helped them. Mir Jafir followed tradition and between 1757 and 1766 gave Clive a total of £234,000 and, during the same period, extended his largesse to other officials in Calcutta, who individually received sums of between £5,000 and £117,000. The goodwill and influence of powerful men were purchasable commodities in Indian political life, as they were in eighteenth-century Britain, and the Company's agents saw no reason why they should not benefit from the accepted practices of a country where they were now power-brokers. Corruption was also endemic in the day-to-day administration of India, and officials who were placed in charge of the tax-collection in Bengal and elsewhere soon 'went native', channelling revenues into their own pockets.

War also generated profits. When the city of Bharatpur fell in January 1826, a private of the 11th Dragoons watched seven cartloads of gold and silver auctioned, and a soldier offer two gold moidores (about £3.50) for a bottle of spirits, which would normally have been sold for a tenth of that amount. He also noticed soldiers carrying off gold necklaces, jewellery and camel-hair shawls, while others dug up the floors of houses in search of cash buried by their owners, a common precaution against looters and tax-collectors.

Late eighteenth-century India was a bustling society, peopled by men on the make whose judgements in Company matters were always swayed by self-interest. The free-for-all which followed Plassey encouraged others to promote thrusting, acquisitive policies from which they had everything to gain. Moreover, as the Company annexed land and infiltrated the princely states, the demand grew for administrators, collectors of revenue, surveyors and residents. All these posts were well-paid and many were filled by ambitious young army officers.

The independent princes of southern and central India knew that survival depended on beating the Company at its own game, by undertaking warfare in the European manner. Tipu (the Tiger) Sultan sent his agents to Paris to procure arms from the Netherlands and, according to Admiralty intelligence sources, had purchased 50 cannon, 80 gun carriages, 100,000 cannon balls, 10,000 muskets and 20,000 'best tempered sabres'. The nizam of Hyderabad had acquired a 14,000-strong corps, armed with muskets and instructed in European methods by French mercenaries, and the princes of the Mahratha Confederacy possessed an estimated 30,000 troops, drilled and organised by freelance European officers.

The late eighteenth-century arms race presented a challenge to the Company, which was accepted with relish by Richard Wellesley, Earl of Mornington and later Marquess Wellesley, when he took up the governor-generalship in 1798. Britain had been at war with Revolutionary France since 1793, and the Company's intelligence officers made much of the fact that French mercenaries in India were all left-wing Jacobin Republicans, and that Tipu, who obligingly called himself 'Citizen Tipu', was begging for French assistance. Invoking the bogey of French Revolutionary subversion made sense in 1798, the year of Napoleon's invasion of Egypt, which was seen in London and Calcutta as a prelude to an overland attack on India. Wellesley, a passionate opponent of the French Revolution, did not wait on events; he struck. Hyderabad was neutralised and neutered by coercive diplomacy, and in 1799 the Company's army overran and conquered Mysore. Tipu died fighting in his capital, Seringapatam, and the nocturnal scene in which Company officers discovered his body became a favourite with British genre painters.

After the conquest of Mysore, it was the turn of the Mahratha states. The initiative came from Wellesley who, by a mixture of force and diplomacy, secured the impoverished and weak Mahratha overlord, the Peshwa, as a Company ally. The result was the Mahratha War of 1803 against the armies of Sindia Daulat Rao of Gwalior and Raghugi Bhonsle of Nagpur. After a whirlwind campaign, their armies were defeated by Arthur Wellesley, later Field-Marshal, the Duke of Wellington and younger brother of the Marquess, at the battles of Assaye and Argaon, while in the north, General Sir Gerard Lake occupied Aligarh, Delhi and Agra. With two of the leading Mahratha princes on their knees, the Marquess snatched at the chance to eliminate the third and declared war on Jaswant Rao Holkar in 1805. The second phase of the war went badly; a Company column was roughly handled near Agra and Lake found Bharatpur too tough a nut to crack. The Marquess Wellesley had overreached himself and in 1806 he was recalled to London.

The Marquess had come unstuck because of over-confidence and temerity. He had not gone to India to enrich himself, but to prove his worth as a dynamic and visionary administrator (he founded a college for Company civil servants at Madras), and hoped that his achievements would qualify him for high office in Britain. He was the first of a breed of high-handed, patrician proconsuls who relished the exercise of absolute power; when he visited Cawnpore in 1802, he rode on a magnificently bedecked elephant and 'in the true style of Eastern pomp, distributed his [the Company's] rupees with a liberal hand' just like an Indian potentate. A man of such temperament had nothing but disdain for balance sheets and the Company's directors who were, he wrote confidentially in 1799, 'held in universal contempt and ridicule in every branch of the service in India'.

By 1815 just over three-quarters of the Company's annual budget was consumed by the expenses of its army, which was now 150,000 strong. The Company has serious financial difficulties with debts of £40 million and it was thought by many to be dangerously overstretched. Major-General James Stuart,

In Clive's footsteps: the raj still needed bold spirits who are promised rich rewards in this recruiting poster for the East India Company's army, c.1810. (© Blair Athol Estate)

Warrior tradition:
Indians from martial
backgrounds freely
enlisted in the Company's
army where they were
well paid and respected.
Like this Madras cavalry-
man of 1840, they were
dressed in the European
style and trained to fight
in the European manner.
(© NAM)

the resident in Tanjore (Thangayu), voiced the widely held anxiety that the Company 'already possesses more Territory and Influence than they well know how to make good use of'. Twenty-five years later, the naturally cautious Arthur Wellesley was convinced that his brother had overstepped himself in his efforts to subdue the Mahrathas. He also believed that there were great risks in making treaties with native princes which left them with the façade of their former power, while real authority was exerted by the Company with the result that they lost respect and their puppet-master gained none.

Critics of expansionism were also uneasy about the swiftness with which senior Company officials resorted to war as an instrument of policy. A quick and unexpectedly arduous foray into Nepal in 1814–15 troubled the Duke of York, the commander-in-chief of the British army, who wondered why 'it was ever necessary'. There was, of course, little that he or anyone else in London could do about it, for the men who made the decisions were thousands of miles away. If challenged, they fell back on a stock explanation which involved local prestige and the refusal of the Company's strategists to tolerate a powerful or obstreperous independent state on their borders.

Behind the debates that had flared up in Britain whenever the men-on-the-spot in India adopted aggressive policies, lay a deep unease. Altogether the events of the fifty years after Plassey suggested that those who held power in India considered themselves beyond the restraint of either the Company or the British government. The growing Indian empire was becoming a state within a state. At the same time, it appeared that those responsible for India underwent a moral transformation, abandoning British habits of mind and codes of public behaviour and embracing those of the subcontinent.

Clive had recognised the temptations, to which he had earlier succumbed, when he returned to Bengal as governor-general in 1765 with a mandate to establish honest and fair government. 'In a country where money is plenty, where fear is the principle of government, and when your arms are ever victorious,' he observed, 'I say it is no wonder that corruption should find its way to a spot so well prepared to receive it.' For the next two years he did what he could to stamp out the worst abuses and the task was taken up by two of his successors, Warren Hastings (1772–85) and Lord Cornwallis (1785–92); but in a country where highly paid posts proliferated, and the opportunities for graft were still plentiful, old attitudes died hard.

There was no reason for the Company's officials to upset the established order in India, a course of action which they lacked the means to undertake and which would have caused untold havoc. Instead, the Company behaved as an inheritor, accepting what it found, and making changes only when practical necessity demanded. This pragmatism involved compromises; religious practices repugnant to Christians were tolerated, and wherever possible Hindu and Muslim legal traditions were accommodated.

There were limits to toleration which were invariably defined by the need to maintain public order. Small-scale campaigns were fought to suppress organised banditry, which was an integral part of the Indian social order, but which interfered with trade and represented a challenge to the Company's authority. Drastic measures such as executions without trial were commonly adopted by officers, who claimed that they were a medicine which both doctor and patient understood. Arthur Wellesley, who never had any qualms about hanging bandits whenever he found them, later commented that the 'liberal' ideals which held sway in Britain were utterly unsuited to a country whose people were conditioned to authoritarian government and expected their rulers to act with a firm hand.

The nature of Indian society and the conditions which Company administrators faced ruled out any importation into India of the freedoms and political rights taken for granted in Britain. And yet, as liberal thinkers in Britain argued, despotic forms of government were corrupting, and the Company was growing into an institution so powerful that it might subvert the British state. Edmund Burke, the most persistent and trenchant critic of the Company and its officials' behaviour, claimed in 1783 that 'a corrupt, private

Opponents of the raj: soldiers from a raja's army, looking as they did a hundred years before and carrying tulwars and obsolete matchlock muskets, c.1860.

A new Rome:
Calcutta's official buildings and triumphal arch (far right) in the early 1800s. They were planned in the grand scale by the Marquess Wellesey to advertise the prestige and permanence of British rule. (© NAM)

BELOW *The*
Company's subjects:
Indian peasants made up the mass of the country's population: they got honest government and a degree of security in return for heavy taxes, efficiently collected, c.1870.

interest' had come into existence 'in direct opposition to the necessity of the state'. This was hyperbole, but it highlighted contemporary misgivings about an institution which seemed outside the control of Parliament. Brakes, not always effective, were placed on the Company by the 1772 and 1784 India Acts which imposed parliamentary control over the board of directors. Gradually a private interest came under public control.

Of probably greater importance than the extension of parliamentary control over the Indian empire was a fundamental change in attitude of that generation of young Company servants who were taking up their posts at the turn of the century. They arrived having been exposed to evangelicalism, a creed which was making considerable headway among the British middle and upper classes during the 1780s and 1790s. Evangelicalism was a form of Protestantism which emphasised personal spiritual regeneration through the acceptance of Providence, and useful service to mankind, undertaken in accordance with Christian humanitarian principles. Cornwallis seems to have been one of the first to have been swayed by evangelical ideals for, on his appointment as governor-general, he listed his priorities as: 'Try to be of some use; serve your country and your friends [and] take the means which God is willing to place in your hands.'

Personal moral uprightness was essential if the evangelical was to perform his duties to the rest of the world. John Malcolm, whose Indian career began in the early 1780s, believed that British power there rested on the gallantry of British troops and the high moral standards of its administrators, in particular their truthfulness and integrity. 'When they condescend to meet the smooth-tongued Mohammedan, or the crafty Hindoo, with the weapons of flattery, dissimulation, and cunning,' he remarked, 'they will to a certainty be vanquished.' In other words, if the British continued to adopt what were taken to be the values of the people they governed, they would be undone.

The momentum to acquire more and more power could not be allowed to slacken. India had become a base from which Britain could dominate southern Asia and the Indian Ocean and promote its commercial interests which were beginning to reach out towards China. The Indian army gave Britain the power with which to protect these interests, and enforce its will throughout a region which extended from the Red Sea to the Malay Peninsula. The potential of the Indian army was first revealed during the wars against Revolutionary and Napoleonic France when a combination of Indian manpower and local naval supremacy enabled the British to wage war in Egypt and conquer Mauritius and Java. After 1807, when it was clear that the French were supreme in Europe, British strategists began to lay plans for the conquest of Spanish America which involved conveying Indian troops across the Pacific to Mexico and Chile.

These schemes were laid in the knowledge that British-trained Indian units were more than up to the task; during the siege of Cuddadur in 1783 Madras sepoys overcame French troops who

had previously repelled a European assault party, and, at Bharatpur in 1805, Indians had advanced into action when the British 76th Regiment had flinched. Nonetheless, those who ruled India had no illusions about the real source of their power, the legend of British invincibility. 'Every European soldier', wrote Cornwallis, 'should be carried in a *dooly* to the scene of action, when, like a panther or a blood hound, he might be let slip against the enemy.' A wave of unrest among native troops during 1809 was an uncomfortable reminder that stability throughout the subcontinent ultimately rested on British troops alone. This fact would never be forgotten, even by those who dreamed of bringing European enlightenment to the people of India.

A conqueror mourned: the memorial to General Sir Eyre Coote. The mourning Indian is a reminder that victories such as Coote's brought enlightened government. (© Crown copyright)

7

THE DESERT OF WATERS:
THE PACIFIC AND AUSTRALASIA

The Pacific Ocean appeared as a huge void on eighteenth-century world maps. In the past two hundred years a handful of sailors had crossed its waters and returned with tantalising but fragmentary reports of islands and one, possibly two continents far to the south. Questions about the region had to remain unanswered. Sailing to and then traversing the Pacific was an extremely perilous enterprise; sailors cooped up for long periods and living on a stodgy diet contracted scurvy, and inexact methods of reckoning longitude sometimes forced captains to sail blindly. In 1741 Anson's officers miscalculated their fleet's position by 300 miles when rounding Cape Horn.

The technical impediments to Pacific reconnaissance were removed by 1765 with the publication of the *Nautical Almanac* and the almost simultaneous invention of an accurate maritime chronometer which together made it possible to measure longitude precisely. Regular rations of lime and lemon juice, laced with rum, reduced but did not eliminate scurvy epidemics. And yet, while these innovations made systematic exploration of the Pacific easier, the voyages undertaken by Captain James Cook and others from the late 1760s onwards remained tests of nervous stamina and physical endurance. Sailors jumped ship before each of Cook's three expeditions, and in 1790 a sixth of the crew of the *Discovery* deserted rather than face an 18,000-mile voyage to the north-west coast of America. What lay ahead of them was described by Captain Sir Henry Byam Martin in a melancholy note added to his ship's log in July 1846. 'The Pacific is the desert of waters – we seem to have sailed out of the inhabited world, and the *Grampus* to have become the Frankenstein of the Ocean.' Isolation, the tensions generated by unchanging companions, the monotony of shipboard routine in an unfamiliar, sometimes frightening seascape were the common lot of the officers and men who first sailed the Pacific.

The intelligence brought back from the Pacific generated enormous public excitement and assured the early navigator-explorers popular heroic status. Cook towered over all. When he set sail for his first voyage in 1768, he was probably the most skilled navigator of his age. He was a patient, highly professional technician who had risen in the Royal Navy through the sheer force of his talent, since he was the son of a Whitby labourer and largely self-educated. Within ten years he had achieved, through his discoveries, international respect. When, in 1778, France declared war on Britain, French naval commanders were ordered not to interfere with his ships for to do so would hinder the advance of human knowledge. After his death in 1779, Cook entered the pantheon of British imperial heroes.

Cook's three voyages between 1768 and 1779 were undertaken to add to universal (i.e. European) enlightenment by the accumulation of geographical, scientific and anthropological observations of a hitherto secret world. But the acquisition of knowledge for its own sake had not been Cook's principle objective. While the eighteenth-century mind prized abstract knowledge, it placed a higher value on that kind which could be used to accelerate human progress. Properly interpreted, the data and specimens which Cook's ships carried back to Britain could be employed to his nation's advantage.

Over two hundred years of overseas expansion had taught Europeans that new worlds contained products desired by the old. Some, like potatoes, tomatoes and spinach, were found to flourish in Europe while others, such as cotton and tobacco, had to be cultivated in the tropics. With Cook sailed teams of experts who, as they discovered and recorded new species of plants, were encouraged to find out whether they might be the cash crops of the future. Since Cook's expeditions served as models for future reconnaissance, subsequent investigations of natural phenomena were always undertaken with an eye to possible profit. In 1790 Captain George Vancouver, bound for Hawaii and the Pacific coast of America, was ordered by the Admiralty to look for evidence of minerals and coal; to record 'what sort of Beasts, Birds, and Fishes' he found; and investigate whether they might 'prove useful, either for food or commerce'. He was also to look out for seals

and whales and undertake industrial espionage by probing the secrets of how the natives dyed cloth.

Details about the breadfruit plants of Tahiti, collected during Cook's visits there, provided the impetus for William Bligh's voyage to the island in 1787. These edible plants had been identified as potential money-spinners by Sir Joseph Banks, Cook's companion, who saw his own speciality, botany, as the handmaiden of British trade. It was Banks who urged the government to secure breadfruit plants which could solve the current economic problems of the West Indian planters who, deprived of American food imports, were looking for a cheap staple with which to feed their slaves. Bligh was ordered to take his breadfruit plants to the botanic gardens at St Vincent, where they were to be replanted and used as a breeding stock. During his outward passage, Bligh was also asked to make a botanic raid on the eastern coast of the Dutch island of Java and carry off cuttings from trees and plants, including rice, which might flourish in the soil of a British tropical colony.

Cook was a pathfinder for British commerce. He was also the representative of British seapower. It was essential if Britain was to remain paramount on *all* the world's oceans that the Admiralty possessed accurate maps of the Pacific, its islands and their anchorages. Furthermore, the appearance in the area

Brilliant but ill-fated: Admiral Bligh, an accomplished navigator and enlightened officer, was dogged by misfortune. He was evicted from the Bounty *by mutineers off Tahiti, and faced another mutiny at Spithead in 1797 and resistance from the New South Wales establishment. (By courtesy of the National Portrait Gallery)* of the French navigator, Louis-Anthoine de Bougainville, in 1766 made it an urgent matter that the British flag was seen there and that the Pacific islanders were apprised of the existence and power of Britain. It was also vital, as international interest in the ocean increased, for Britain to find out more about the mysterious southern continents and possibly lay claim to them.

When Cook left England in 1768 he was seeking to do more than satisfy his own natural inquisitiveness and push back the frontiers of knowledge. He was an instrument of national commercial and strategic ambitions, and his most distinguished passenger, the gentleman naturalist and botanic pirate Banks, viewed their destination as a secret garden whose fruits might be harvested to Britain's advantage. During the next three years their ship, the *Endeavour*, visited Tahiti and then turned southwards to New Zealand and the eastern seaboard of Australia, which Cook named New South Wales. He then proceeded northwards, steering along the Great Barrier Reef and through the Torres Strait to prove that Australia was an island.

Cook carried with him a mandate to declare British sovereignty over any territory which he found to be unpopulated or whose inhabitants were manifestly making no use of their land. His right to do so had the backing of the law, at least as it was interpreted by Chief Justice Blackstone, for whom anyone who owned but did not exploit land forfeited his claim to it. So, with a clear conscience, Cook declared Australia *terra nullus* (land of no one) and annexed it. What Banks saw of George III's latest dominion convinced him that its climate and soil made it suitable for future colonisation. Its natives, the aborigines, could be discounted. They were nomads who did not till the ground and lacked any discernible form of social organisation or religion. Cook characterised them as 'the most wretched people' in the world, although well contented in their condition.

His second expedition to the Pacific (1772–5) was dominated by the search for the second southern continent. He skirted the edge of the Antarctic ice pack, got as far as latitude 71° 10′, exclaimed 'Ne Plus Ultra', and steered towards New Zealand and Australia. His final voyage, begun in 1776, was intended as a reconnaissance of the coastline of north-west America and Alaska, where, it was hoped, he might discover the outlet of the North-West Passage. Ever since the late sixteenth century navigators had pursued this geographic will-o'-the-wisp, a channel around the edge of northern Canada which linked the Atlantic and Pacific oceans. Like his predecessors Cook was unsuccessful, although, while charting Nootka Sound, his sailors accidentally came across large numbers of sea otters, whose pelts fetched a high price in China.

This was Cook's last discovery; he was killed in a brawl with Hawaiian natives in February 1779 while his ships were wintering by the island. His greatest achievements were the breaking of psychological barriers that had hitherto prevented Pacific exploration and filling in large areas of the map of the ocean. The commercial results of his discoveries were disappointing, but British entrepreneurs were grateful for any new markets, however small. Within a few years the East India Company was developing the sea otter fur trade with China and, sixty years after Cook's death, Hawaii was importing British manufactured goods worth between £30,000 and £50,000 a year.

It was the people of the Pacific rather than prospects for trade there which captivated the imagination of Cook's contemporaries. Revelation of their existence and way of life coincided with a period of intellectual ferment in which questions were being asked about the basic assumptions of the European moral and social order. Since the late seventeenth century thinkers had contemplated a semi-abstract creature called the 'noble savage'. He existed in a state of nature beyond the boundaries of Europe, where he lived without its elaborate social codes and, most important of all, that system of rewards and punishments laid down by the Christian religion. In this condition he was imagined a happier man than his European counterpart.

The account of Tahiti by de Bougainville and his surgeon, Philibert Commerson, which appeared in 1772, presented Europe with the living version of the noble savage. Tahiti, the Frenchmen insisted, was an Edenic world in which men and women thrived and found unparalleled happiness by living according to their own reason and consciences rather than following the injunctions of revealed religion. Nature, in the form of abundant fruits and wild creatures, provided for their needs and so the greater part of their time was spent in pleasure, mostly uninhibited sex. The existence of this Utopia (the word was used by de Bougainville) appeared to challenge the entire social-religious order of Europe.

The level-headed Cook was sceptical of de Bougainville's claims, which bordered on fantasy. The Tahitians were not without vices, and during Cook's visit were actually in the middle of a long-drawn-out civil war. As for the free and open sexuality of their women, of which the rakish Banks took advantage, Cook drily observed that the Tahitian beauties who tempted his men were not so different from their equivalents who enticed sailors on the quaysides of Chatham or Plymouth, save that the former took payment in iron nails rather than cash. Cook was, however, dismayed that the Tahitians called venereal disease 'Apa no Britannia' or, an unfortunate pun, 'Brit-tanne' (British disease) and, as a point of national honour, he insisted that it had been introduced to the islands by French sailors.

While Cook noticed that the peoples he encountered appeared happy, he never subscribed to the notion of the noble savage. Nonetheless, what he and others had reported provided ammunition for the increasingly powerful humanitarian and evangelical lobby which demanded the abolition of slavery throughout the British empire. Those evangelicals opposed to slavery took on board the evidence of the existence of noble savages to strengthen their case that the negro was not a morally inferior man. There was also some concern for the protection of vulnerable societies from outside oppression and abuse, but this weighed less with the evangelicals than the fear that their Christian countrymen might become contaminated by alien vices. Cook and Bligh were accused of having compromised themselves by the 'complacency with which they assisted at idolatrous ceremonies' on Tahiti. Their corruption had parallels with that of slavers, slave-owners and venal and despotic officials in India.

Christian consciences were appalled by reports of what one missionary apologist called the 'lasciviousness which degrades the Tahitians even below brute beasts'. The evangelical imperative demanded the moral reformation of the South Sea islands and their conversion. The first missionary came ashore in Tahiti early in 1797, bringing with him the Mosaic and Pauline 'thou-shall-nots' and a determination to enforce the Protestant work ethic. Within the next ten years others fanned out among the Polynesian islands and were soon sending back reports of tribal wars, torture and cannibalism, which gave the lie to the concept of the noble savage, and appeals for additional missions. Reassuringly, the inhabitants of Tongatabu were found to have a patriarchy, no priests and a legal code which treated adultery as a crime, all factors which made conversion easy.

Missionary activity in the Pacific, well underway by 1815, was an extension of colonisation. By exposure to Western Christianity, the Pacific islanders were made aware of their own apparent deficiencies and the superior culture of their instructors. The process was outlined in a review of an account of New South Wales published in 1803. 'The savage no sooner becomes ashamed of his nakedness, than the loom is ready to clothe him; the forge prepares for him more perfect tools' and so on until he is dependent on the artefacts and techniques of Europe. Cook had been disheartened when Omai, a Tahitian whom he had taken to Britain, returned to the island without any wish to apply what he had seen and learnt to his homeland. The missionaries changed this for ever; through their efforts the Pacific islanders were integrated into the British commercial system. They supplied coconut oil, arrowroot and fresh pork and in return received guns, metalwares and cloth. It is one of the ironies of history that Cook's Hawaiian assailants may have been armed with blades manufactured in Matthew Boulton's Birmingham steelworks, which had been given them as examples of the products of Britain's new industrial technology.

Cook had not been given a warrant to annex those islands whose natives cultivated their land, but, as trade with them developed, Britain's naval presence in the Pacific increased. From 1790 onwards warships regularly cruised among the islands and their captains assured chiefs of George III's goodwill, gave some medals showing his features (a thousand were specially minted for Vancouver's 1790 voyage), and warned them not to harm European sailors and missionaries. This naval activity provoked the Spanish government to claim prior rights to the Pacific under the terms of the 1494 Treaty of Tordesillas, a scrap of paper which meant nothing to Britain. A Spanish threat to enforce sovereignty over Nootka Sound in 1787 was answered by a partial mobilisation of the fleet which was enough to bring about a sullen but prudent climb-down. It was an admission of weakness by a fading imperial power all too aware of Britain's proven ability to hurt her trade and by 1800 the Pacific had become a British lake. French interest in the region dwindled after 1789 and American interest had yet to be awakened. The outbreak of the Anglo-American War of 1812 led to a foray into the ocean by the commerce raider, USS *Essex*, but, outgunned, it was forced to surrender after an encounter with a small British squadron.

It is possible that if the *Essex* had not been intercepted it would have headed for Britain's new colony of New South Wales. Banks had spotted New South Wales's economic potential in 1769, and ten years later urged the government to use one of its harbours, Botany Bay, as a penal settlement. His suggestion was well-timed: the American War had halted the flow of convicts to the tobacco colonies and the early 1780s witnessed a crime wave which swamped the inadequate and often privately owned prisons. Official thinking favoured transportation as the only way out of the problem, and in August 1786 selected New South Wales as the felons' destination.

The choice had been dictated by Banks's description of local conditions; the need to have even a small settlement in Australia as a token of British ownership; and the possible strategic value of a base which might serve as a launching pad for a seaborne invasion of the undefended western coast of Spanish America. This was not as far-fetched as it seemed. At the time, conflicting Anglo-Spanish claims in the Pacific were unresolved, and there was a chance that the two powers might fight a naval war in the region. The scheme was revived in 1806–7, when an influential circle of strategists and businessmen laid plans for a naval descent on Mexico and Chile, Spain then being an ally of France. Among the suggestions was one which proposed shipping Indian troops to New South Wales on the first leg of their journey to Chile.

A further consideration was the convicts. They were to provide the sinews of a new colony that, in time, would profit Britain, which was preferable to having them idling in prison cells or the hulks (dismasted battleships anchored in the Thames) at considerable cost to the government. Transportation was a utilitarian and, according to its supporters, humane form of punishment which offered the criminal the chance of redemption and a return to society. Although today transportation may appear harsh, and conditions on board ship and in New South Wales were harsh, the men who ruled Britain in the late eighteenth century sincerely believed it was both an effective check on crime and a device by which criminals could be reformed.

The first flotilla of ships with their cargoes of male and female convicts, soldiers, free settlers and officials sailed from England in May 1787 and cast anchor off Botany Bay in January 1788. Its commander and the first governor, Captain Arthur Phillip, found the harbour unsatisfactory and shifted his ships to a better one nearby, which was named Sydney in honour of the Colonial Secretary. Landfall appears to have been marked by a night-long bout of drinking and sexual excess by the convicts and those sent to guard them. Later, a clergyman regretted that the long ocean voyage encouraged torpor and a taste for wine and spirits which immigrants found hard to lose once they were in Australia.

The making of early Australia was an extremely complex process. It had been officially assumed that convict muscle would carve out an agrarian colony which would be self-supporting and possibly profitable. Australian society would be pyramidal and paternalist. Executive and judicial power would be in the hands of former officers, whose service experience had presumably prepared them for exercising authority over men from the lower classes who were easily led astray. From the beginning there were three kinds of Australians: officials and guards, free settlers and convicts. The last made up the bulk of the population and were there unwillingly. Analyses of the backgrounds of the criminals who found themselves in Australia after 1788 indicate that the typical convict was an urban recidivist, aged under twenty-five, who had existed on the margins of society, and lived by theft of one kind or another. In their new environment, such creatures had to sink or swim; or, as Phillip put it, 'Men able to support themselves, if able and industrious, I think cannot fail,' while those without the 'spur to industry' will starve.

Phillip and his successors hoped that a spur to hard work might be the presence of female convicts. In 1794, the arrival of sixty women, all under forty, was welcomed by Lieutenant-Governor Francis Grose who told the Colonial Secretary that 'there can be no doubt, but that they will be the means by intermarriage of rendering the men more diligent *and* laborious.' This may have been over-optimistic; one passenger on a convict ship was horrified by the 'shamefully indecent' behaviour and 'abundantly gross' language of the women convicts which drove the respectable to shun the decks whenever they took their daily exercise.

The convicts were allotted to various duties after disembarkation. The canny never revealed any particular skill when asked their trade, for this might mean detachment to onerous labour up-country. For this reason, perhaps, rather than truthfulness, many gave their occupation as 'thief',

Master mariner:
Captain James Cook
whose voyages opened up
the Pacific, New Zealand
and Australia.
(By courtesy of the
National Portrait Gallery)

which was rendered as 'labourer' in the official register. Labour, skilled or unskilled, was undertaken for the government or the handful of free settlers. Discipline was rigorously enforced; flogging was the common corrective for most offences, and on Norfolk Island in 1790 three runaways were warned that they would be shot as outlaws if they did not surrender.

Escape was perilous and rarely attempted, although the geographically ignorant imagined that by plunging inland into the bush they would reach China. In 1791, the government made it plain that every hurdle was to be placed in the way of those convicts who wished to return home after the end of their sentences. Instead, they were to be offered grants of land in the hope that they might become self-supporting farmers, and in 1794 men still serving their sentences were allowed to earn 10d (5p) an hour for work done in their spare time. On Norfolk Island, convicts and their marine guards were given twenty-four acres and some pigs, with the intention that the settlement would become self-supporting.

By 1821 the colony was flourishing; its population had risen to 38,000 and its economy was sound. This owed much to the thriving wool trade, sheep fortuitously being introduced to the colony just as the mechanised Yorkshire cloth industry had been deprived of Saxon and Spanish imports. New South Wales merino was judged finer than its former rivals and demand soared. There were 290,000 sheep in Australia in 1821 and within twenty years raw wool exports topped 10 million pounds annually. Sheep had been to the colony what tobacco had been to Virginia and sugar to the West Indies.

8

WEALTH AND VICTORY:
THE STRUGGLE AGAINST FRANCE

1793–1815

Until 1914 the war against Revolutionary and Napoleonic France was sometimes called the Great War. It began in February 1793 and lasted until June 1815 with a thirteen-month break, which was little more than an armed truce, between April 1802 and May 1803. Historically, this war appeared to be an extension of the Franco-British conflict which had started in 1689, but it was markedly different from its predecessors, not least in the scale of the fighting and the aims of the contestants.

First, it was seen by both antagonists as a struggle for survival, a Roman-Carthaginian duel that could only end with one side stripped of its overseas empire, commerce and independence. The French had learned from previous struggles that Britain's greatest strength was its system of government credit which rested on public confidence. This confidence could be eroded to the point of collapse if, as both Revolutionary governments and Napoleon believed, Britain lost her Continental trade, which was the chief source of her wealth. With nothing to sell, the 'nation of shopkeepers' would have no surplus money to advance their government.

From 1795 to 1805 Britain was threatened by invasion, and with it the prospect of occupation by a power bent on remodelling every nation it conquered according to Revolutionary principles. The monarchy would have been removed, the constitution dissolved and a republic established. The pattern changed somewhat after 1803, when Napoleon crowned himself emperor. States under his control were transformed into military dictatorships governed by puppet princes, whose main task was to supply men and cash for the French war machine. Individual freedom would have vanished had Britain become a Napoleonic satrapy, a point based on the experience of other countries in Europe, and repeatedly made by government propagandists.

This, unlike previous Franco-British wars, was a contest of ideologies. The French, at least during the 1790s, were animated by an urge to emancipate the people of Europe, and share with them the blessings of the new Revolutionary order based on equal rights for all men and government by the general will. The ideals of the Revolution appealed to many in Britain, particularly those excluded from power, who saw them as the blueprint for a new political order in their own country. Jacobin theories of equality also won converts, but they and more moderate apostles of the Revolution were soon driven underground. In 1794–5, the government, desperate to secure national unity and fearing the existence of what later would be called a fifth column, began the legal persecution of anyone suspected of Revolutionary sympathies. Their numbers and powers of persuasion were exaggerated, but nevertheless they became, like their French counterparts, bogey men intoxicated by wild fancies. And yet, in the political climate of the late 1790s, such a figure had a potential for mischief-making. War-weariness, food and anti-militia riots, the naval mutinies of 1797 and their successors, and the 1798 insurrection in Ireland were reminders that, at times, British political unity was brittle.

Political propaganda which emphasised national solidarity was vital in what quickly became a total war in a modern sense. Sustained and effective resistance to France required the greatest ever mobilisation of Britain's manpower and financial resources. Just over a tenth of Britain's adult males were drafted into the armed services during the war, and even then there were continual complaints from commanders of shortages of men. By 1810 there were 145,000 sailors and 31,000 marines, 300,000 regular soldiers and militiamen, and 189,000 volunteers, an early version of the Home Guard.

The total cost of the war was just over £1000 million of which £830 million was consumed by the army and navy. Part of this sum came from increased customs and excise duties, which was why it was so important to maintain the flow of British trade, and from new imposts, including income tax which was first introduced in 1798 and had yielded £142 million by the end of the war. Government borrowing spiralled, and by 1815 the national debt stood at £834 million. It was not surprising that the rich were willing to invest so much of their money in government stock for it was, in a way, an insurance against imported, levelling Jacobinism.

The British government looked to the sea as the means of bringing about the breakdown of France and, incidentally, the strengthening of Britain. The process was explained to the Commons in March 1801 by Henry Dundas, the Secretary of State for War, who had been one of its stoutest advocates:

> *. . . the primary object of our attention ought to be, by what means we can most effectively increase those resources upon which depend our naval superiority, and at the same time diminish or appropriate to ourselves those which might otherwise enable the enemy to contend with us in this respect.*

It was, he continued, therefore imperative to 'cut off the commercial resources of our enemy, as by doing so we infallibly weaken and destroy their naval resources.'

Dundas's war was an imperial contest, waged in the manner of the elder Pitt, in which Britain picked off her opponent's colonies and swept her merchantmen from the seas at the same time as preserving, even enlarging, her own commerce. Some of the loot would be kept and the rest bartered for a European settlement designed to restrain France.

The results of the naval war were up to expectations. In 1793 the French fleet was bottled up in its harbours, and a blockade imposed on its Atlantic and Mediterranean seaboards. There followed a series of seaborne offensives against the French West Indian colonies and, after 1795, when Holland surrendered, the Dutch. As supporters of these operations predicted, they were highly profitable; the prize money from Demerara and Essequibo (now part of Guyana) was £200,000 and the invasion forces were followed by British planters keen to buy up sugar estates at knock-down prices. The cost in lives was enormous with a death rate of 70 per cent among sailors and soldiers, nearly all of them victims of malaria and yellow fever exacerbated by alcoholism. As the wastage rate among fighting men rose, local commanders decided to recruit free negroes, despite the protests of planters horrified by the idea of any black men trained in arms. In 1798 a new expedient was tried to increase the numbers of the West India Regiment and the army began buying slaves to fill its ranks; within nine years just over 6,800 had been purchased at a cost to the Treasury of £484,000.

The fruits of this campaign fought by slave-soldiers and fever-ridden redcoats were listed by Dundas in 1801. In eight years, Britain had acquired Tobago, Martinique, Guadeloupe, St Lucia and the Saintes from the French, Curaçao, Demerara and Essequibo from Holland, and Trinidad from Spain, which had

Matchless Heroes still we own; Crown'd with honourable spoils From the leagued Nations won On their high prows they proudly stand The God-like Guardians of their native Land Lords of the mighty Deep triumphant ride, Wealth and Victory at their side.

ANTI-JACOBIN MAGAZINE, 1798

entered into an alliance with France in 1795. Further overseas gains were Malta, Minorca, and the Dutch colonies in the East Indies, Trincomalee on the coast of Ceylon (Sri-Lanka) and Cape Town. It was, by the standards of any previous war, an impressive haul and deeply satisfying to the commercial community who welcomed new markets.

These were desperately needed in 1801. On the Continent the war had gone the French way, despite early prophecies that the makeshift Revolutionary armies would quickly fall apart when they encountered regular troops. The reverse had happened, with Austrian, Prussian and Russian armies coming off worse in nearly every engagement. What was more, the French had discovered how to compensate for their financial weakness by making war pay for itself; as they fanned out into the Low Countries, the Rhineland, Switzerland and northern Italy, French armies lived off the land, and topped up their war-chests with forced contributions from the people they had liberated. At the same time French soldiers, learning as they fought, developed a tough professionalism and the Revolutionary principle of making talent the sole criterion for promotion encouraged the emergence of a cadre of highly able and intelligent commanders.

Britain's contribution to the land war in Europe had been negligible. Following earlier precedents, the younger Pitt had despatched expeditionary forces to the Low Countries but, undermanned and

India preserved:

the storming of Seringapatam (1799). A Frenchman (behind battlements and wearing a cocked hat) in the service of Tipu Sultan vainly encourages the Mysorean defenders. (Collection of A.V. Williams)

mismanaged, they were quickly sent packing. Another old expedient had to be reluctantly revived in 1794–5, when Pitt was forced to offer subsidies and loans to Austria and Prussia for whom the financial strain of the war had been too great. British credit kept Austrian, Prussian and, in 1799, Russian armies in the fight, but it did not improve their performance on the battlefield. France's armies remained unbeatable, and by 1801 it had absorbed the Austrian Netherlands (Belgium) and the Rhineland and established satellite republics in Holland, Switzerland and northern Italy.

The fortunes of the land war in western Europe affected the naval balance of power in the Atlantic and Mediterranean. In 1793 this had strongly favoured the Royal Navy, which mustered 115 line-of-

battle ships against France's 76. The conquest of the Netherlands in 1795 added 59 battleships to the French total, and the Spanish alliance a further 76. The risk of an overwhelming Franco-Dutch-Spanish concentration in home waters was so great that, early in 1797, the Mediterranean fleet withdrew to deploy off Spain's Atlantic coastline. The alarm proved premature; in February 1797 Admiral Sir John Jervis led his heavily outnumbered fleet in an attack on the Spanish off Cape St Vincent and took four battleships, and in October, Admiral Lord Duncan severely mauled the Dutch at Camperdown.

The victories of 1797 confirmed British paramountcy in the Channel and Atlantic, but the French held the initiative in the Mediterranean. By the beginning of 1798, the Toulon fleet had been refurbished and transports were assembling in the harbour to take on board a 17,000-strong army, commanded by Napoleon. Its purpose was to strike a knock-out blow against Britain, but a question mark hung over its destination. There were two alternatives: an invasion of Ireland, where the French landfall would be a signal for a mass uprising by the Gaelic, Catholic Irish, or Egypt. Egypt was chosen on strategic grounds since its occupation would jeopardise Britain's considerable commercial interests in the Middle East, and place a French army within striking distance of India.

The empire's saviour: Admiral Lord Nelson. (By courtesy of the National Portrait Gallery)

The sheer boldness of Napoleon's plan still astonishes. Yet it was taken seriously by Dundas, whose specialist advisers agreed that an attack on India, either overland across Syria and Iraq or through the Red Sea, was perfectly feasible, and that Napoleon might expect assistance from the Shah of Persia (Iran) and the Amir of Afghanistan. Moreover, it was imagined that even a small force of European troops could easily tilt the Indian balance of power against Britain. All this was a nasty shock for the cabinet, and Dundas, who was certain that the loss of India would prove 'fatal' to Britain, ordered reinforcements to be rushed there.

They were not needed. Napoleon's master-stroke was frustrated when his fleet and transports were destroyed by Admiral Sir Horatio, later Lord, Nelson at Abukir Bay in August. The French army, abandoned by its general, who hurried back to Paris to further his political career, was left isolated in

Supremacy secured:

the closing phase of

the Battle of Trafalgar

(1805) which confirmed

Britain's mastery of

the seas and removed

the threat of invasion.

(© NMM)

Egypt. It was finally evicted by a British expeditionary force sent for the purpose in 1801. In India the Marquess Wellesley moved quickly to eliminate France's potential ally, Tipu Sultan, and prepared to do likewise to the Mahrathas who employed French mercenaries.

The episode had been nerve-wracking for British ministers, who had been given an object lesson in the vulnerability of India and its communications. Even if Napoleon had simply stayed put in Egypt, he would have severed the so-called 'overland route' to India. This stretched from Port Said across the Suez isthmus to Alexandria and provided the fastest means of communication between Britain and India. It was clear from the events of 1798 that the future security of India required British control of the Mediterranean and political domination of the Ottoman empire, whose territories now became a vast *glacis* defending India's western frontiers. Furthermore, the possibility that the rulers of Persia and Afghanistan might have connived with Napoleon made it imperative that both countries were drawn into Britain's orbit. Napoleon's Egyptian adventure had laid the foundations of British policy in the Mediterranean and Middle East for the next hundred and fifty years. It had also opened up a new region for Franco-British imperial rivalry which gathered pace after 1815.

For the moment, France's war aims were confined to Europe. There had been a brief peace, signed at Amiens in the spring of 1802, which was no more than a breathing space during which Britain and

France bickered and recovered their strength. When the war reopened just over a year later, Napoleon set his mind on the conquest of Britain, which he recognised as his most formidable and implacable enemy. His invasion plans demanded mastery of the Channel by the Franco-Spanish fleet based at Toulon. This broke through the blockade in May 1805, made a feint towards the West Indies, but was intercepted by Nelson off Cape Trafalgar in October and destroyed. Eighteen battleships were taken or sunk and with them went all hopes of France ever again challenging Britain at sea. Stringent measures were taken to hinder the rebuilding of the French navy, including a pre-emptive attack on Copenhagen and the seizure of the Danish fleet in 1807. Fears of an invasion receded, France's overseas trade was choked and Britain was free to continue engorging itself on her enemies' colonies.

On land, Napoleon was triumphant. His Grande Armée, originally earmarked for the invasion of Britain, turned against her allies, Austria, Prussia and Russia. Between 1805 and 1807 he chalked up an amazing sequence of victories: Ulm, Austerlitz, Jena-Auerstädt, Eylau and Friedland. As a result, Austria, Prussia and Russia were impelled, literally at gunpoint, to accept a new European order devised by Napoleon. The Continent was now dominated by an enlarged France and its satellites, the Kingdoms of Italy and Westphalia, the Confederation of the Rhine

and the Grand Duchy of Warsaw. Whether or not directly under Napoleon's heel, all the states of Europe were forced to adopt his 1806 Berlin Decrees which forbade all commerce with Britain.

Britain answered with an embargo of its own, enforced by the Royal Navy, which brought Europe's overseas trade to a virtual standstill. Europeans were denied such products as tobacco and sugar, which had been re-exported by Britain, and British manufactured goods such as cotton. France could not make up the shortfall since her industry lacked the capacity to satisfy Europe's markets, and her import trade had been all but extinguished by the blockade. While Europe's trade stagnated, Britain's actually expanded as merchants penetrated new markets in the United States (until the war of 1812), Asia, the Middle East and, despite resistance, Spanish South America. Fresh outlets for British goods obviously offset the loss of older markets, but they did not entirely replace them. By the winter of 1811–12 a recession seemed likely as exports were in the doldrums and manufacturing output was falling.

The search for new commercial advantage was carried on with great vigour. After the reoccupation of Cape Town in 1806, the local commander, Admiral Sir Home Popham, delivered a *coup de main* against Buenos Aires in May of that year. News of his exploit aroused enormous excitement in London, where senior army and naval officers combined with business interests to promote a profitable war of conquest against the whole of Spanish America. Dreams of a new American empire with vast markets

Sepoy general: the Duke of Wellington who, by his own admission, learned the art of war in India, and later commanded the British army in the Peninsula and the Allies at Waterloo. (Collection of Michael Staniforth)

proved illusory; nerveless command and mismanagement led to an ignominious evacuation of the River Plate by midsummer 1807.

By this time events in Europe were taking a new turn. Napoleon's attempts to browbeat Portugal and set his featherbrained brother, Joseph, on the throne of Spain dragged him into an unfamiliar type of war. The Spanish insurrection of May 1808 was a spontaneous, popular uprising, which took the French by surprise, and forced their generals to fight a guerrilla war in a countryside where food and fodder were scarce. The Portuguese and Spanish appealed to Britain, and the government immediately pledged cash, arms and an army. Pitt had been dead for two years, but his ideas still formed the framework of British policy, which was to offer unqualified help to anyone who promised to fight France.

The resulting Anglo-Spanish-Portuguese alliance was one of convenience rather than conviction. Portugal was transformed into a British dependency for the next six years, and the Spanish, suspecting that Britain coveted their American possessions and commerce, steadfastly resisted demands to open their markets to British merchants. Old hatreds died hard; in 1814 British merchants in Buenos Aires complained that local officials were 'arbitrary, insulting and vexatious', and that they suffered the 'bigotted Zeal and vindictive rage of the soldiery', and in the same year a British sloop was fired on by the guns of the fort at Cartagena. Nevertheless the alliance held, thanks to the tact and firmness of the British commander-in-chief, Arthur Wellesley. He was a consummate strategist who saw from the first that he was about to conduct a war of attrition in which the winning army would be that which was well-fed and supplied. The navy escorted convoys of merchantmen to Lisbon, where cargoes of grain and fodder were unloaded for distribution up country. There were many nail-biting moments, but on the whole Wellesley's troops did not starve. The French, living off the land, did.

Moreover, Wellesley repeatedly beat French armies. His string of victories between 1808 and 1812 made the Iberian peninsula the graveyard of French marshals' reputations, and dispelled for ever the myth of French invincibility. Disengagement from an unwinnable war was unthinkable for Napoleon, since it would be a confession of weakness which was bound to encourage resistance elsewhere. He was politically bankrupt, with nothing to offer Europe but economic stagnation, heavy taxes and conscription, the last two necessary to preserve the war machine with which he menaced anyone who opposed his will. His confidence, one could almost say hubris, remained high, and at the beginning of 1812 he was preparing to solve his problems in the only way he knew how, by war. He intended to overawe Russia, which was showing disconcerting signs of independence, and then, in person, take charge of affairs in Spain.

The invasion of Russia, designed as an exercise in intimidation, went awry. French muddle, miscalculation and over-confidence combined with Russian doggedness to cause first the disintegration and then the destruction of the Grande Armée during the autumn and winter of 1812–13. Prussia broke ranks and joined Russia, and so too did Austria after a little hesitation. Britain was swift to rebuild a new coalition, delivering its members just over £26 million in subsidies and loan guarantees as well as cannon and muskets from her foundries and workshops.

Napoleon's European *imperium* fell apart quickly. Founded on victories, it could not survive the defeats inflicted on its master's armies in the autumn and winter of 1813–14. Joseph Bonaparte was finally turned out of Spain, and in January 1814 Wellesley, now Duke of Wellington, led an Anglo-Portuguese army into southern France. Squeezed between Wellington and the Austrians, Prussians and Russians who were striking deep into eastern France, Napoleon abdicated in April. A year later he returned from Elba, convinced that he could again mesmerise his countrymen with fresh dreams of martial glory. The end came at Waterloo where he suffered a decisive defeat at the hands of Wellington and Marshal Blücher's Prussians. At the end of June, Napoleon surrendered to the British, and was sent in exile to their remotest colony, St Helena, where, unchastened, he brooded on his mistakes.

Winning the war against France had been a Herculean effort. The conventional wisdom, then and later, attributed final victory to seapower because, above all, it ensured that Britain stayed in the ring. The ships of the Royal Navy had prevented invasion; they had confined French power to Europe and allowed Britain to occupy nearly all the overseas possessions of her adversaries; they had guarded the convoys which sustained Wellington's army in the peninsula; and they had guaranteed the survival of Britain's global commerce, which generated the wealth needed to pay for her war effort, and underwrite those of the three big European powers with armies large enough to engage Napoleon on equal terms.

Victory bred arrogance and a feeling that Britain represented, in its system of government and the industry of its people, the highest state yet reached by civilisation. The possession of overseas territories contributed little as yet to this national pride. The peace treaties of 1814–15 had added to British possessions with confirmation of ownership of Malta, the Ionian Islands, Trinidad, Tobago, St Lucia, what is now Guyana, Cape Colony and Mauritius. With the exception of the West Indian islands, the chief fruits of conquest were naval bases sited to secure future control over the Mediterranean and Indian Ocean. Significantly, Britain was prepared to hand back some of her spoils, all of commercial value. Guadeloupe and Réunion were returned to France, and Java and Surinam to the Netherlands, which helped bring about concessions on the Continent which favoured British interests.

The post-war bargaining over colonies is instructive. Britain was a maritime power which lived by international trade. Her by now rapidly expanding manufacturing industries and her older commerce in re-exported tropical commodities found their largest markets in Europe. European peace and stability were therefore essential for British commerce; as for the rest of the world, all that was required was a permanent naval presence which would safeguard the sea-lanes and, on occasions, assert the rights of British businessmen. In 1815 captive, colonial markets and sources of raw materials were a bonus to the country which dominated every area of world trade. The war had helped Britain achieve this ascendancy and it had fostered a belligerent, often self-righteous outlook which made it relatively easy for the British to exploit their advantages at the same time as representing themselves as mankind's benefactors.

Beating Napoleon: the French army surrenders to a smaller Spanish force at Baylen in 1808.
(© Mary Evans Picture Library)

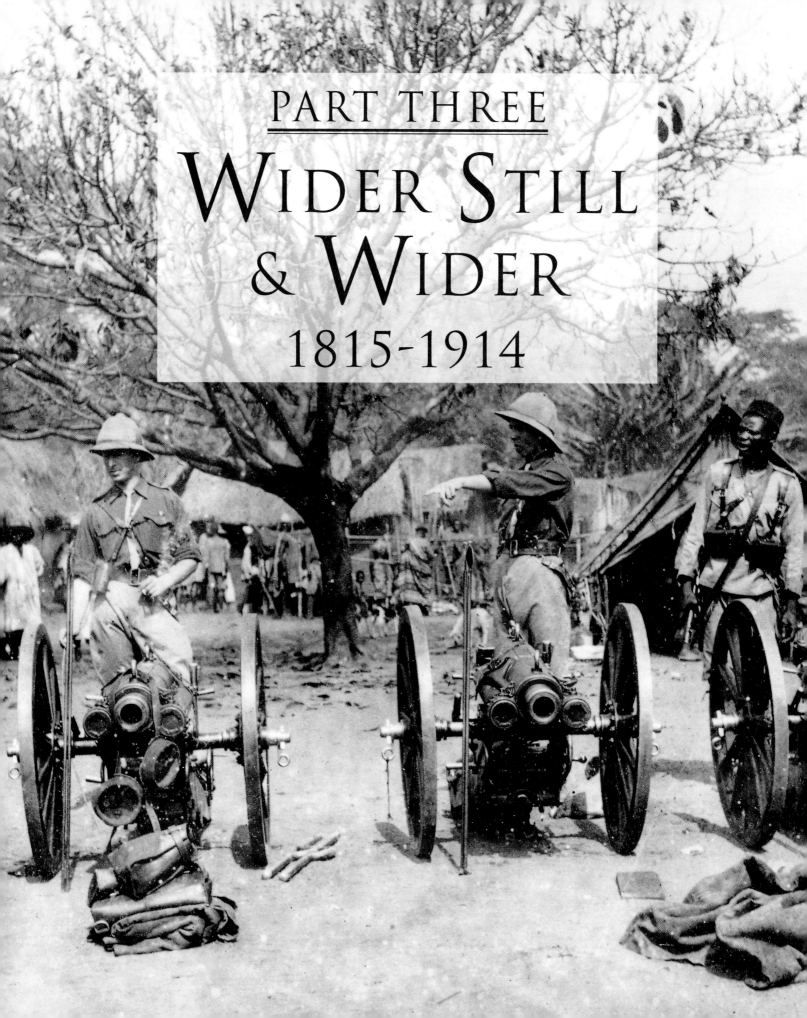

PART THREE
WIDER STILL & WIDER
1815-1914

I

POWER AND GREATNESS:

COMMERCE, SEAPOWER AND STRATEGY

1815–1870

For the first three-quarters of the nineteenth century Britain appeared as a colossus astride the world. Britain dominated every field of human activity and its people seemed to possess an almost demonic energy. On seeing the thriving port of Sydney in January 1836, Charles Darwin wrote, 'My first feeling was to congratulate myself that I was born an Englishman.' The city's buildings and bustle were evidence of 'the power of the British nation' and a contrast to the lassitude of the Spanish and Portuguese, whose former colonies he had just visited and where, he concluded, little progress had been made over the past three hundred years.

Men of Darwin's generation recognised three sources of that peculiarly British power which was currently transforming the world. The first was the native inventiveness and application of its people which had been the moving force behind the second, the growth of Britain's manufacturing industry. Finally, there was naval supremacy, which made it possible for Britain to penetrate new markets and to count for something in the affairs of the world.

There was also, and this was continually announced from the pulpit and set down in tracts and editorials, that inner strength and purposefulness that individuals derived from a Christian faith which set a high store on personal integrity, hard work and a dedication to the general welfare of all mankind.

Edward Pine, a surgeon who served in China and New South Wales wrote, 'the greatest satisfaction results from the strict performance of one's duty – I pray God that my best efforts may be directed to that end.' This and similar private creeds collectively strengthened what was to become a national conviction: Britain had been chosen by Providence as an instrument of universal progress.

Progress was inseparable from the Industrial Revolution. It had proceeded slowly and unevenly from the middle of the eighteenth century and would be more or less complete by 1860. The growth of large-scale manufacturing industry had coincided with a population explosion: in 1801 there were roughly ten million people in Britain, a total which had risen to over twenty-two million by 1871 despite emigration and the Irish famine of 1845–7. Had Britain remained a largely agrarian country, the inevitable outcome of growth on this scale would have been famines of the kind seen today in parts of Africa. The Industrial Revolution proved Britain's salvation for it absorbed its surplus population.

This process solved one problem, but created others. In the thirty years after Waterloo the new workforce faced a precarious existence, since its only hope of survival lay in an ever-increasing market for

The moral force of empire: David Livingstone, missionary, explorer and crusader against African slavery. (© Church of Scotland World Missions)

PREVIOUS PAGES

Firepower: collapsible artillery: these mobile pieces could be broken down and carried by mules, or, in malarial districts where they perished, by native porters, Nigeria, 1905. (© NAM)

manufactured goods. This could only be achieved as long as products remained cheap, and so wages were depressed. Here industrialists were assisted by the 1834 Poor Law, which was deliberately contrived to make conditions for the unemployed so unbearable that they were driven to seek work or emigrate. Sometimes there was no work available even for the willing. Recessions, which occurred regularly between 1815 and the mid-1840s, were accompanied by mass lay-offs, public disorders and outbursts of often violent political radicalism. Matters were made worse by the fact that by 1840 Britain could no longer produce enough food to sustain its population.

Free trade offered an escape from these difficulties, or so it was argued, and this belief coincided with a determined effort to open up new markets. The volume of Britain's overseas trade expanded steadily for the next forty years, with the largest outlets being Europe and the United States.

For a time it was imagined that free trade would irreparably damage those colonial economies which relied on preferential treatment for their raw materials. This was true for the West Indian sugar producers who were the victims of a breathtaking example of contemporary humbug, for they had been forced to emancipate their slaves in 1833 and then, by the 1846 Sugar Duties Act, had to compete in a free market with sugar imported from the slave-operated plantations of Cuba and Brazil. Not surprisingly, the economy of the British West Indies collapsed. Other colonial economies survived the loss of their old commercial privileges, a phenomenon which puzzled some observers who believed them incapable of surviving in a free market.

The empire was a valuable outlet for British products. In 1867, India imported goods worth £21 million, which made it a market equal to Britain's largest foreign customer, the United States. The other totals were impressive; exports to Australia totalled £8 million, Canada £5.8 million, Hong Kong £2.5 million, Singapore £2 million and New Zealand £1.6 million. Of course given that Britain possessed just under half the world's industrial capacity at the time, her colonies, like everyone else, had little choice but to import British manufactures.

The expression 'workshop of the world' is now a cliché, but it still best describes Britain's international trading position from 1815 to 1870. There were some free trade enthusiasts in the 1840s who looked forward to a time in the near future when all Britain's energies would be devoted to industry, whose workforce would live off cheap imported food from America and Europe. As in the seventeenth and eighteenth centuries, Britain's commercial success rested on the export of inexpensive staple goods. Machine-produced cotton dominated; during the 1830s cottonware from the Lancashire mills made up more than half of Britain's exports. In 1867 the value of all kinds of cotton, including yarn for weaving elsewhere, was £55.9 million. Next in importance came woollen cloth (£18 million), coal (£5.4 million), railway track (£4.8 million) and steam engines (£1.9 million). The last items indicate that by this time Britain was exporting her technology to other countries to assist their programmes of industrialisation.

Britain also exported capital. The accumulated private wealth of the country, drawn from both industrial and agricultural profits, was channelled into foreign and imperial investments. Raising capital for foreign governments and commercial enterprises, along with banking, marine insurance and stockbroking were the work of the City of London. These specialisms, experience and the sheer volume of money available in Britain for overseas investment assured London pre-eminence among the world's financial centres.

Money-lending complemented manufacturing. By injecting large sums of money into undeveloped and developing economies, British investors were stimulating new demands. British-funded enterprises

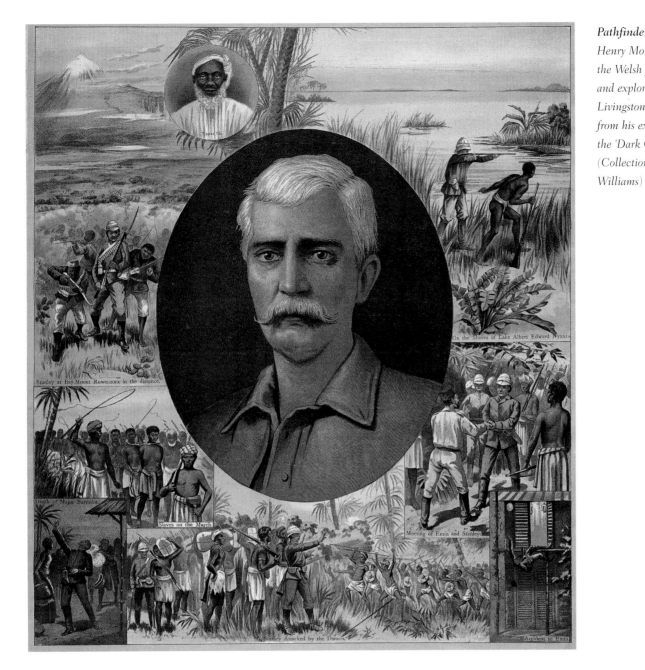

Pathfinder:
Henry Morton Stanley,
the Welsh journalist
and explorer who 'found'
Livingstone, with scenes
from his expeditions in
the 'Dark Continent'.
(Collection of A.V.
Williams)

such as cattle ranches in Uruguay, railroads in America and Indian cotton plantations drew new countries into her global network of trade. At the same time, although this was not immediately apparent, British investment was also creating industries which would, in time, compete with her own.

The export of goods and money led to the creation of what had been called an 'unofficial' or 'informal' empire. In the scramble for new markets it was inevitable that British merchants faced local opposition or found themselves in countries where governments were either too feeble or lazy to take measures to protect them or their goods. Britain's response was what became known as 'gunboat diplomacy'. Whenever a crisis occurred, a warship would be summoned by the local consul and its commander would keep watch. Direct engagement, save in an emergency, was discouraged since the British government preferred to persuade the local authorities to do their duty. It was the Sultan of Pahang's police who rounded up the murderers of some British tin-mining engineers in 1892, prompted by the appearance of two gunboats off his coast.

By 1870 the apparatus of informal empire was in place in every quarter of the world. Asian and African princes were bound by treaties in which they pledged themselves not to molest missionaries and merchants, and to suppress slave-trading and piracy; Latin America was safe for business and investment; and it was possible to speak of Britain's 'practical protectorate' over the Turkish empire. Even though the primary purpose of informal empire was to make the world a safe place for the British to trade in, it was also the imposition of a higher morality. Slavery and piracy were wrong, and, when they moved abroad, the British expected to find the same standards of official honesty and detachment as obtained at home.

Informal empire depended on British maritime supremacy. The Royal Navy possessed 214 battleships and nearly 800 smaller vessels in 1815. There were considerable post-war cuts, but in 1817 the Foreign Secretary, Viscount Castlereagh,

Ruling the waves:
the ironclad battleship
HMS Sultan *at full*
speed, c.1880.
(© IWM)

insisted that Britain's security required her to maintain 'a navy equal to the navies of any two powers that can be brought against us'. This principle was more or less upheld for the rest of the century, despite regular calls for cheeseparing from lobbies who held that it was the government's first duty to keep down expenditure and taxation. Invasion scares, which occurred frequently throughout Victoria's reign, silenced demands for a reduced naval budget and usually triggered a crash programme of ship-building.

Send a gunboat!:
a sloop at anchor c.1850.
Small vessels of this kind
upheld British interests
on every ocean until
superseded by purpose-
built gunboats.
(© IWM)

By the middle of the nineteenth century the empire had given Britain a power and self-confidence which was satirised by Charles Dickens in his novel, *Dombey and Son*:

> *The earth was made for Dombey and Son to trade in, the sun and the moon were made to give them light. Rivers and seas were formed to float their ships; rainbows to give them the promise of fair weather; winds blew for or against their enterprises; stars and planets circled in their orbits, to preserve inviolate a system of which they were the centre.*

The British Empire, 1850

‡ Naval Bases and Depôts

2

WE ARE GOING AS CIVILISERS:
EMPIRE AND PUBLIC OPINION
1815–1880

What did the empire mean to the British public? This question became a vital one as the nineteenth century proceeded. The thoughts and feelings of the people on this and other subjects of national concern mattered more and more as the country moved towards democracy. The 1832 Parliamentary Reform Act created a middle-class electorate, and the Reform and Redistribution Acts of 1867 and 1884–5 extended the vote to most urban and rural working men. Contemporaries sensed that they were living in an age of political progress, in which reasoned debate between educated men was being proved

A godly nation under Providence: shipboard service on board a liner bound for India. The Union Jack serves as an altar cloth, c.1890. (© P&O)

Fighting the slave trade: a Royal Navy frigate pursuing a slaver, c.1840. (© Wilberforce House Museum/Bridgeman Art Library)

as the most perfect means of solving all human problems. Simultaneously, there was a growth in the numbers and readership of daily newspapers and weekly journals which disseminated information and fostered discussion of national issues. The London press took advantage of the extension of the railway network between 1840 and 1860 to build up a national circulation, and with it the ability to influence opinion throughout the country.

Views on the empire differed enormously during this period, and there was much passionate debate about how it should be managed, the best treatment for its subjects, and whether or not it should be extended. There was, on the whole, general agreement that the empire was a powerful force for the spread of civilisation through trade and the imposition of superior codes of behaviour on its 'savage' inhabitants. Few would have disagreed with an editorial in the *Sun*, which welcomed the announcement of the form of government chosen for Britain's newest colony, New Zealand, in January 1847. 'So speedy an attainment of the choicest fruits of civilisation, in a country where, a few years since, a hardy race of savages alone ranged free, ignorant of their better nature, is without parallel in history.'

There were, however, profound differences of opinion as to whether the Maoris and other races possessed a 'better nature', and how it could be cultivated. On one side there were the pragmatists, who were for the most part soldiers, sailors and administrators (often former servicemen), colonists and their adherents in Britain who were sceptical about the capacity of native peoples for advancement. On the other hand there was a powerful body of Christian philanthropists who believed that these races could be raised to standards of education and conduct which would place them alongside Europeans. Members of this group tended to be Nonconformists, middle-class, and Liberal or Radical in their politics. Their opponents were largely Anglicans with aristocratic or gentry backgrounds and Whig or Tory sympathies, although this was a period when party labels mattered far less than they did later.

At the beginning of the century the great imperial issue was slavery. The movement for its abolition had gained impetus during the 1770s and won considerable support from all classes. Evangelicals, with their strong belief in salvation through saving others, were attracted towards a campaign which was pledged to release the slaves from bondage and convert them. Much anti-slavery propaganda

Liberated slaves:
Africans rescued from
Arab slavers, Zanzibar,
c.1870.

*Satisfying the
nation's taste:*
the house of an Indian
tea planter. Since the
early eighteenth century
the demand for tea had
extended to all classes
in Britain.
(© e.t. archive)

A model for a dark continent:

a family group from Sierra Leone wearing European clothes in a colony founded by evangelicals bent on proving that Africans were capable of enlightenment and advancement, 1898. (© NAM)

was emotional, highlighting the callous treatment of slaves and their inner suffering, and this appealed to those under the influence of the Romantic Movement. Reason might and did argue that slavery was vital to the economy, but sentiment replied that the misery it inflicted alone justified its abolition.

The power of the anti-slavery movement owed much to the energy and singlemindedness of its leaders, William Wilberforce and Thomas Clarkson. To demonstrate their faith in the ability of the negro to regenerate himself, they joined the sponsors of an experimental colony, Sierra Leone, founded in 1787. The Sierra Leone Company's object was to 'introduce civilisation among the natives and to cultivate the soil by means of free labour' and to educate them to a level which proved them the equals of Europeans in accomplishments and civilisation. Sierra Leone flourished and, in 1808, became a Crown colony and its capital, Freetown, one of the bases for the new Royal Navy anti-slaving squadron.

Britain's abolition of the slave trade in 1807 was the movement's first triumph. Thereafter, British statesmen and diplomats did their utmost to induce other governments to follow Britain's example. Squadrons of warships were deployed to arrest slavers, first off the West African and Congo coasts, and later in the Indian Ocean and Persian Gulf to suppress the Arab slave trade. The global war against the slave trade was advertised as the most glowing example of Britain's humanity and enlightenment. The concept of slavery had become abhorrent to a people which, thanks to the propaganda of the French wars, was increasingly aware that personal freedom was their birthright.

It proved easier to outlaw the traffic in slaves than it did to abolish the institution of slavery in the British empire. There was unremitting resistance from the West Indian plantocracy and its allies in Parliament. Some of their apologists sniffed hypocrisy, and asked why those who made so much fuss about the slaves did so little about the sufferings of their destitute countrymen. According to one pro-slavery pamphlet of the early 1800s, 'Many a Gentleman's gelding, or high-mettled racer, and many a Lady's pad, in England, is looked after and tended with kinder treatment than some of our own poor.' Moreover, as the Tory *Anti-Jacobin* claimed in 1807, the 'Crying, methodistical philanthropists' were mistaken in their assumption that every planter mistreated his slaves. Plantation owners went to some lengths to present themselves as humane men; in 1816 those of Barbados pointed out that pregnant women were excused field work and added, with unintentional irony, that when they gave birth they received a payment.

Imperial matriarch:
Queen Victoria's
declaration as Empress
of India in 1876 added
prestige to the empire and
lustre to the monarchy
which would become a
focus of imperial loyalty.
(© Opie)

A reformed Commons, in which Whigs and Radicals dominated, abolished slavery in 1833, allowing several years for the transition from unpaid to paid labour on the plantations. Throughout the debate over slavery the issue of what would happen to the slaves after emancipation had been central. Supporters of slavery had repeatedly argued that the slaves would 'soon sink into miserable penury, and languishingly pine away in their old African laziness, inaction and want'. As a result, the local economy would dissolve.

Abolitionists had always held that the end of slavery was the first stage in the elevation of the West Indians. Released from servitude, they would be free to make their own future and raise themselves by their own efforts. An abolitionist who visited Antigua in 1839–40 found encouraging signs that this was happening. Seven thousand children were attending schools, where there was regular Bible-reading, and the Methodist meeting house at St John's was filled with a congregation of 'respectable-looking' worshippers drawn from a community of busy smallholders. Equally gratifying was the evidence of a long overdue sexual reformation. 'Even the overseers are ceasing, one after another, from the sinful mode of life, and are forming reputable connexions and marriages.'

The view from the top was less sanguine. Giving evidence to a Commons committee in 1849, Sir James Light, the governor of British Guiana, feared that many ex-slaves had imagined that emancipation meant equality with the white man. He lamented the decay of deference within his colony, where he and other men of substance were now exposed to the 'jeering and impertinent remarks of loungers' as they rode through the capital, Georgetown. What was worse was that former slaves shunned plantation work, forcing the owners to look elsewhere for labour. An early seventeenth-century precedent was resurrected and indentured servants were imported. In what was one of the first internal migrations within the empire, poor Indians and Chinese were hired and shipped to the West Indies. By 1857 well over a half of the 14,000-strong workforce on the Trinidadian plantations were from China and India. The number would have been larger, but many immigrants died during the six-month voyage in insanitary and ill-ventilated ships.

The campaign to end slavery within the British empire coincided with the growth of organisations devoted to Christian missions throughout the world. Conversion was one of the highest forms of Christian service. The 'soul of a poor heathen was as valuable as his own to God' claimed Thomas Kendall, who, from the moment of his salvation, was determined to bring others to that grace he had found within himself. He began missionary work among the Maoris of New Zealand in 1817.

The Christian missions of the nineteenth century not only redeemed souls, they regenerated whole races. An account of Cape Colony written in 1819 praised the work there of the Moravian missionaries, who 'have converted the indolent degraded Hottentot into an active moral member of society'. 'We were going as civilisers as well as preachers,' wrote James Stewart in 1874. He was one of a new generation of evangelists, having studied medicine as well as theology, who set off into Central Africa with a party of practically qualified men to carry on the work of his mentor, the missionary-explorer David Livingstone. He had taken artisans to teach new crafts to his flock and to build a new, self-sufficient, ordered Christian society where there had once been chaos.

As well as preaching the gospel, missionaries were also responsible for bringing their congregations into contact with the values of the West. George Brown, a stout-hearted Methodist missionary who began his work on the island of New Britain, west of Papua, in 1875 was more than a saver of souls. Within three years he 'succeeded in opening up a large extent of the coast of New Britain and New Ireland to the influence of Civilisation and Christianity so that Traders were allowed to land and live on the islands in comparative safety.' This praise came from a naval officer who warmly endorsed his methods. When tribal chiefs had threatened to kill him, his flock and every European they could find, Brown attacked and defeated them with a small force of Fijian converts armed with two fowling pieces and a revolver.

Missionaries were not only pathfinders of empire, and even, at times, pacifiers. Through their connections with British churches they linked the empire with the ordinary men, women and children who collected money for and promoted their activities. One of these helpers, Mrs Jellyby, was caricatured by Dickens in *Bleak House* (1851) as a creature who 'could see nothing nearer than Africa' and neglected her family duties in favour of work for the mission settlement of 'Borrioboola-Gha' on the banks of the Niger. But then Dickens had no time for the noble savage – 'His virtues are a fable; his happiness is a delusion; his nobility, nonsense.' Nonetheless, thousands of Dickens's countrymen went to considerable effort to provide for the metamorphosis of such creatures into useful Christians.

Subscribers to missions were encouraged to donate money, Bibles and material by sheaves of tracts which outlined the wretchedness and depravity of the heathen. Lurid accounts were presented of Indian infanticide, sati, idolatry and superstitions. From the Pacific and Africa came stories of tribal warfare, cannibalism, domestic slavery and thinly veiled details of sexual promiscuity. There were in central Africa vices which 'cannot be explained or named for shame'. According to one exasperated missionary, 'The imagination of the Kaffir runs to seed after puberty. It would be safer to say it runs to sex', which explained why, after the age of fifteen, white pupils surpassed blacks!

The lion's roar: Britain leaps to the defence of Turkey and warns Russia to keep out of the Ottoman Empire on the cover of a 'jingo' popular song, 1877. (© NLS)

The soldier, like the missionary, was also seen as a civiliser. This was a period of almost continual imperial warfare. Between 1817 and 1878 there were intermittent campaigns against the tribes of the eastern Cape, known indiscriminately as Kaffirs, and in 1879 a British army invaded Zululand. In 1867 an expedition entered Abyssinia to rescue hostages held by the Emperor Theodore, and in 1873–4 there was a large-scale punitive war against the Asante of the Gold Coast. The army in India fought campaigns in Burma (1824 and 1853), Afghanistan (1838–42 and 1878–80), conquered the Sind (1843) and the Punjab (1845–6 and 1848–9), and suppressed the Mutiny (1857–8).

From time to time large columns penetrated the North-West Frontier, punishing its notoriously recalcitrant tribesmen. There were also campaigns in New Zealand fought on behalf of the colonists against the Maoris between 1846 and 1870. A rebellion was put down in Canada in 1837, China was attacked three times between 1839 and 1860, and Persia once in 1856.

The British press gave extensive coverage to the campaigns, usually reproducing stories from local papers, official despatches and letters from men serving at the front. During the Crimean War of 1854–6 the pressmen, the first war correspondents, were able to follow the army, compile reports and send them back by fast steamer and train for publication ten to fourteen days later. The time lapse was reduced to forty-eight hours in May 1855, when a telegraph office was established at Balaklava, the army's base. Henceforward, the wars of empire were covered first-hand. War correspondents accompanied British forces during the Indian Mutiny, the 1859–60 China War, and the Abyssinian, Asante, Afghan and Zulu campaigns. Each of these wars gained a further immediacy through the reproduction as engravings of on-the-spot sketches and photographs in the *Illustrated London News*, which had been founded in 1842. The popularity of these illustrations was so great that by the 1870s specially commissioned war artists were being sent to the front alongside reporters.

Accounts by the journalists were horrific; the *News of the World* promised its readers the 'fullest and exclusive details of Indian atrocities' in November 1857. Its pages and those of the other papers were full of blood-chilling accounts of the random slaughter of men, women and children and hints of darker, unprintable outrages by the mutinous sepoys. Assailed by these hideous tales, there was a universal demand for retribution. Thus a speaker in the usually sedate Cambridge Union: 'When the rebellion has been crushed from the Himalayas to Comorin; when every gibbet is red with blood; when every bayonet creaks beneath its ghastly burden; when the ground in front of every cannon is strewn with rags, and flesh, and shattered bone – then talk of mercy.' Similar bloodthirsty rhetoric poured from editorials and pulpits.

What happened in India during 1857 and 1858 had a profound impact on British thinking about the empire and its peoples. According to their masters, the Indians had for many years been the beneficiaries of a humane system of government, deliberately contrived to uplift them and modernise their country. In the light of this, the Mutiny was both an act of betrayal and a wilful rejection of progress. Had the British failed to penetrate into the interior of the Indian mind? The *National Review* thought so: 'The CHILD and the SAVAGE lie very deep at the foundations of their [the Indians'] being. The varnish of civilisation is very thin, and is put off as promptly as a garment.' If this were so, and the events in India strongly suggested it, then much humanitarian endeavour had been in vain. Furthermore, the premises on which it had been based were false. Reclamation of the 'savage' through exposure to European religion and knowledge might not be possible because of indelible flaws within his character. The Indian Mutiny strengthened British racism and threw doubt on the gospel of the philanthropists.

In Liberal, Nonconformist and free trade circles it was feared that the empire engendered belligerent nationalism and militarism, which undermined what they saw as Britain's real national virtues, thrift and industriousness. John Bright took a characteristically extreme standpoint when he claimed that, 'Inasmuch as supremacy of the seas means arrogance and the assumption of dictatorial power on the part of this country, the sooner it becomes obsolete the better.' Waving cudgels had no justification in a world where free trade was increasing the interdependence of nations and reducing the friction which had

The lion's teeth: British and Indian troops parade above Malta's Grand Harbour early in 1878. The presence of a large Indian contingent was a sign that Britain could deploy its Asian power in a European crisis. (© NAM)

formerly been the source of wars. As for the colonies, they had no economic value and the bill for their defence and administration was an expensive luxury.

Canada, Australia, New Zealand and Cape Colony were all moving towards self-government and there seemed no reason why, in the near future, they should not detach themselves from Britain as America had done. *The Times* rejected this argument and, in an editorial of 4 February 1862, asserted that the white colonies were 'uniformly prosperous, and desirous of maintaining their connexion with the mother country and each other', and that their present felicitous state was 'a triumph of civilisation' of which Britain ought to be proud. Many colonists agreed. A New Zealand settler predicted that his colony would 'rise as a community to the enviable status of their forefathers, and then they would form the stoutest of all bulwarks to guard our noblest of privileges, civil and religious liberty.' Potential colonists were anxious that Britain kept its empire. The working-class journal, the *Bee Hive*, believed that the colonies belonged to the whole nation and collected 100,000 signatures for a petition which asked the Queen to promote state-funded emigration schemes for the unemployed.

The nearest the government came to taking imperial disengagement seriously was in 1865, when a parliamentary committee recommended the evacuation of tiny stations on the West African coast.

Nothing came of the proposal, largely because of the practical difficulties and uncertainty about what would replace British rule. The anti-imperialists had always been a small lobby making a great deal of noise about an issue which aroused little public interest. Moreover, predictions that the world was about to enter a golden age of harmony and free trade were dramatically disproved by the Franco-Austrian war of 1859, the Danish war of 1863, and the Austro-Prussian war of 1866. Nor did it make much political sense to contemplate disbandment of empire when Britain's rivals were engaged in empire-building: Russia was advancing into central Asia and France had completed the subjugation of Algeria in 1860 and Cochin China (Viet Nam) in 1867.

Benjamin Disraeli viewed the mutable world of the 1860s with misgivings. He was the most striking and influential figure within the Conservative party, which he led after 1868. His advancement within a party in which cleverness was mistrusted had not been easy. Flamboyant, Jewish, a novelist by profession and frequently strapped for cash, Disraeli once likened his career to the ascent of a 'greasy pole'. But he was, as he would have been the first to admit, the most talented figure in a party which had not won a general election since 1841, and whose only taste of power in the intervening years had been as partners in a couple of coalitions. It entered office again in July 1866 with Lord Derby as Prime Minister and Disraeli as Chancellor of the Exchequer and the power behind the throne.

Hurrah for our soldiers!: imperial campaigns had echoes in patriotic parlours; this piano piece was written shortly after the 1845–6 Sikh war. (© NAM)

OPPOSITE *Undaunted and defiant*: the flag is defended in a music-hall song of 1879, inspired by the Zulu war. (© NLS)

Disraeli had been angered by every turn of Liberal foreign and imperial policy, which he considered fainthearted. As a pragmatist, he realised that Britain had to maintain its standing as a global power actively, and if necessary forcefully, pursuing its interests. This could only be done if Britain maintained and strengthened her overseas empire for it was these possessions, particularly India, which made Britain strong and respected. The empire was an asset to be cherished. Disraeli the politician detected a reservoir of imperial and patriotic sentiment among the electorate, and he intended to tap it in the interests of his party. Within a year of taking office, and with Disraeli's encouragement, the government demonstrated that Britain was still a power to be reckoned with. In the summer of 1867 an Anglo-Indian army landed on the Abyssinian coast, marched inland, and stormed Magdala, where the Emperor Theodore had been holding a number of European prisoners, including British officials. The Abyssinian expedition was a minor triumph and proved that the spirit of Palmerston was alive and his mantle had fallen on Disraeli.

Success in Africa did not bring Disraeli an election victory. In 1868 the Liberals under Gladstone were returned and with them a foreign and imperial policy based upon high-minded abstract principles.

Images of conquest: since Waterloo, the government has awarded medals to ordinary soldiers as a token of the nation's gratitude. The iconography of these campaign medals is distinctly imperial.

FROM LEFT TO RIGHT
Britannia: Naval General Service Medal, 1848.

The British lion defying assegais: Matebele War Medal, 1896.

Jungle ambush: Africa Service Medal, 1887.

The Indian tiger roars: Indian General Service Medal, 1937.

We don't want to fight, but, by Jingo if we do, We've got the ships; we've got the men; we've got the money too!

MUSIC-HALL SONG, 1877

However, by 1874 the Liberals had run out of steam and the Conservatives regained power. The next six years revealed the nature of Disraeli's populist imperialism. In practice it followed lines laid down by Palmerston: Ottoman integrity and Indian security had to be upheld at all costs and informal empire enforced with vigour. The completion of the Franco-Egyptian-financed Suez Canal in 1869 had increased the need for Britain to remain the dominant power in the Middle East, since it was now India's lifeline. By a feat of legerdemain, Disraeli secured a controlling interest in the Suez Canal Company in 1875 and added the Canal to Britain's unofficial empire.

It was fears for the Canal as well as an urge to fracture the recent unity between Russia, Germany and Austria-Hungary which drove Disraeli to intervene in the affairs of Turkey. A rebellion of its Balkan subjects in 1875 had led to a war of massacre and counter-massacre, which the European powers and the Liberals in Britain blamed on the Turkish government. British moral outrage at Turkish atrocities in what today is Bulgaria was orchestrated by the Liberals, with Gladstone leading the denunciation and calling on the government to abandon its support for the decrepit and callous régime in Constantinople. The interests of humanity outweighed those of India's safety. Fortunately for Disraeli, Russia invaded the Balkans and by the end of 1877 its army was within sight of the Straits.

Public opinion began to swing behind Disraeli. A British fleet, led by the most up-to-date battleship in the world, the splendidly named HMS *Devastation*, anchored in the Dardanelles and, just to make sure that no one forgot that India's security was at stake, Indian troops were shipped to Malta. The empire was mobilising for war, and music hall audiences, infected with war fever, bellowed out the song of the moment.

Thereafter the word 'jingoism' came to stand for every form of clamorous, pugnacious and intestinally inspired patriotism. Neither it nor its manifestations were novel; there had been 'jingoes' in 1759 and throughout the Napoleonic and Crimean wars. The 1877 crisis was solved by diplomacy and not war. Russia, severely debilitated by its war effort, withdrew from the Straits, and Britain received Cyprus, a potential sentry post for the Suez Canal.

What had been demonstrated by the war scare during 1877 was the fickleness of public opinion, which had swung between the emotional poles of extreme moral indignation against Turkey and an equally passionate urge to fight on its behalf against Russia. The pendulum swung again in 1879, this time against Disraeli.

He was not by instinct an annexationist, preferring policies which affirmed and consolidated British power where it was already established, rather than those that enlarged it. For instance, in 1877 he had Queen Victoria proclaimed Empress of India, a gesture designed to link the monarchy with the empire, to bind India more closely to Britain and to serve as a sign of the permanence of British government there. It was very much against Disraeli's wishes that his ministry became embroiled in the takeover of the Transvaal in 1877, the invasion of Afghanistan in 1878 and the war against the Zulu kingdom which began in January 1879. All had their roots in the responses to local crises by individual officials who believed, mistakenly, that the home government would support belligerent policies. Matters were made worse by the near annihilation of a British column at Isandlwana in Zululand in the first month of the war, and there were some near-run things in Afghanistan.

This rash of aggressive wars was a signal to Gladstone to abandon semi-retirement and the study of theology and to arouse the conscience of the nation against the iniquities of what he called 'Beaconsfieldism' – Disraeli having taken the title Earl of Beaconsfield in 1877. Beaconsfieldism was an unwholesome political cocktail whose main ingredients were amoral opportunism, military adventures and a disregard for the rights of others. During the winter of 1879–80 Gladstone, brimming with energy and moral indignation, traversed southern Scotland and denounced the policies which were destroying Britain's reputation for fair play and justice. Ten thousand Zulus had died, he told a Glaswegian audience, for 'no other offence than their attempt to defend against your artillery their homes and families'. Villages had been razed in Afghanistan and their inhabitants left to starve, victims of a government bent on conquest.

The Liberal victory in the 1880 general election was, for Gladstone, a sign that the nation had turned its back on flag-waving jingoism and lost whatever taste it may have had for conquest. Under the new Liberal government the country would return to its old ways; through free trade and self-help its people would gain in prosperity and moral strength, and Britain, through example, would continue to reshape the world in its own image.

The soldier sentimentalised: newspaper reports of his gallantry on imperial battlefields transformed the private soldier from a social pariah, addicted to strong drink, into a hero and family man, early 1880s.
(© Opie)

INDUSTRIAL TECHNOLOGY AND SCIENCE ON THE IMPERIAL BATTLEFIELD

After 1850, technical and medical developments provided immense advantages for British troops fighting overseas. Firepower increased, enabling relatively small forces to engage far larger native armies, and medical breakthroughs reduced wastage from disease.

RIGHT *Heliograph operating in the Malakand Pass, 1895: this device flashed messages from hilltop to hilltop, provided there was sunshine.*

BELOW *Nigerian askari oiling a Maxim machine-gun, 1905: these weapons dominated the imperial battlefield from 1879 onwards and underwrote the conquest of Rhodesia (Zimbabwe), the Sudan and Nigeria.*
(© NAM)

OPPOSITE ABOVE
An X-ray machine probing for a bullet or fracture, the Sudan, 1898.
(© NAM)

OPPOSITE BELOW
Water purification plant, South Africa, 1901.

3

THE MISSION OF OUR RACE:

BRITAIN AND THE 'NEW IMPERIALISM'

1880–1902

In 1880 the British could still regard the world as their oyster, but with marginally less confidence than twenty or thirty years earlier. Britain was still the world's only global power and much, perhaps the greater part, of its international strength lay in its ability to influence weaker, less developed states rather than in the possession of a territorial empire. India was, of course, a priceless asset. During the past twenty years, Indian troops had undertaken the coercive work of unofficial empire in China, Malaya and Abyssinia and had been summoned by Disraeli to defend Turkey from Russian aggression.

In some areas the need for the old-style informal empire was disappearing. In 1886 the commander of the Cape Squadron told the Admiralty that it was no longer necessary for warships to police the waters off the Plate. The days of violent revolutions and civil wars had passed and the slave trade had been ended. Now governments kept order and, even during the tensions of presidential elections, British lives and property were respected. He added that the navy's ships in this part of the world were obsolete and 'objects of ridicule', unlike the modern men-o'-war which guarded local French and Italian interests. This observation was a reminder that other European powers were following Britain's example and providing world-wide naval protection for their businesses and investments. German and French warships now cruised regularly in the Atlantic, Indian and Pacific oceans.

The appearance of foreign warships in areas which had been almost wholly under British surveillance was a token of a greater change that was occurring throughout the world. Contemporaries called it the 'new imperialism', a phrase that was subsequently taken up by historians to describe the sudden surge of annexations by the great powers, chiefly in Africa, the Far East and the Pacific. In point of fact, there was little that was novel about this phenomenon save its frenzied pace and the participation of Germany, Italy, the United States and Japan, states which had previously avoided overseas expansion.

The reasons for this outbreak of conquest and occupation of underdeveloped and militarily weak countries by the industrial nations were complex. Everywhere, there was plenty of heady talk about the progress of mankind and the spread of civilisation. After America's annexation of the Philippines in 1899, Senator A. J. Beveridge proclaimed his faith in 'the mission of our race, trustees under God, of the civilisation of the world'. The same sentiments were expressed by German, French and Italian imperialists, and in Britain they had been uttered repeatedly over the past sixty years.

Behind the bombast of late nineteenth-century imperialism lay economic uncertainties and self-doubts which troubled both old and new imperial powers. From 1872 the patterns of world trade were changing in ways which hurt all countries, particularly Britain. From then until 1896 there was a world-wide recession whose effect was tempered by sporadic, short-lived booms. The French, German, Italian, Russian and United States governments reacted by dropping free trade in favour of protection. As the tariff barriers went up, British exports to these countries tumbled. Yet in Britain the old faith in free trade remained strong, especially in the Liberal party. There were objections from the fainthearted and realists, like the Liberal-Radical Joseph Chamberlain, but they never overrode the simple belief that the golden age of free trade would somehow return and with it Britain's dominance of world trade.

So, in 1880, the new Liberal government was stuck with free trade, faced with slackening exports (they fell from an annual average of £234 million in the first half of the decade to £226 million in the second), rising imports, a growing population and an increase in urban deprivation. Furthermore, Britain was no longer the world's only industrial power and her rivals were gradually catching up and overtaking her. Between 1880 and 1910 Britain's portion of the world's trade shrank from 23 to 17 per cent, and by the latter date her share of the world's industrial capacity was 15 per cent, compared to the United States's 35 per cent and Germany's 16 per cent.

These figures reflected industrial stagnation, the decline of the entrepreneurial spirit, and the lack of that inventiveness which had marked the early phases of the Industrial Revolution. Britain lagged

And God shall save the Queen: the 1887 Golden Jubilee procession leaves Trafalgar Square. This and the 1897 Diamond Jubilee were imperial state theatre on the grand scale, designed to strengthen the bonds of unity through loyalty to the Crown. (© e.t. archive)

GENERAL GORDON'S MARCH.

COMPOSED FOR THE PIANOFORTE, BY
ETIENNE CLAUDET.
LONDON: ROBERT COCKS & Cº NEW BURLINGTON STREET, REGENT STREET.

*Imperial martyr:
Gordon's 1884 mission
to Khartoum and death
there transformed him
into an imperial super-
hero whose features
adorned commemorative
pottery (below), sheet-
music covers (left)
and prints. In the
popular imagination
he had been a champion
of Christianity and
civilisation.
(Both © NAM)*

OPPOSITE *An
unstarchy monarchy:
protocol did not forbid
royal images to be used
in advertising and so
the Queen and her
family regularly
appeared to endorse
household products.
(© Opie)*

behind in the development of new industrial technologies and production methods, leaving the United States and Germany to make the pace in chemicals, oil, electrical engineering and motor cars. It was paradoxical that during the 1870s and 1880s those vital accessories for Britain's imperial campaigns, Gatling and Nordenfelt machine-guns, were manufactured in America. Those two innovations of the early 1880s, telephones and electric lighting, were both promoted in Britain by American-owned companies. Nevertheless, Britain was cushioned against the effects of diminishing exports and backward production methods by the 'invisible' earnings from banking, shipping, insurance and investments. By 1913 these last totalled £3,780 million.

Britain had to come to terms with cutthroat competition in a contracting world market. As the 1880s proceeded, export outlets were further reduced as her protectionist rivals began to stake out stretches of the world, occupy them and then declare them exclusively reserved for their own traders and investors. Britain attempted to deflect this process, but with limited success. Diplomatic pressure ensured that in 1884 the markets of the privately owned Congo Free State were open for all comers. Again, in 1898, the British government protested when Germany and Russia were negotiating with China for concessions in Shantung and Manchuria which would give each power a monopoly of trade and investment in its province.

Disapproving diplomatic noises were not enough. While adhering to the dogma of free trade, Britain had to keep abreast of her rivals. Businessmen, often acting through their local chambers of commerce, began urging a policy of annexation on the government to prevent existing or potential markets from being lost to competitors. Colonial lobbying became a growth industry during the last years of the nineteenth century with well-organised and funded expansionist pressure groups springing up in Germany and France. In these countries and in Britain the imperialists made alliances with the owners of the new, cheap, mass-circulation press which had the power to sway lower-middle- and working-class opinion.

The popular press invited the public to participate in the international bargaining for territory and occasional head-on collisions which marked the period of the new imperialism. It was soon found that the masses could be whipped into a belligerent frenzy whenever it appeared that their country was being flouted. Lord Harmsworth, owner of the *Daily Mail* (founded 1896), once remarked that his readers relished a 'good hate'. There were plenty of opportunities for this pleasure as the 1880s and 1890s unfolded and imperial rivalries intensified.

How could Britain adjust to and survive in a world which was rapidly changing and where the dice were no longer loaded in its favour? It could, as many Liberals believed, rely on the old formula of free trade and unofficial empire. But the latter was no longer practical in an age when other countries were establishing their own, jealously guarded spheres of influence across the world, and in many instances taking control of so-called 'empty' areas in Africa and the Pacific. The practical response was to jettison old shibboleths and join in the rush to acquire territory, if only to forestall rivals.

When unofficial empire collapsed in Egypt in 1882, Gladstone's government substituted direct control, occupying the country by force. Likewise when, in 1884, it seemed that German settlers in South-West Africa (Namibia) might join forces with the Boers of the Transvaal and take over Bechuana-land (Botswana), hitherto loosely controlled through British missionaries, the government stepped in and declared a protectorate. It was all very galling for Gladstone, who had so firmly set his face against imperial filibustering, but he could not allow power to slip from Britain's grasp. Moreover, he could not ignore strategic arguments put forward by imperialists within his own cabinet or public opinion.

In broad terms, Britain was committed to hanging on to its old influence, even if this meant replacing informal with direct control. There was no imperial masterplan beyond a determination to ensure the absolute security of India. 'As long as we rule India we are the greatest power in the world,' claimed Lord Curzon in 1901. 'If we lose it we shall drop straight away to a third rate power.' No one would have seriously challenged this assertion nor the policies designed to protect the subcontinent. They were pursued ruthlessly to the point when, during the winter of 1898–9, Britain was willing to go to war to prevent France from keeping a toehold in the Nile valley. Less than a year later, in October 1899, Britain did go to war against the Transvaal and the Orange Free State to defend its paramountcy in South Africa. Loss of control over the Nile valley would have jeopardised Egypt and weakened Britain's grip on India's lifeline, the Suez Canal. Similarly, the dilution of British power in southern Africa would have imperilled the Cape and with it British naval supremacy in the South Atlantic and Indian oceans. Elsewhere Britain could afford to compromise. The partition of East and West Africa, the sharing out of Pacific islands, and the balancing of the great powers' interests in China were managed diplomatically, if not always cordially.

The enlargement of the empire and the wars which accompanied it attracted enormous public interest in Britain. The process coincided with a widespread revision of ideas about the empire and its future. Rethinking the empire had been stimulated by two speculative books, Sir Charles Dilke's *Greater Britain* (1869) and the best-selling *The Expansion of England* (1882) by Sir John Seeley. Both offered consolation for those who were apprehensive about Britain's future. For Seeley the empire was the main source of British strength and its expansion and unity were vital for the nation's survival as a great power. In the modern world size equalled strength and vitality; both America and Germany had grown in area and population during the past twenty years and had accordingly increased in strength. The sinews of British power were its colonies, particularly the white dominions, which were an extension of Britain. If, as Seeley hoped, they continued to expand, then Britain could hold her own in the world and eventually outdistance her new rivals.

The British empire was an expression of what Seeley considered to be the special genius of the Anglo-Saxon race, that is the British. Social Darwinism was now fashionable and its theories, a rough and ready transfer of Darwin's principles from the world of plants and animals to that of men, suggested that certain races were better fitted to survive and flourish than others. Leaving on one side the pertinent question as to who exactly were the Anglo-Saxons, and late nineteenth-century imperialists usually did, there was a common agreement that their assumed progeny, the British, represented a super-race. This conclusion could be justified in terms of material, scientific and intellectual progress and adaptability. The fact that the Anglo-Saxons had dispersed across the globe and mastered their environment added to the general feeling that they were ideally qualified to rule.

Notions of racial superiority blended with arguments for imperial unity to produce an ideology for the new imperialism. It suited the times, since it offered Britain a chance to reverse the decline of its international power and revive a torpid economy. After all, in 1884 three million Australians consumed £23 million pounds' worth of British goods. Here was not only a valuable market, but a country whose ties of kinship, language and institutions were with Britain. Striking proof of this was provided the following year when New South Wales sent troops to serve alongside British and Indian units in the Sudan.

Civilisation imagined: a cartoonist's view of Kumasi (Ghana) after British occupation in 1896. The Asante town has become a British suburb dominated by the street advertisements which disfigured contemporary streets.

The most significant convert to the imperial creed of Dilke and Seeley was Joseph Chamberlain. He was probably the most able politician of his time and certainly the most restless and difficult to label. Chamberlain looked like an archetypal aristocrat with elegant features, a monocle and a fresh orchid in his buttonhole. He was in fact a Birmingham businessman who progressed from a Radical Lord Mayor with fierce republican views to a Liberal minister under Gladstone, and, in 1895, Colonial Secretary in a Conservative government. During the course of his political career he split two parties, the Liberals in 1886 and the Conservatives in 1904, a unique achievement which says much for his influence.

Of all the causes which Chamberlain embraced, that of the empire was the most deeply felt and longest lasting. Attachment to the ideal of imperial unity, as well as frustration with Gladstone's indifference towards social reform, drove Chamberlain to desert the Liberals over Irish Home Rule in

1886. Thereafter, he led his splinter Unionists towards a coalition with the Conservatives, reserving for himself what had hitherto been a minor cabinet office, Colonial Secretary. His brand of imperialism was an amalgam of older notions of disseminating civilisation and modern concepts of race. In 1893, when Britain had accepted a protectorate over Uganda, he told the Commons that the country welcomed the new addition to the empire. The people, he continued, were well matched to the tasks of spreading civilisation since they were animated by the traditions of the past, and by what he called 'that spirit . . . of adventure and enterprise distinguishing the Anglo-Saxon race [which] has made us peculiarly fit to carry out the working of colonisation.'

It was essential that the Anglo-Saxon race should understand the qualities that it needed to foster if it was to fulfil its historic destiny. Most importantly, the young had to be given models of how the Anglo-Saxon

Only the best:
coffee fit for
heroes, c.1880.
(© Opie)

Catching them
young:
a boys' magazine
cover.
(© Opie)

should behave and which of his innate virtues he should cultivate and how. A generation of university teachers, schoolmasters, clergymen, poets, journalists and boys' fiction writers concentrated their minds and energies on popularising the cult of the new imperialism. At its heart lay the concept of 'Anglo-Saxon manhood', an abstraction compounded in equal parts of patriotism, physical toughness, skill at team games, a sense of fair play (sometimes called 'sportsmanship'), self-discipline, selflessness, bravery and daring.

The ground had been well prepared for the apostles of the Anglo-Saxon ideal. Since the 1840s the public schools had undergone a revolution, started by Dr Thomas Arnold of Rugby, which transformed the habits of mind of the middle and upper classes. Arnold and his acolytes sought to instil Christian altruism into their

PRICE ONE PENNY.] **"A PIRATE'S LEGACY" BEGINS THIS WEEK.**

No. 295.—Vol. VI.]   MAY 4, 1898.   [ALL RIGHTS RESERVED.

"THE LIEUTENANT, STILL CARRYING PINGA-PINGA, CAME DOWN THE HILL" (See page 578.)

A tale for plucky lads:
North-West Frontier
derring-do, 1898.
(© NLS)

pupils and direct their ambition and aggression towards the playing field. The public schoolboy, educated according to the Arnoldian code, also learned how to control himself and others through the prefectorial system, a perfect preparation for ruling and chastising the empire's 'lesser breeds'. Intelligence mattered less than the acquisition of 'character', and intellectual activity was largely restricted to otiose and repetitive exercises in the languages of two former imperial powers, Greece and Rome. The end product was a Christian gentleman with a stunted imagination, who played by the rules and whose highest aim was to serve others. If he had to earn his living, he elected to become an army or navy officer, a senior civil servant, a clergyman, a barrister or joined a branch of the Indian or Colonial administration.

By 1880 a generation had passed into manhood with an outlook which made them ideally suited to govern the empire and fight its wars. By the turn of the century the obsession with games had become a mania. It was the belief of J. E. C. Welldon, headmaster of Harrow (1881–95) and later Bishop of Calcutta, that, 'If there is in the British race, as I think there is, a special aptitude for "taking up the white man's burden" . . . it may be ascribed, above all other causes, to the spirit of organised games.' These fostered team spirit from which sprang self-sacrifice.

Throughout the 1890s schoolboys were bombarded by popular magazines written specially for them and steeped in the ideas of the new imperialism. They interwove thrilling adventure yarns with patriotism and reminders of imperial duty. The older, evangelical *Boys' Own Paper* was joined by *Chums*, *Pluck* and *Union Jack*, the last two both of 1894, whose titles reflected their contents. *Chums* was packed with tales of imperial derring-do and coloured illustrations, including 'Storming the Heights of Dargai', which showed an incident in the 1897 North-West Frontier campaign in which Highlanders rushed a Pathan position, spurred on by the playing of a wounded piper who was later awarded the Victoria Cross. The cover of the *Young England* annual for 1902 symbolised its own and its competitors' values; alongside a cavalryman dressed to fight the Boers were rowing oars, cricket bats, stumps, tennis racquets and a fisherman's basket.

Those who read *Young England* would also have enjoyed the many full-length tales of derring-do which poured relentlessly from publishers during the 1890s. Of these, the best were the yarns of G. A. Henty, a dyed-in-the-wool imperialist who had served as a war correspondent during the 1873–4 Asante War. Henty turned out on average three boys' stories a year, which appeared in time for the Christmas market and cost five or six shillings (25–30p) each. In his earlier works, Henty addressed his readers as 'My dear lads' and confessed that he found it painful to write of any campaign in which the British were defeated. Mercifully, there were plenty of victories for him to work into straightforward narratives in which a resourceful young man finds himself caught up in the events of history.

Just how his younger readers should behave was laid down by Henty in *Through the Sikh War*, in a passage where the hero is told what would be expected of him when he joined the East India Company's army:

> *Think it over yourself, Percy. Can you thrash most fellows your own age? Can you run as far and as fast as most of them? Can you take a caning without whimpering over it? Do you feel, in fact, that you are able to go through fully as much as any of your companions? Are you good at planning a piece of mischief, and ready to take the lead in carrying it out? . . . It is pluck and endurance and the downright love of adventure and danger, that have made us the masters of the great part of India, and ere long makes us the rulers of the whole of it.*

The huge public fascination with the early stages of the Boer War was a godsend to Henty and his imitators. Christmas 1900 saw a cascade of boys' tales set in South Africa, including Henty's *With Buller in Natal*. The politics of these books was crude; Henty represented Britain as the 'greatest civilised power on earth' fighting against one 'without even the elements of civilisation, ignorant and brutal beyond any existing white community'. Readers of Captain F. S. Brereton's *One of Our Fighting Scouts* (1903) were urged to follow the hero's example: 'If it is your fortune to take a rifle and go forth to fight for your king and country – may you keep your face to the enemy, and ride as boldly as did George Ransome, one of the Fighting Scouts.' Many had not needed such bidding. In the winter of 1899–1900 thousands came forward to volunteer for service in South Africa as imperial yeomanrymen like the 'large limbed Anglo-Saxon heroes' who sailed for the Cape with the future novelist and Irish patriot, Erskine Childers.

Imperial propaganda of the gripping kind produced by Henty and his fellow wordsmiths was deliberately spread to all classes. Henty's publishers encouraged state and Sunday-school teachers to present his books as prizes, and thousands were duly presented. Working-class children could share in the adventures of their social superiors, learn about the deeds which shaped the empire, and absorb some of the imperial ideas. The new imperial ideology was already penetrating the elementary-school classrooms through the curriculum. Nearly all the geography learned by trainee teachers at Cavendish College, Cambridge in 1896 consisted of lists of colonies, details of how they were obtained, their products and accounts of their native inhabitants, all of which were passed on for their pupils to memorise. In the same year the recommended outlines of a lesson on South Africa drew attention to the primitive Calvinism of the Boers and their reluctance to wash frequently. As for the blacks, they 'have become reconciled to the inevitable supremacy of the whites' and had been taught to be 'useful servants'.

Even the nursery was not closed to imperialism. While the infant mouthed *An ABC for Baby Patriots*, published in 1899, its elder brothers and sisters battled with the brightly painted lead soldiers which became so popular after 1890. There were plenty of imperial units: red-coated British infantrymen, sailors in straw hats, Sudanese in fezes, Bengal cavalry in turbans, and colonial horsemen in khaki and broad hats with turned-up brims. The fighting men came complete with the paraphernalia of modern war: cannon, machine-guns, heliographs and field ambulances.

There were plenty of real soldiers in exotic uniforms marching through London to celebrate Queen Victoria's Diamond Jubilee in 1897. Troops from every part of the empire took part in the festivities, which also included a review of the fleet at Spithead. The Jubilee was more than a display of imperial muscle; the Queen was at the heart of the empire and it was loyalty to her which helped give it a sense of cohesion. There was no other obvious bond to hold together white settlers from Canada or Australia who were now managing their own affairs; Indians governed from Delhi; Nigerians ruled by the privately owned Royal Niger Company; and the subjects of protectorates and colonies ruled from Whitehall through local officials with the cooperation of their own chiefs. The Queen whose head appeared on their stamps and coins symbolised the unity of the empire. Her genuine,

Saviour of India:
Sir Henry Havelock, the evangelical general who contained the Indian Mutiny, overlooks Trafalgar Square. As the empire expanded, other leaders found their way onto plinths in London and other cities.
(© Courtauld Institute)

C is for Colonies
Rightly we boast,
That of all the great nations
Great Britain has the most.

AN ABC FOR BABY
PATRIOTS, 1899

maternal care for her subjects (she had deliberately chosen Indian attendants for her household) was widely publicised.

Newsreels from the front, including shots of the battle of Spion Kop in January 1900, were the inevitable outcome of the intense public interest in imperial campaigns. The new cheap press offered extensive coverage by war correspondents whose style was vivid and punchy. Moreover, the spread of the telegraph network meant that details from even the most far-flung battlefields could reach Britain within twenty-four hours, the time it took for news of the Ndebele rebellion in Rhodesia (Zimbabwe) to appear in the London newspapers in June 1896.

Thrilling front-line reports in mass circulation newspapers, like the popular boys' magazines and stories, coloured the public's view of the empire. Photographs and sketches in the *Daily Graphic* during the 1896–8 Sudan War showed various battle scenes, British and Egyptian medical orderlies treating wounded Dervishes and, by way of a contrast, skeletons of tribesmen massacred at the orders of the Khalifah Abdullah. Further confirmation that Britain was fighting for civilisation came with an illustration in June 1896 of Muslim chiefs in northern Nigeria, swearing on the Koran to renounce slavery.

Imperial themes and images were hijacked by advertising artists and copywriters. The results were often remarkably durable: a bearded sailor and an ironclad of the 1890s still appear on the Players Navy Cut cigarette packet, and another Victorian warship is the trademark of England's Glory matches. It was the Boer War which gave advertisers their chance, and the public was soon swamped with cheery

The civilising mission in action: fumigation of houses in Bombay during the 1897 bubonic plague epidemic. (© Christie's Images)

soldiers and sailors endorsing patent cure-alls, beef extracts and Colman's mustard. Manly, firm-jawed and moustachioed fighting men in khaki bestowed *machismo* on various brands of tobacco and cigarettes. Bovril led the field in patriotic puffs, offering a print of the relief of Ladysmith to buyers of a product which, if the testimonials from men at the front were to be believed, more or less kept alive the entire army in South Africa. One ingenious copywriter alleged that the letters BOVRIL traced out the lines of Lord Roberts's march through the Orange Free State.

The Boer War saw an unprecedented boom in the manufacture of every kind of patriotic souvenir. There were buttons with portraits of the leading commanders, whose features also stared from all kinds of commemorative pottery and cigarette cards. There were songs for music-hall patriots ranging from the sentimental 'The Boers have got my Daddy' to the swaggering 'Soldiers of the Queen'. What was an explosion of mass patriotism came to a hysterical climax in May 1900 when news came through that the town of Mafeking had been relieved. Everywhere the announcement prompted spontaneous and often abandoned celebrations, a nationwide street party which produced, hangovers apart, the word 'mafficking'.

Homage from Zanzibar: every corner of the empire celebrated the Diamond Jubilee of 1897. (© F & CO)

Those who 'mafficked' were celebrating something more than the rescue of a comparatively insignificant garrison. The high jinks that May night were a mass release of tensions and a momentary dispersal of fears that had been deepened by the war. During the winter of 1899–1900 the army had suffered a series of unexpected and humiliating reverses, and the British people discovered that they were no longer invincible. Furthermore they were friendless, for all the great powers were hostile, particularly France and Germany. There had been a recovery on the battlefield in the spring of 1900, which raised national morale to the point where festivities were in order, but their clamour did not drive away self-doubt.

To a large extent those who proclaimed the triumphs of empire were whistling in the dark. A nation which had been so full of self-confidence forty to fifty years earlier, when it had appeared the supreme force for mankind's improvement, was now tormented by apprehension. It was true that between 1890 and 1900 the empire had grown at

'A gentleman in Kharki': Kipling's Tommy stands embattled on a commemorative jug and suggests, indirectly, his nation's isolation during the Boer War.

an unprecedented rate; in Africa Britain had secured control over the Sudan, Uganda, Kenya, Nyasaland, Nigeria, Rhodesia, the Transvaal and the Orange Free State, making it the largest imperial power on the continent. And yet the newspapers and journals which chronicled these acquisitions were also filled with baleful analyses of what was wrong with the country.

The psychological roots of this critical introspection stretched back well into the century. Invasion scares were a regular occurrence and were usually accompanied by hair-raising tales of how Britain, for all its outward strength, could be overrun by a daring enemy. For instance, in 1871, a best-seller, Sir George Chesney's *The Battle of Dorking*, described a Prussian invasion and a whirlwind campaign that ended with the occupation of London. Soon after the end of the Boer War, Erskine Childers' thriller *The Riddle of the Sands* cleverly showed how a German fleet could steal across the North Sea undetected and support landings on the British coast. These were fantasies, usually written to shock the country into demanding extra cash for the army and navy's budget. But there were also plenty of sober appraisals of underlying weaknesses in Britain's economy and unfavourable comparisons of its performance with those of its rivals. There was, for instance, much heart-searching during the 1890s about the shortcomings in Britain's educational system which seemed to be producing a workforce inferior in aptitude to those of Germany and the United States.

'Bobs':

a bronze bust of Field Marshal Lord Roberts of Kandahar who reversed the humiliating defeats in South Africa in 1900.

As ever, the strength of the navy became the ultimate yardstick for Britain's relative power in the world. From 1878 France, Russia and Italy had adopted ambitious programmes of naval rearmament that soon had alarm bells ringing in Britain. The result was the 1889 Naval Defence Act, which confirmed the traditional two-power standard by which the Royal Navy's total of battleships equalled that of its two closest rivals. A naval race was now on, with Britain vying against France and Russia in building battleships. The margin was always tight; in 1898 Britain possessed 52 battleships with 12 under construction, France and Russia 39, but with a further 18 on the stocks. Within six years, naval intelligence estimated, Britain's two rivals would have overtaken her. These disturbing figures took no account of Germany, which had 17 battleships and 5 being built.

As the pace of the naval race gathered momentum, British strategists realised that their country no longer had enough ships to be strong everywhere. The shortfall was most apparent and dangerous in the Mediterranean. In 1892 a Russian squadron had sailed through the Bosphorus and joined the French Mediterranean fleet at its Toulon base, a gesture designed to advertise the new alliance between the two powers and unnerve Britain. It did; the Admiralty was forced to admit that, given a war against France and Russia, the British fleet could not seize the Bosphorus, and so the Russian fleet was free to join their ally's whenever an emergency occurred. A year later Chamberlain declared to the Commons that the Royal Navy had ceased to control the Mediterranean.

The shifting balance of power in the Mediterranean endangered the Suez Canal and therefore threatened India. Here the appearance of Russian troops on the Afghan border in 1885 had re-awakened fears of an invasion. This was now more feasible than ever since railway construction in Central Asia directly linked the region with the Russian heartlands to the north. Most menacing of all, from an Indian standpoint, was the Orenburg to Tashkent line which was started in 1901. Within three years it was within 240 miles of its terminus, bringing the Russian rail network to within striking distance of the Afghan frontier. As Russia acquired the means to transport and supply a mass army for an attack on India, strategic planners in Delhi and London wrestled with the problems of defending the subcontinent. They came to no definite conclusions save that if local Anglo-Indian forces were to hold the Afghan passes, they would need substantial reinforcements from Britain, which would have to be carried by sea by way of the Suez Canal or the Cape. Additional forces would also be needed to keep order in India where, it was predicted, a Russian invasion would trigger mass disturbances.

There remained the uncomfortable fact that, in the event of an assault on India, Russia could mobilise 300,000 men within three months and launch them against an Anglo-Indian army of 95,000 holding a line between Kabul and Kandahar. Prestige demanded an aggressive stance in Afghanistan, but there was no way of knowing how the volatile Afghans would react to the intrusion. The Boer War further exposed India's vulnerability, since by the end of operations in South Africa Britain had had to commit 295,000 regular, reservist and volunteer troops. The presence of thousands of Canadians, New Zealanders and Australians helped, but they could not disguise the fact that the imperial battleline was stretched to breaking point. There was a bad, but not unexpected attack of jitters when, in February 1900, the War Office received intelligence of Russian concentrations near the Afghan border. The attack did not materialise, but the lesson was clear; had the Russians moved against India there would not have been enough troops to counter them.

Keeping up with the enemy: HMS Nile, *one of the ironclad battleships built in the 1890s as part of a programme to keep the Royal Navy ahead of the Russian and French fleets. The cost of these ships was increasingly burdensome. (© IWM)*

Britain entered the twentieth century as the world's greatest imperial power at least in terms of territory and population. The fact was widely trumpeted by politicians and journalists, along with platitudes about dispensing civilisation to those who lacked it. There was also a steady stream of reassuring propaganda which emphasised national greatness and the innate strengths of the Anglo-Saxon character. What effect all this had is difficult to measure precisely. Certainly, many exposed to the writings of Henty and his fellows emerged convinced that brawn mattered more than brains, and large numbers of them acted in a manner of which their boyhood heroes would have approved when they volunteered for war in 1914 and 1915.

Some, mostly on the left, were distressed by the brashness and belligerence of the new imperialism which, they believed, had made militarism fashionable and undermined national moral values. One critic regretted that the businessman of the 1890s asked the question 'is it expedient and profitable?' unlike his mid-Victorian predecessor, who asked 'is it right?' It is extremely doubtful whether the latter was ever so high-minded, but the middle years of the century had already become a golden age in the eyes of old-style, free trade Liberals. Among other faults of the new age was a middle class that indulged in 'speculation which necessitates new conquests of territories and constant acts of aggression' and 'that modern monstrosity and anachronism, the Conservative Working Man', who had 'exchanged his birthright of freedom and free thought for a pat on the head from any rump-fed lord that steps his way and spouts the platitudes of Cockney patriotism.'

'Cockney patriotism' could drown the voices of those who believed they spoke with reason, but it quickly fell silent when there was nothing to celebrate. There was no mafficking during the tedious anti-guerrilla campaign in South Africa, which dragged on during 1901 and half of 1902. Indeed, politicians sometimes wondered whether the capriciousness of public opinion would prevent them from ever following through the long-term policies which were needed to renovate the country and consolidate the empire. Both were urgently required as the new century opened for, despite all the jingoes' rhetoric, Britain's former global pre-eminence could no longer be taken for granted.

4

THE MIRACLE
OF THE WORLD:
INDIA
1815–1905

The Empire of India Exhibition, which opened at Earl's Court in 1895, captivated Londoners. It was a colourful imperial extravaganza, which suited the mood of the times and both educated and entertained. Indian scenery was reproduced and there were displays which reflected the country's past and present states. The overall theme was clear: modern India was the product of British patience and genius. This truth was spectacularly illustrated by 'India', a pageant performed daily in the adjacent Empress Theatre. The climax of the show was a glittering tableau entitled 'Grand Apotheosis: The Glorification of Victoria, the Empress Queen'. The Queen-Empress appeared in 'an allegorical car', drawn by white horses and accompanied by the symbolic figures of Love, Mercy, Wisdom, Science, Art, Commerce, Prosperity and Happiness. Dazzled, the audience would have left to stroll through the Indian gardens or eat at the curry house where, no doubt, they would have felt a thrill of pride in their country's achievements. British India was nothing less than 'the miracle of the world' according to the Marquess Curzon, who was appointed Viceroy in 1898.

There was indeed something miraculous about the way in which less than 100,000 soldiers and administrators held in thrall 250 million Indians. India also possessed elements of glamour and mystery which entranced the Victorians, and everyone sensed that ruling it gave Britain power and prestige. Furthermore, and this was made clear in the Earl's Court displays, everything that was good in India derived from Britain's influence and was inspiring evidence of Britain's civilising mission.

What the Indians called the *angrezi raj* (English rule) was not, however, an exercise in higher national altruism, although many such as Curzon liked to think so. Britain had become economically dependent on India during the nineteenth century. India had become an unequalled market for British manufactured goods, particularly cottonware, and by 1913 60 per cent of all Indian imports came from Britain and it had absorbed £380 million in British capital, one tenth of all the country's overseas investments. India had rescued British commerce during the lean years of the late nineteenth century, taking goods which had previously been sold in European markets. The process of modernising India, which gave so much satisfaction to the Victorians, was vital for balancing the books at home.

The history of India since 1815, as chronicled by the British, was a steady ascent from the depths of chaos, ignorance and backwardness towards the heights of peace, order and material progress. And yet, in many quarters, doubts lingered about the ambiguity of Britain's position in the country. How was it that

I do not see how Englishmen, contrasting India as it is with what it was or might have been, can fail to see that we came here in obedience to what I call a decree of Providence, for the lasting benefit of millions of the human race.

MARQUESS CURZON

OPPOSITE
Bharatpur falls:
the capture of this princely stronghold in 1825 was a reminder of what happened to those rajas who crossed the East India Company.
(© *British Library*)

a nation with liberal traditions and deeply held convictions about personal liberty could maintain an authoritarian empire which ultimately rested on force? The answer was that the constraints on Indians were applied humanely by a régime devoted to their best interests. Autocratic paternalism was defended by Herbert Edwardes, who had been guided by its principles as a commissioner in the Punjab in 1848–9.

Variations on this theme became a standard defence of the British raj for the next hundred years. The framework of Indian government meant the concentration of power in the hands of a few men, but their sense of duty and standards of honesty were such that they never acted capriciously or oppressed their subjects. This self-image of the men who ruled India was tirelessly promoted both in Britain and the subcontinent, and it contained much truth. And yet in the application of enlightenment, the administrators of India found themselves confronted with resistance from subjects who did not see things in the same way, and were deeply devoted to customs which their masters despised. A collision between rulers and ruled became inevitable as the Indian government turned its attention towards what it imagined to be the emancipation of India from its past.

After 1815 the old Company live-and-let-live approach to the governing of India was replaced by one which set great store by remoulding the country along Western lines. India became a sort of laboratory for current British liberal, evangelical and utilitarian theorists who sought, in various ways, to regenerate all mankind. James Mill, historian, pamphleteer, philosopher and, from 1823, a Company bureaucrat based in London, wanted above all to liberate the Indian mind. Native religions were the chief obstacle to this process:

> *By a system of priestcraft, built upon the most enormous and tormenting superstition that ever harnessed and degraded any portion of mankind, their [the Indians'] minds were enchained more intolerably than their bodies; in short; despotism and priestcraft taken together, the Hindus, in mind and body, were the most enslaved portion of the human race.*

There laws exist not, and he who rules, must rule the people by his will. If his will be evil, the people will be far more miserable than it is possible for any people to be . . . but if his will be good as well as strong, happy are the people . . . for a benevolent despotism is the best of all governments.

HERBERT EDWARDES

Using their dictatorial powers, humane British officials would sweep away these supernatural encumbrances on Indian thought. The poet and historian Thomas Macaulay, who was chairman of a committee formed in 1833 to consider future educational policy in India, predicted that Hinduism would wither away as Western learning spread across the country. To accelerate this process, he insisted that all teaching was in English and based on English texts. With remarkable foresight, he claimed that exposure to British ideas and patterns of thinking would, in time, create an Indian élite which would demand self-government. Some years later, the governor-general, Lord Ellenborough, remarked to a babu (an English-speaking Indian clerk), 'You know, if these gentlemen succeed in educating the natives of India, to the utmost extent of their desire, we should not remain in the country three months.' 'Not three weeks,' was the reply.

British-style schools, run by missionaries, had been established in India by the mid-1820s. Evangelical pressure from, among others, Wilberforce, had persuaded the Company to allow missions in its territories despite fears of a Muslim backlash. Nevertheless, the directors allowed themselves to be overwhelmed by the familiar missionary lobby arguments that conversion would advance civilisation and create new customers for British products.

There was much that was crass in the thinking of those who imagined that they could remake India in the British mould. High-mindedness and an urge to improve often appeared like meddlesome arrogance, and this was all too apparent in the almost universal contempt shown towards India's existing culture and religions. Hinduism and its caste system were singled out for the worst abuse; one exasperated champion of progress declared that its polytheist followers displayed 'an ignorance and a credulity almost approaching idiocy'. What was worse was that some Hindus stuck resolutely to their faith despite Western instruction. In 1824 Reginald Heber, hymn-writer and Bishop of Calcutta, sensed divided loyalties after an Indian pupil at a mission school had shown him a shrine of Shiva, and explained the

Nineteenth-Century India

////// Under British rule

::::::: Princely States

legends of different Hindu gods and goddesses. The enthusiasm of his discourse perturbed the cleric, who afterwards wondered whether Indian boys might become 'accomplished hypocrites, playing the part of Christian with us, and with their own people of zealous followers of Brahma'.

The agitation of British political and religious theorists did push the Company in the direction of benevolent, paternalist policies which, by their nature, disturbed Indian society. Non-interference with native customs was abandoned and campaigns undertaken against religious rituals which offended European sensibilities. Under Lord William Bentinck, governor-general from 1828 to 1835, systematic measures were adopted to eradicate thagi (the Hindu cult of assassin-priests who preyed on travellers) and sati. The Thugs, as they were called, were all but eliminated by condign methods, as was sati, although there were still isolated cases being uncovered in the 1920s. At the same time Company employees were encouraged to dissociate themselves from Hindu ceremonies and involvement in the administration of temples.

Conquering heroes:
ABOVE LEFT *General Sir Charles James Napier who annexed the Scind in 1843 having defeated its Baluchi rulers. These photographs were taken by Captain John McCosh, probably in 1849. (Both © NAM)*

ABOVE RIGHT *Viscount Gough defeated the Sikhs in 1845–6 and 1848–9, when he told his soldiers that they had succeeded where Alexander the Great had failed. An Irishman with a brogue, he favoured near suicidal frontal attacks, but was loved by his men on account of his concern for their welfare.*

H. Vibart.

Soldiers of the raj:
LEFT *A Madras sepoy in shako, c.1850. (© NAM)*

RIGHT *Cadet Vibart learning the art of war and the languages of India at the Company's officer's training school, Addiscombe College, c.1850.*

BELOW *An officer of the Bengal Horse Artillery in full dress uniform with a highly appropriate crested Graeco-Roman style helmet, c.1855. (Both © British Library)*

Nonetheless, passive tolerance had to be shown publicly to native religions. A handbook of advice for young officers, published in 1833, suggested that they would have to show forebearance towards their men's religions even though they were unwholesome. This had obviously been hard for the author, who later commented disparagingly about the 'self-venerating Hindu' and 'the bigotted Mussulman [Muslim]'. Such expressions became commoner in British works on India in the 1820s and 1830s, and provide hints of a growing gulf between the British and the Indians.

One indicator of shifting racial attitudes was a reduction of sexual contacts between British men and Indian women, which had been extremely frequent throughout the eighteenth century. On one level such behaviour was seen as condoning an indigenous morality and therefore unfitting for men whose duty was to serve as detached administrators and commanders. Indian sensuality revolted British churchmen who saw it as debilitating and potentially subversive. In 1816 one complained that young Christian men were morally undermined by India, succumbing to all its temptations even to the point of letting their faith lapse. Eight years later Bishop Heber was glad to notice that keeping native mistresses was longer 'a fashionable vice' among younger officials in Calcutta, although laxity of this and other kinds was thriving in remote districts. The high-principled Metcalf, despite prizing that 'pure love which exists between man and man', had three sons by his native mistress, and General Ochterlony, the Resident in Delhi from 1803 to 1825, had a harem of thirteen concubines.

There were plenty of busybodies who did what they could to stamp out such indulgences, but old habits proved resilient; a young officer who first arrived in India in 1834 recalled how he 'commenced a regular course of fucking' with delightfully uninhibited native girls who understood 'in perfection all the arts and wiles of love'. His example was later followed by, among others, the explorer and anthropologist Sir Richard Burton, and the future field-marshals, Lords Roberts and Wolseley.

These officers' conduct could be justified by the fact that they needed to know the languages of those they commanded, and a concubine could also serve as a schoolmistress. The sepoy army was, even in the era of reform, the chief prop of the British raj, as many of its officers were quick to point out. In 1837, one dismissed as nonsense any suggestion that the empire was one 'of opinion', that is, resting on native goodwill, rather than armed force.

The era of tentative internal reform inside India was also one in which the Company consolidated and extended its authority. In 1818 the Mahrathas had been forced to submit, and in 1824 a part of the independent kingdom of Burma was annexed after a short war. By the 1830s attention was turning towards India's northern borders, the powerful Sikh state of the Punjab, and the possibility of a Russian invasion. The question was whether the Indian frontier should lie on the Indus or be pushed forward into the Himalayan foothills.

It was generally agreed in Calcutta that India's safety required a *cordon sanitaire* which encompassed Afghanistan. An attempt in 1838 to transform that country into an Indian dependency ended in catastrophe three years later, when the Kabul garrison was evicted and all but wiped out during a harrowing winter retreat down the Khyber Pass. It was a humiliating reverse which tarnished British prestige. The governor-general, Lord Ellenborough, ordered General Sir George Pollock to restore its lustre through a series of raids deep into Afghan territory where villages, crops and livestock were destroyed.

The Afghan débâcle provided a pressing reason for the government to flex its muscles against the Baluchi amirs of Sind and the Sikhs. The latter were the most menacing, since they possessed the Khalsa, a well-disciplined and equipped modern army trained by imported European specialists, which astonished those who encountered it. General Sir Harry Smith reckoned the rapidity of fire and accuracy of the Sikh gunners equal to those of their French counterparts during the Peninsular War. Another officer, present during the siege of Multan in 1848–9, paid the Sikh infantry the highest compliment possible by saying that they charged into battle 'like Britons'.

The taming of the Baluchi tribesmen and the emasculation of Sikh power required three hard-fought campaigns: one against the Sind in 1843, and two against the Sikhs in 1845–6 and 1848–9. All were undertaken by commanders brimming with a self-confidence and an offensive spirit as strong as those of their eighteenth-century predecessors. 'Never give way to barbarians' was the motto of General Sir Charles Napier when his 2,400-strong army was faced with 35,000 Baluchis at the battle of Meanee. He placed his men behind barricades of straw bales and kneeling baggage camels, and put his faith in the Irishmen of his only British regiment, the 22nd. They were 'strong of body, high-blooded, fierce, impetuous soldiers' who, as he expected, terrified their adversaries with volleys of musketry and bayonet charges. Beaten, the amirs submitted.

A tiger caged: Mulraj, leader of the Sikh rebellion of 1848, which concluded with the annexation of the Punjab. He was photographed in captivity. (© NAM)

Not all Indians were prepared to submit to British rule. Early in 1832, a frightening conspiracy to massacre Europeans was discovered at Bangalore. The ringleaders had exploited fears that the government was preparing for the mass conversion of Muslims to Christianity. Jolted by this unpleasant reminder of the fragility of British power, the local authorities turned the punishment of the chief culprits into a sombre public display of retribution. Four condemned men, all sepoys, were escorted to the place of execution by military bands playing the 'Dead March' from Handel's *Saul* and were tied to cannon barrels and blown to pieces. According to the superintendent of police, this spectacle 'struck much terror into all Classes, Civil and Military', and he felt certain that it would be a long time before further signs of resistance manifested themselves.

This incident was quickly dismissed as an example of the waywardness of the native character and the particular naïveté of Muslims, who readily swallowed any rumour, however preposterous. The method of execution, traditional in India, also dramatically illustrated the internal contradictions of a 'despotism' which simultaneously boasted of its humanity and enlightenment.

By this time, the spread of Western enlightenment was becoming one of the chief purposes of the government. It was a task for which it was not well-fitted. There was no uniform administration throughout the subcontinent: in the old Company presidencies of Bengal, Madras, Bombay and their dependencies authority was exercised by district judges and collectors, while in other regions, native princes ruled under the guidance of British residents. A considerable part of administrative energy was consumed by the collection of land revenue from the rural peasantry. At the lowest level this was undertaken by local proprietors, the zamindars and taluqdars. Their powers had been confirmed and enhanced during the late eighteenth century when the government wanted to enlist the support of men of substance and influence. Reformers, including John Stuart Mill, questioned this system, comparing the tax-collectors to leeches. But there was no alternative; in the fiscal year 1856–7, the Indian government's income was approximately £30 million, of which £16.7 million came from land revenues and nearly £7 million from salt and opium monopolies.

The raj therefore rested on the ability of its servants to extract the small surpluses made by peasant farmers, who at best lived a hand-to-mouth existence. Their cash provided the wherewithal for schemes designed to transform and regenerate their country. Land taxes funded the schools, and the metalled roads which from 1836 onwards radiated out from and connected the large centres of commerce and administration. Twenty years later, the government's investment programme included a railway network 3,000 miles in length and linking Calcutta with Delhi, Delhi with

Peshawar, and Bombay with Nagpur. By the beginning of 1857 nearly three hundred miles of track had been laid and, in advance of the railway gangs, engineers had criss-crossed the country with 4,000 miles of telegraph lines.

Roads, railways and telegraph wires symbolised the irreversible march of progress, probably more than the schools, colleges and teaching hospitals which were springing up in provincial capitals. For Indians who tried to fathom their meaning, these novelties were a source of unease. As the tempo of change quickened and the results began to affect new areas of everyday life, the old, persistent fear of forced conversion became stronger. When, in January 1857, a mob burned down the new telegraph office at Barrackpore, it did so because the building symbolised change imposed from above by an alien power.

In the winter of 1856–7 two new twists were given to the familiar tale of impending conversion. There was one widely credited report that the cartridges for the new Enfield rifle were greased with a blend of pork and beef fat, and another which alleged that the powdered bones of pigs and cows had been surreptitiously added to ration flour issued to the sepoys of the Bengal army. Both rumours were false, but what mattered was that they gave substance to vague fears that Christianity was about to be imposed.

Hauteur and resignation: an Indian nobleman, c.1850. As the Company became paramount throughout the sub-continent, men of his background chose cooperation rather than extinction. By temporising and making themselves clients of the British, India's rajas and maharajas preserved their dynasties and lands. (© NAM)

OPPOSITE *Military quickstep*: *General Sir Colin Campbell leads Highlanders on the last push to relieve Lucknow, a sheet-music cover of 1858. (© NAM)*

Muslims and high-caste Hindus of the Bengal army were particularly susceptible to misgivings. Their elevated self-esteem had been eroded by new military regulations designed to promote efficiency, and they were perturbed by the new policy of recruitment of the 'traditional' warrior races of the Sind and Punjab. Sepoys born in Oude, where soldiering had long been regarded as an honourable occupation for Brahmins, for whom no other source of dignified labour existed, had an additional grievance. In 1853 the province had been peremptorily annexed by the governor-general, Lord Dalhousie, who had ridden roughshod over Indian customary law by ignoring the rights of the nawab's adopted heir, Nana Sahib. This offered further proof that the government would stop at nothing to get its way.

These undercurrents of apprehension and anger broke surface at Meerut in the last week of May 1857 after sepoys had been publicly humiliated and punished for refusing to touch the by now infamous cartridges. One cavalry and three infantry regiments spontaneously rebelled, ransacked the European cantonment and murdered several officers and their families. The insurgents fled to Delhi, seized the city and proclaimed the aged Badahur Shah, a descendant of the Mughals, Emperor of India. Then the mutineers paused to await the reactions of their countrymen and their rulers.

The raj had been challenged by its own soldiers with a suddenness which left everyone momentarily dazed. Prestige was at stake and the classic British response would have been a counter-attack, whatever the risks. But no hammer-blow struck Delhi until the second week of June, when a scratch force of 4,000 men, hastily assembled in the Punjab, arrived outside the city walls and began a blockade. Elsewhere administrators and generals decided to sit tight and, like the first mutineers, wait on events. Their pusillanimity was later condemned, but there was little else they could have done given the vast local disparity in numbers between British and Indian troops. In all there were 45,000 white and 232,000 Indian soldiers dispersed across the subcontinent. Of the 23,000 British and 136,000 Indians in Bengal and northern India, nearly all the British were concentrated in the newly annexed Punjab. There were only four white battalions scattered across the potentially disaffected districts, and no local commander was willing to relinquish his only insurance against a sepoy mutiny to attack Delhi.

So, at Agra, Cawnpore (Kanpur) and Lucknow the British withdrew behind makeshift defences, having wherever possible disarmed any sepoys whose loyalty looked shaky. The spirit of insurrection slowly spread out from Delhi, and by early July there had been uprisings in Aligahr, Benares, Jhansi, Gwalior and Indore. Sepoys attacked and murdered their officers and their wives and children, and they were joined by civilians who had in various ways been losers as a result of recent government changes. The dispossessed, like Nana Sahib and the Rani of Jhansi, were augmented by peasants whose marginal lands were overtaxed, soldiers from the disbanded army of Oude, Muslim holy men, and petty criminals and bandits for whom any collapse of authority was a chance to make a profit. One group, the Gujars, a caste of pastoral nomads living in the neighbourhood of Meerut and Delhi, stole from both sides. Everywhere there prevailed a feeling that the raj, like the defenders of the three cities, was at bay.

It took roughly six weeks for British authority to dissolve throughout the upper Ganges and in the northern areas of central India. Then the Mutiny appeared to lose direction and run out of steam. This was probably inevitable since from the beginning it had lacked both overall leadership and a sense of purpose. Those who revolted were united only in what they hated and, for this reason, converged on the three beleaguered outposts of Agra, Cawnpore and Lucknow. These cities acted like magnets and embroiled the greater number of the rebels in prolonged sieges. At the same time, a large body of mutineers allowed itself to be trapped inside Delhi by a smaller British army. The insurgents' advantages of surprise and numbers were therefore thrown away. There were two possible explanations for this inertia: the first the fact that perhaps the majority of rebels wanted loot, of which the greatest quantities lay within the cities, and the other was the nature of their movement. It was essentially a *jacquerie*, whose supporters were hitting back randomly against the figures and symbols of an authority they believed was

The Mutiny defeated:
British redcoats with
turbans around their caps
stand amid the ruins of
Lucknow, 1858.
(© NAM)

changing their lives for the worse. They possessed no ideology, beyond Muslim appeals for an anti-British jihad, and from what is known had no alternative system of government for the districts they had temporarily liberated.

From the end of July British troops began to pour into India. The nature of the revolt made it obvious that white soldiers would restore a white man's raj, but there was invaluable assistance from Ghurkas and Sikhs, of whom there were 23,000 in arms by the end of the revolt.

Manpower shortages and innumerable transport hitches made life difficult for the commanders of field armies during the first counter-offensives in June, July and August. It was the hot season and when bullock carts, palanquins, river-boats and elephants were unavailable, men marched. Lieutenant George Barker of the 78th Highlanders, attached to General Sir Henry Havelock's column between Allahad and Cawnpore, estimated that more men died from sunstroke than mutineers' fire. Casualties from all causes, but mainly heat exhaustion and dysentery, were exceptionally high during the siege of Delhi, where in four weeks the 52nd Light Infantry were reduced from 600 to 242.

Only a superhuman will kept men in the field during these and later phases of the campaign. This was fuelled by a universal desire to take revenge on an inhuman foe who had murdered women and children. Worst of all was the mass murder of civilians in Cawnpore, after they had been promised safe conduct by Nana Sahib at the end of June. Prisoners and anyone suspected of sympathising with or assisting the rebels were executed randomly, and at Cawnpore all those implicated in the massacre were defiled or stripped of their caste before being hanged. In the eyes of their captors the rebels were less than wild beasts and many eyewitness accounts of operations used hunting metaphors to describe the fighting. A gunner officer approvingly recorded the actions of a colleague who, on the march near Bareilly, suspected some mutineers of taking refuge in a field of corn. 'Forming his line precisely as he would have beaten a field of turnips for game, a scene commences which baffles all description: pea fowl, partridges, and Pandie [mutineers] rose together: the latter giving the best sport.'

Through ruthlessness and iron stamina the British were getting the upper hand by early autumn. The turning point was the capture of Delhi on 19 September, a psychological blow which 30,000 or more rebels had anticipated when they deserted the city in the four weeks before the final assault. Further south, Havelock and General Sir James Outram cut their way through to Cawnpore and relieved Lucknow, but were trapped there by superior numbers of the mutineers. In October, the siege of Agra was raised by a column from Delhi and a month later the garrison and civilian population of Lucknow was evacuated. The war of containment was ending, and as the new year approached preparations were in hand for the campaign of pacification under the new commander-in-chief, General Sir Colin Campbell, a grizzled Glaswegian veteran who had first seen action as a fifteen-year-old ensign in Portugal in 1808.

1858 saw the crushing of almost all the remaining resistance, and Lucknow was retaken in March. Participants in the war had no doubt as to why the raj had triumphed. One evening during the campaign in Oude, Garnet Wolseley, then a junior officer, had watched some Sikhs exercising with clubs and had been impressed by their physiques and dexterity. He turned to the strongest British soldier in his company and asked if he could match them. 'No sir,' was the reply. 'But I'll fight any three of those fellows.' Remembering the episode over forty years later, Wolseley concluded, 'It is that belief in the superior pluck and fighting qualities of our race that won us India and still enables us to hold it. Had our men no such confidence in themselves we should never have relieved Lucknow nor retaken Delhi.' And yet, as his anecdote suggests, there were plenty of Indians willing to stand by the raj.

The Indian Mutiny was a civil war. Thousands of Indians fought alongside the British, including traditionally militant Pathans from the North-West Frontier, who defied calls to fight for Islam against the infidels. Dost Muhammad, the Afghan amir and no friend of Britain, made no hostile move. Others who had suffered at the hands of the British also refused to commit themselves; Judge George Edmondson, a fugitive in June 1857, found one prince willing to assist him even though the government 'had reduced his army and taken away his guns'. Like many other benevolent neutrals, this magnate recognised that the Mutiny was primarily a soldiers' rebellion, which had temporarily got out of hand because the government lacked the forces to contain it. It was localised, negative in its objectives, destructive in nature and therefore limited in appeal.

The Mutiny pushed India into the forefront of British political life and there was much heart-searching as to what had gone wrong and why. The immediate result was the dissolution of the East India Company in 1858. Henceforward, a secretary of state and ultimately Parliament were responsible for the government of India, with local law and policy-making in the hands of a viceroy and provincial governor-generals, assisted by councils composed of bureaucrats and a handful of Indian princes. Admission to a reconstituted Indian civil service was through an examination and was, theoretically, open to educated Indians.

In the year of the Mutiny twelve Indian doctors had graduated from the newly founded medical school at Agra, a fact which would have more long-term significance for India's future than the battles in the Oude. These doctors would join a steadily growing élite of educated Indians who had undergone instruction in English in government schools, colleges and universities. By the mid-1880s it was estimated that there were 8,000 Indians with degrees and a further half a million who had graduated from secondary schools. All had been taught in English and had been exposed to British political ideas.

However, there were widespread protests in 1883 at a government proposal to extend the jurisdiction of Indian local magistrates to Europeans, and the Viceroy, Lord Ripon, was forced to withdraw the measure. Educated Indians felt affronted at what was an assertion of racial superiority. This slight led indirectly to the formation in 1885 of the Indian National Congress, an association of educated Indians from all professions, which met annually to discuss issues relating to their country. In its early days it was compared to an earnest public-school debating club, but its membership soon grew and by the end of the century it had become an influential forum for Indian opinion.

The Queen-Empress's peace: British mounted infantrymen with captured dacoits shortly after the annexation of Burma, 1885. (© British Library)

The emergence of what was essentially a highly respectable and respectful assembly of Indians imbued with British political ideas caused some alarm. Ripon's successor, Lord Dufferin, a Liberal appointee, had no time for the 'Bengali Babu', whom he found 'a most irritating and troublesome gentleman'. The Indians' demands, however, were at this point moderate and were largely confined to the assimilation of more of their educated countrymen into the middle and higher ranks of the government.

Of course, this was rightly seen as the prelude to Indian self-government, which was why Curzon (Viceroy from 1898 to 1905) steadfastly refused to consider greater Indian participation in government. He rejected in forthright terms the request made by Romesh Chunder Dutt, Congress president in 1901, for the appointment of Indians to the viceregal council. The Marquess's unyielding position on the advancement of Indians to senior posts, and his well-known view that the Congress was an unrepresentative and disruptive body, had the effect of beginning its metamorphosis into a focus for active political opposition to the raj.

A collision between westernised Indians and the government had been predicted at the onset of the government's educational reforms in the 1830s. Although in many ways a despotism, British India had never been a totalitarian state in which the government proscribed books, newspapers and foreign travel and banned political debate. If Indians were allowed free access to British political and philosophical writers, it was inevitable that they would apply what they read to their own country, and ask why they were excluded from those political rights which were their rulers' birthright. It was a tricky question which Curzon and those of like mind could only answer with reference to the peculiar conditions of India. Divisions of religion, wealth, caste and clan were so profound and a source of so much division that only a disinterested and fair-minded British government could command the loyalty of all Indians, protect them and secure internal order. Reference was often made to the state of India before British rule when life had been precarious and anarchy was endemic. Above all was the fear that democracy and moves towards self-determination would, in the words of Sir Michael O'Dwyer, a rigorous and plain-dealing administrator who served in India from 1885 to 1919, release 'the demon of discord' so that the country would be convulsed by 'all the latent feuds and hatreds' hitherto reined in by men of his stamp.

On another and all-too-common level, Indian aspirations towards self-determination were countered on racial grounds. These were candidly expressed by Major-General Sir George Younghusband, who served with the Indian army intermittently between 1878 and 1918.

> *It is never wise to stand studied impertinence, or even the semblance of it, from any Oriental. Politeness, and courtesy, by all means, and even camaraderie, as long as these are reciprocated, and all is fair, and square, and above board. But the moment there is a sign of revolt, mutiny, or treachery, of which the symptoms not unusually are a swollen head, and a tendency to incivility, it is wise to hit the Oriental straight between the eyes, and to keep on hitting him thus, till he appreciates exactly what he is, and who is who.*

Younghusband spent some time putting this doctrine into practice on the northern frontiers of India in the endless small wars of punishment and pacification. Their common purpose was summed up by one of Younghusband's colleagues after a bout with the Chins of the Assam frontier when he had taught them 'that the only thing that mattered was the Great White Queen across the waters'. Resistance was toughest and most persistent among the tribes along the North-West Frontier, a remote, mountainous region where British control was always precarious.

There was a special romance about the North-West Frontier campaigns largely because they were contests in which the British usually managed to overcome brave, resourceful and daring warriors on their home ground. Of course technology mattered and probably tipped the balance, but there were plenty of close shaves, since the tribesmen were adept at ambushes. Two campaigns were needed in 1888 and 1890 against the recidivists of the Hazara district, who defiantly refused to pay fines for raiding and sniped at patrols. On the first occasion 14,000 men were sent against them, and on the second, 8,000, of whom at least a quarter were British, a custom established after the Mutiny.

This was a highly specialised form of warfare in which every use was made of up-to-date technology. The two Hazara forces used the field telegraph for communication between commanders and columns, and were armed with Gatling machine-guns, breech-loading rifles with a range of up to 1,000 yards, and small, collapsible mountain guns (the 'screw guns' of Kipling's poem) which were carried by mules. Despite the weight of firepower, charging tribesmen armed with swords and knives sometimes careered into British lines and caused havoc. In 1895, seasoned frontier fighters were perturbed by the allegations that the new .303 rifle bullet lacked the stopping power of the old .457. Secret forensic tests were therefore carried out on the corpses of Pathan mullahs, who had been executed by firing squads using the two types of ammunition, to discover their relative merits.

Grisly details like this were deliberately kept from the public in Britain, who were also kept in the dark about the full extent of the systematic burning of villages, crops and granaries, and the slaughter of livestock which marked every frontier operation. Instead, newspaper reports and eyewitness accounts like Winston Churchill's popular *Malakand Field Force* (1897) presented the wars as tales of derring-do and adventure. When justification was offered it was in familiar terms of quite literally pushing back the frontiers of civilisation. The North-West Frontier wars (there were nearly twenty between 1863 and 1901) were a glamorous and headline-catching feature of a grander, often more mundane business, the government and regeneration of India.

Famine relief:
the railways introduced
by the British facilitated
the transport of food
from areas of abundance
to those of dearth, but
major famines, like
that of 1896, required
a programme of public
works. Here Indian men
and women are building
a water tank (reservoir)
for which they were paid
by the government.
(© Blair Athol Estate)

MEMSAHIBS

From the 1820s onwards more and more British women accompanied their husbands to India, preferring the risks of climate and disease to extended separation. They were also joined by an annual boatload of eligible ladies, armed with letters of introduction and in search of husbands. The arrival of British women contributed to a minor social and moral revolution: civilians and officers spent less time dining together and enjoying local entertainments. Native mistresses were frowned upon. These memsahibs were photographed by Captain McCosh between 1849 and 1852.

Miss Scott

Mrs Currie

Mrs Tuson

Mrs Weston
(All © NAM)

5

THEY LITTLE
KNOW OUR
STRENGTH:
THE FAR EAST AND
THE PACIFIC

In the eighteenth century men of discrimination looked on China with awe and wonderment. It was an ancient, orderly civilisation whose artefacts, particularly porcelain, were prized by collectors and imitated by craftsmen employed in English country houses. China tea, imported by the East India Company, was well on the way to becoming a daily palliative for all classes. By the nineteenth century attitudes to China had changed radically. A popular encyclopaedia published in 1842 said little on Chinese civilisation, but instead described China as 'an unbounded mart' with a population clamouring for British goods. These were denied them by their rulers, who refused to recognise the benefits of free trade and had gone as far as to exclude British commerce.

Opium rather than manufactured goods was what the Chinese people demanded. The felicitous combination of the British taste for tea and the Chinese for opium had been exploited by the East India Company which, since 1773, had enjoyed a monopoly over the drug's production. The rise of the opium trade coincided with a period of Chinese decline. By 1800 China had become a static, introverted society governed by an intensely conservative and ossified bureaucracy. The Ching dynasty of emperors were Manchus, outsiders who found it hard to rally their Chinese subjects at moments of crisis. But rulers and ruled were united by a common mistrust of all foreigners, whom they designated 'barbarians' and treated with condescension. This had been amply demonstrated in 1793 and 1816 when two British missions, headed by Lords Macartney and Amherst, had travelled to Peking in an attempt to establish formal diplomatic relations between Britain and China. Both embassies were politely cold-shouldered, and departed in no doubt that they had been regarded as representatives of some distant, tributary state.

Given Chinese insularity and apprehension of all things alien, it was inevitable that a clash would occur with Britain, which believed it had a right to conduct unrestricted trade throughout the world. The first collision occurred in the spring of 1839 at Canton, the main port open to foreign commerce. The Chinese imperial government, disturbed by the harmful social and economic consequences of opium addiction, decided to curtail the trade and instructed Commissioner Lin Tse-hsü to cut it off at its source, Canton. His measures provoked an angry response from Captain Charles Elliot, the Superintendent of Trade, and when news of them reached London, the government came under pressure from companies with Chinese interests. Lin's behaviour was represented as another example of Chinese obstructiveness and a direct challenge to the principles of free trade. The Foreign Secretary,

Lord Palmerston, therefore authorised the despatch of a seaborne expeditionary force to the mouth of the Canton River.

Today the First Opium War (1839–42) is commonly portrayed as a shameful act of aggression contrived to promote a trade which was immoral, and to which the Chinese government had rightly taken exception. Contemporaries regarded the war and its successors as highly praiseworthy enterprises undertaken as a final resort. The fault lay with the Chinese who had formerly connived at the trade at the same time as treating Britain and its merchants in a high-handed manner. The war was therefore seen as a showdown in which Britain, its patience exhausted, revealed its muscle in the hope that, thereafter, a chastened Chinese government would prove more amenable to perfectly reasonable demands.

The war was a severe shock to the Chinese who knew nothing of the technology of their adversaries. In every engagement the Chinese were, in the words of an eyewitness, 'unable to contend against the fearful weapons of their determined foe'. He had been astonished when, during the early fighting, a Congreve war rocket struck a junk which then caught fire and exploded, killing all its crew. When the British landed at Amoy in September 1841 they suffered no losses, but their musket volleys killed at least a hundred Chinese who were armed with matchlocks and bladed weapons.

Initially operations were confined to the Canton River. Hong Kong island was annexed as a future naval base and commercial centre. There followed a sustained demonstration of firepower on the Yangtze River, devised to show the imperial government the hopelessness of resistance. During June and July 1842 Woosung, Shanghai and Chinkiang were shelled and taken by landing forces. It was a tough campaign, fought in the hot season, and there were heavy British losses from sunstroke, malaria, dysentery and cholera. Of the thirty-four men killed during the capture of Chinkiang, sixteen died from heat exhaustion.

The Yangtze campaign paid off politically. A stunned Chinese government signed the Treaty of Nanking which confirmed British possession of Hong Kong and opened Canton, Amoy, Foochow,

In the Chinese fashion: the Chinese room at Claydon House, Buckinghamshire, c.1765 reflects the passion of the contemporary bon ton for all things Chinese. (© Country Life)

China 1839-1900

⚑ 1842 Treaty ports

Shanghai and Ningpo to British commerce. The apparatus of unofficial empire was soon in place: consulates were established; British subjects were allowed exemption from Chinese jurisdiction; a naval base with coaling facilities was set up at Shanghai; and British men-o'-war were permitted to patrol Chinese rivers and coastal waters. France and the United States quickly followed Britain's example and were granted similar privileges.

The Opium War had far-reaching consequences for the history of the Far East. China's technical backwardness and vulnerability had been exposed and Britain had made itself the major commercial and military power in the region. In 1853, when the American Admiral Perry visited Japan to persuade its rulers to open their country to Western trade, he warned them if they did not, then the British would appear and treat Japan as they had China. The Japanese wisely conceded, and within a few years had made commercial agreements with the Western powers, including Britain.

Having dragged China into the informal empire, Britain turned its attention to making it safe for trade by the suppression of riverine and coastal piracy. This was exciting and rewarding work; in 1849 one squadron of warships earned £42,000 in head-money which was calculated at £20 for each dead or captured pirate and £5 for each of those who escaped. Actions were brief and brisk and their flavour is captured in an official report of an engagement between the steamer HMS *Hermes* and five junks near Hong Kong in March 1853. Proceeding under sail, the *Hermes* lured the pirates towards her until, realising their mistake, they scattered and three got away. The remaining two:

> *Finding they could not escape, closed and lashed themselves together, prepared to*
> *fight, and sent men aloft to throw stink pots [primitive hand-grenades which emitted*
> *a noisome smoke] as we ranged up alongside them, firing musketry; as we closed*
> *they put their helms hard over and got under our bows, and commenced throwing*
> *stink pots most furiously, when we backed off and opened fire on them ... offering*
> *to cease if they would yield, but they would not. Finally, having driven them below*
> *with Grape, Canister and Musketry, Lieutenant Burton boarded and got possession.*

Twenty-eight pirates had been shot or drowned and a further fifty-seven, all in red turbans and red-trimmed robes, were taken prisoner. Forty-five pirates were estimated to have escaped and so, in all, the *Hermes*'s crew were entitled to £1,755. Save for a few sailors scalded by the stink pots, there were no British casualties.

This incident in the war against piracy occurred at a time when Sino-British relations were deteriorating. The flashpoint came in 1856 when Cantonese soldiers, searching for a pirate, boarded the British-registered *Arrow* and hauled down its flag. The legal grounds for claiming the *Arrow* as British were flimsy, but this did not deter John Bowring, the consul in Canton, from using the affair to provoke a trial of strength with the local Chinese commissioner, Yeh Ming-chin. Yeh had never hidden his disdain for all foreigners, and for some time had done everything in his power to exclude them and their goods from Canton. Bowring was equally stiffnecked and summoned a flotilla which shelled the city to show Yeh and its inhabitants the folly of interrupting trade.

Like its predecessor, the Second Opium War of 1856–8 was an exercise in intimidation. This time, however, the French collaborated, using as their excuse the murder of a missionary, a ploy they adopted to justify simultaneous aggression in Annam and Cambodia. While Anglo-French forces battered ports along the Canton River, Lord Elgin was ordered to China with powers to settle outstanding differences between Britain and its government. The result was the Treaty of Tientsin of 1858 which granted fresh concessions to foreign business interests and legalised the opium trade.

What the British and French interpreted as Chinese stone-walling and prevarication over enforcing various clauses in this treaty led to a final application of *force majeure* in 1859–60. An Anglo-Indian and French army landed in north China and marched on Peking. Again modern weaponry triumphed over medieval: Robert Swinhoe, an interpreter, was impressed by the unflinching fortitude of the Tartar cavalry who refused to retire under close-range shellfire. 'Poor heathens!' he wrote later. 'They little know our strength although they have shown themselves brave fellows.'

During the advance on Peking looting became endemic and Swinhoe was amused to see provost-sergeants joining in. The big prizes lay inside the imperial palaces in Peking which were precipitately abandoned by the Emperor Hsien-feng and his court in October 1860. According to Swinhoe, the French were first off the mark in what soon became a general free-for-all. On entering the Emperor's throne room he found 'the floor covered with the choicest curios' which were being sifted through by General de Montauban, who was making piles of presents for Queen Victoria and Napoleon III. Shortly after, the summer palace was burned down at the instructions of Elgin as a reprisal for the torture and murder of several emissaries and their escort.

The plundering of Peking and the destruction of the summer palace symbolised the prostration of China. She had been hammered in three wars and driven to submit to forces which few of her people or rulers could comprehend. As the country with most to gain from a pliant China, Britain had taken the

Trading freely:
Hong Kong's waterfront and harbour eighteen years after it was ceded to Britain, 1860.
(© NAM)

Scourge of the
foreign devils:
Mandarin Yeh Ming-
chin, who attempted
to halt opium imports
and provoked the wrath
of Lord Palmerston,
c.1860.
(© NAM)

lead in this process of humiliation, although by 1860 she had been joined by France, which was already infiltrating Indo-China, and Russia, which had its eyes on Korea and territory along China's northern boundaries. Britain had no interest in annexation, save for Hong Kong and the adjacent Kowloon peninsula; all she had ever wanted was unrestricted access to China's trade.

For forty years after 1860 Britain dominated China's commerce. In 1895 Britain enjoyed two-thirds of all China's foreign trade, which then totalled £53.2 million. Opium remained at the head of the list of China's imports, accounting for an average of £10 million a year during the 1880s, with Lancashire cottonware in second place with an annual value of about £3 million. As well as having a near-monopoly of China's markets, Britain had a stranglehold on the Chinese customs. These had passed under foreign control in 1853 as an emergency measure when Taiping insurgents threatened Shanghai. Twenty years later the entire Chinese customs service was managed by Sir Robert Hart, who had a staff of eighty-nine Europeans of whom more than half were British. This supervision guaranteed the government a reliable source of revenue and was also a safeguard for foreign capitalists. In a passage which gives an insight into the mind of British investors, the *Economist* of 15 January 1898 commented that, 'The Customs Houses of China are within reach of British shells', which presumably might be fired if its government defaulted on its loans.

British political paramountcy in China ended in 1895. The sudden and complete collapse of China in the 1894–5 Sino-Japanese War signalled the country's weakness to the rest of the world. Japan was the first to take advantage, with demands for sovereignty over Formosa (Taiwan), a £35-million indemnity and the Liaotung Peninsula. This last was withdrawn after protests from France, Russia and Germany, who had combined in a cynical conspiracy to protect China. In return, a grateful Chinese government granted France mineral rights in Yunnan, Kwangsi and Kwantung, and Hankow was delivered to Germany. Russia, already dreaming of an empire in Manchuria, was allowed a controlling stake (paid for by the Czar's treasury) in the Chinese Eastern Railway which, when finished, would connect northern China with the eastern terminus of the projected Trans-Siberian Railway.

In 1897 Germany put in a bid for more territory, using the by now well-worn excuse of murdered missionaries, this time in Shantung. Their deaths opened the way for the German occupation of Kiachow, which was turned into a naval base, and a monopoly of investment in mines and railways in Shantung. Russia, sensing that the 'scramble for China' had begun, slipped into Port Arthur in March 1898, two years after she had helped shift the Japanese out.

These brutal manifestations of the new imperialism caused dismay in Britain. Hitherto British governments, confident in the knowledge that their businessmen enjoyed supremacy in China, had supported a free-trade-for-all-comers policy, and turned a blind eye to French and Russian efforts to lop off China's outlying tributary provinces, Indo-China and Korea. The events of 1897–8 suggested that China, like Africa, would be partitioned with the result that Britain would lose markets. The encroachments of protectionist Russia posed the most serious threat; the Trans-Siberian railway would facilitate mass emigration to underpopulated eastern Russia and, once its branch lines to the south had been laid, would serve as a conduit for China's trade with Europe, which had previously been carried by British ships.

After statements that it had no territorial claims to China, the Marquess of Salisbury's government announced in April 1898 that it had leased Wei-heiwei on the coast of north China as a naval base. At the same time a promise that no other power would be allowed concessions in the Yangtze basin had been extracted from Peking. Not that this counted for much, since soon afterwards China approved the Russian-funded Hankow-Peking railway which infringed Britain's local investment monopoly. Fears of further con-frontations led to the reinforcement of the Far Eastern squadron, which was increased to three battleships and ten cruisers, making it equal to combined Franco-Russian fleets in the area.

Salisbury feared that defending Britain's informal, commercial empire in China would stretch resources to breaking point. Britain was currently embroiled in the conquest of the Sudan, was preparing for a showdown with France on the upper Nile, and was on a collision course with the Boer republics in South Africa. The transfer of warships to the China station depleted the home and Mediterranean fleets, but Britain could not afford to let Germany, Russia and France do as they wished in China.

China bound:
British soldiers relax en route to Tientsin during the Third Opium War, 1860.
(© NAM)

The quickening pace of foreign penetration provoked popular resistance inside China. There had been spasms of violent xenophobia, largely directed against missionaries in 1891–2, and by the end of 1898 a new anti-foreigner movement had emerged, the I-ho chuän (Righteous and Harmonious Fists), or Boxers. Its members hated all Europeans, Chinese Christians and anyone who used alien manufactures. The Boxers boasted magical powers which made them immune to bullets, and possessed what turned out to be a suicidal addiction to fighting with traditional swords and spears. They were, initially, anti-Manchu, but their obscurantist ideology won them friends among the ultra-conservatives at court and in the government. The sympathetic governor of Shansi, Yü-hsien, incorporated the Boxers in the local militia and then unleashed them on foreign missionaries and their converts.

By the beginning of 1900 the Dowager Empress, Tzu-hsi, had cobbled together an alliance with the Boxers in order to deflect popular anger away from the dynasty and towards the foreigners. It was a shortsighted and self-defeating policy since the Chinese government's ambivalence towards the Boxers was already serving to draw more and more British, French, German, Russian and American warships to the Gulf of Chihli. Fearing an allied advance on Peking, Tzu-hsi finally took the plunge on 18 June and committed imperial troops to join 30,000 Boxers in an attack on the walled legation quarter of Peking.

This was madness and the Empress's pro-Boxer policy was swiftly repudiated by the more realistic provincial mandarins. More importantly, from the viewpoint of the few hundred defenders of the legations, General Jung-lu refused to lend the defenders his modern artillery. On 14 August an international army, 18,000-strong, entered Peking and relieved the legations.

These troubles were a godsend for Russia. They provided the excuse to pour 200,000 troops into Manchuria and to transfer warships from the Baltic to Vladivostok and Port Arthur. Mutual distrust between Britain and Russia was as strong as ever, but there were strategic restraints on how far the British government could go to frustrate the annexation of Manchuria and preserve the *status quo* in China. During 1900 and 1901 the Admiralty just managed to maintain naval parity with France and Russia, but at the cost of reducing the numbers of the home and Mediterranean fleets. The only answer lay in reaching an accommodation with Japan, which was forcefully contesting Russian claims to Manchuria and Korea.

The Anglo-Japanese alliance of January 1902 allowed Britain to withdraw from the Far Eastern naval race. Each power promised to assist its partner if it was attacked by two or more countries, an arrangement which left Japan free to go to war with Russia without fear of French intervention. In terms of the history of the British empire, the accord with Japan was a turning point. Britain had been forced to admit that she could no longer maintain her paramountcy in China singlehandedly, and henceforward her informal empire there would depend upon the goodwill and cooperation of Japan.

Nevertheless, the short-term results of the alliance were invaluable. In February 1904 Japanese warships made a pre-emptive strike against the Russian squadron at Port Arthur, the first of an amazing sequence of land and sea actions which shattered Russia's dreams of a Far Eastern empire and overturned the local balance of power. Russia's humiliation was greeted with undisguised pleasure throughout Britain and the alliance with Japan, now a vital prop to British pretensions in the Far East, was renewed in 1911. For the people of this region, and for that matter the rest of Asia, Japan's victory had a far greater

Peking burns: the view from the legation quarter during the siege, 1900. (© NAM)

OPPOSITE *A new friend beats an old enemy: a prostrate Russia is finished off by Japan, while a pipe-smoking Englishman looks on approvingly. A German view of the Russian-Japanese War, 1904.*

„Wenn ich gewiß wüßte, daß der Kerl nicht mehr aufstehen kann, gäbe ich ihm auch einen Tritt."

significance. Japan, an Asiatic power, had proved that European armies and navies were not invincible; the trend of over a hundred years had been reversed.

Elsewhere in the Far East and in the Pacific the nineteenth century witnessed the gradual replacement of informal by formal empire. In the early 1800s Malaya and the islands of the East Indies had attracted a handful of energetic, ambitious young opportunists: Sir Stamford Raffles, John Clunies-Ross, Alexander Hare and Sir James Brooke. All were animated by the spirit and vision of Clive and, like him, had a peculiar knack of turning local circumstances to their own and their country's advantage. Dutch power was in eclipse and the small independent states of Malaya and Borneo were fragile and therefore keen to obtain British friendship and armed assistance.

Raffles, frustrated of the chance of starting an empire for the East India Company in Java, laid the foundations of another in Malaya by acquiring Singapore island in 1819. Placed athwart trade routes between India and China, Singapore soon became a major free trade *entrepôt* for South-East Asia and the East Indies. Hare tried to establish himself as an independent prince in southern Borneo, but failed, while his partner, Clunies-Ross, finally ended up as 'king' of the Cocos-Keeling islands in the Indian Ocean. Their enterprise inspired another romantic swashbuckler, James Brooke. Something of a misfit in England, Brooke had sought service with the East India Company's army and had been invalided out as a result of wounds received leading a charge of irregular horse in the Burma War.

Brooke's lucky break came in 1833, when he inherited £10,000 which provided him with the wherewithal to launch a venture designed to acquire territory and open trade on the coasts of northern Borneo. There was something distinctly Elizabethan about Brooke and his scheme, but it had the passive support of the East India Company and the Admiralty. Brooke's greatest assets were his audacity, singlemindedness and the well-armed, 142-ton schooner, appropriately named *Royalist*, which made him

Piracy punished:
Royal Navy steamers, one pulling boatloads of marines and bluejackets, attack a pirates' lair, Borneo, c.1848.

a power to be reckoned with in regional politics. Between his first reconnaissance of the shores and creeks of northern Borneo in 1839 and 1841, Brooke had made himself indispensable to Hasim Jeal, the regent of Brunei, who was attempting to bring the province of Sarawak to heel. When Hasim feared that Brooke might desert him, he installed him as Rajah of Sarawak.

Appointed as a strong man to rule an un-governable territory, Brooke set about restoring peace and laying the foundations of a stable government and economy. The suppression of coastal piracy was his hardest task, despite regular assistance from British men-o'-war based at Singapore. The Malay and Borneo pirates were persistent and elusive, although their light craft were no match for modern ships' guns. During one riverine engagement in 1843 Brooke recorded how a single round of grapeshot 'swept all the men from paddles on one side' and forced the rest of the crew to jump into the water, where they were shot.

The British government approved Brooke's new position, although he had many enemies among humanitarians, who deplored his vigorous methods of handling pirates. He and his tiny state were a useful addition to Britain's local unofficial empire. Territorial ambitions in the area were confined to the occupation of islands and land for naval bases and commercial centres, such as the Straits Settlements – Penang Island, Port Wellesley, Singapore and Malacca, secured

Nineteenth-Century Malaya

between 1785 and 1824 – from which influence was exerted over Malaya, Siam and the East Indies.

Informal empire in Malaya depended on the cooperation of the local hereditary princes who were expected to keep the peace and safeguard British lives, property and investment. After 1870 these duties proved beyond the capacities of the Malay rulers as the region slid into a period of violent political and economic upheavals. Since the mid-1850s, Selangor and Perak had enjoyed a tin-mining boom, which had brought a mass influx of Chinese immigrants. There were 40,000 in Perak by 1870, and they, like their countrymen in Selangor, were passionately attached to various, mutually hostile secret societies. The Chinese faction struggle in Selangor had deteriorated into a civil war by 1870, and a year later a succession contest broke out in Perak.

Successive governors of the Straits were faced with a dilemma: they had to do all in their power to restore stability inside Malaya while, in the best traditions of informal empire, staying neutral. It proved practically impossible for the British to keep out of Malaya's internecine conflicts, not least because they had triggered a revival of piracy. In 1870 gunboats had been driven to shell the stockades of a contender to the throne of Selangor after his adherents had impeded the arrest of some Chinese pirates. Such incidents multiplied until, by 1873, the Straits' authorities had become completely entangled in Malayan politics. Long before, the men-on-the-spot had concluded that the apparatus of informal empire was inadequate to settle the crisis, which could only be resolved by direct intervention.

A tug-of-war consequently developed between British officials and the Liberal Colonial Secretary, Lord Kimberley, who was determined to stop the drift towards Britain taking full responsibility for Malaya. In the end he gave up when the annexationists warned that inactivity would invite German or Dutch intervention. Then and later, even outwardly anti-imperialist governments like Gladstone's would not dare take the political risk of allowing Britain's informal power to be superseded by that of another country. The colonial officials got their way; Britain threw its weight behind one of the pretenders in Selangor and Anglo-Indian forces were ordered to pacify Perak and Sungei-Ujong in 1875.

The result of the 1873–4 crisis was Britain's assumption of formal protection over Perak, Selangor, Negri Sembilan and Pahang. Existing political structures remained in place with the local princes, like

Barter:
British sailors do business with South Sea islanders, c.1840.

their Indian counterparts, submitting to guidance by British residents. In time, under British direction, debt and domestic slavery were abolished and the princes were actively encouraged to become improving, paternalist rulers. As part of this process of enlightenment, a college was established at Kuala Kangsor in 1905 where the prince's sons underwent a British public-school régime which, it was believed, would teach them how to govern responsibly.

Events in Malaya were paralleled by those in Fiji, where informal empire also disintegrated under the pressure of changes brought about by economic development and contact with Europeans. The complex and serpentine politics of Fiji had, by 1871, given rise to a bizarre situation in which King Thakombau was ruling as a constitutional monarch advised by a cabinet of European cotton-planters and merchants (including a bankrupt Sydney auctioneer on the run from his creditors) and two native chiefs. The government's many internal problems were made worse by the existence of a local lobby which claimed that the only solution to Fiji's difficulties was British rule.

The annexationists had allies in New Zealand, New South Wales and Britain. In the former two, Fiji was represented as a country ripe for colonisation, an argument which Australian expansionists extended to Papua and New Guinea. In Britain, Gladstone's ministry had to contend with pressure from humanitarian and missionary groups. Between 1835 and 1860 the Fijian missions had made 60,000 converts, but it was believed that only British rule would extirpate cannibalism and ritual sacrifice from among the islands' remaining animists. There was also concern about the spread of 'blackbirding', a form of slave trading in which Pacific islanders were cajoled or forced aboard ships, and then transported as indentured labourers to the Peruvian guano fields or the Queensland sugar plantations. The Royal Navy had tried to interrupt this traffic during the 1860s, but had been hampered by the refusal of Australian juries to convict kidnappers.

A combination of commercial and philanthropic arguments persuaded an unwilling British government to investigate the alleged collapse of central authority in Fiji. The naval officers on the spot were easily convinced that the islands would slide into anarchy if the British flag was not hoisted, and in 1874 the government approved annexation. There was a strong and understandable feeling in anti-imperialist Liberal circles that ministers had been outmanoeuvred by a determined coalition of interest groups.

After 1874 British policy in the Pacific reverted to the old pattern of policing the islands by warships and careful avoidance of any action that might lead to permanent occupation. Australian adventurers, keen to do a Rajah Brooke in Papua and New Guinea, were frowned on by the Colonial Office which, however, made it clear that steps to acquire these regions would be taken if there were signs that another power was considering their annexation.

The coming of the new imperialism in the 1880s saw Germany and France preparing to stake out claims to various South Sea islands. German interest in the region went back thirty years, and during the 1860s the Hamburg-based Goddeffroy and Son had outstripped all its rivals as general traders in the Pacific. The firm collapsed in 1879, but Bismarck was happy to subsidise its successors, the New Guinea

Blackbirds:

Polynesian indentured labourers on a Queensland sugar plantation, 1860s.

Colonial Company, and the Deutsche-See-Handels-Gesellschaft, in order to win political favours from the business community and the colonial lobby. He also approved a series of annexations of islands between 1883 and 1886.

There was something surreal about the German procedure of establishing sovereignty. In 1886 a German gunboat hove to off one of the Solomon Islands and sent a landing party ashore. Local chiefs were given trading flags and a proclamation in a presentation box, while a board inscribed 'German Imperial Protectorate' was set up. A German flag was then raised and lowered, and the officials and sailors returned to the ship. Whether or not they understood exactly what was happening to them, the Solomon Islanders were deeply impressed by this display, for they related its every detail to a British naval officer fourteen years later. As they sailed through the islands the Germans also renamed them: New Britain became New Pommern, and so on.

The island names were changed again when Britain, Germany, France and the United States haggled over a final settlement of who kept what. Britain got Papua, the Solomon and Gilbert and Ellice Islands, while the Germans were satisfied with Samoa, New Guinea, the Bismarck Archipelago and the Caroline and Marianna Islands. The Chancellor, Prince von Bülow, was delighted and predicted that this sprinkling of islands and atolls would become 'milestones along the road ... to *Weltpolitik*'. Global power of this kind was an expensive luxury for, in 1913, Germany had to pay a 1.8 million mark subsidy to sustain its Pacific empire.

Britain's scattering of Pacific islands remained for many years the most backward and forgotten of her colonies. None had any great economic potential and all were afflicted by falling population levels; Fiji's dropped by 30,000 between 1860 and 1873 and the decline only ceased in 1921. Imported diseases, against which the islanders possessed no effective immune systems, were largely responsible for these losses. Efforts were made to reverse this process with some success. The death rate of indentured labourers on the Solomons was cut from five to three per hundred between 1906 and 1921, thanks to the work of a colonial medical officer and the building of a hospital.

The new colonial administrations were also concerned with the moral welfare of the Pacific islanders, but attempts to eradicate such disruptive customs as inter-tribal warfare met with resistance. Feuding continued on the Solomons well into the 1920s, despite frequent hangings of warriors found guilty of murder. The Malaita fighting men, or ramos, were proud of their warlike traditions, and when they were challenged by a local district officer, who styled himself 'super ramo', the result was a skirmish in which he and thirteen native policemen were killed in October 1929. Another source of irritation to the authorities was the islanders' unwillingness to integrate into the newly introduced market economy. A 1932 official account of the Solomons' development regretted that the Gela islanders were still refusing to grow more than was needed for themselves and the purchase of tobacco and a few other necessities. Nevertheless nearly 7,000 islanders had become part of the new economy by taking work as indentured labourers on the European-owned copra plantations. Conditions appear to have been severe: in 1922 three native overseers were charged with murdering a worker, but were acquitted, as was a Mr C. V. Maxwell, a plantation manager who had been accused of beating to death a servant boy. There were some very dark and unpleasant corners in the remotest parts of the empire.

A shot across the bows: HMS Rosario *in close pursuit of a schooner engaged in what amounted to the Pacific slave trade, the kidnapping of Polynesian labourers. If caught, the crew would expect sympathetic treatment from Australian juries, 1867.*

6

A GREAT ENGLISH-SPEAKING COUNTRY:
SOUTH AFRICA

In 1809 Lord Caledon, governor of Cape Colony, wrote, 'The true value of this colony is its being considered an outpost subservient to the protecting and security of our East Indian possessions.' This view of what otherwise was an unprofitable and turbulent backwater explained why the British had occupied the Cape three years before, and why they insisted on its retention at the end of the French wars. The strategic value of the Cape remained unaltered for the next hundred years. In the early 1900s, Admiral Lord Fisher, the First Sea Lord, designated Cape Town, along with Singapore, Alexandria, Gibraltar and Dover as one of the 'Five strategic keys [which] lock up the world'. In 1887, nearly twenty years after the opening of the Suez Canal, Cape Town was chosen as the principle staging post for reinforcements bound for India in the event of a war with Russia. At that time the Cape was guarded by 4,200 regular troops, supported by 3,000 local volunteers.

If Britannia was to rule the waves, Britain had to keep the Cape. This was neither an easy nor rewarding task since the Cape lay in a region where racial tensions were acute and, for the first seventy years of the nineteenth century, economic growth was sluggish. Britain had inherited a dispersed population of whites of Dutch and French ancestry, who called themselves Boers or Afrikaners, 25,000 black slaves who worked for them, and 15,000 Khoikhois (Hottentots). On the colony's eastern borders lived 17,000 Xhosa, whose lands the Europeans coveted, and who had been at war to defend them since 1779.

The Boers were the dominant race. They had first come to the Cape in 1652 and saw their past, present and future in terms of an unending struggle to subdue the land and its black inhabitants. Both had been willed to the Boers by God who, according to their primitive Calvinist theology, had chosen them, as He had the Israelites of the Old Testament, to be the masters of a new Canaan. Like the British, the Boers imagined themselves the blessed instruments of Providence, a belief which gave them extraordinary resilience and reserves of inner strength.

Under the minimalist administration of the Dutch East India Company, the Boers had been largely left to their own devices and were allowed a free hand with the natives. This state of affairs ended with the installation of British colonial administration, which felt morally obliged to deal even-handedly with all its subjects, and extend basic legal rights to those who were black or of mixed race. Therefore no partnership emerged between the Boers and a régime which attempted to apply liberal and humanitarian principles, which the former found incomprehensible. There were further sources of misunderstanding and friction between rulers and ruled. The governors of the Cape were patricians, some, like Sir Benjamin D'Urban and Sir Harry Smith, with illustrious records of service in the French wars, and they and their equally well-connected staffs could distinguish no marks of civilisation among Boers, who appeared uncouth, obstructive and extremely touchy. Missionaries were horrified by the practice of slavery, and by the raiding parties who preyed on native communities whenever the need occurred to replenish the Boer labour force.

Relations between the colonial authorities and the Boers deteriorated rapidly after 1815 to the point in 1834 when thousands of Boers decided to withdraw into the South African hinterland. What subsequent Boer mythology called 'the Great Trek' was a slow and uneven process which lasted several years. In part it was a reaction to the British Parliament's abolition of slavery in 1833, although pressure on the land in the Cape forced many Boers to emigrate. At first, the Cape government feared that the mass exodus would lead to a widespread war once the Boers collided with the expanding Ndebele and Zulu states which lay in their path, and in 1842 the new Boer republic of Natalia was annexed as a precautionary measure. In fact, the well-armed Boers were able to take care of themselves, and their spectacular victories over the Ndebele and Zulus in the late 1830s assured them occupation of what became the Transvaal and Orange Free State republics.

Given that the overriding aim of British policy in southern Africa was the achievement of local stability, the government saw no useful purpose in attempting to coerce the Boer republics. In 1854 Britain officially recognised their independence, with the proviso that they acknowledged British sovereignty, which made them, on paper at least, part of Britain's informal empire.

One persistent Boer complaint had been that the British had failed to deal firmly with the Xhosa on the Cape's volatile eastern frontier. The recent history of the Xhosa, or Kaffirs as they and other South African blacks were indiscriminately and contemptuously called, was one of intermittent wars to protect their land from settler encroachment. This conflict continued and intensified after the arrival of the British; there were major campaigns in 1811–12, 1819, 1834–5, 1846–7 and 1850–3. The Xhosa were in the same position as the Red Indians of North America and, if the colonists had their way, were destined for the same fate. This was brutally outlined in a letter written to the War Office by a commander during the 1846 campaign: 'The Kaffir must be driven across the Kei; he must be made your subject; he is wanted to till the Colonists' land.' Another officer went further, and predicted the elimination

Southern Africa 1815–1902

[map showing Southern Africa with labels including SOUTH WEST AFRICA, BECHUANALAND PROTECTORATE (1884–5), BRITISH BECHUANALAND, CAPE COLONY, ORANGE FREE STATE, SOUTH AFRICAN REPUBLIC (TRANSVAAL), NATAL, BASUTOLAND (1884), MATABELELAND, MASHONALAND [RHODESIA], MOZAMBIQUE, with towns Salisbury, Fort Charter, Fort Victoria, Shangani, Bulawayo, Pietersburg, Pretoria, Johannesburg, Mafeking, Pitsani, Goschen, Vryburg, Harrismith, Newcastle, Ladysmith, Colenso, Durban, De Aar, Kingwilliamstown, East London, Port Elizabeth, Cape Town, Simon's Bay, Angra-Pequeña (Luдеritz), Delagoa Bay; rivers R. Orange, R. Vaal, R. Modder, Gt. Kei R.; campaign notes: 1893 Campaign, British South Africa Column 1890, Jameson's Raid, Doorn Kop 1896, Sekukuni's Fighting Kopje 1879, 1899–1900, 1899, 1846–54, Kaffir Wars 1815–53, 1878 Campaign, Gaika, 1885; Miles scale 0 100 200]

Bushwacked:
Highlanders ambushed
by Xhosas during the
1851 uprising in
eastern Cape Colony.
(© NAM)

of the Xhosa as the only outcome of the contest for land. 'They must recede before the white man – all attempts at civilisation are futile. The great want here is a body of energetic colonists to follow in the back of the troops.' Irksome frontier wars against an elusive enemy always hardened consciences, but these remarks make it clear that some British were beginning to think in the Boer fashion. South Africa belonged to the white man and the black had a stark choice between submission or extinction.

The business of grinding down the Xhosa was fraught with difficulties since they were ingenious guerrillas, fighting in rough country which they knew intimately. Explaining this to his superiors in London, a British commander in the 1846 campaign characterised the Xhosa warrior as 'a greasy savage, whose full dress consists of a feather in his head and a sheaf for his organ of generation, who runs about as quick as a horse'. Getting to grips with such an opponent was hard and frustrating work. Nevertheless, bush-fighting came as a relief from tedious garrison duties. 'I can scarcely keep myself from jumping out of joy at the idea of really being a soldier,' Lieutenant Fleming of the 45th Regiment told his family as he prepared for action in July 1846. Six months later he was suffering from dysentery, loss of appetite and a hacking cough, and was keeping himself alive with doses of quinine and port. When the war ended, he had had his fill of excitement and returned to England to take holy orders.

As in so many imperial frontier wars, there were natives who were willing to place their local knowledge and skills at their conquerors' disposal. Khoikhoi were widely employed as scouts and skirmishers, although large numbers deserted during the 1850–3 operations against the Ngquika Xhosa. Gradually, and by a scorched earth policy which starved out their opponents, the British soldiers, known as 'amarwexu' (small-pox Satans), got the upper hand, but the spirit of resistance remained strong. In 1855 the Xhosa were heartened by rumours that Britain had been beaten in the Crimea, and that Russian troops would shortly appear and drive all the British from the Cape. Soldiers did arrive from the Crimea, but they were former German mercenaries who had been employed to make up the wartime shortfall of British recruits. The War Office, sick of costly frontier campaigns in the Cape, had resurrected a precedent used by the Romans to keep order on chaotic frontiers. The mercenaries, like ex-legionaries, were given farms in return for defending fortified villages in districts recently seized from the Xhosa.

Seen from the perspective of London, the Cape and its tiny offshoot, Natal, were Cinderella colonies, continually disturbed by internal and external ructions. Both were unrewarding as markets for British manufactures; in 1855 South Africa imported British goods worth £922,000, which put it on the same level as Peru and well behind the Argentine and Chile. The political development of the two colonies followed the same course as that of the Canadian provinces and Australian states: under Colonial Office guidance, elected parliaments were established in the Cape in 1854 and Natal two years later. Pressure from British and local liberals devised a franchise which included richer black and mixed-race voters. This was done in the hope that a non-white middle class would eventually emerge and join with the white to form a stable, responsible electorate like that in contemporary Britain.

The late 1860s witnessed an economic revolution in the Cape, the repercussions of which soon affected every part of southern Africa. The discovery of diamonds in Griqualand, which was swiftly annexed as a Crown colony in 1871, attracted investment and immigrants on an unprecedented scale. British imports into the Cape soared from £2 million in 1871 to £7.7 million twenty years later, when the total of the Cape's exports stood at £9.5 million, a third of which came from diamonds. Between 1871 and 1875, the Cape government inaugurated an ambitious programme of railway construction that, by 1890, gave the colony a network which extended for over 2,000 miles.

Digging for diamonds and laying railway tracks were both labour-intensive activities requiring a vast, unskilled workforce, which could only be found among the black population. If industrialisation was to proceed, the blacks of southern Africa had to be completely pacified and brought under white control. The need for a final assertion of white supremacy was becoming urgent by the mid-1870s as black migrant workers, particularly Pedi from the Transvaal, and Basotho, were using the wages they earned on the diamond fields to buy guns. Obsolete muskets and modern breech-loaders, some imported through Natal, were becoming widely available, and for some years the Zulu kings had been building up an arsenal of firearms.

A chosen people:
Boer wagons parked
outside a church,
Pretoria, 1880.
(© NAM)

A passive black population was necessary to implement the Colonial Secretary Lord Carnarvon's plan for a federation comprising the Cape, Natal and the two Boer republics. This appeared an ideal solution to regional problems since it would create a stable unit which, thanks to the Cape's mineral revenues, would be self-supporting. Cautiously welcomed in the two British colonies, the scheme found little favour with the Boers, who saw it as a stratagem by which Britain could dominate the entire region.

Progress towards a South African federation was halted in 1876–8 by a sequence of native rebellions and wars, which were, as it turned out, the last major effort by South Africa's blacks to stem the advance of white power. There was unrest among the Griquas in the northern Cape, the Pedi and Basotho in the Transvaal, and the Ngquika and Gcaleka Xhosas in the eastern Cape. Local British and troops, bluejackets and marines were able to handle the unrest in the Cape, employing the latest military technology, including the new Martini-Henry breech-loading rifle and Gatling machine-guns. The Boer campaign against Sekhukhuni's Pedi soon ran out of steam and into trouble when a kommando (unit of mounted volunteer riflemen) was beaten. This reverse exposed the fragility of the Transvaal, and gave Carnarvon a welcome pretext to order its annexation in January 1877. The Boers were grateful for British intervention which, for the time being, guaranteed their safety.

The coup against the Transvaal was delivered by Sir Theophilus Shepstone, a single-minded colonial bureaucrat with a flair for native languages and a taste for intrigue. While the Boers may have seen him as a saviour, Shepstone saw the occupation of their republic as the prelude to its incorporation into the proposed South African federation. An enthusiast for the federation, Shepstone had convinced himself that measures for its creation could not proceed until the Zulu state had been emasculated. The overthrow of the Zulu kingdom was also the objective of Sir Bartle Frere, the new governor of the Cape, whose Indian experience had taught him that it was dangerous to tolerate the existence of any independent and well-organised native state on an imperial frontier.

During 1878, Frere and Shepstone conspired to engineer a war with the Zulu king Cetshwayo, ignoring the fact that he showed no hostility towards his southern neighbour, Natal. The two proconsuls doctored their reports to the Colonial Office to make Cetshwayo appear a warlike tyrant, and exaggerated the size of his army, which they falsely alleged was a standing force, rather than a body of men who were only mobilised in an emergency. Behind their cynical machinations was the hope that once Cetshwayo's

Enthroned: the installation of Cetshwayo as King of Zululand in the presence of British officials, whose white sun helmets can be seen in the middle ground. Behind are British cavalrymen and, in the left foreground, seated Zulu warriors wearing headrings and carrying assegais. Within a year they would go into battle against a British army. (© NAM)

kingdom had been dismantled, his subjects would become a subservient labour force at the disposal of Natal's white farmers and the mining companies.

Having manoeuvred Cetshwayo into a corner, Frere and Shepstone got the war they wanted in January 1879. It started badly thanks to ill-luck and the slipshod generalship of the commander-in-chief, Lord Chelmsford. At the end of the month, a 1,200-strong column of British troops and native auxiliaries was all but wiped out at Isandlwana. Immediately after, and in defiance of Cetshwayo's orders, an impi of between three and four thousand warriors crossed into Natal and attacked the mission station at Rorke's Drift, which was defended by 139 men from the 24th Regiment, many of them invalids. In the epic battle which lasted for over twenty-four hours the attackers were repelled with losses of over 500 dead. The Zulus were exhausted and had not eaten for two days, and British firepower more than compensated for the imbalance in numbers. One survivor, Colour-Sergeant, later Colonel Bourne, remembered how a few Zulus had managed to reach the improvised defences. Those who did, 'to show their fearlessness and their contempt for red coats and small numbers ... tried to leap the parapet, and at times seized our bayonets, only to be shot down.' Nonetheless the defenders showed extraordinary steadiness and eleven were awarded the Victoria Cross.

The trouble for the Zulus was that their indunas (generals) were fatally addicted to the traditional headlong charge of assegai-armed warriors. It had succeeded, just, at Isandlwana, but at a cost of 5,000 casualties. Nevertheless, similar tactics were repeated throughout the war, although Cetshwayo urged his commanders to adopt a guerrilla strategy and attack the extended and vulnerable British lines of communication. The British government was also disappointed by its servants' performance and sacked Shepstone, Frere and Chelmsford, who was replaced by the abler and more methodical Sir Garnet Wolseley. He arrived in Zululand too late for the final destruction of the Zulu army at the battle of Ulundi in July. By this time everyone involved knew what to expect; the British deployed in a Napoleonic-style square, the better to concentrate their firepower, and the Zulus, who had been progressively disheartened, launched their usual charge, but, observers noticed, without much conviction. The overthrow of the Zulu kingdom had required a tremendous effort, which indicated the importance the government attached to the achievement of paramountcy in southern Africa. 17,000 reinforcements had been rushed to Natal and the two invasions of Zululand had required 27,000 oxen, 5,500 mules and 30,000 native porters and labourers. The final bill was £4.9 million.

With Zululand prostrate, Wolseley turned his attention to Sekhukhuni, whose Pedi were defeated by a mixed force of Highlanders and Swazis. The Basotho, who copied the Boers and fought as rifle-armed mounted infantry, proved a harder nut to crack. The result was that Basutoland became a British protectorate governed through local native

Dethroned:

Cetshwayo after his flight and capture, 1879.

(© NAM)

Spellbound:

an alleged Zulu sorceress photographed in 1879. The extinction of witchcraft was one of the reasons offered by the British press for the invasion of Zululand. (© NAM) chiefs. Experiments of a similar kind in Zululand failed and it was finally absorbed by Natal. The campaigns of 1877–9 had achieved their purpose: large-scale black resistance had been extinguished and white supremacy, which would last for just over a hundred years, was confirmed.

The pacification of South Africa's black population by the British army marked the start of a new power struggle between the British and the Boers. Once it became clear that Britain's occupation of the Transvaal was not a stopgap measure, but a preparation for its amalgamation into a South African federation, the Boers rebelled. The Transvaal's war of independence of 1880–1 ended with the defeat of a small British force, which had been trapped on the summit of Majuba Hill in northern Natal. Rapid, long-range rifle fire had done for the British infantrymen, but the Boers celebrated their victory as the judgement of God in favour of His elect and against a race commonly considered impious. The newly elected Liberal ministry saw the battle as the outcome of an amoral policy, which Gladstone had campaigned against during the general election. Plans for a federation, which the Boers had so forcefully rejected, were dropped and the Transvaal's independence was restored. And yet, during negotiations at Pretoria in 1881 and London three years later, the government clung to pretensions of sovereignty over the Boer republics, and with it the right to interfere in the shaping of their domestic and foreign policies.

What at the time was no more than an academic legal point assumed enormous significance during the next twenty years. It was a period which witnessed tentative Boer expansion northwards and east-wards, and, after the discovery of gold on the Witwatersrand in 1886, the transformation of the Transvaal's economy. Once in production, the Rand mines provided a quarter of the world's supply of gold and ensured that the centre of economic power in southern Africa shifted away from the Cape to the Transvaal. By 1896 the Transvaal government was the richest in Africa with annual revenues of over £8 million from minerals. British credit underwrote this economic revolution: in 1899 British investment in the Transvaal totalled £350 million, and two-thirds of the Rand's mines were owned by British stockholders.

The questions which hung over southern Africa during the last two decades of the nineteenth century were: how would the Transvaal's new wealth be used, and what effect would it have on Britain's

Across the Tugela: a British base camp on the Zulu border. Sacks of meal await transportation by a Cape wagon (left foreground). By not harassing the extended lines of communication, the Zulus missed a tactical opportunity which might have severely hampered the British, 1879. (© NAM)

position in the area? This last was very much the concern of Cecil Rhodes, who, while still in his early thirties, had made himself a multi-millionaire by an accumulation of diamond-mining concessions. A shrewd manipulator, he had by 1891 secured a monopoly over the Kimberley diamond fields for his Rhodes De Beers Consolidated Company and had extensive investments on the Rand.

Rhodes became the most famous, many would have said notorious imperialist of his age. He was amoral, instinctively acquisitive (sleeping in the open during the 1884 Bechuanaland campaign, he had contrived to get for himself a blanket he was sharing with a British officer) and a brilliant businessman. His fortune was the servant of his dreams. These were inspired by contemporary Social-Darwinism and the new imperialism, which convinced him that it was the destiny of the Anglo-Saxon races to civilise the world. Nothing could withstand the force of this destiny, certainly not the rights of those who stood in its way. In a revealing episode, he listened to Kaiser Wilhelm II's complaint that Germany had entered the race for empire too late and that there was nothing worthwhile left for her anywhere. 'Yes, your Majesty there is,' Rhodes responded. 'There is Asia Minor and Mesopotamia.' That these belonged to Turkey did not trouble Rhodes. The compass of Rhodes's temerity and ambitions startled contemporaries. Viscount Milner observed, 'Men are ruled by foibles and Rhodes's foible is *size*.'

Like other mavericks, such as Clive, Brooke and, later, T. E. Lawrence, who came to empire-building by chance, Rhodes's imagination and talents were not apparent in his earlier life. He also shared the former trio's good luck by being the right man in the right place at the right time and, of course, had the singular advantage of a private fortune with which to fulfil his dreams. He also had, at every turn, the assistance of successive British governments which, while many of their members did not share Rhodes's breadth of vision, saw him as an extremely useful instrument for the preservation and extension of Britain's influence in southern Africa at a time when it was in jeopardy.

Rhodes's first coup, achieved with the cooperation of Gladstone's ministry, was the annexation of Bechuanaland in 1884–5. During the past five or so years, parties of Boer settlers had been penetrating this region, where they established the miniature republics of Goschen and Stellaland. Simultaneously, German colonists were moving inland from the embryo settlement of Angra Pequeña, and there were fears in Cape Town and London that they would eventually link up with the Boers. The result would be the blocking of the 'Missionaries Road', which ran northwards towards what was then known as Zambesia (roughly modern Zimbabwe and Zambia), a region widely believed to be rich in minerals. There was also, and this caused the greatest anxiety to the British government, the possibility of the emergence of a German-Transvaal axis. In April 1884, when Paul Kruger, the Transvaal's president, had visited Berlin he had spoken publicly of his people's affinity with Germany. 'Just as a child seeks support from his parents so shall the young Transvaal state seek, and hopefully find, protection from its strong and mighty motherland, Germany, and its glorious dynasty.'

This was enough to arouse the British government, already uneasy about the appearance of German settlements in South-West Africa (Namibia), and under pressure from an alliance of Rhodes and the missionary lobby, which feared for the future of the Tswana of Bechuanaland under Boer rule. In December 1884 a small, well-armed force was ordered into the area to evict the Boers and declare a protectorate over Bechuanaland, which it did without resistance.

Rhodes was the ultimate beneficiary from the acquisition of Bechuanaland, a colony of little economic value, which was costing Britain £100,000 a year in subsidies during the 1890s. Bechuanaland was the springboard for Rhodes's incursion into Zambesia, an undertaking that would be accomplished by his British South Africa Company, which was officially chartered in 1889. This company, like its contemporaries the Royal Niger Company, the British Imperial East Africa Company and the North Borneo Company, represented a revival of seventeenth-century, private enterprise colonisation and trading. The government gained overlordship of new territories on the cheap since their day-to-day administration and policing were in the hands of the company's staff. The British South Africa Company's mandate was for farming and mining in Mashonaland, where mineral and settlement rights had been granted by the Ndebele king, Lobengula, in return for a company pension, 1,000 now obsolescent Martini-Henry rifles and a gunboat for the Zambesi River, which was never delivered.

At the end of 1890, the first column of settlers, less than 400 in number but heavily armed with machine-guns and artillery, entered Lobengula's kingdom. The events of the next ten years paralleled those which had been played out in North America during the previous two centuries. Lobengula gradually realised that by making concessions to the company he had weakened his own authority, which he attempted to reassert in the autumn of 1893 by ordering his impis to raid Shona villages close to British settlements. He played straight into the hands of the company's chief magistrate, an extremely foxy and belligerent former physician, Dr Leander Starr Jameson. Jameson had long believed that two sources of power could not co-exist in the region, and that the company's future would never be assured until the formidable Ndebele war machine was dismantled. The raids were therefore just what Jameson wanted and gave him the excuse for a war against Lobengula.

The first Matabele War of 1893–4 was a one-sided affair, for Ndebele generals, like their Zulu counterparts, stuck to traditional frontal attacks. These were suicidal against the company's Maxim

Unwelcomed guests: British soldiers wearing sun helmets are among the clients of a Pretoria hotel during the occupation of the Transvaal, 1880. (© NAM).

LEFT *Nightriders*:
*Dr Leander Starr Jameson
and British South Africa
Company policemen
ambushed near their goal,
Johannesburg, 1896.
(Collection of A. V.
Williams)*

Digging in:
*British troops improvise
trenches and parapets, a
vital precaution in the
face of intense, long-
range Boer rifle fire that
had overwhelmed three
armies in the winter of
1899–1900.
(© IWM)*

machine-guns, the latest and most deadly of their kind, which fired six hundred rounds of .45 ammunition a minute. The Maxims terrified the Ndebele, who saw them as some awesome kind of magic; a native baby, born at this time and alive in the 1970s, explained his unusual name, Zigga-Zigga, as being based on the sound made by the machine-guns, and therefore believed by his parents as having some supernatural power. Ndebele resistance did not end with the overthrow of Lobengula's state, for there was a further uprising in the spring of 1896, in which settlers and their families were attacked and murdered.

The killing of the colonists generated bitter racial passions in Britain and Rhodesia (Zimbabwe), as the company's territories were now generally known. 'Permanent peace there cannot be in countries like Mashona and Matabeleland until the blacks are either exterminated or driven back into the centre of Africa,' proclaimed the *Saturday Review*. Its forthrightness echoed the views of settlers, like the big-game hunter Sir Frederick Selous, who thought that armchair imperialists were mistaken if they expected gratitude from natives who had been freed from oppressive rulers and the powers of the witch-doctors. Only condign chastisement repeatedly applied would teach the Ndebele 'the uselessness of rebelling against the white man'. Delivering these lessons in quiet-ism was a horrifying business. Rifleman John Rose, one of the 1,200 British soldiers hurried to Rhodesia from the Cape, described the storming of a kraal during mopping-up operations in August 1896:

. . . all over the place it was nothing but dead or dying niggers. We burnt all the huts and a lot of niggers that could not come out were burnt to death, you could hear them screaming, but it served them right. We took about 5 women prisoners, but let them go again; one woman was holding a baby and some one shot the baby through the leg and through the woman's side, but it was nothing [and] our doctor bandaged the wounds up.

Relaxation:
Tommies refresh
themselves in a river;
some may well pick
up infections from
polluted water, 1901.

Details of this nature shocked Liberals and Radicals at home, and there were some sharp exchanges in the Commons between Chamberlain and the company's critics. Henry Labouchere questioned him on Rhodes's stated intention of 'thoroughly thrashing the natives and giving them an everlasting lesson', executions without trial and village-burning. The last, Chamberlain insisted, was 'according to the usages of South African warfare', which must have puzzled those who believed that the advance of Anglo-Saxon civilisation in Africa would bring an end to such practices. Parliamentary protests did little to change the nature or the course of the war, which dragged on into 1897, when the last guerrilla groups were finally hunted down.

A secondary, equally bloody campaign of pacification was being fought to the north-west of Rhodesia on the eastern shores of Lake Nyasa. British penetration of this region had followed Livingstone, whose early missions had been superseded by the Scottish Presbyterian African Lakes Company. It received government patronage in its armed struggle against Arab slave-traders, who operated from Zanzibar and supplied slaves to the tribal potentates of Arabia and the Persian Gulf. A British protectorate was declared over the area in 1891 to forestall acquisition by the Portuguese, who were, with good reason, suspected of not pulling their weight in the international effort to suppress Arab slaving. There followed four years of small-scale wars, subsidised by Rhodes, and fought by Sikh troops, commanded by Sir Harry Johnston, and a flotilla of tiny gunboats. Arab slavers and those tribal chiefs who had refused to accept Britain's paramountcy were successively defeated; the latter were characterised by Johnston as slavers, which made it easier for him to justify his rigorous measures to the Foreign Office.

Those who took part in the small wars waged across southern Africa during the 1890s believed they were the pathfinders of the vast new British dominion with its own iron racial order. 'Africa south of the Zambezi must be settled by the white and whitish races,' claimed Johnston in 1893, 'and that Africa which is well within the tropics must be ruled by whites, developed by Indians, and worked by blacks.' William Brown, an American naturalist-turned-colonist who had been captivated by Rhodes's dreams and helped to make them reality, believed the process of conquest and settlement was inexorable since it was an expression of 'the spirit of the age'. This, he insisted, 'decrees that South and Central Africa shall become a great English-speaking country', perhaps another United States, which in time would fulfil 'the destiny for which Providence seems to have chosen the Anglo-Saxon race'.

By 1914 the process seemed well underway. Southern Rhodesia had a white population of 34,000, with an elected legislative council which lorded it over the 732,000 blacks, half of whom lived in reservations. Many whites were Boers, who brought with them the racial prejudices of South Africa. In 1903 a law was made which punished a black man found guilty of raping a white woman with death – a protection not available to black women. In Northern Rhodesia (Zambia), where white settlement was sparse, British law obtained under a separate and, by and large, a more humane form of government which owed its form to British rather than South African influence. In 1924 it was taken over by the Colonial Office.

On the track of the Boers:

imperial yeomanrymen, all volunteers, mount up for another day of hunting Boer kommandos, 1901. (© IWM)

The period that saw the establishment of British supremacy in Rhodesia and Nyasaland was one during which it was under assault in South Africa. The British government continued to regard South Africa as its exclusive sphere of influence, and hoped that its constituent parts would eventually merge in a federation within the empire. Rhodes was of the same opinion and, on becoming Prime Minister of the Cape in 1891, he endeavoured by charm and cheque book to convince its Boer population to accept the permanence and value of the British connection. There was, however, an alternative future for South Africa as part of a predominantly Boer federation in which the Transvaal would be paramount.

Such an arrangement was wormwood to Britain. Neither Rosebery's Liberal ministry (1893–5) nor its Conservative successor under Salisbury could allow a strategically vital region to slip from Britain's grasp into Germany's. It was argued that a United States of South Africa under the Trans-

Round-up: Boer women and children and their belongings are packed into a wagon while their farm is torched. They would be sent to a camp as part of measures to cut off Boer kommandos from assistance and supplies, 1901. (© IWM)

vaal would be too weak to resist German encroachments, and might easily become a German satellite. The Transvaal had now become a pawn in the game of international imperial power politics, which was being played by Germany in order to extract concessions elsewhere. German political interest and investment strengthened the Transvaal's sense of independence and, seen from both London and Cape Town, were evidence of the urgent need for measures to reassert British prestige and authority.

Developments in 1894 and 1895 heightened tension. The completion of the Delagoa Railway gave the Transvaal free access to the sea (German warships attended the opening celebrations at Lourenço

Prisoners: Boer POWs in camp: some would offer their service to the British, others would be sent to Ceylon or St Helena, 1902.

Marques) and was followed by a brief trade war in which hindrances were officially placed in the way of British businessmen in the Transvaal. This petulant display of independence helped concentrate the mind of the British government on how to bring the Transvaal to heel. Rhodes's answer was a *coup de main* delivered by mounted forces of the Rhodesian and Bechuanaland *gendarmerie*, who would descend on Johannesburg in support of an uprising there. The rebels were drawn from the largely British Uitlander (outsider) community of miners, engineers and entrepreneurs, who outnumbered the Boers and, for this reason, had been denied political rights.

What became known as the Jameson Raid was botched from the start. Rhodes's private army began assembling at Pitsani on the frontier with Transvaal in November 1895 amid conflicting rumours that it would attack either the Transvaal or a local native chief. There was no security here, nor in Johannesburg, which meant that the Transvaal authorities had warning of what was in hand. Spurred on by abundant supplies of whisky and promises of high wages, the troopers launched their attack at the very end of December, were intercepted, and forced to surrender early in January 1896. President Kruger had the ringleaders sent back to Britain for trial, and Rhodes, his political integrity compromised, withdrew from public life.

Just how much Chamberlain, the new Colonial Secretary, knew of Rhodes's plans is not known for certain, although there can be no doubt that he would have warmly applauded the coup had it succeeded. Inside South Africa, the raid raised the political temperature and was widely seen as the first round in a contest between Britain and the Transvaal. Lewis Michael, manager of the Standard Chartered Bank in Cape Town, believed that the issue could now only be resolved by war. 'The ambition of the Transvaal to become the rising power in the land is beyond doubt,' he wrote in April 1896, 'and I don't think we shall all quiet down again until the question is settled one way or another. The whole school is looking at the "two big boys" who aspire to be "cock of the school", and I fear there is only one way of settling the dispute; viz. the old school way.'

Chamberlain agreed, but he knew that if war came it would have to have the wholehearted support of the British electorate. He had been a populist politician, and was therefore more aware than his aristocratic colleagues of the need to proceed with the backing of public opinion, particularly in the provinces. What was needed to prepare the ground for a war against the Transvaal was a moral cause which would win wide support. One was available: Kruger's steadfast refusal to allow the vote to the Uitlanders was presented as an affront to those democratic principles which were now the basis of Britain's government. Chamberlain's efforts to swing British opinion behind a strong line with the Transvaal were helped by an ill-judged telegram of congratulations and a pledge of support sent to Kruger by the Kaiser after the Jameson Raid. From 1896 until the outbreak of the Boer War in October 1899, Chamberlain was able to pose both as a champion of democratic rights and the defender of Britain's historic influence in southern Africa against Germany, which was already being publicly identified as an international rival. But it was the Uitlanders who always held centre stage; in May 1899, when the drift to war seemed unstoppable, Lord Selbourne, the Under-Secretary of State for the Colonies, summed up Britain's moral case (*left*).

Ironically, both British and Boers imagined themselves specially chosen races whose right to govern rested on the dispensation of Providence. Boer preachers and newspapers constantly reiterated claims that the British were an ungodly people, while British propagandists dismissed the Boers as a backward, semi-barbaric race. Viscount Milner, High Commissioner in South Africa since February 1897 and a fervent apostle of Britain's imperial destiny, perceptively summed up the Transvaal's government as a 'mediaeval race oligarchy', which existed solely to perpetuate Boer dominance. During the war British soldiers were struck by Boer naïveté (which included the acceptance of elaborately printed biscuit-box labels as five-pound notes), callousness towards the blacks ('Johnny Boer, he used to shoot niggers like you'd shoot a dog') and coarseness.

We take our stand on . . . the duty and right of every civilised government to protect its subjects resident in foreign countries when they are oppressed and our own especial interest in everything South African as the Paramount power there.

LORD SELBOURNE

War broke out in October 1899 after the breakdown of negotiations between Kruger and Milner over the Uitlanders' franchise. The only strategy open to the Boers was the seizure of railway lines in the Cape and Natal and the occupation of Durban and Cape Town, which would frustrate the landing and dispersal of British reinforcements. Successful at first, the Boer offensive soon ran out of momentum, and by the end of the year the Boer armies were bogged down besieging Ladysmith, Kimberley and Mafeking. British attempts to relieve the former two were beaten back at the battles of Stormberg, Magersfontein and Colenso during the second week of December.

The loss of ground and the three defeats stunned the British public, which had grown used to its army winning spectacular victories over poorly armed natives. In South Africa it faced opponents who were mobile, adept in bushcraft and armed with modern rifles and artillery. It was fortunate that during the winter of 1899–1900 the Boer high command threw away these advantages and chose static warfare, giving their opponents a breathing space in which to collect armies and develop a strategy. This was the responsibility of a new commander, Field Marshal Lord Roberts and his chief-of-staff, General Lord Kitchener.

It was Roberts who masterminded the downfall of the Transvaal and the Orange Free State by adapting Boer principles of mobility. Using massed cavalry, he swiftly outflanked his enemies, occupying Kimberley and trapping Piet Cronjé's army at Paardeberg, where it surrendered on 28 February 1900, Majuba Day. A cavalcade followed in which Roberts's forces successively took Pretoria and Johannesburg. Further east, in Natal, General Sir Redvers Buller, a courageous but intellectually limited soldier, relieved Ladysmith, and then advanced to the Transvaal frontier.

By midsummer 1900 many fighting men believed the war was over, won by superior manpower and matériel. It was not; a younger generation of Boer commanders came to the fore with a new, war-winning strategy of attrition. Kommandos, disencumbered from their wagon trains, would maintain a continual pressure on the British by lightning raids on camps and lines of communication. Ceaseless guerrilla warfare would make South Africa ungovernable and force the war-weary British to restore' independence.

ABOVE LEFT *Beefing up the army*: Bovril was among the many firms which used the 1899–1902 Boer War in advertising copy.

ABOVE RIGHT *Puffing the victor*: Field Marshal Lord Roberts, whose victories in 1900 led to the annexation of the Transvaal and Orange Free State. (Both © Opie)

During the next two years the nature of the war changed radically. Kitchener, who replaced Roberts as commander-in-chief, devised a counter-strategy, which was also based on attrition, but designed to make life unbearable for those who continued to resist. Disaffected areas were criss-crossed with barbed wire and blockhouses; carefully coordinated mounted columns rode to and fro in search of kommandos; and Boer farms and livestock, which provided sustenance for the partisans, were destroyed. Boer women and children and their black servants were coralled into internment camps.

In the early days of the war, British public opinion had rallied to the government with an upsurge of patriotic clamour. Domestic jingoism did not reach the front line, where the 'soldiers' songs of the death and glory quality' which pleased music-hall audiences were actively discouraged around campfires. The tedium of garrison duties, long hours in the saddle, thin and irregular rations, extremes of heat and cold, and disease quickly disenchanted even the most zealous patriot. In a book kept in Cape Town, the ardent young men who volunteered as Imperial Yeomanrymen during the winter of 1899–1900 were asked to fill in their reasons for their arrival in and departure from South Africa. One, who must have spoken for thousands, wrote 'Patriotic Fever' and 'Enteric Fever'.

Kitchener's campaign inspired no patriotic fever in Britain, rather unease about what the war's critics described as 'methods of barbarism'. The phrase rang true as Britain heard reports of epidemics sweeping through the internment camps, killing women and children. Contrary to Boer legend, these were not a consequence of deliberate British policy, but the result of contemporary medical and sanitary ignorance. The same distempers which decimated the inmates of the camps also laid low over 16,000 British soldiers, nearly three times as many as died from enemy action. Nonetheless, there was mounting concern at home among humanitarians, left-wing Liberals and Socialists who refused to believe that the ends justified the means.

They did, at least for Kitchener, and in the spring of 1902, when both sides were approaching exhaustion, peace negotiations began. The Treaty of Vereeniging, signed at the end of May, gave the British what they had always wanted, political supremacy. The Boers got £3 million, which they needed to rebuild and restock their farms, and the promise that self-government would eventually be restored to the Transvaal and the Orange Free State. The Boer *volk* was also assured that Britain would not make an issue of legal rights for blacks when it came to framing a constitutional settlement for the region.

Britain's largest imperial war had cost £200 million and had witnessed the mobilisation of 295,000 soldiers, which was evidence of the lengths the government was prepared to go to to uphold paramountcy in South Africa. In a sense, Britain had been defending the imperial *status quo*, which from 1895 onwards appeared imperilled by the Transvaal's bid for independence and German meddling. To have ignored both would have been to admit weakness, which would have been unthinkable at a time when Britain was under pressure from France, Germany and Russia, who were challenging her position elsewhere in Africa and the Far East. The war was, in international terms, a demonstration of Britain's imperial will and determination to retain global power, whatever the cost.

Practitioners of the conspiracy school of history, mostly on the left, believed that the war had been secretly engineered by a handful of capitalists, some Jewish, to advance their interests on the Rand. This theory was superficially attractive, but failed to show exactly how the plotters had benefited, something which did not prevent it from becoming widely accepted by those already convinced that capitalism was wicked. In one sense, however, the war assisted business interests by perpetuating the system which relegated the black population to the role of a passive labour force. When the British army rode into Pretoria and Johannesburg, black workers burned their passes, the hated symbol of Boer oppression. They had acted prematurely, as the documents would be needed under the new order. Hundreds of thousands of blacks had been employed by the British during the war, often for wages higher than those commonly on offer. Smaller numbers had been used as armed scouts by column commanders, much to the fury of the Boers who naturally insisted that the war, like the future of South Africa, was the white man's affair.

7

THAT
HEROIC SOUL:
THE STRUGGLE
FOR THE NILE

In 1882 Egypt appeared on the way to becoming a thriving, modern state. Its improvement owed much to the ambition and energy of Khedive Muhammad Ali and his successors who, for the past sixty years, had run the country as a private estate. They had encouraged investment in irrigation, railways, ship-building, cotton plantations, schools and universities. Two-fifths of Egypt's cultivated land was given over to the growing of cotton, most of which was exported to Britain, Egypt's major trading partner. The remaking of Egypt had been paid for by British and French capital, and by 1880 its total debt topped £100 million, a huge amount for a country whose annual exports averaged £13 million.

In spite of Khedive Ismail's sale of his 44 per cent holding in the Suez Canal to Britain for £4 million in 1875, Egypt was sliding into insolvency. Various expedients were adopted by the great powers to keep her afloat: in 1876 an international commission was imposed on the government with a mandate to enforce financial stringency, and three years later the new Khedive Tawfiq was persuaded to accept Anglo-French control of his treasury, customs, post offices, telegraphs, railways, ports and even museums. What added up to the gradual erosion of Egyptian sovereignty and the commandeering of its government by foreigners was bound to provoke a nationalist backlash. It first manifested itself in February 1881 with a protest by unpaid army officers, led by Urabi Pasha who, the following September, carried out a *coup d'état* and made himself Minister for War with full control of the army. Urabi was a nationalist who united the fellah class of smallholders, from which he came, with the educated effendi class of landowners and officials. The fellahin were being squeezed off their lands by capitalist agriculture, much of it practised by foreigners who had purchased land in Egypt, and the effendiya were alarmed by the irruption of foreigners into government posts. There were also fears, natural enough, that Egypt would be directly taken over; during the spring and early summer of 1881 the French were putting the finishing touches to their annexation of Tunis.

The appearance of a popular national movement inside Egypt, and with it a government which might not dance to a tune played by foreign functionaries and composed by British and French bankers, took the British and French governments by surprise. The British government was in a quandary. Gladstone and his cabinet were operating under considerable constraints since, two years before, their party had campaigned against the amoral adventurism of the Tories and in favour of a pacific foreign policy based on international cooperation. For this to work in the case of Egypt, Britain and France would have to proceed in tandem and with the backing of the rest of Europe. Attempts to produce a joint Anglo-French policy aimed at restoring the *status quo* were, however, overtaken by events in Egypt.

On 11 June 1882 a row over a fare between an Egyptian donkey boy and a Maltese led to a riot in Alexandria in which nearly fifty foreigners were murdered and their property plundered. What was interpreted as the first step towards anarchy in Egypt shook the money markets in London and Paris, where panicky French investors were beginning to offload Egyptian stock. Unease among the business community was reflected in the *Economist*, which predicted on 17 June that 'very great losses must be incurred and great disturbances to business must arise' if no effort was made to contain the disorders in Egypt. In Parliament there was an angry mood and demands for action. 'Our side of the Commons is very jingo about Egypt,' wrote Sir Charles Dilke, a member of the cabinet. 'They badly want to kill somebody. They don't know who.' If there was killing to be done, Gladstone hoped that the French would lend a hand, but on 1 July the French assembly voted decisively against armed intervention.

Britain was now alone and facing further defiance from Urabi. After his troops had restored order in Alexandria, he ordered the strengthening of the port's defences with modern Krupp cannon. A substantial British squadron was lying in the roads, and on 3 July its commander, Admiral Sir Beauchamp Seymour, demanded the dismounting of the new batteries. Urabi refused, and eight days later the cabinet approved the bombardment of the gun emplacements. On 13 July landing parties of sailors and marines entered Alexandria, where law and order had collapsed after the departure of Urabi's soldiers.

Defending the attack, Gladstone claimed that Egypt was 'in a state of military violence, without any law whatsoever'. This being so, his government was prepared to send an expeditionary force which would restore order and install a new administration. During August two armies, one 24,000-strong from Britain and the other 7,000-strong from India, converged on Egypt under the command of Wolseley. Warships occupied the canal unopposed and the British landed at Ismailia on 18 August. Four weeks later, Urabi's fortified camp at Tel-el-Kebir (al-Tall al-Kabir) was stormed and overrun, opening the way for a triumphal march on Cairo. Urabi was taken prisoner, court-martialled and banished to Ceylon.

Gladstone's government was deeply embarrassed by what had happened, and argued that it had no other choice but to rescue Egypt from self-destruction. Having done so, Britain would, in the same spirit of high-minded altruism, supervise the regeneration of Egypt. This would be accomplished by a cadre of British bureaucrats who would oversee the country's administration under the direction of Sir Evelyn Baring, later Lord Cromer. At the same time, the Egyptian army would be revitalised by a body of senior British officers, assisted by a corps of drill-sergeants. At its inception, it was claimed that this system of control was a temporary measure which would last as long as Egypt required tutelage.

What had been created in Egypt was an imperial hybrid. It was neither a colony nor an official protectorate, and outwardly it remained an independent country ruled by a khedive, whose overlord was, in purely legal terms, the Sultan of Turkey. In reality Egypt was, after 1882, a state where power rested in the hands of a higher civil service staffed by British officials, whose first priority was to bring the country to solvency.

This orthodox view of the occupation of Egypt as a service to its people was challenged by those who saw the Anglo-Egyptian War of 1882 as having been foisted on the government by a clique of investors. Interestingly, traditionalist Tories and left-wing Radicals both identified the manifestations of the new imperialism of the 1880s and 1890s with the backstairs influence of capital.

Inside Egypt, British occupation provoked sullen resentment. Cromer, while publicly boasting that the fellahin were thankful for even-handed British government, confessed to the Committee of Imperial Defence in 1902 that little loyalty could be expected from Egyptians if their country was invaded by France or Russia. During the winter of 1914–15, the Turko-German high command felt confident that an attack on Egypt would immediately trigger an anti-British rebellion. Such conclusions were not surprising; Britain had entered Egypt to suppress a national movement, and the sentiments behind it did not just evaporate after the battle of Tel-el-Kebir, where, incidentally, the fellah soldiers had fought stubbornly. Nationalism remained a strong emotional force among all Egyptians, especially the educated class, who had the added grievance of finding themselves largely excluded from the highest ranks of the civil service, judiciary and army. Despite an energetic and highly competent police intelligence service, run by the British, nationalist agitation continued during the 1880s and 1890s and was covertly fomented by Tawfiq's successor, Abbas II. In January 1900 Egyptian officers stationed at Khartoum, heartened by the news of British defeats in South Africa and rumours of a Russian advance on India, encouraged their Sudanese askaris to mutiny in the hope that the rebellion might lead to the expulsion of the British.

The jugular vein of the empire: the Suez Canal, c.1880. (© NAM)

What then kept the British in Egypt? Free passage through the Suez Canal appeared a compelling reason, since most of its traffic was British-registered shipping; of the 2,727 vessels which used the Canal in 1881, 2,250 were British. And yet at no time did Urabi indicate that he would interfere with the running of the Canal, and it was the British administration in Egypt which terminated the Canal's status as an international waterway at the outbreak of war in August 1914. Of course, in 1882 there was no way of knowing what Urabi might do in the future, and if Britain did nothing, another power could step in.

In the end, as in so many other areas where the machinery of informal empire broke down, formal, and in this case extremely swift occupation by Britain was the only alternative to annexation by another country. Moreover, there was no way of knowing whether the mood of the French deputies would change and a majority would emerge in favour of intervention, with or without British assistance. Subsequent international developments added weight to this argument. The growth of Anglo-French colonial jealousies after 1885, the Franco-Russian alliance of 1892, and with it the prospect that the Mediterranean might become 'le lac français' of French imperialist dreams, justified the decisions taken in 1882 and ruled out any withdrawal from Egypt. A firm grip on Egypt could also be defended when it became clear, as it did in the late 1880s, that Turkey could no longer be relied on to stop the Russian navy from passing through the Bosphorus. The cost of Egypt was high in terms of Britain's international influence. To obtain support for her position there, Britain was compelled to make compromises and offer concessions to Germany and France which, had the circumstances been different, she might have refused.

Possession of Egypt gave Britain responsibility for the Egyptian empire in the Sudan. After sixty years of gradual conquest and pacification, the Sudan was still a turbulent province where Egyptian authority was fragile. Forty thousand soldiers and officials struggled to hold the lid down on unrest and gather the taxes needed to sustain the khedive's credit. Most recently the Egyptian administration had been engaged in the suppression of slave trading, a duty undertaken by foreign governors, including the famous General Charles ('Chinese') Gordon.

On to Cairo:

an armoured train, improvised by the future Admiral Fisher, steams out of Alexandria, 1882. (© NAM)

In 1881 the Egyptian authorities faced a new rebellion, led by Muhammad Ahmad, a thirty-seven-year-old messianic holy man, who called himself the Mahdi. As a chosen servant of Muhammad, it was his mission to purify Islam and chastise those whose faith had lapsed or become contaminated. His simple piety, powerful faith and message of spiritual rebirth won him thousands of converts, the ansars (servants), with whom he took the town of El Obeid. With the permission of Cromer, a well-equipped Egyptian army commanded by Colonel William Hicks was sent south to crush the insurrection. In November 1883, led on a desert wild goose chase, Hicks was ambushed at Shaykan, where his army was overwhelmed and its rifles, machine-guns and modern artillery captured. In the winter of 1883–4, one of the Mahdi's adherents, Uthman Diqna, started a new front in the vicinity of the Red Sea port of Suakin with attacks on local Egyptian garrisons.

It was now obvious that the Egyptian army could not contain let alone suppress the Mahdist movement, and that Egyptian administration in the Sudan was falling apart. Rather than waste resources and men fighting a desert war to put it together again, the cabinet agreed in January 1884 to the evacuation of all Egyptian garrisons and personnel. Imperial disengagement proved as complex and vexatious an undertaking as imperial conquest. Forces rushed to Suakin in February 1884 soon found themselves drawn into a trial of strength with Uthman Diqna, and were consequently forced to make a series of limited offensives to uphold British prestige. This was preserved by victories at El Teb and Tamai, where the British soldier had his first and unnerving experiences of the tenacity and courage of the ansars, or Dervishes as they were usually called.

Supervision of the withdrawal from the Sudan was given to General Gordon. It was a controversial appointment, ostensibly made because of his previous local experience, but in fact engineered by the press. Gordon was already a popular hero, whose combination of bravery and intense evangelical fervour was bound to appeal to the Victorian public. Wilful and confident of his own charisma, Gordon saw himself as an agent of Providence, and, like Gladstone, answered to God for his decisions. He also had a peculiar talent for inspiring non-European soldiers: in the 1860s he commanded the 'Ever Victorious Army', which crushed the Taiping rebellion on behalf of the Chinese emperor, and in the 1870s he led Egyptian troops against Sudanese slave-traders. He spoke hardly any Arabic, but, despite his Christian zeal, believed that he had the hearts of the Sudanese. Their devotion to him was apparently confirmed by the enthusiastic reception he was given when he arrived in Khartoum in February. What he failed to understand was that the city's population imagined that he had the

The Nile Valley, 1882-98

power to summon British soldiers who, as events around Suakin had shown, could beat the Mahdi's ansars. Not that Gordon was unduly worried by Mahdism, which he mistakenly believed was shallow-rooted and unlikely to make much headway. He therefore jettisoned his orders to evacuate the Sudan, and instead prepared to defend Khartoum and resist the Mahdi.

Gordon singlehandedly reversed the government's policy. From Khartoum he issued a series of highly emotional but powerful appeals to the public conscience in which he called upon his countrymen to shoulder the burden of civilisation, and save the Sudan from being overwhelmed by what he considered the forces of darkness. His pleas and predicament captured the public imagination; he was an embattled warrior in a remote land who had placed Christian duty and service to humanity before expediency. Early in August public opinion impelled a reluctant government to send an army to rescue him.

Gordon's position was becoming more and more precarious. Mahdist forces had been concentrating near Khartoum since May, which made evacuation of the city impossible. The main Mahdist army converged on the city in September and a month later the Mahdi took command of the siege. In the meantime, a 10,500-strong expeditionary force, commanded by Wolseley, had mustered and was beginning a cautious advance down the Nile. The press and the public saw the campaign as a race, but Wolseley, as ever, proceeded with care, in the knowledge that the desert had already swallowed up Hicks's army.

By early January 1885, the advance guard of the army had reached Kurti, from where the Desert Column would move across the Bayuda desert to al Matamma. Here, a token detachment would embark on three steamers sent from Khartoum. At Gordon's instructions, it was to contain some men in the traditional scarlet jackets rather than khaki in order to convince the Sudanese that the British really had arrived. The Mahdi, alarmed by the nearness of the relief force, ordered his generals to intercept the Desert Column at the wells of Abu Klea (Abu Tulayh).

What followed was a classic imperial battle. The British force of just over 1,000 men, many cavalrymen mounted on camels, had been told by the intelligence department not to expect serious resistance and was unaware of its opponent's numbers and dedication. Its first sight of the enemy was the appearance of green, red and black banners, inscribed with Koranic texts, waving above a hidden ravine. Skirmishers ran back to the square, which opened to receive them, making a gap through which some Dervishes surged. Infantrymen were unable to discern their attackers until the last moment, and sand and mechanical faults jammed machine-guns and rifles. Where the square had fractured there was 'a mass of yelling men and camels – alive, dead and dying'. What saved the day was the presence of mind of men on an unengaged side of the square, who turned about and fired volleys into the mêlée. The breach was then sealed and the attackers driven off. It was all over in less than twenty minutes, but casualties had been high and all involved were stunned by the ferocity and daring of the ansars.

Among the dead was Colonel Frederick Burnaby of the Blues, whose famous portrait by Tissot represents him as the embodiment of the elegant and devil-may-care insouciance which was the distinguishing mark of a perfect British officer. He would doubtless have approved of colleagues who remarked after the battle that it would have been awful to have been killed without knowing the results of the Derby. Burnaby had taken part in the fighting near Suakin a year before, when newspaper reports of his 'potting' Dervishes as if they had been partridges shocked left-wing Liberals and humanitarians. That Burnaby was also a Tory candidate for Parliament probably added to their indignation.

After Abu Klea, the Desert Column moved on to al Matamma. Further Dervish attacks forced the commander to take defensive measures, and it was only on 24 January that the steamers sailed for Khartoum. The ululations of the women whose husbands had been killed at Abu Klea were heard in Khartoum, now in its last extremity, and news of the battle drove the Mahdi to risk storming the city. The assault succeeded and on 28 January, as the steamers closed in, it was obvious that it had fallen.

What had become of Gordon? The Mahdi, who admired his steadfastness and courage, had wanted him taken alive. Forty years later, ansar eyewitnesses to his last moments testified that he had been killed fighting, one claiming that he had shot several adversaries with his revolver before being shot himself. This evidence bore out the account of Karl Neufeld, who was taken prisoner in Khartoum, and described Gordon as displaying 'superhuman strength' during the fighting. Information along these lines reached Wolseley's intelligence department during February, but it was contradicted later by unreliable sources which offered an altogether more dramatic story. These described how Gordon had stood, aloof, unarmed and in full dress, on the steps of the Khartoum residency, and stared contemptuously at a mass of ansars. Turning disdainfully away, he had been speared and killed.

This version of Gordon's death was promulgated by Sir Reginald Wingate of the intelligence department, who realised that it was the only fitting end for a Christian hero. He knew that the 'martyrdom' of Gordon would inspire his countrymen to reconquer the Sudan as an act of vengeance. So emerged the familiar icon of Gordon facing his enemies and making the ultimate self-sacrifice for the cause of civilisation. This was how his death was seen in Britain; 'a grave misfortune has fallen on civilisation',

All of a sudden the banners were in motion towards us at a rapid pace led by spearmen on horseback. The enemy advanced against our square at a very rapid pace and in a dense black mass, keeping capital order.

LORD DUNDONALD

Fuzzy-wuzzies: Hadanduwa Dervishes pose for a British photographer. The soldiers' nickname for them was taken from their characteristic bushy hairstyle. (© NAM)

announced the *Spectator* on 7 February 1885 as a wave of dismay and anger swept the country. Gladstone took the brunt of the blame, and was left with no choice but to pledge a full-scale campaign to recover Khartoum and punish the Sudanese.

Gladstone was let off the hook in March, when a Russian incursion across the Afghan border led to a general mobilisation. Troops were withdrawn from Sudan for shipment to India, leaving only a garrison at Suakin. In June the Mahdi died, probably from typhus, and the government of the Sudan passed to the Khalifah (successor) Abdullah bin Muhammad. His militant Islamic state posed no threat to Egypt after 1889, when an invasion force was decisively routed at the battle of Toski (Tushki).

Late-Victorian statesmen and strategists were haunted by a fear that the flow of the Nile could be artificially stopped with the result that Egypt's agriculture would be destroyed and the country ruined. It was agreed that blocking the Nile was well beyond the capabilities of the Khalifah's Sudan, but it could be managed by European engineers. This was the opinion of Victor Prompt, a French hydrologist who, in January 1893, published a technical paper that described how a dam could be constructed on the Upper Nile which would effectively cut off Egypt's lifeline. It was, in fact, an unworkable plan, but its possibilities fascinated Théophile Delcassé, the French Under-Secretary for the Colonies. Prompt's scheme, and French official interest in it, caused consternation in Britain which had for some time been endeavouring to secure international recognition of an exclusive sphere of influence which extended down the Nile Valley. There were also simultaneous attempts to secure control over the northern shores of the White Nile's headwaters, Lake Victoria.

Between 1888 and 1898 the headwaters of the Nile were the prize in an extended and at times convoluted game of chess played by the governments of Britain, Germany, Italy and France, and King Leopold II of the Belgians, the owner of what was, in effect, a private estate known as the Congo Free State. As virtual ruler of Egypt, Britain claimed to have inherited that country's historic claims to the Nile Valley as far as Lake Victoria, and was anxious to secure its shores. This region, modern Uganda, had already been penetrated by British missionaries, and in 1888 one of their sponsors, a self-made Scottish businessman, Sir William Mackinnon, founded the British Imperial East Africa Company. Chartered by the government, this firm was empowered to develop trade and extend British influence. Hitherto, the dominant power in East Africa had been Germany. Its interests were represented by an energetic explorer,

Carl Peters, who in 1884–5 had gathered a sheaf of treaties with native rulers in the hinterland of Dar-es-Salaam, which provided the legal foundation for what would become German East Africa (Tanganyika). Italy, keen to acquire the prestige which went with overseas possessions, concentrated its efforts on Ethiopia and the horn of Africa. France was, to start with at least, on the periphery of the contest since her ambitions lay in the Western Sahara, although in 1885 she had acquired the French Congo, a small colony on the north bank of the Congo River. The southern shores of that river and its vast, inland basin were the personal property of Leopold II. His ownership was the result of a compromise made by the European powers in 1885 at the Berlin Conference, but there was no way of knowing whether the company he formed to exploit the area would flourish. If it failed, then France hoped to step in.

1888 saw the first moves in the contest for central Africa. Each of the players was concerned to rescue Eduard Schnitzer, a Silesian Jew who had taken the title Emin Pasha when he had been appointed one of the khedive's governors in the Sudan. After the fall of Khartoum, he had led the detritus of his staff and army southwards into Equatoria, where he was stranded. Mackinnon and Peters planned armed expeditions to extricate him in the name of humanity, and at the same time plant their national flags close to the headwaters of the Nile. They were overtaken by Sir Henry Stanley, the Welsh workhouse boy who had become successively war correspondent, explorer, discoverer of Livingstone and, from 1885, administrator of the Congo Free State. Stanley brought back the none-too-willing Emin, and, by his brief presence in Equatoria, established his royal master's claim to the region.

This episode jolted Lord Salisbury's government into action. Through a series of determined diplomatic gambits, it obtained a bundle of agreements with Italy, Germany and Leopold II which, on paper at least, affirmed British supremacy over the Nile Valley. The Anglo-German agreement of 1890

The death of Gordon: a reconstruction of the fall of the Khartoum residency (1885) from the 1939 film The Four Feathers. *This image of Gordon's death, unarmed and facing Dervish hordes, was used by contemporary artists and became a familiar imperial icon. Before the battle of Omdurman (1898), Kitchener urged his troops to 'Avenge Gordon'. (© Kobal)*

affirmed British claims to Uganda and what is now Kenya, and German to Tanganyika, an arrangement made possible by Britain's willingness to barter the North Sea island of Heligoland for Zanzibar. Next, an accommodation was reached with Italy. Since 1885 Britain had encouraged her ambitions in Ethiopia, and had even delivered her the Egyptian Red Sea port of Massawa to facilitate operations in Eritrea. In gratitude, the Italians promised in 1891 to keep clear of the Nile Valley. Three years later, Lord Rosebery's Liberal government agreed, after considerable internal debate, to declare a protectorate over Uganda, where the financial collapse of the British Imperial East Africa Company had coincided with the spread of tribal war. Soon after, King Leopold pledged not to push his estate's boundaries to the Upper Nile. So, by 1894, the state of play was in Britain's favour. At this stage France entered the game.

France's bid for territory on the shores of the White Nile was intended to overturn the new political order in Egypt. Once it was clear that Britain was not going to abandon her position there in the foreseeable future, France became increasingly embittered and resentful. Hostility towards Britain was orchestrated by a powerful lobby of predominantly right-wing, ultra-nationalist politicians, officials, soldiers and newspaper editors, who claimed that France had been deliberately tricked by her rapacious neighbour. The only way for France to regain her rightful influence in Egypt was by an aggressive challenge to Britain somewhere on the Upper Nile. If successful, this would either compel Britain to evacuate Egypt or concede the sharing of power there. Such an outcome would immeasurably raise France's international prestige and tilt the balance of power in the Mediterranean in her favour. Not everyone in French political circles was convinced; it was argued that if Britain was somehow forced out of Egypt then the entire Near and Middle East would be destabilised, which would hurt French interests.

Nevertheless, the anglophobe faction within the government, army and colonial service were determined to play their hand. Towards the end of 1894, Victor Liotard, the administrator of Upper Ubangi, was instructed to make his way to the Upper Nile, but a change of ministry led to his orders being countermanded. A second expedition was under consideration during the summer of 1895 which was to be commanded by Captain Jean-Baptiste Marchand. He was an officer of immense resolution and an experienced colonial soldier of that breed which, for the past decade, had been busy planting the *tricolore* across the Western Sahara, often in defiance of the wishes of Paris. In March 1897 he set off from Gabon with 163 officers and askaris and orders to negotiate '*alliances sérieuses et des titres indiscutables*' with whomever he encountered on his trek to the Upper Nile. He was engaged upon what he and his sponsors knew to be a gamble, and which some of the latter revealingly compared to the Jameson Raid.

In July 1898 Marchand's party arrived at Fashoda (Kokok) on the shores of the Upper Nile after an epic journey during which, on occasions, he had ridden on a solid-wheeled bicycle, now preserved in the museum of St Cyr Military Academy. While he was pedalling across the southern Sahara, the governor of French Somaliland was making clandestine offers of protection and friendship to the Ethiopian Emperor, Menelik II. The possibility of French intrusion in an area which was nominally a British sphere of influence was one of the reasons why the government sanctioned the first stage of the reconquest of the Sudan in March 1896. Another was the recent defeat of an Italian army by Menelik at Aduwa, which had changed the balance of power in the Upper Nile basin and gravely damaged European prestige. The advance southwards towards Khartoum was undertaken in the name of Egypt by a largely Egyptian and Sudanese army under the command of Sir Herbert Kitchener. From Protestant Ulster stock, Kitchener was a soldier of considerable energies, most of which were channelled into the furtherance of his career. He was a dedicated imperialist who believed that he was waging war in the Sudan in the name of civilisation; this did not, however, prevent him from treating his enemies with extreme ruthlessness.

Kitchener's war was, of necessity, a slow, piecemeal advance down the Nile. It was also a model of logistic efficiency with a single-track railway following the fighting line, which impressed the host of war correspondents who accompanied the army and sent back enthusiastic reports for the public. Press versions of the war contrasted the modern technology of the conquerors with the barbarism of their opponents and continually emphasised the loftiness of Britain's motives. The invasion of the Sudan was a crusade for civilisation and vengeance for the death of Gordon.

Public interest in the war intensified during the winter of 1897–8 as more British troops were sent out at Kitchener's request in readiness for a final, decisive battle with the Khalifah's main army, believed to be 60,000-strong. The government expected a victory and was already contemplating the future political settlement of the Sudan. Salisbury put aside his reservations about the burden of governing a profitless and vast province, and accepted that British occupation of the entire Sudan was inevitable. He approved a counterstroke to Marchand's expedition at the end of 1897 when Major J. R. L. Macdonald was instructed to advance northwards along the White Nile from Uganda with a force of Sudanese askaris. His purpose was to forestall a meeting between Marchand and another French detachment, which was wrongly imagined to be travelling from Ethiopia to the

Muscle power:
Egyptian labourers unload supplies from a Nile steamer during the 1898 advance of Khartoum.
(© NAM)

river. There was no collision; at the outset of Marchand's expedition most of the Sudanese mutinied and the campaign was abandoned.

Further north, Kitchener was making steady progress with an army of 7,500 British and 12,500 Egyptian troops, supported by a flotilla of river gunboats. The climax of the war came on 2 September 1898 on a plain near Omdurman where the Khalifah's army delivered a sequence of frontal attacks. All were repelled by long-range rifle, machine-gun and artillery fire which killed 11,000 ansars and wounded a further 16,000. It was tantamount to a massacre which, more than any other encounter between European and native armies, illustrated the gulf between the technology of the industrialised powers and that of their opponents in Africa and Asia. The difference was summed up by Winston Churchill, then a young subaltern, and combining the duties of a staff officer with those of war correspondent. On first seeing the ansar host with its banners, mailed

cavalry and masses of spear- and swordsmen, he immediately recalled pictures he had seen of twelfth-century Crusader armies.

Two rulers, one country: Abbas II, the Egyptian khedive (mounted centre) reviews his army in the company of its British officers (far right), 1901. (© NAM)

The day after Omdurman, the British and Egyptian flags were ceremonially raised over the ruins of the governor-general's palace in Khartoum, and a memorial service was held for its last occupant, Gordon. A Catholic chaplain prayed that God might 'look down … with eyes of pity and compassion on this land so loved by that heroic soul'. There was no sign of divine mercy on the battlefield where, much to Churchill's disgust, Kitchener had left the wounded ansars to die. Inside Khartoum there was looting with Kitchener leading the way. At the same time, many of the Khalifah's leading followers were summarily shot, some at the orders of Major, later General Sir John Maxwell, who commented afterwards that he regarded 'a dead fanatic as the only one to extend any sympathy to'. As commander-in-chief in Ireland in 1916, he applied the same principle to Irish nationalists after the Easter Rising.

Accounts of the outrages at Omdurman and Khartoum provoked a group of MPs to take the unprecedented step of opposing the payment of a £30,000 reward to Kitchener for his work in the Sudan. There were acerbic exchanges over his exhumation of the Mahdi's bones, which he had had thrown into the Nile, after having briefly considered having the skull mounted as a cup. One Tory MP, a former officer, pooh-poohed the allegations of inhumanity, and reminded the House that 'we are bringing into the Dark Continent Civilisation' and it was 'a fatal thing to get in the way of a nation that is fulfilling its destiny'. 'Murder, rapine, whisky and – the Bible' were the ingredients of this civilisation, retorted an Irish Nationalist, Michael Dillon, while a Liberal asserted that 'imperialism is nothing but organised selfishness'. The debate, like others of its kind, may have served as a warning to commanders not to jettison the rules of civilised conduct whenever they waged the wars of civilisation, but the vote went Kitchener's way and he got his cash.

He contributed some of it to the Gordon Memorial College at Khartoum, his brainchild and a visible symbol of Britain's civilising mission. Among the other subscribers to this institution were the machine-gun manufacturers, Vickers Son and Maxim, who had done as much as anyone to facilitate the triumph of civilisation in the Sudan.

Defeat:
Colonel Wingate chats with the captured Dervish emir, Mahmud, after the battle of Atbara (1898); Mahmud wears the patched jibbah which symbolised the poverty of the Madhist ansar. Afterwards he was tried and executed by the Anglo-Egyptian authorities.
(© NAM)

The political future of the Sudan was sealed after the capture of Khartoum; henceforward the province would be governed jointly by Britain and Egypt through a British governor-general. There remained the problem of Marchand, whose presence at Fashoda had been revealed by Mahdist prisoners. The commander-in-chief had been given secret orders on how to proceed if he encountered French intruders in the southern Sudan. They were to be evicted, but without the direct use of force. Privately, Kitchener thought that Marchand's escapade was not to be taken seriously, but when he met the Frenchman he treated him courteously, and, tactfully, had the Egyptian rather than the British flag hoisted over Fashoda. Faced with firmness and overwhelming force, Marchand withdrew, believing that he had upheld his own and his country's honour.

An international row followed between Britain and France. Checkmated and humiliated at Fashoda, the French government accused Britain of flouting its rights in the southern Sudan and bullying its representative there. Britain rejected these charges and insisted that France possessed no claim whatsoever to any portion of the Upper Nile. The public, which was both elated by the victory at Omdurman and displeased by recent concessions in the Far East, backed the government's unbending policy. A stand had to be made over Fashoda because Britain's rivals would certainly interpret any compromise as evidence of irresolution and would be encouraged to challenge British power elsewhere.

Britain's imperial will appeared unshakeable and France stepped down. She had little choice, for her people were divided by the Dreyfus scandal and her ally, Russia, refused to become entangled in a dispute over Africa. Moreover, as the French Foreign Minister Delcassé appreciated, British naval superiority would make any war an unequal contest, with France's overseas trade suffering damage similar to that inflicted by Britain during the eighteenth century. He also had the wisdom to realise that by turning Britain into an enemy, perhaps even an ally of Germany, France's power in Europe would be undermined.

Having emerged the winner of the struggle for the Nile, Britain and its partner, Egypt, had to confront the task of pacifying and ruling a huge and still largely unexplored region, inhabited by people who had hitherto known little or no outside government. There was also the Khalifah who, with a force of about 10,000 ansars, had fled south after Omdurman. He was finally run to earth in November 1899 and defeated at the battle of Umm Diwaykarat. Apparently having learnt nothing from Omdurman, the ansars again threw themselves into the killing zone created by rifle and machine-gun fire and were cut down in hundreds. It would not be too far-fetched to see this engagement, like its forerunner at Omdurman, as a form of mass suicide by men who preferred death to submission to the new, infidel order. The Khalifah certainly possessed the means partly to redress the military imbalance, since he had carefully preserved the modern weaponry captured during the 1884–5 campaigns. Equally extraordinary was the failure of British commanders to understand the significance of what they had witnessed during the Sudan campaign. Major, later Field Marshal Lord Haig saw for himself the devastating effects of modern firepower at Omdurman and yet, as commander-in-chief on the Western Front between 1915 and 1918, he sanctioned offensives in which British troops faced the same odds as the Dervishes.

There were sporadic Mahdist and pan-Islamic insurrections for nearly twenty years after Omdurman. The most threatening was in 1916 and led by Ali Dinar, the semi-autonomous Sultan of Darfur, who hoped for but did not receive Turko-German assistance. British propaganda dismissed him as insane, a diagnosis that was extended to nearly every Muslim who rejected British rule in Africa and Asia. Muhammad Abdille Hassan, who persistently resisted the British in Somaliland between 1898 and 1920, was called the 'Mad Mullah', and there were other 'mad' faquirs and mullahs on the North-West Frontier. Their excesses do not appear to have matched those of Ali Dinar who, Sir Reginald Wingate confided to an American newsman, had once forced a mother to eat her own baby. It is not known whether the journalist asked why the British had tolerated the presence of this monster in Darfur for the past eighteen years.

It took over thirty years to subdue the animist tribes of the southern Sudan who objected to the naturally unwelcome novelty of taxation, and refused to renounce such customs as stock rustling and inter-tribal feuds. Thirty-three punitive expeditions were needed to persuade the tribesmen of the remote Nuba Mountains to accept the new order. No newspapermen accompanied the small detachments, and so the public remained ignorant about what occurred during these campaigns, which was just as well for the authorities in Khartoum and Cairo. 'The less attention is drawn to these matters the better,' observed Lord Cromer after he had read a report of the summary public hangings that had followed the suppression of a small uprising in the Sudan in 1908. Another form of deterrent was applied in 1928 when a party of Dinka and Guer chiefs were treated to an exhibition of machine-gun and artillery fire during a visit to Khartoum.

Gordon's avenger and national saviour: Field-Marshal Lord Kitchener of Khartoum. After his Sudanese campaign, he took command in South Africa and, between 1914 and his death in 1916, was the architect of Britain's new army. (Collection of A. V. Williams)

Impatient and exasperated officials often resorted to more forceful methods of coercion. During the 1917–18 operations in the Nuba Mountains, villages and crops were burned, and tribesmen and their families driven into the bush to die of thirst. At Wingate's suggestion, aircraft had been brought from Egypt to bomb and strafe Ali Dinar's army, and thereafter they were often deployed against tribes in the deep south of the Sudan. The results were horrendous; in February 1920 incendiary bombs were dropped to start bush fires and flush out Nuer warriors, and they and their herds of cattle were regularly bombed and machine-gunned.

The official justification for these harsh measures was that they brought stability to remote and turbulent districts. And yet there was something profoundly incongruous and distasteful about the employment of aircraft to intimidate people whom Britain claimed she wished to regenerate. Administrators, who had been taught to believe in their country's civilising mission and who dedicated their lives to its fulfilment, were ashamed of what was euphemistically called 'air control'. It was suspended after 1930, although flights continued over potentially disaffected areas as a reminder of what lay in store for the insubordinate. The brief resort to air power as a means of punishment revealed, as did the episodes that followed the fall of Khartoum, the gulf which separated the lofty, humanitarian ideals of British imperialism and the methods of its agents.

8

THE GREATEST
BLESSING THAT
AFRICA HAS KNOWN:
EAST AND
WEST AFRICA

There were two 'scrambles' for Africa during the 1880s and 1890s. The first was a sedate, although sometimes acrimonious, diplomatic game in which statesmen pored over maps and drew lines across them. The second was a more robust business in which individuals ventured into largely unknown hostile regions and cajoled or coerced their inhabitants into accepting new masters and new laws. This activity was confined to a handful of men whose fixity of purpose gave them the strength to endure extremes of discomfort and danger. One described Africa as 'a training ground for young men' with a taste for reckless adventure for, 'once started on *safari* – i.e. the line of march in Africa, one never knows where it may lead to, nor does one very much care.' Some did; for Kitchener and his equally ambitious French counterparts,

Palava:
Sir Gilbert Carter,
governor of Lagos, and
his staff with the ruler
of Abeokuta. Behind
stand Hausa troops, 1893.
(© F & CO)

Joseph Simon Gallieni and Joseph Jacques Joffre (the conqueror of Timbuktu), the byways of Africa led to the highest commands in the First World War. Others, like Louis Hubert Lyautey, Wingate and Frederick, later Lord Lugard, stepped sideways and became senior proconsuls.

Lugard set his stamp on East and West Africa. He was a tough, lean officer with a straggling walrus moustache, which was exceptionally extravagant at a time when no self-respecting fighting man went bare-lipped in the tropics. Kitchener's growth may have been more famous, but Lugard's was more striking. It helped give him, and other bristly officers, a fearsome appearance, which may have been advantageous when he had to overawe natives. In 1887 Lugard, with three campaigns under his belt, was at a loose end. Having been diagnosed by his physician as exhausted, he decided, 'What I needed was active hard work – rather than rest.' Africa would provide his cure, and his sword was accepted by the missionary Lakes Company. During 1888 and 1889 Lugard commanded their levies in a war against slavers around the shores of Lake Nyasa.

He liked the way the Scottish missionaries ran their affairs and he learned much from them. The neat, clean mission houses and the schools with their tidy, well-dressed pupils were an 'object lesson' in European civilisation. White men in Africa, Lugard concluded, should always stick to a separate way of life that was an 'assertion of superiority which commands the respect and excites the emulation of the savage'. 'Insolent familiarity' by blacks was never to be tolerated and would be rebuffed by a 'gentleman'. Like the British lower classes, the African instinctively recognised and respected a 'gentleman' and followed his lead.

This opinion was widely shared by British officers and administrators. The gallant, public school-educated British officer, who commanded by force of character and innate self-confidence, could secure the loyalty of simpleminded black men who recognised him as a true warrior. Sporting prowess, particularly the singlehanded stalking of big game, added to the appeal of the British officer. In an intelligence report of 1906 on German East Africa a British official noted that, 'The Germans never move off the roads, they don't care for sport, and have no idea of the word as used by the British.' Moreover, they hunted in a distinctly ungentlemanly manner, ordering askaris to fire volleys at elephants, rhinoceroses and buffalo. French colonial officers, like the British, imagined they had an interior quality which won them the hearts of natives. This was baraka, an inner spiritual charisma possessed by Muslim holy men which brought luck. The officer with baraka had, quite literally, a charmed life and appeared miraculously preserved in battle; it was General Franco's baraka which saved his life in battles in Morocco in the 1920s and won him the loyalty of Moroccan troops.

East Africa in the Nineteenth Century

African allies:
*Chief Will Braide, his
ministers and bodyguard.
The chief has acquired a
European-style cocked hat
and the soldier on the far
left wears a skirt with a
tartan design, perhaps
cotton imported from
Lancashire, 1899.
(© Unilever)*

Liquid assets:
*Ibo women carry
containers of palm oil
for the Royal Niger
Company, 1901.
(© Unilever)*

Survival in Africa needed physical as well as moral stamina. Lugard devised his own eccentric, but, as events turned out, effective regimen for daily life in the tropics. He wore a broad-brimmed hat and drank large amounts of weak tea or water, often indifferent as to the latter's source. For Lugard the vital organs were the stomach, spleen and liver, which he kept covered with a flannel cummerbund at all times since their chilling was the cause of 'most of the fever, dysentery, diarrhoea and cholera' which laid men low in Africa. A substantial breakfast, taken just after sunrise, prevented fever which could arise from the sun overheating an empty stomach. When this precaution failed and he contracted fever, Lugard took doses of quinine and buried himself under a pile of clothing to sweat it out. These rough and ready nostrums appear to have worked successfully.

Healthy exercise further reinforced the white man's constitution. Lieutenant Richard Meinertzhagen, posted to the King's African Rifles in Kenya in 1902, recommended 'vigorous hunting', which not only tested 'manliness', but developed bushcraft and marksmanship. Not everyone was so dedicated; he observed disapprovingly that while he stretched nerves and muscles 'many of my brother officers were drinking rot-gut or running about with somebody else's wife'. But this was to be expected in a mess which contained homosexuals and men who boasted about their native mistresses.

Self-discipline and a stringent régime kept Lugard fit and enabled him to play a crucial part in the remaking of East and West Africa. Between 1889 and 1893, he was employed by the British Imperial East Africa Company, first to establish a military presence in its territory by building stockades and making treaties with native rulers, with whom he sometimes made pacts of blood brotherhood. Later he was a peace-keeper, suppressing slavery and intervening for the Protestants in a civil war between them and Catholic converts in Uganda.

Lugard was profoundly affected by what he saw as he traversed East Africa. The region was collapsing into anarchy from which it could only be rescued by Britain:

> *The African knows no peace. One day you may see peace and plenty, well-tilled fields, and children playing in the sun; on the next you may find the corpses of the men, the bodies of the children half burnt in the flames which consumed the village, while the women are captives of the victorious raiders. Not against the slave-trade alone are our efforts needed ... The* Pax Britannica *which shall stop this lawless raiding and this constant inter-tribal war will be the greatest blessing that Africa has known since the Flood.*

Such descriptions of the uncertainty and violence of African life were the stock-in-trade of the first-hand accounts of the continent which appeared in late-Victorian Britain. Readers were introduced to a land of contrasts in which all that was good was of European origin and all that was bad was of African. For instance, two eyewitness descriptions of Nigeria, published in the 1890s, refer to 'vile pagan customs', 'wild lawless people' and a 'kingdom of darkness'. One author was struck by the coastal town of Bonny where the cleanness and order of the missionary settlement highlighted the grossness and depravity of the native township, where, ironically, the streets were littered with discarded bottles of 'trader gin'. Like the mission tracts of an earlier generation, such material provided a call to duty; the British people had to give their wholehearted support to men like Lugard, who had shouldered what Kipling called 'the white man's burden'. It was appropriate that his employer, the British Imperial East Africa Company, set its device of a lightbulb on their postage stamps: it symbolised modernity and bringing light to a benighted region.

Lugard had developed his own views on how enlightenment should be spread in Africa, based on his experiences there and as a soldier in India. He wanted government along the lines that had evolved in India in which the administration would be impartial, firm, and respect local institutions and conventions. 'An arbitrary and despotic rule, which takes no account of native customs, traditions and prejudices,' he wrote, 'is not suited to the successful development of infant civilisation nor, in my view, in accordance with the spirit of British colonial rule.' He had in mind the Indian practice of indirect rule by which Britain had adopted and sometimes adjusted existing political structures and cooperated with established rulers. It was an attractive alternative to the infinitely more expensive and wearisome process of creating an entirely new system of government, which was bound to provoke upheavals and resentment.

The Bonny army: an improvised force armed with spears and outdated flintlocks under British officers: troops of this sort served as auxiliaries for the Royal Niger Company. (© Unilever)

This theory was not of course new but, as applied by Lugard to Africa, proved very influential. There, as elsewhere, Britain entered into an alliance of convenience with local rulers who, in return for concessions such as the extirpation of slavery, were allowed to continue in positions of authority so long as they exercised their power in a manner approved by British advisers. By the early 1920s schools had been set up in East Africa where chiefs' sons were educated for future responsibility. At these and other government schools, boys and girls wore a uniform based upon African rather than European dress, which had once been *de rigueur* for an African seeking a European-style education. In some areas, missionaries were adapting pagan initiation rites so that the traditional period of preparation for circumcision became one in which the youth learned the virtues of Christian 'manliness'.

Money-making as well as civilising had been a function of the British Imperial East Africa Company. The two were not as compatible as they had once been in India, and by 1891 the company was tottering on the verge of bankruptcy. The upshot was that Uganda and British East Africa (Kenya), which had fallen to Britain's lot after the 1890 agreement with Germany, passed into Foreign and then Colonial Office control. The misfortunes of the company were evidence that claims that Africa offered an unlimited outlet for British manufactures were overblown. They had, however, helped provide the original impetus for African colonisation and had given hope to British businessmen trapped in a recession. The *Leeds Mercury* of 28 February 1885 had predicted that Africa would become a 'vast market' for 'cotton goods, blankets, crockery, muskets [this was true enough], hardware of all kinds, and cheap finery of every description'. But how were the Africans to pay for all these goods?

This irritating question was ignored during the optimistic period when Africa was being opened up, but it returned to trouble governments and businessmen at the turn of the century, by which time everyone was wiser about the actual conditions on the continent. Outside South Africa there were no

Benevolent imperialism: government school at Bonny, Nigeria, 1907. (© Unilever)

Full steam ahead:
the line is cleared for
an East African railway
train, somewhere
between Mombasa and
Nairobi, c.1910.
(© PRO)

King Solomon's mines. An economic revolution was clearly needed to create customers and, given that nearly all of them were under foreign government, the change would have to be imposed from above. A favourite metaphor of the 1890s, and one used by Chamberlain, was that the colonies were outlying 'estates' which, through careful management and investment, could be made profitable both to their owner and their inhabitants. This process was, however, complicated by the fact that the Colonial Office had inherited and cherished the old liberal tradition that it and its agents were trustees for gullible and child-like native populations, who needed protection from the unscrupulous and from each other.

At the same time, current economic orthodoxy insisted that capital investment in any enterprise was the task of individuals, not governments. There had been considerable opposition to demands by the British Imperial East Africa Company for a subsidy to help fund a railway from Mombasa to the shores of the Indian Ocean, which would both serve as a conduit for trade and tighten Britain's grip on the source of the White Nile. In 1896, Chamberlain recognised the line's potential and agreed to underwrite some of its costs. By 1913, when the arrangement ended, the British government had paid £2.8 million in grants for the development of East Africa.

The railway was completed in 1903 and five years later was making a respectable annual profit of £60,000. By this time the economic development of Kenya was well underway, the local authorities having, in 1903, agreed to set aside a huge upland region of temperate climate and fertile soil for white settlement. Agriculture, practised by Europeans using modern methods, offered the only means of making the region self-supporting and, incidentally, of helping make the railway pay. As in Southern Rhodesia, land on either side of the track was reserved for Europeans who therefore had easy access to transport and outside markets.

Richard Meinertzhagen encountered one of the first white pioneers in Nairobi in 1902, and heard from him that in Kenya 'the white man is the master race and that the black man must forever remain cheap labour and slaves'. It was a view which, in various and often less trenchant forms, was held by successive settlers. In 1916 they numbered 8,000 and included a sprinkling of Boers who had trekked up from South Africa, bringing with them the racial attitudes of their homeland. Matters were further complicated in East Africa by another consequence of economic changes, the presence of Indians. They had been shipped there as indentured labourers to help build the railway, and afterwards settled as shopkeepers and clerks; they were also undertaking skilled work for which there were no qualified Africans. By 1920, there were 23,000 Indians in Kenya squeezed between 10,000 whites, mostly settlers and their families, and nearly three million Africans.

The colonial government faced a dilemma. Although no money-spinning staple such as cotton, sugar or tobacco had emerged to provide an early boost for the Kenyan economy, coffee- and maize-growing and ranching were flourishing and the 1914–19 war in East Africa had provided a welcomed impetus for growth. In the latter year there were two million acres earmarked for white farmers, and the government was extensively advertising a scheme to attract British ex-officers to invest their gratuities in Kenyan farms. Private capital was essential for the Kenyan settler, as it had been for his North American predecessor (£2,000 was considered the minimum in 1919), and he needed abundant, cheap labour.

Since the start of white colonisation, the colonial authorities had had to concoct ways in which to push sections of the black population towards regular wage-earning and the market economy. The annual Hut Tax of three rupees (20p) a hut, with a further three rupees per wife for hut-owners with more than one, and a poll tax of three rupees for every adult non-householder, forced Africans to seek cash. Kenya also adopted in 1918 a measure that had its origins in South Africa, and which had been copied in Southern Rhodesia and Nyasaland, by which blacks were banned from living in areas set aside for Europeans unless they undertook to work for the owner.

Unskilled labour for Europeans was at this period highly unpopular for understandable reasons. For years the prevailing wisdom had been that the reason why most Africans kept out of the Western economy was ingrained laziness. Hard work for regular hours appeared not to come naturally to them, nor did they appreciate its moral value. An explorer who had crossed East Africa in 1884 with a party of unwilling porters, congratulated himself on his return for having driven them forcefully, for they had come back 'as men, with their moral and physical defects cast off'. Lugard, faced with malingerers among his porters, dosed them with a mixture of water, salt and mustard, which one, who was cured, pronounced 'a very fierce medicine'. A more common astringent was the sjambok, a rhino-hide whip which was commonly used on black miners at the Wankie colliery in Southern Rhodesia during the early 1900s. It had been a frequent form of punishment for insubordinate black labourers during the Boer War, and in November 1914 the commander of HMS *Dartmouth* at Cape Town asked Admiralty permission to flog striking Arab and Indian lascars, on the grounds that no other correction would have any effect.

Lord Cranworth, in his guidebook for would-be farmers in Kenya published in 1919, warned against too many beatings; but for offences such as lying, petty pilfering, cruelty to children and animals, 'the whip is the best and kindest preventive and cure'. Lady Cranworth, counselling the new settler's wife, strongly recommended regular inspections of the kitchen, a disagreeable chore which invariably ended with 'a feeling of soreness on the part, the posterior part, of the cook'. It appears that Swahili (part African, part Arab) and native cooks were never fastidious about washing utensils.

Not surprisingly, given their needs, a substantial minority of Kenyan settlers favoured a union with South Africa, whose government would, they believed, treat them more sympathetically than the Colonial Office. Despite regular polo and soccer matches between teams of officials and farmers, tension remained high. It reached breaking point in 1921 after the announcement that Indian representatives were to be added to the governor's council. This measure was interpreted as a step towards a multi-racial Kenya in which the outnumbered settlers might soon find their interests overridden.

A resistance movement sprang up and there was heady talk of rebellion. The man of the moment was Brigadier-General Philip Wheatley, an ex-officer in the Indian army with a hearty dislike of Indian

West Africa in the Nineteenth Century

nationalism, whose blustering, extreme right-wing views made him a living prototype of David Low's cartoon figure, Colonel Blimp. Kenya was a natural sanctuary for Blimps, and they rallied round Wheatley and concocted a hare-brained plan for a settlers' *coup d'état* with the slogan 'For King and Kenya'. What in many respects was a trailer for the unilateral declaration of independence by Rhodesia in 1964, turned out to be a damp squib with the settlers pulling back at the last moment. The episode did provoke the Colonial Office to issue a white paper in 1922 that set out official policy in an unambiguous manner: 'Primarily Kenya is an African territory' in which 'the interests of the African natives must be paramount'.

West Africa was also a black man's country. It was an inhospitable region where a combination of humidity, heat and a febriferous coastline combined to give it the notorious reputation of 'the white man's grave'. In the late eighteenth century convicted criminals were sentenced to undertake garrison duty there as a form of delayed death sentence, and during most of the nineteenth, the mortality rate among troops in Sierra Leone was the highest in the empire. Advances in medical knowledge increased a European's chances of survival, but in the years immediately before the First World War, officials in the Gold Coast were expected to spend no more than twelve months there before being sent on leave. Their colleagues in Northern Nigeria did eighteen-month stints and, one observed, they counted themselves unlucky if they had more than three bouts of fever in a year.

For most of the nineteenth century, Britain's West African colonies were derelict outposts. The Gambia and Gold Coast settlements were relics of the slave-trading era, no longer of economic value, but Sierra Leone, a major coaling station for the Royal Navy, was a glowing example of what could be achieved by black men and women with a Christian education. A visitor in 1898 found it a 'most terrifically civilised place', even though the sight of black people going to church in European clothes, which would have so pleased earlier philanthropists, struck him as 'grotesque'. Lagos, acquired in 1861 as a base for anti-slaving operations and a toehold in Nigeria, was the only part of this region to attract British commerce.

A German cartoonist's impressions of the different styles of colonisation in Africa:

RIGHT *The German: discipline and regimentation.*

OPPOSITE TOP *The British: whisky, exploitation and conversion.*

OPPOSITE CENTRE *The French: seduction.*

OPPOSITE BELOW *The Belgian: brutality and extortion.*

So kolonisiert der Deutsche,

The magnet here was palm oil, a vital commodity for British industry which used it as a lubricant and the basis for making soap and candles. The profitable trade in palm oil was dominated by Liverpool entrepreneurs whose interests were guarded by a network of consuls, backed by intermittent naval patrols, some of which penetrated the Niger and Benue rivers. The natives here and elsewhere in West Africa were enthusiastic consumers of 'trader gin', a noxious but potent narcotic; in 1889 1.35 million gallons were imported into Nigeria and, despite protests from temperance and missionary groups in Britain, the flow steadily increased. In 1908 the total West African gin trade was worth £1.2 million, with nearly 90 per cent going to Nigeria. So long as palm oil poured out of Nigeria and gin poured in, Britain had no interest whatsoever in acquiring additional territory there or elsewhere in West Africa. Until the early 1880s, it was a region where the machinery of informal empire functioned more or less effectively. If a local ruler proved obstructive, as did Kofi, Asantehene of the Asante ('King Coffee'), in 1873, a small but well-armed military force delivered a rap over the knuckles.

This local equilibrium was upset by France. From the mid-1870s a small, highly motivated clique of French soldiers and politicians became entranced by the idea of creating a sprawling empire, which would stretch from West Africa across the western Sahara. This province might prove another India, enriching France and enhancing its status in the world, which had been diminished by the humiliations of the Franco-Prussian War. The key to the region's economic exploitation was thought to be a railway that would cross from West Africa to the Red Sea, never leaving French soil, and which would serve as a conduit for the entire trade of Africa north of the Sahara. The inspiration for this trans-continental railway was the American Union Pacific Railroad, which had been completed in 1869 and was currently opening up the West. Rhodes had also recognised the potential of a railway bisecting Africa and, from the 1890s, planned a Cape to Cairo line which would, needless to say, run across British territory.

The French took their first steps towards a West African empire in the late 1870s. The impetus came from two highly placed imperialists, Admiral Jean de Jauréguiberry, the Minister for Marine, and Charles de Freycinet, a railway enthusiast, who was Minister for Public Works. They approved probes inland from Senegal, while the gunboat *Voltigeur* was ordered into Nigerian waters to make contact with and extract treaties from local chiefs. Simultaneously the explorer Savorgnan de Brazza was making agreements with rulers in the Congo basin. Confronted with trespassers in regions hitherto under the loose control of Britain, British consuls started to collect treaties.

So kolonisiert der Engländer,

So der Franzose

These pledges were ammunition for British and French statesmen and diplomats to whom fell the task of haggling over who had what. Britain's main fear was that the protectionist French would obtain swathes of the West African hinterland, which would leave the Gambia, Sierra Leone and the Gold Coast as stranded coastal colonies without any inland trade. Furthermore, France might secure the Upper Niger and so strangle the trade that passed down the river from northern Nigeria and the western Sudan. British commercial interests got some safeguards from the settlement made at Berlin during 1885: Britain was allowed a sphere of influence which stretched up the Niger and inland from the Gold Coast.

The British government now faced the problem of giving substance to its authority over paper protectorates. It was, as in southern and eastern Africa, lucky to find a private corporation that was willing to undertake what otherwise was a tiresome and costly business. The Royal Niger Company was chartered in 1886 to trade and govern along the lower and mid-Niger. The company was the creation of George Taubman Goldie, a Manxman who had, until 1877, led a directionless life as a diffident professional soldier and wanderer. In that year he visited the Niger coast and saw the chance to make his mark on the world. A childhood worshipper of Rajah Brooke, Goldie later claimed that, 'My dream as a child was to colour the map red,' and there is no reason to disbelieve him. In Nigeria he found a convenient blank and, like Brooke, he had the cash to fulfil his ambitions. Within a few years he had organised the local merchants and laid the foundations for his own company.

During the late 1880s and early 1890s, there were plenty of Goldies, and for that matter Lugards among the young French officers who were pursuing pro-motion and medals in West Africa. Their collective motto was '*Prenez l'initiative*', even if that meant, and it often did, ignoring orders from hesitant bureaucrats in Paris. By the early 1890s, the French conquest of West Africa and the western Sahara had entered a decisive phase, with the momentum sustained by soldiers

und so der Belgier.

Tea party:
British officials and
their wives take tea
while curious Nigerians
watch, 1905.
(© NAM)

convinced that they knew better than their masters, one of whom once remarked that colonial commanders constituted what was in effect an independent state, answerable to no one. Perhaps so, but politicians were wary of asserting authority over the French army which, in right-wing, ultra-nationalist circles was seen as the embodiment of the country's honour.

French aggression in West Africa had never unduly troubled Salisbury, who sardonically questioned the ultimate value of vast areas of 'light soil', his euphemism for sand. This view was quietly held by many in France, and was reflected in the failure of the projected trans-Saharan railway to attract any investment. It was less easy, however, for British ministers to dismiss France's West African adventures after 1894, when it had become plain that they might end with the seizure of the Upper Niger. Goldie had been among the first to sense the danger, and in July 1894 he hired Lugard to lead a small expedition deep into northern Nigeria and negotiate treaties which would bring its rulers into Britain's orbit. Almost simultaneously, Captain Decouer had been commissioned to proceed from Dahomey into the same area and for the same purpose, and there was a rumour that the Germans were also preparing an expedition.

Lugard's treaty-gathering trek through Borgu during the autumn and early winter of 1894 was a superhuman feat of perseverance. He and his party endured extremes of temperature (his dog died of heat exhaustion), torrential rain, an ambush and bouts of fever. Lugard overcame the latter by self-medication in the form of a course of antipyrin and a thirteen-mile march in the blazing sun, which produced a curative sweat. Native medicines, whose ingredients he did not investigate too closely, provided an apparent antidote to poison from an arrowhead which had pierced his skull. Lugard deserved and got what he wanted, an agreement in which the aged and decrepit King of Nikki accepted the protection and friendship of Britain and its agent, the Royal Niger Company. The trouble was that just over a fortnight later Decoeur arrived at Nikki and went away, like Lugard, with a treaty.

The Upper Niger now became a focus for Anglo-French rivalry. The chief protagonists were Chamberlain, who became Colonial Secretary in June 1895, and Gabriel Hanotaux, who took over France's Foreign Ministry in April 1896. Chamberlain refused on principle to relinquish an inch of African territory to which Britain had a legal claim, while Hanotaux sought to prevent Africa from becoming another India in which French ambitions were checked by a combination of British guile and bullying. The British, he believed, used their language as a cover for deception ('*elle affirme, elle n'explique pas*') and therefore France would have to resort to action to get her way rather than waste time on otiose negotiations over the validity of treaties. Only Marchand on the banks of the Nile and Senegalese *tirailleurs* on the banks of the Niger would stop Britain in her tracks.

Britain was first off the mark in the confrontation on the Niger. With Chamberlain's blessing, Goldie launched a war against Bida and Ilorin, whose rulers had refused to fulfil their promises to abandon slave-raiding. The campaign of January 1897 was not just a humanitarian crusade, it was a fearsome demonstration of the military power of the company and Britain. A twelve-pounder gun was manhandled, with considerable difficulty, through the bush to hurl shells against the walls of Bida at a range of two miles. But what really struck terror into the spearmen and mailed cavalry were the company's six Maxim guns, the 'bindigat ruiva' (water guns) or 'piss guns'. They enabled an army of 500 men, mostly Hausa constabulary, to beat a medieval horde, believed to outnumber them by thirty to one.

Goldie's little war alerted the French to British intentions, and during 1896–7 advance parties of their colonial forces filtered into Borgu, where *tricolores* were hoisted over native villages and old treaties waved about as proof that they were now French property. Chamberlain foresaw a collision, and began taking precautions. In June 1897 he proposed the immediate formation of a 2,000-strong black army, the West Africa Frontier Force, and appointed Lugard its commander and Britain's special commissioner for northern Nigeria. Obviously Lugard's experience counted, but Chamberlain was also making a gesture designed to show the French that Britain was going to take a tough line. In France, Lugard was detested on account of his alleged massacre of Catholic converts in Uganda and, more recently, his coup at Nikki. When Lugard arrived in Nigeria in the spring of 1898, *The Times* reported that for Frenchmen he 'symbolised … the fierce and grasping spirit of perfidious Albion. He is for them the stuff of which legends are made.'

A comedy of manners rather than a legend emerged from the Anglo-French stand-off in Borgu during the summer of 1898. Lugard had officered the West Africa Frontier Force with men of his own kidney, all of whom could have stepped from the pages of a G. A. Henty yarn. They were young, ex-public-school boys with a love of sport and taste for adventure. Field command was in the hands of Colonel James Willcocks, another sportsman and veteran of several Indian campaigns. It was he who set out from Jebba into Borgu where, at Lugard's instructions, he was to hoist the Union Jack wherever he thought fit, taking care to avoid villages over which the *tricolore* was already flying.

Africa partioned, 1914

There followed a bizarre charade in which British units sidestepped French villages and occasionally collided with French detachments. There were some wrangles, usually about such niceties of protocol as saluting flags, but the prevailing mood on both sides was one of nervous good humour. International rivalries were forgotten as professional empire-builders discovered, over drinks and cigarettes by a campfire, that they had much in common as soldiers and gentlemen.

There were a few fire-eaters on both sides, including some of the native troops, who yearned for a fight. The French position was, in fact, precarious, since their rule was still being resisted in other parts of West Africa. During the confrontation on the Niger, troops had had to be hurried to the Ivory Coast to deal with Samory Touré, France's most tenacious adversary in West Africa, and to suppress an uprising in Soudan (Mali). Furthermore, as Lugard appreciated, a shooting war on the Niger would leave the French isolated throughout the region since the navy would blockade their West African ports.

Throughout the crisis, Chamberlain remained in full control as the telegraph line had been extended from Lagos to Jebba so that the men-on-the-spot could not take matters into their own hands. It was diplomatic camel-trading that finally ended the confrontation and Britain, who got the best of the deal, secured Borgu and with it all the territory which now lies within the boundaries of modern Nigeria. All that remained was for Chamberlain to tie up the administrative loose ends. Lagos and the coastal Oil Rivers Protectorate were amalgamated in 1900 as Southern Nigeria, the company was abolished, and its territories passed into the government of the new colony of Northern Nigeria, whose first governor was Lugard.

Similar consolidation occurred in Sierra Leone and the Gold Coast where, boundaries having been fixed with the French, pacification followed. Regions where British control had hitherto been fitful or non-existent were brought to heel. In 1887, at the conclusion of a campaign against the Yonni of Sierra Leone, the British commander told their chiefs, 'The Queen has shown you her power by sending her force and taking the country, which now belongs to me and the governor.' The message was punched home with a demonstration of Maxim-gun fire which 'much surprised' them. It took two expeditions, in 1895 and 1900, to convince the Asante of the strength and permanence of the new order in the Gold Coast. The last was a particularly brutal affair in which British officers had the utmost difficulty in restraining their native troops, who seemed to have regarded the campaign as a licence to plunder and rape.

As the terrifying lessons of conquest sank in, the conquerors often found it easy to overawe their new subjects. When Captain George Abadie arrived in Ilorin a year after Goldie's campaign, he found its people submissive, and remarked on 'two very hot and dirty, begrimed, badly clothed Englishmen dictating to a crowd of about six hundred Muhammadans, all big swells, and kicking them out.' A clue to their reaction was soon revealed; when Abadie set up his camera to photograph the local prince, his attendants fled at the sight of the tripod which reminded them of the mounting for a machine-gun.

British social attitudes were exported to Africa, where the orthodoxy that the government of naïve native peoples was best entrusted to gentlemen was already taking root. Lieutenant Ladislaus Pope-Hennessey took an instant dislike to the colonial government officials, who were all 'bounders' and 'cads' addicted to 'cocktails', a novelty which the young officer found distasteful. Lugard shared these prejudices and feared that the conduct of men who were not gentlemen lowered respect for all white men.

He and Goldie had separately discovered 'gentlemen' among the Fulani Muslim princes of central and northern Nigeria and were impressed by their sophistication, bearing and the orderly procedures of their law courts and administration. Here were men with whom the British could cooperate, and Islamic institutions could be adopted to suit British needs. The first preliminary was the by now ritual trial of strength which occurred between 1902 and 1904, when the states of Sokoto and Kano were invaded and their armies defeated by Lugard.

Resistance from the ruling élite ceased, but there was a sudden upsurge of popular opposition to the British in February 1905 under the banner of Mahdist millennialism. The followers of this movement, including many slaves and ex-slaves, identified the British and French armies which had entered their

The type of English-man in the shape of the trader, whom we meet in these parts, is too awful for words to describe; they are all more-or-less counter-jumpers of the worst type and biggest bounders into the bargain.

LIEUTENANT ARCHIBALD
EDEN, 1898

country during the past decade with Baggal, an anti-Christ figure who, in Islamic eschatology, would appear before the coming of the Mahdi. The rebels surprised and overcame a British column at Satiru, capturing a slightly damaged Maxim gun, rifles and ammunition. No use was made of these spoils. Like its counterpart in the Sudan, the Nigerian Mahdist movement was backward-looking. The insurgents disdained to use the implements of modern, infidel war, relying instead on faith and traditional weaponry. In their next engagement, they adopted a mass charge and were defeated with over 2,000 dead.

The Fulani aristocracy cooperated with the British in the suppression of this uprising, which threatened their own as well as their conqueror's authority. The two were now working in tandem as Lugard had introduced the system known as 'indirect rule' or 'dual control'. He wanted to maintain a continuity of government and assure Britain's new subjects that, with the exception of slavery, Islamic practices were to be preserved and respected. Once this was clear, Muslim princes and clergy rallied behind the new order and the old courts and civil service continued to function under the eye of a British resident. This form of government suited the circumstances of Northern Nigeria for it was inexpensive and required limited manpower. An instinctive rapport developed between the princes and the conservative, public school- and university-educated administrators who were filling the ranks of the civil service during the 1900s. Interestingly, the Colonial Office recruiters preferred sportsmen, who were presumably fitter and knew how to play by the rules.

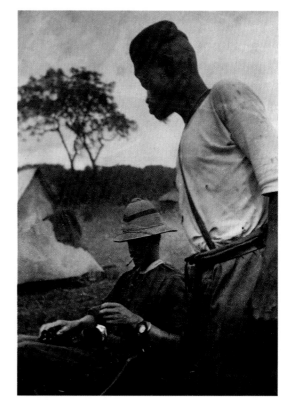

Alongside the emir and his Muslim staff was a new élite which had been created over the past forty years by British educators in Sierra Leone and southern Nigeria. Early colonial government depended on this body of literate blacks. Lugard admitted the value of such men, but insisted that they should never usurp or interfere with the functions of men whose power derived from tradition. No African clerk or constable could override the judgement of, say, a village headman. As in India, the British faced the dilemma of how to handle a class of educated natives who were vital for everyday administration, but who knew something of the outside world and the political values which obtained in it. They were not always compliant collaborators, and it is not surprising that British administrators preferred the old hierarchies.

9

YE SONS OF THE SOUTHERN CROSS:

THE WHITE DOMINIONS

In his patriotic vision, *The Poets' Pilgrimage to Waterloo*, Robert Southey wrote of 'those distant lands, where Britain blest with her redundant life the East and West'. He was thinking of Canada and Australia, which, like many of his countrymen, he saw as repositories for superfluous men and women, unwanted by reason of their poverty or criminality. This was the age of Robert Malthus, the parson-schoolmaster who devoted his life to studying the calculus of population growth, and concluded that a spiralling birth rate could only be checked by cyclical famines. This bleak prognosis was widely accepted and appeared confirmed by the starvation that followed bad harvests during the 1810s.

Emigration to Canada, Australia, South Africa and, after 1840, New Zealand offered salvation for those who might otherwise have languished and died in a homeland which could not provide for them. The government concurred and, between 1819 and 1825, allocated £95,000 in subsidies for pauper emigration. Local authorities followed suit; in 1826 the Board of Guardians of Benenden in Kent paid £14.10 shillings (£14.50p) each to twenty-seven men, women and children for their passage to New York. This was a large outlay, but it was a once and for all measure which relieved ratepayers of people who would have been a burden for many years to come. For this reason, the 1834 Poor Law included provisions for assisting poor emigrants. The 1891 Reformatory and Industrial Schools Act gave their governors the power to send delinquent children to the colonies. Private charities did likewise: the Salvation Army and Dr Barnado's paid for the passage of orphans to the colonies and, in the sixty years after 1870, 100,000 were settled in Canada alone. As in previous centuries, enforced emigration provided a solution to domestic social problems.

Most nineteenth-century emigrants were not state-funded. When they did receive help, it came from voluntary charities set up for the purpose and based upon the principles of self-help. Typical of this sort of body was the Highlands and Islands Emigration Society which assisted crofters from an economically moribund region to settle on farms in Australia during the 1850s. It was axiomatic that anyone who was industrious and thrifty would prosper in the colonies. A prospectus for the Canadian province of New Brunswick, issued in 1842, claimed that a workman there, drawing wages of between twenty and thirty pounds annually, could in a few years accumulate enough capital to buy his own farm since average land prices were about three shillings (15p) an acre. 'Were young persons of either sex to engage themselves in this way,' the author concluded, 'they would ... become useful members of society'.

Many underwent this process of regeneration, and some who did wrote home letters which were circulated to encourage other emigrants. Typical was that sent by James Dobbie of Lanark, Canada, to his father and friends in 1826:

> *I really bless God every day I rise, that He was ever pleased in the course of his providence to send me and my family to this place. We are not without difficulties here, but they are nothing to your wants in Glasgow; we have always plenty to eat and drink, and have always a little to spare ... I wish you would try and do all you can to come out: you will find plenty of work, and hard work, but be assured it will pay well. My stock of cattle consists of one yoke of oxen, three milk cows and three young ones. I have got up a very handsome new house, with the assistance of fifteen young men, it was raised in one day; it is 24 feet in length and 15 in breadth.*

This must have been very tempting since Clydeside was suffering badly from a trade recession. In January 1827, when handloom weavers' wages had dropped to four shillings (20p) a week, reports that five times that amount were being paid in America persuaded 800 heads of families to ask the local authorities for assisted passage. High wages also acted as a magnet for immigrants.

In 1834 transatlantic fares from Liverpool and Glasgow were as little as twenty-seven shillings (£1.35), for which the passenger endured the misery of sleeping on the deck, and cabins were between £14 and £35. The 12,000-mile journey to Australia and New Zealand cost £23 steerage and £50 with a cabin and, as on all other voyages, passengers had to provide their own food. Those who paid the lowest fares suffered much discomfort. A well-to-do passenger crossing the Atlantic in 1834 peeped into the steerage-class quarters and saw 'children crying, women screaming, and all tossing about from side to side as the vessel pitched: butter, biscuit, treacle, beef and potatoes all lying higgledy-piggledy or rolling from side to side.' Conditions improved and fares fell after 1840, when steamships superseded sailing vessels: in 1898 a single ticket to Australia could cost as little as thirteen guineas (£13.65p).

It is estimated that 16 million emigrants sailed from Britain between 1815 and 1914, of whom about one in four went to the United States, the rest to the colonies. Periods of recession witnessed

DIGGER'S HUT OF CANVASS AND BARK.

*Roughing it:
an immigrant and
his family on the
Australian gold
fields, c.1850.*

the largest exoduses; 1.8 million left Britain between 1901 and 1910, half settling in the white dominions, whose popularity rose steadily during the next sixty years. Ireland provided a large proportion of these immigrants: about 800,000 between 1815 and the 1845–6 famine and an astonishing one million in the seven years after, most of whom were destined for the United States.

There were also smaller flows of immigration within the empire. When Scots left Clydeside in the 1820s, they were replaced by Gaelic, Catholic Irish (there were 27,000 in Glasgow in 1827), who were willing to take lower wages and so contributed to further emigration from Scotland. A combination of overpopulation, chronic poverty and demands for cheap unskilled labour lay behind the Irish migration as it did that of Indians and Chinese. Indian labourers were recruited for plantation work in the West Indies from the 1850s onwards and Fiji from the 1880s, where they balanced the fall in the native birth rate. The agricultural, mining and railroad boom on the west coast of the United States and Canada drew Chinese, Japanese and, by the turn of the century, Sikhs. In 1852 there were 52,000 Hong Kong Chinese alone in California, and by 1900 15 per cent of the population of British Columbia was Asian.

The influx of Chinese and Japanese into Canada stirred up racial tensions and official efforts were made to ban Asians. This was possible because since the mid-1890s the government had been encouraging mass immigration from central Europe and Russia, where there were plenty of destitute men and women who were glad to accept low wages in the expanding lumber, construction and mining industries of Canada's mid-west. There was racial friction in Australia following the import of Chinese labourers after the gold rush of 1852. For the next forty or so years the Australian trade union movement and later the Labour party agitated against further Chinese immigration on the grounds that it would drive down wages. The result of this campaign was the 1901 Immigration Restriction Act which codified what became known as the 'White Australia' policy.

Non-white labour was required for work which was shunned by British immigrants. Most emigrants had been enticed to the colonies by official promises of cheap land and with it the chance to achieve financial independence. It was universally accepted in Australia and New Zealand, as it had been in North America, that the original occupants of the land had forfeited their rights of possession by their failure to use it productively. Landing in New Zealand in 1845, Surgeon Pine was dismayed to find, 'Its fields are uncultivated ... its mines unworked; its rivers unnavigated.' He automatically concluded that the country should become the property of 'intelligent people of the old world.' They were already there, introduced by the New Zealand Company, whose guiding spirit was Colonel Edward Gibbon Wakefield. He was a singleminded enthusiast for emigration which, he believed, had to be practised with scientific precision so that the fledgling colony would have a proper balance of men and women, landowners and labourers. Gibbon had an elastic conscience (he had once allegedly abducted an heiress) which made it easy for him to persuade the Maoris to forsake their lands in return for such cheapjack trifles as razors, ribbons, looking-glasses and Jew's harps.

These and other British manufactures were among the loot British soldiers carried off from the pah (fortified camp) of Paramatta in 1845. Paramatta had refused to accept the new order and his resistance started twenty-six years of intermittent wars between the Maoris and the settlers, backed until the mid-1860s by the British army. The Maoris could not hope to win and, like other South Sea islanders, their population fell as they came into contact with alien diseases, but they held their own with a courage and skill which impressed their adversaries. They were not, like the Australian aborigines, driven into the wastelands and hunted like kangaroos, but allowed to become integrated into New Zealand. Maoris who passed the property-owning hurdle were given the vote when New Zealand received its constitution in 1852, and British soldiers paid them a unique tribute by erecting a war memorial to their dead in Christ Church Cathedral.

Men and women contemplating emigration to Canada in the 1820s were assured that on arrival they would enjoy the same rights there as they had in Britain, whatever this may have meant to the poor of that time. In a similar vein, an invitation to immigrants issued by the Queensland government in 1908 offered them the chance to help 'lay the foundation of a nation of brave, diligent, and liberty-loving men'.

Between these two dates the internal government of the white colonies had been transformed. The process had started in 1839 with the publication of a report by Lord Durham of an investigation he had conducted in Canada after small-scale disturbance there two years before. The Whig peer's recommendations for local self-determination were the basis for a policy which his party implemented between 1847 and 1867. The Canadian provinces, the Australian states, New Zealand and Cape Colony were each given constitutions that provided them with elected governments with powers to make laws and distribute land. From the early 1840s there had been a flow of former Chartists to Australia and New

Zealand and their radical ideas provided a leaven for political life in both colonies. Without an aristocracy to act as a brake on reform and with a large population drawn from the British working class, it was inevitable that the colonies soon had a wider franchise than Britain and governments willing to undertake novel and far-reaching social reforms.

Local autonomy led the way to the voluntary creation of nation states: in 1867 Canada became a confederation, Australia a federation in 1901, and South Africa in 1910, including the Transvaal and the Orange Free State, which had been granted self-government in 1906. Here there were no liberal franchises, for to obtain political peace the British government had been forced to accept the exclusion of black and mixed-race voters from the Transvaal and Orange Free State electorate. Non-white voters made up 1 per cent of Natal's voters and 15 per cent of Cape Colony's. The price paid by Britain for a stable and tractable dominion in South Africa was toleration of what, in 1910, was a customary apartheid, a system of discrimination and segregation that would, in thirty-eight years' time, be given the force of law.

The compromise in South Africa was a reminder that political expediency as well as liberal principles had shaped Britain's policies towards her white colonies. The Whig dogmas of *laissez faire* and public economy, as well as the belief that British political rights should be enjoyed by all British subjects, wherever they lived, had dictated the first moves towards colonial self-determination. Self-governing

ABOVE LEFT
Steerage class:
cheap fares for Scottish emigrants: the United States is given special prominence as it, rather than Canada, was the destination of the majority who crossed the Atlantic, c.1880.

ABOVE RIGHT
Paradise waiting:
a Victorian emigrant's guide to New Zealand. (Both © SRO)

colonists could raise their own taxes and pay for their own administration and, most importantly, protection; in 1858 the Canadian garrison had cost the Treasury £261,000. By 1871, the redcoats had been recalled from all the colonies save the volatile Cape, and the colonists had to raise and fund their own militias.

As administrative bonds were severed, the question was raised as to the future relationship between Britain and her colonies. Despite predictions that home rule was the first step along a road that led towards complete independence, there were few signs that any of the colonies wished to break their remaining political ties with Britain. Queen Victoria remained the head of state in each dominion, as the self-governing colonies were called, and her features appeared on their postage stamps and coins.

Alongside such advertisements of attachment to Britain, there were indications that the colonies were developing a distinctive identity and culture of their own. These were most pronounced in Australia. A prospector who arrived at the Victoria gold diggings in 1853 found himself in the middle of 'an American type of society'. 'All aristocratic feelings and associations of the old country are at once annihilated,' he observed. 'Plebianism of the rankest, and, in many instances, of the lowest kind, at present dwells in Australia, and riches are now becoming the test of a man's position.' Digger egalitarianism soon became part of the Australian consciousness. The Anzac (Australia and New Zealand Army Corps) soldier 'is no lover of privilege of class. He does not understand it,' proudly announced the Queensland *School Paper* in November 1917. According to the official Australian history of the war, the classless Australian fighting men were also independent-minded, refusing 'to take for granted the prescribed opinions' and were ready always to take the 'vigorous and unfettered initiative'. Individualism was balanced by a powerful sense of brotherhood which lay at the heart of the Australian male psyche. It was known as 'mateship' and its only rule was that 'a man should at all times and at any cost stand by his mate'. These qualities did not endear Australians to that stick-necked breed of Englishmen, often army commanders, who believed in an orderly, disciplined society in which everyone stuck to the rules. A gentleman cricketer, writing in 1888, regretted that players in Australian touring XIs tended to contest umpires' decisions.

There was a small but clamorous group of Australians who rejected British standards. The Sydney *Bulletin* regularly poured scorn on what it called 'colonial cringe', a mass inferiority complex which accepted the innate superiority of all things British. The *Bulletin* also denounced attempts to promote imperial consciousness in Australia as a ploy to further Britain's selfish interests, and accordingly renamed Empire Day as 'Vampire Day'. The *Bulletin*'s carping did not seriously weaken Australian imperial sentiment nor convince Australians that Britain's interests were not necessarily their own.

The *Bulletin*'s anti-British shafts were being launched at a time when Australia and the other dominions were becoming increasingly aware of the political and strategic value of the imperial connection. So too was Britain which, since the mid-1870s, was endeavouring to survive in a mutable and none too friendly world. As she entered into competition with hostile powers whose strength matched her own, it became imperative for Britain to cultivate colonial goodwill. The colonies were becoming valuable assets, since their assistance might prove vital in the event of conflict with France and Russia. Shifts in the global balance of power generated anxieties within the dominions, which had for the first time to come to terms with their own isolation and vulnerability. The possibility of an Anglo-Russian war in 1877–8, and with it seaborne raids by Russian warships on the Pacific coastlines of Canada, Australia and New Zealand, made the governments of each appreciate the extent of their dependence upon the Royal Navy.

One immediate consequence of this scare was the purchase of warships by Victoria and Queensland in 1882–3 and a greater willingness on behalf of these and other dominion governments to contribute to Britain's naval budget. A sense of common purpose and shared responsibilities prompted the New South Wales government to send 700 volunteers, all in red coats, to join the British army in the Sudan in May 1885. These soldiers, and offers of help from South Australia, Victoria and New Zealand, impressed Wolseley. He wrote warmly to Lord Loch, the governor of Victoria, and said that he had

Aussies lend a hand: *volunteers from New South Wales embark from Sydney for the Sudan to reinforce British and Indian troops during 1885. This was the first example of Britain deploying dominion manpower in its wars.* (© *Australian War Memorial*)

welcomed the Australians 'not only as comrades, but as countrymen'. Their disembarkation at Suakin was an event of tremendous significance for Britain, which was far beyond the blinkered 'vestry who ruled in Downing Street and there pose as the successors of Pitt, Palmerston and Beaconsfield.' For Wolseley, the common ministerial failing was that lack of imperial imagination which made it impossible for them to appreciate the power of the empire. Nor could they see its future potential as Britain's partner. And yet he predicted, 'When war with Russia comes, as come it must before many years pass away, we shall have help from all our Colonies.'

The idea of some kind of imperial unity was superficially attractive, especially to those disturbed by Britain's comparative decline as a world power. But practical attempts to facilitate closer relations between Britain and the dominions and the creation of a coordinated imperial defence policy ended in failure. A series of conferences of dominion prime ministers, held intermittently between 1887 and 1907, produced much talk but no results. There was an understandable suspicion that Britain was promoting imperial unity to further her own international interests, and dominion leaders were chary about committing their armed forces to British control. In Canada there were deep misgivings among the French-speaking population about becoming embroiled in a war with France, and in 1898, when such a war appeared likely, the Canadian government doubted whether *Canadien* militiamen could be persuaded to take part in the seizure of St Pierre and Miquelon islands. Again, in 1899, French-Canadians were reluctant to support Britain in what they saw as a war of imperial aggression against the Boers.

Looming large over the British government's endeavours to secure imperial cooperation was the Irish Question. Before 1800, Ireland had had its own parliament, which was to a large extent the mouthpiece of the Protestant landowners. In 1801 this parliament was dissolved and thereafter Irish MPs went

Britain reproduced:
Prices Street, Dunedin
(c.1900) could be a
replica of any high street
in the mother country.

to Westminster. This arrangement was continually challenged by Irish nationalists, who grew stronger in numbers and determination as the franchise was extended to the majority of Gaelic, Catholic Irishmen. Militancy increased dramatically after 1870 with the foundation of the Irish Home Rule Party and the Irish issue was pushed into the forefront of British politics.

The Irish Question was debated on two levels. On one, it was a purely domestic matter concerned with the restoration of a measure of internal self-government to Ireland. On the other, it was an imperial issue of the greatest significance since it involved the future integrity of the empire. The enemies of Irish autonomy feared that it would fragment the United Kingdom and thereby wreck any chances of wider imperial union. Opposing Gladstone's first Home Rule Bill in May 1886, a Tory MP argued that if it was passed 'the colonies would not come to join such a federation if the United Kingdom was first broken up . . . [for] if we could not keep our own kith and kin together we could not be expected to keep our Colonies, which were at so great a distance from us, together.' Gladstone, defending his measure, hoped that a self-governing Ireland would become a friendly and loyal dominion like Canada. This was wishful thinking; the legacy of hatred for England and the passionate anglophobia of nationalist rhetoric made it extremely unlikely that Anglo-Irish relations would ever be cordial. A semi-independent Ireland would always pose a danger in any future war, and one MP reminded the Commons how, in 1798, Irish nationalists had made common cause with France.

The threat to national security and possible harm to the empire convinced a substantial body of Liberal MPs, including Joseph Chamberlain, to defect and vote against the bill. Its successor, presented in the spring of 1893, passed the Commons but was thrown out by the Lords. It had been denounced by Chamberlain as 'the Bill for creating Little England', which would advertise irresolution to a jealous world. Defence of the Union was fiercest among those, like Chamberlain, who favoured tighter links between Britain and the dominions. Although in political terms these appeared unobtainable during the 1890s, there were gratifying signs that loyalty to the Crown was a powerful emotional force throughout the dominions. Its strength was publicly revealed during the 1897 Diamond Jubilee celebrations which witnessed not only dominion troops marching through London, but a cascade of congratulations from every corner of the empire.

When war between Britain and the Transvaal became unavoidable, Australia and New Zealand immediately offered troops, as did Canada, despite considerable misgivings among the *Canadien* community. The raising and departures of the contingents were the cause for much celebration, and the mood of the men who paraded through the streets and those who cheered them was captured by a New Zealand poet. Just over 30,000 colonial troops fought in the Boer War and their activities were closely followed in the dominion newspapers, recorded in letters home or in reports from war correspondents. Public interest in the war and their countrymen's part in it was most intense in New Zealand and Australia.

Military pomp and a pride in achievements on the battlefield were part and parcel of nationalism everywhere in the late nineteenth and twentieth centuries, and so it was both natural and inevitable that the Boer War gave a fresh vigour to dominion patriotism. Participation in the war also contributed to a sense that the dominions had 'come of age', that is, had reached a stage of maturity which entitled them to consider themselves nations rather than colonies. Waving flags at parades and sending volunteers to fight the Boers was not merely an affirmation of youthful nationhood. Australia and New Zealand stood to lose from the extinction of British influence in South Africa, which would have led to a shift in the balance of power throughout the southern hemisphere.

Dominion help benefited Britain, both militarily and psychologically. Large numbers of tough, enthusiastic young men who had learned to ride and shoot in the outback were exactly what the British army needed in 1899, and in a world where Britain was conspicuously friendless, dominion support was a boost to national morale. None were happier than supporters of imperial federation, who believed their creed had been vindicated and looked forward to a post-war world in which the partnership formed on the battlefield would become permanent. In any new emergency Britain would have to depend heavily on dominion manpower to fill the ranks of its armies. Mass emigration meant that by the beginning of the twentieth century 20 per cent of the empire's white population was living in the dominions.

*The signal had flash'd
oe'r the water,
The word that old
England wants help;
The Mother has cried
to her daughter;
The lion has roared to
its whelp.
Cast away any dread
that appals ye,
Any doubts to the sea
winds toss –
'Tis the Old, Old
Country that calls ye,
Ye sons of the
Southern Cross.*

NEW ZEALAND POET

*Growth point:
the newly built docks
and warehouses at Port
Chalmers, New Zealand
(c.1900), which handled
imports and exports. As
the dominions prospered,
they were recognised as
invaluable markets for
British goods which were
facing stiff American and
European competition.*

PLAYING THE GREAT GAME

Between 1838 and 1904, British strategists feared that Russian penetration of central Asia would lead to an invasion of India. Explorers and spies (they were usually synonymous) investigated what the Russians were up to and mapped the passes of Afghanistan and the Himalayas. A combination of local crises and alarmism in London and Calcutta led to two full-scale wars against Afghanistan, the invasion of Tibet and numerous minor campaigns in the foothills of the Himalayas. The whole business was known as the 'Great Game'.

Logistics:

RIGHT ABOVE *British cavalrymen, horse artillery batteries and a dog waiting to escort Yakub Khan, the puppet ruler of Afghanistan, 1879. (© IWM)*

RIGHT BELOW *The Indian army's base camp at the head of the Malakand pass during operations to relieve the besieged residency at Chitral, 1895.*

Even minor operations in remote regions required an enormous effort:

RIGHT *A rope and wooden bridge being constructed during the Chitral campaign.*

BELOW *Transport mules are coaxed across a river, Tibet, 1904.*
(© NAM)

BOTTOM *No longer forbidden: British troops approach Lhasa, 1904.*
(© NAM)

10

BE BRAVE,
BE BOLD,
DO RIGHT!:
THE EDWARDIAN EMPIRE
AND THE PEOPLE

The year 1902 ought to have been one for hubristic celebration. It was not; imperial soldiers may have marched in step during the coronation procession of the new King, Edward VII, but the mood of the Imperial Conference was one of polite disharmony as dominion prime ministers rejected suggestions for closer links with Britain. Peace in South Africa gave no cause for jubilation. It had taken two exhausting years to overcome the Boers in a tedious campaign which had inspired no headlines, save ones which highlighted 'methods of barbarism'. The fighting over, a royal commission convened to hear evidence of how the war had been conducted. Much of it was a catalogue of mischance and muddle.

What was revealed to the commissioners on such matters as the lack of an army intelligence service, mismanaged hospitals and the rejection of thousands of young, working-class volunteers because of their physical debility appeared to confirm the fears of those who had been warning their countrymen of the dangers of national decline. Their jeremiads may have sounded ironic at a time of unparalleled imperial expansion but, as they were always pointing out, appearances were misleading. The empire may have grown, but it had also become infected with a malaise which, if untreated, would end with its dissolution. Extreme pessimists, such as Major-General Sir Robert Baden-Powell, the hero of Mafeking, imagined that Britain, like Rome, would be destroyed from within by a moral virus, which he believed was already spreading among the young.

There was also an external threat. Could Britain continue to survive as a global power under the pressure of challenges from Germany, the United States and Russia (now in the process of rapid industrialisation)? Nervous sidelong glances at the progress of those rivals revealed nations with greater populations and resources, and, in the case of the former two, economies that were outpacing Britain's in terms of productivity and growth. Social-Darwinism had intruded so far into the collective thought of the major powers that it was taken for granted that they now existed in a permanent state of acute competition. For this reason, periods of intense rivalry were commonly likened to races (the race for the Nile, or, after 1906, the Anglo-German naval race) which suggested a winning post, a prize and a string of also-rans. By this analogy, Britain had led the field for most of the previous century, but after 1900 seemed to be losing ground to stronger, healthier beasts.

The disturbing possibility that Britain might find itself among the also-rans prompted a bout of intense national soul-searching among politicians, economists, social commentators and journalists. Their diagnoses of national ills were usually accompanied by a quest for remedies that would revitalise the country, restore its self-confidence and reinforce its power abroad. Analysts of the right and left concluded that only radical nostrums had any hope of success. The old Liberal orthodoxies of free trade, *laissez faire* and the sovereignty of market forces had failed; indeed, had contributed to Britain's present misfortunes. Milner, who had returned in 1906 from his controversial period as high commissioner in South Africa determined to play a part in the rebirth of Britain and the empire, blamed the sad state of both on the 'old maidenly hands' of the Liberal leadership.

The Fabian socialist, Sydney Webb, believed that Liberal individualism had become obsolete. Writing in 1901, he insisted that, 'We have become aware, almost in a flash, that we are not merely individuals, but members of a community, nay citizens of the world.' The man in the street now appreciated that 'the good government of his city, the efficiency with which his nation is organised, and the influence which his Empire is able to exercise in the councils, and consequently in the commerce of nations' were vital for his and his childrens' survival and prosperity. For Webb and imperialists on the right 'efficiency' became a talismanic word, holding the key to the restoration of national well-being and competitiveness.

The application of efficiency required strong government, willing to plan ahead and intervene when necessary in all areas of national life to promote better education and state-funded pension and medical programmes. 'The building up of the nervous and muscular vitality of our race' was for Webb 'the principal plank of any Imperial programme'. A Liberal MP, stating the case for child welfare and school meals in 1906, said that while, in theory, it sounded like 'rank Socialism' it was in reality 'first rate Imperialism', for the 'Empire cannot be built on rickety and flat-chested citizens'. Indeed it could not, and concern with high infant mortality rates and the need to foster a sturdy 'imperial race' led to the first steps being taken

ABOVE LEFT
Anti-imperialist:
a Tory postcard reminds voters in 1910 of how the pro-Boer Lloyd George had to flee in disguise from a meeting in Birmingham Town Hall. By contrast, his present enemies, the peers, were laying down their lives in South Africa.

ABOVE RIGHT *Nursery of the empire*:
imperial themes appeared in books for children of all ages.
(© Opie)

to provide widespread child care in the 1900s. What was in effect the foundation of the welfare state was in many respects an imperial measure. The district nurses and health visitors who instructed working-class mothers on how to bring up vigorous children were seen as serving the greater good of the empire. Supporters of such activities argued that they had been undertaken in Germany and Japan for some time.

The pursuit of efficiency in the name of empire demanded the discarding of old shibboleths, breaking up vested interests and the abandonment of systems which had become arthritic. 'Something businesslike' would have to replace the 'smartness, gilt braid and gallantry' which had hitherto characterised the army, insisted Leo Amery in 1900. He was *The Times*'s correspondent in South Africa and so knew at first hand the shortcomings of the old army system. He was also a dedicated imperialist who admired Milner, and became one of a knot of impatient young politicians who were appalled by their elders' failure to grasp the imperial vision and make it reality.

Imperial issues were now in the forefront of British political life. They became the focus of a national debate in the spring of 1903 when Chamberlain, inspired and invigorated by a tour of South Africa, launched his tariff reform campaign. It was based upon the assumption that free trade had failed disastrously and the British economy would only thrive again if all foreign imports were taxed throughout the empire. Imperial products, chiefly foodstuffs, would be admitted duty-free so creating an empire-wide free trade system. The benefits were twofold: the imperial customs union would pave the way for an imperial federation, and the revenues raised would pay for the social reforms needed to create a robust imperial race. 'The ideals of national strength and imperial consolidation' were complementary to those of 'domestic and social progress', claimed Milner, a keen tariff reformer. National greatness, he believed, rested ultimately on 'the welfare and contentedness of the mass of the people' and he felt sure that working men took more pride in being members of the vast empire than their social superiors. But, he warned, patriotism could be 'choked . . . in the squalor and degradation of the slums of our great cities.'

The sheer boldness of this dual programme for imperial unity and national regeneration was its political undoing. It proved too far-reaching and radical for most of Chamberlain's Conservative and Unionist colleagues, who split, with Churchill crossing the floor of the Commons to line up with the Liberals. The tariff debate was a godsend for the Liberals, who had spent the past eight years out of office and divided over policy, particularly towards the empire. Now they rallied behind the old battlecry of free trade and won the general election of January 1906 with a massive overall majority, their last this century. The Liberal victory owed much to their having frightened the working-class electorate into believing that the Conservatives would tax imported cereals and raise the price of bread. The most telling image of the election was a poster which showed a plump and substantial 'Free Trade' loaf alongside a miniature, bun-sized 'Tariff Reform' loaf.

Liberal vote-catching was not only aimed at the nation's stomach. Another imperial issue, the employment conditions of Chinese indentured labourers in South Africa, was invoked to stir the nation's conscience. What was by now an antique imperial expedient to provide cheap and abundant labour had been adopted as a stopgap measure to raise productivity in the gold mines. The scheme had Milner's blessing and he had, imprudently as it turned out, approved flogging as a means of imposing discipline on the Chinese. The cry of 'slavery' was immediately raised by Liberals, the Labour party and sundry Nonconformist clergy, and with some justification. British sexual morality was offended by the official banning of women from the mineworkers' compounds, a restriction which, it was alleged, would cause a mass outbreak of sodomy among the frustrated Chinese. This proved not to be the case as a government enquiry of 1906 discovered. Among the evidence were the tart remarks of the Medical Officer of Health for the Rand, in whose opinion there was, per head, more sodomy among the men of London than the Chinese in Johannesburg. Understandably, the report was never published.

The affair of the Chinese coolies had aroused the passion of the Labour party, for which the 1906 general election had been a breakthrough. Labour politicians had been and would remain ambivalent in their attitudes towards the empire. The middle-class intellectual Fabians such as G. B. Shaw and Sydney and Beatrice Webb considered the empire a national asset which, properly managed, could benefit all its subjects. On the other hand, Labour leaders, whose origins were in the working class and whose ideology had its roots in mid-Victorian Nonconformity and Radicalism were apprehensive about an institution that was authoritarian in its nature and seemingly devoted to the world-wide extension of capitalism, often by force.

For this reason James Keir Hardie, a Scottish ex-miner who had become the Labour party's first MP, joined forces with left-wing Liberals to denounce the Boer War as capitalist aggression unleashed on a race of farmers, whom he likened to the now extinct, independent English yeomen. Like other Socialists, Keir Hardie was distressed by music-hall jingoism, which he believed was deliberately fomented by the bosses in the hope that working men, intoxicated by belligerent patriotism, might forget such knife-and-fork issues as wages and unemployment. This did not happen; the Labour party managed to increase its vote despite the clamour of the Jubilee and the street junketings during the early phases of the Boer War. More importantly, the party flourished in the face of a cheap popular press which, by 1910, had become for the most part Conservative and imperialist in outlook.

In determining its policy towards the empire, the Labour party was strongly influenced by parallels between its own struggles and those of contemporary embryonic democratic, nationalist and trade union movements in India, Egypt and South Africa. This consideration, a socialist faith in the brotherhood of man and an instinctive sympathy for the underdog made the Labour party the natural ally of what a later generation would call colonial freedom movements. Links were quickly established between the Labour leadership and nationalist politicians in India, where the anti-colonial opposition was strongest, Egypt and South Africa. Ramsay MacDonald, the future leader of the party, toured India and was dismayed by the racial aloofness of his countrymen and the lack of official energy in extending education for Indians. Keir Hardie, who visited India in 1907, consorted with Bengali nationalists and was received by Hindus as a holy man, much to his secret satisfaction, for he was a vain man.

Keir Hardie also had first-hand knowledge of South Africa, which he used to champion the blacks during the debate on the bill granting the country a federal constitution in 1909. The government's willingness to accommodate the Boers and disbar blacks from the franchise would, he predicted, sour relations between the races and reduce the blacks to a 'landless proletariat', forced to accept the lowest wages to keep alive. In the same year, Keir Hardie lectured representatives of the Young Egypt party in Geneva and urged them to forge an alliance between students and fellahin. This accomplished, the

Food for patriots:
imperial images
continued to boost sales.
(© Opie)

Imperial preference:
patriots were encouraged
to buy goods made or
grown in the empire.
(© Opie)

Egyptians could proceed to press Britain for self-determination, but, as Keir Hardie insisted, in an orderly manner.

The significance of these statements and the links between colonial liberation movements and what was, in the 1900s, still a small party lay in the future. Nonetheless, the educated élite who led the nascent nationalist movements in Asia, the Middle East and Africa believed that they would always receive a sympathetic hearing from the Labour leadership. In a letter of August 1917, which was intercepted by military intelligence, an Iraqi nationalist exile warned the Labour MP and member of the war cabinet, Arthur Henderson, that the government was mistaken in funding Hussain, sharif of Mecca, on the grounds that he was an untrustworthy reactionary. He added with premature and naïve optimism that he hoped Britain would withdraw from Iraq when the war was over.

There was a wide gulf of attitude and temperament between the Labour party and the men who ran the empire and Conservative and Liberal imperialists at home. The Indian government smeared Keir Hardie as a firebrand and sedition-monger during his visit to the country, and Ramsay MacDonald wondered whether the empire's rulers would return home with their heads full of authoritarian ideas. This fear was not new; it had been expressed by Burke in the late eighteenth century and had been repeated intermittently in the next century by Liberals and Radicals disturbed by the fact that their countrymen, mostly from the upper classes, governed the colonies as autocrats.

Authoritarian imperialist sentiments were also strongly held amongst officers in the armed forces and this was dramatically revealed by events in Ireland during the spring of 1914 after Herbert Asquith's government had been driven to contemplate measures for the enforcement of the Irish Home Rule Act. Necessity rather than conviction had forced the Liberals to introduce this measure in 1912 as a payment for Irish Nationalist support in the Commons, after their majority had been swept away by the two general elections of 1910. As in 1886 and 1893, Conservatives and Unionists denounced Irish self-government as a potentially lethal blow to imperial integrity. This time, however, the Lords could only postpone the bill's enactment, and so, having exhausted the customary forms of political opposition, its adversaries resorted to force. The Protestant majority in Northern Ireland screamed 'Home Rule! Home Rule!'; affirmed their wish to remain part of the British empire; formed a volunteer army and, early in 1914, began procuring rifles and machine-guns. Mainland Conservative and Unionist leaders applauded what they saw as a gallant defence of imperial solidarity.

Faced with a rebellion, the cabinet proposed at the end of March 1914 that troops from the Irish garrison (concentrated in the Catholic south of the island) might be used to guard arsenals, and prevent the Ulstermen from getting more weapons. The majority of officers involved promptly resigned; such a duty was against their consciences, as it was against those of officers on board the warships that had been ordered to take stations off Belfast. Senior officers openly sympathised with their subordinates' gesture, and a distraught cabinet was compelled to temporise. The outcome was a pledge that British soldiers would not be deployed to disarm the Ulster Volunteers, which was a victory for them and the officers.

What was called with discreet understatement the Curragh Incident (after the name of the camp where the first batch of resignations had occurred) was a testament to the depth and passion of imperial loyalty within the army. It was also revealing that those who approved the officers' actions believed that imperial considerations outweighed the traditional obedience of the military to the civil power.

Imperialists on the right saw the moral issue as clear cut. One argued that the disaffected officers behaved as they did because they had realised that 'the Ulstermen are loyal subjects who refused to be placed under the heel of a faction which Mr Gladstone [before his conversion to Home Rule] asserted to be "marching through rapine to the dismemberment of the Empire."' It was unthinkable that officers of an army which had by a hundred years of exertion and sacrifice enlarged and protected the empire, should have allowed themselves to become accomplices to what was widely seen as a betrayal of empire. They could not remain true to themselves if they made war against men who wished to remain part of the empire on behalf of those who wished to leave.

A private soldier, watching events at the Curragh from the sidelines, wondered why the officers of the 'aristocratic and plutocratic' army had previously shown not the slightest qualm about using force against those of their fellow countrymen who happened to be industrial workers on strike. This was the language of class politics, a recent phenomenon in British life which was a direct consequence of the growth of the Labour party and militant trade unionism. Class politics were wormwood to the Conservative and Liberal imperialists who saw them as undermining national unity and therefore weakening the empire. Out of a population of 45 million, 34 million were working class and it was therefore imperative that an antidote be found to the poison of class antagonism.

Chamberlain had hoped that his personal programme which melded dynamic imperialism and tariff reform would win over the working classes. Even the most

A healthy empire: imperial images still conveyed excellence. (Both © Opie)

Kindergarten for
proconsuls:
Harrovian sportsmen
and their headmaster;
the values taught in
such schools, including
sportsmanship, were
the moral bedrock
of those who would
govern the empire,
c.1925.

traditionalist Conservatives were of the same mind. 'The greatest resource of the Empire is the British character,' proclaimed Lord Wylloughby de Broke, a right-wing Tory racing peer. But he admitted that the inner strengths of the Briton could only be sustained if everyone was allowed free access to what he described as 'the moral and material essentials of life'. Only then, no one could complain, 'The British Empire has done nothing for me.' So long as there were large sections of society which felt no benefit from the empire, Britain could never obtain the national solidarity needed to guarantee its maintenance. Or, as Robert Blatchford, an ex-soldier who was both an imperialist and a Socialist, once observed, while the sun was said never to set on the empire, there were city slums over which it had never risen.

The working classes had, therefore, to be made aware of the empire, taught to feel pride in it, understand how its existence was to their advantage, and most important of all, learn the special virtues that would be expected of them as its citizens. What today might be called raising imperial consciousness was a task undertaken by a collection of voluntary organisations founded and funded by the middle and upper classes. The lists of patrons and subscribers were roll calls of imperialists from all parties, former proconsuls and senior army and navy officers. Together they directed and paid for a formidable propaganda machine which operated throughout the years between the Boer and the First World Wars.

One of the largest and most influential of the bodies which broadcast the imperial message was the Primrose League. It had been established in 1883, was named after Disraeli's favourite flower, and claimed to be apolitical, although atheists and enemies of the empire were denied membership. In 1900 it had 1.5 million members, nearly all working class. It promoted a robust imperial patriotism (one of its heroes was Gordon) through a mixture of entertainments and instruction, paying for lectures, lantern-slide shows, exhibitions and public rallies. A more forceful pressure group was the National Service League whose supporters campaigned across the country for compulsory military training for all schoolboys, and conscription. A living national hero, the aged but still sprightly Field Marshal Lord Roberts, frequently addressed its public meetings. The National Service League had accumulated 200,000 members by 1914, including some formerly attached to the Lads Drill Association with which it had merged in 1906.

The Lads Drill Association was the brainchild of Reginald Brabazon, Earl of Meath, an Anglo-Irish Tory who had dedicated his old age to spreading the gospel of empire to the young. His conversion to imperialism had occurred one winter's day in the 1850s when he had been a schoolboy at Eton. Wiping snow from his knees, he was upbraided by a schoolmaster, who used the occasion for an off-the-cuff sermon on imperial manliness:

> *Do you call yourselves British, boys? . . . Your fathers are the rulers of England, and your forefathers have made England what she is now. Do you imagine that if they had minded a little snow that Canada would have been added to the Empire, or if they had minded heat we should ever possess India or tropical Africa? Never let me see you shrink from heat or cold. You will have to maintain the Empire which they made.*

This harangue affected the young Meath deeply, and later he set about making sure that future generations would keep faith with their ancestors.

Homage to the imperial past and commitment to its future were the objects of Empire Day, which Meath wanted celebrated annually in schools throughout the empire on 24 May, Queen Victoria's birthday. Empire Day was commemorated first in 1902 and within four years was being observed in 6,000 schools. A parliamentary attempt to secure it official recognition failed in 1908, to the audible delight of Labour and Irish MPs, and Labour councils such as Battersea banned it from their schools as militaristic. Nevertheless, Empire Day increased in popularity, especially in south-eastern England and rural areas everywhere. In 1916 a wartime government, willing to do anything that would encourage popular patriotism, gave Empire Day official recognition.

Something of the flavour of an Edwardian Empire Day is conveyed by a pamphlet issued by the Empire Day League in 1912 with suggestions for uplifting entertainments. For older schoolchildren there was an abridged version of *Henry V* which centred on the scenes before, during and after Agincourt. Younger pupils were offered a simple pageant in which a procession of heroes, whose 'noble deeds' had contributed to the growth of the empire, paid homage to Britannia. Clive and Nelson rubbed shoulders with symbolic figures representing the army, navy and, an up-to-date touch, 'air power'. As each appeared, they were greeted with rehearsed cheers from the spectators – 'Hurrah to our brave soldiers!' and so on. In conclusion, Britannia made a short, inspiring speech: 'My Empire shall hold; and, like summer roses, perfume the world with freedom's gladsome fragrance. Be brave, be bold, do right!' In an alternative and equally colourful *tableau vivant* children dressed to represent the dominions and colonies paid their respects to their mother, Britannia. Recommended costume for South African blacks consisted of 'two fur rugs', 'strings of melon seeds' and an improvised assegai. The spectacles were a climax to a morning during which children learned patriotic songs and memorised facts about the empire. Work and fun were not enough, and Meath emphasised that pupils should be given the rest of the day off. The young, he wrote, 'do not readily appreciate the importance of any event unless it brings a holiday in its train.'

Everyday lessons were constructed around imperial themes. The Prince and Princess of Wales's Indian tour of 1906 was an opportunity for elementary schoolchildren to learn about the subcontinent and the firm and fair way in which it was governed. Nationalist agitation, which had recently flared up in Bengal, was brushed aside with the statement, 'The British rule has brought peace . . . and the native police and soldiers are usually able to preserve order among a people who are naturally docile.'

Public schoolboys continued to be bombarded with imperial propaganda, relentlessly delivered by headmasters who were invariably Anglican clerics of the muscular Christian persuasion. Themes of athletic prowess and warrior patriotism mingled in the rousing school songs which became so popular at this time. The sentiments of Harrow's 'Forty Years On', which always brought tears to Churchill's eyes, were typical. Stiffened by such appeals and brought to a high pitch of fitness on the playing field, the public school man was ready to do his duty by the empire; but what of boys from other classes?

The question was asked continually in Edwardian Britain. The answers were often disquieting; in 1898 one commentator summed up working-class youth as 'stunted, narrow chested, easily wearied, yet voluble, excitable, with little ballast, stamina and endurance'. Generalisations of this sort were confirmed

God gives us bases to guard or beleaguer, Games to play out in earnest or fun, Fights for the fearless and goals for the eager, Twenty and thirty and forty years on.

'FORTY YEARS ON'

by the cold statistics gathered by army doctors who examined would-be recruits, and the surveys undertaken in the urban slums by proto-sociologists like Seebohm Rowntree. The underfed, sickly sons of the industrial cities were evidence that Anglo-Saxon manhood was in decline. On one level, this fact was ammunition for social reformers of all persuasions, and on another, it provided the impetus for a body of determined imperialists to launch programmes for the regeneration of the masses. What was needed, claimed Baden-Powell, was the 'hardening of the nation' and the 'building up of self-reliant, energetic manhood' which would, in time, be able to populate and defend the empire.

'Wishy-washy slackers' were Baden-Powell's target. A public celebrity, he used his considerable influence to awaken the nation's youth to its duty and prepare it for its fulfilment. In an appeal which echoed that of Meath's schoolmaster, he invoked the exploits of past heroes to shame their lethargic descendants. In December 1904 he exhorted the readers of *Union Jack* and the *Marvel* to learn how to drill and shoot. He concluded with an appeal for letters from captains of soccer and cricket XIs whose teams were keen to learn how to fight. Baden-Powell's ideas were translated into action in 1908 with the foundation of the Boy Scouts who, two years later, totalled 100,000. The scouting movement's philosophy was simple patriotism, and its activities, largely undertaken outdoors, were derived from Baden-Powell's textbook on fieldcraft and survival which was based on his experiences fighting the Ndebele in Rhodesia. Appropriately, scouts wore a khaki uniform, complete with broad-brimmed bush hat and bandanna.

The Boy Scouts joined a number of other organisations dedicated to the proper diversion and instruction of youth. The well-established Boys Brigade drilled its largely working-class members with wooden rifles; dressed them in uniforms, which included the same pill-box hat that was then worn by soldiers; and instilled doctrines of Christian manliness and loyalty to Crown and country. There were other, smaller bodies dedicated to the creation of upright and sturdy sons of empire, including the Anti-Smoking League and the League of St George. The latter campaigned against pornography and masturbation, which was also a source of anguish to Baden-Powell, who warned his scouts that, quite literally, it weakened the imperial seed, led to general debility and even madness.

The future mothers of the imperial breed received their own indoctrination. The Church of England Girls' Friendly Society which, in 1913, had 200,000 members, was primarily concerned with giving moral guidance to young working-class women. As well as counselling deference, chastity and quietism, this society helped unmarried women to emigrate, and its leaflets contained a scattering of imperialist propaganda. 'I look on imperialism as a means of eradicating the selfishness of Socialism,' announced the Honourable Mrs Joyce, the society's emigration secretary, in 1913. The Girl Guides, an offshoot of the scouting movement, adopted similar patriotic values. A leaflet issued for Guides in 1910 drew their attention to a role that they might have to play in defence of the empire:

> *Girls! Imagine that a battle has taken place in and around your town or village ... what are you going to do? Are you going to sit down and wring your hands and cry, or are you going to be plucky, and go and do something to help your fathers and brothers ...?*

Just how far those on the receiving end of Edwardian patriotic and imperial propaganda were converted by it cannot be known. It contained, and this was recognised and regretted by those on the left, elements designed to smother class politics. There were also charges that the emphasis placed on such military values as obedience and duty fostered militarism, which was true up to a point. Admiration for the services had grown throughout the nineteenth century, but the British cult of the warrior hero had always laid great stress on his Christian faith which, as with Gordon, was the basis for his superior courage. The fighting man was respected not just because he was physically strong and brave, but because of that interior moral stamina which made him perform his duty.

Like his predecessor, the Edwardian soldier was essentially a bringer of civilisation. This was how he was depicted in newspaper reports of the small and rather unglamorous campaigns fought between

Your forefathers worked hard, fought hard, and died hard to make this empire for you. Don't let them look down from heaven, and see you loafing about with your hands in your pockets, doing nothing to keep it up.

MAJOR-GENERAL SIR
ROBERT BADEN-POWELL

1902 and 1914 on various frontiers. The *Daily Mail*, now with a daily circulation of three-quarters of a million, gave coverage to operations in Somaliland during 1902 and 1903, and the invasion of Tibet in 1903. In each case the old formula was adopted, with the empire's adversaries being represented as wild, brave and reckless savages engaged in a hopeless struggle against civilisation. Incidentally, in its reporting of the Somaliland war, the *Mail* astonishingly asserted that the Mad Mullah's near victory at Erigo in 1902 was certain proof of his clinical insanity. Presumably only a lunatic could expect to defeat a British army!

The patrician high priests of imperialism, while they approved of attempts to widen the public's knowledge of the empire, had always been disdainful of the sudden upsurges of popular patriotism that had been triggered by victories in colonial wars. For the likes of Chamberlain and Milner, jingoism distracted the public from the more serious but less romantic aspects of empire, and was an uncomfortable reminder of the fickleness of public opinion. It was a drawback of democracy that the public at large was easily bored and could not be persuaded to concentrate on any issue for long. For this reason, such figures as Milner were anxious to convert to the imperial creed those who really mattered, the young men who would be the future rulers of Britain and the empire.

In South Africa, Milner had collected around himself a knot of young, zealous imperialists who had, between 1900 and 1906, worked with him towards the country's reconstruction. Known as the kindergarten, this band of talented Oxonians included the journalist and future novelist John Buchan, Philip Kerr and Lionel Curtis, all of whom would dedicate their lives to the promotion of imperialism. Their circle was joined by Leo Amery and formed the nucleus for the Round Table, a cross-party, imperial pressure group founded in 1910 and partly financed by the Rhodes Trust. The Round Table's object was to influence those who shaped public opinion in Britain and the empire by press articles, pamphlets, discussion groups and individual contacts.

An imperial federation was the Round Table's goal. Its members believed that Britain could not survive economically and remain a global power unless it became the dominant force within a closely bonded empire. They feared that this 'big' issue could easily get lost amid public debates over tariffs and the price of a loaf of bread. Just what the Round Table achieved is hard to judge, at least before 1914. Lionel Curtis, the Round Table's roving ambassador to the dominions was cordially welcomed by their leaders, but his message cut no ice with them. As in the colonial conferences, they identified manoeuvres to secure a formal imperial unity with the machinations of the British ruling class. There was also an understandable fear that if a federation was formed, the dominions would find themselves relegated to the role of passive junior partners. So, while dominions were sincere in their profession of emotional attachment to Britain, they remained extremely lukewarm towards the forging of more tangible links.

By 1914 imperial union was as far off as ever. There had been greater progress in making the public and the working class in particular more aware of the empire. It is impossible to know how far the catchwords of those organisations which promoted various forms of patriotism and imperialism entered the national consciousness. Many who heard them became the rank and file of the mass volunteer army formed between 1914 and 1916 to fight on the Western Front. Then, as in the Boer War, the slogans of popular patriotism did not travel to the fighting line; the letters home written by working-class soldiers reflected little of the strident patriotism whipped up by the press and the recruiters or the lower key pre-war imperial propaganda. What they did reveal was an acute sense of duty, a determination to persevere and an intense loyalty to comrades and unit.

'Speak for empire, Leo':
Leo Emery, Conservative
politician and imperialist,
prepares to address the
problems of empire in this
caricature by David Low.
(By courtesy of the
National Portrait Gallery)

SPORT AND THE EMPIRE

Playing games and hunting developed stamina and character, qualities vital for those who ran the empire. This was the gospel of the public schools and it had many converts. Oxford and Cambridge blues were preferred as candidates for the Sudan and colonial civil services: they understood the quality of fair play, which was the essence of sportsmanship, were physically tough and knew how to work in a team. Equestrian sports and hunting were essential for the imperial soldier, for they developed horsemanship and an eye for country.

ABOVE *Deck cricket,*
c.1890.
(© P&O)

LEFT *Tennis party,*
India, c.1890.
(© NAM)

RIGHT *Polo chukka,*
India, c.1920.

ABOVE *Mysore hunt moving off, India, c.1920.*

LEFT *Big game shooting, India, c.1920.*

II

TO JOIN
THE KHAKI LINE:
THE EMPIRE AND THE
COMING OF WAR

Hints that a major war was imminent, even welcome, were implicit in much Edwardian imperial propaganda. In a pamphlet of 1911 the National Service League reminded the British 'lad' that he alone stood between 'his mother and sister, his sweetheart and his girlfriend' and the 'inconceivable infamy of alien invasion'. Any ethical or physical qualms which he might have had about taking up arms were swept aside by the glib assertions that 'war is not murder, as some fancy, war is sacrifice – which is the soul of Christianity', and 'fighting and killing are not of the essence of it [war], but are accidents'.

From 1906 onwards the country was convulsed by spasmodic bouts of spy mania, with rumours of an underground army of German secret agents and equally ridiculous reports of nocturnal Zeppelin flights over Yorkshire. The conscription lobby carefully exploited that intense, irrational fear of sudden invasion which had long been embedded in the national psyche. It had broken surface intermittently throughout the past century with invasion alarms and accompanying calls for national vigilance and rearmament. There was, however, an important difference between Victorian and early twentieth-century invasion scares which made the latter far more convincing: the growing German navy.

The Kaiser was convinced that if Germany, like Britain, possessed a large fleet, she could become a world power on the same scale and with equal, if not greater influence. At first, Wilhelm II had regarded the German navy as a necessary counterbalance to those of France and Russia, but it was soon apparent to him that it could be used as the servant of Germany's new *Weltpolitik*. If, as he and his advisers wished, Germany was to acquire colonies and international power commensurate with its growing wealth, it would have to be prepared to challenge Britain on more-or-less equal terms.

The creation of the German navy, its presence 400 miles from Britain's coastline, and the possibility that it might be used as a bludgeon to extort overseas concessions, presented the government with three problems. The first two were practical: new ships had to be laid down to preserve the Royal Navy's advantage in numbers, and the existing fleet would have to be redistributed to provide squadrons for home defence. Calling home men-o'-war from overseas stations demanded a complete overhaul of Britain's relations with those powers against which they had hitherto been deployed, France and Russia. Rearmament and diplomacy therefore proceeded side by side in what became a search for world-wide security. The first phase of this new course in British policy opened with the Japanese alliance of 1902, which cleared the way for the reduction of the Far Eastern fleet.

The radical restructuring and modernising of the navy began in 1904 under the direction of the First Sea Lord, Admiral Lord Fisher. Fisher's greatest contribution to the remaking of the Royal Navy was pushing through the design and building of a new type of battleship, HMS *Dreadnought*. *Dreadnought* took a record eleven months to construct, was completed in October 1906, and rendered all other battleships obsolete. Three more Dreadnought-class battleships were laid down in 1906–7, along with two battlecruisers, HMS *Inflexible* and *Indomitable*. These were also faster than conventional battleships thanks to lighter armour-plating and represented a revolution in naval architecture. *Dreadnought* and its immediate successors gave Britain a head start in what was a new contest with Germany; but the Germans possessed the will, technology, and most importantly the cash to narrow the gap. As German naval planners realised, the Anglo-German naval race was an economic marathon, rather like the American Star Wars project of the 1980s, in which victory would ultimately go to the power with the longest purse.

Nearly every Dreadnought-class battleship and battlecruiser built between 1906 and 1914 was earmarked for service in the reconstituted Home and Channel fleets, which were now the empire's first line of defence. Between 1904 and 1910 Fisher completely changed the disposition of Britain's navy: in 1896 there had been 74 ships stationed in home waters and 142 overseas; fourteen years later these totals were 480 and 83 respectively.

Such a sweeping change in the Royal Navy's deployment had been facilitated by the new course in Britain's foreign policy. In April 1904, Britain agreed the *entente cordiale* with France, a collection of accommodations which ended twenty years of acrimony and sabre-rattling over colonial boundaries and spheres of influence. Most important in terms of imperial security was French recognition of Britain's position in Egypt, a concession paid for by Britain's acknowledgement of France's paramountcy in Morocco. This was put to the test in 1905 and 1911, when Britain stood by France in resisting German encroachments in this region.

It was less easy to come to a similar understanding with Russia, despite French encouragement. There was profound suspicion of Russian expansionism among British diplomats and strategists, and fears of a Russian attack on

India were as strong as ever. Despite an Anglo-Russian Convention of August 1907 misgivings about Russia remained strong in British official circles, fuelled by evidence of renewed Russian interest in Mesopotamia, Persia and Turkestan.

Britain had done comparatively well from its *détentes* with France and Russia, even if Russian goodwill was brittle. Disentanglement from old disputes had left successive British governments free to adjust their overall strategy to meet the threat of the German fleet in the North Sea. This had been achieved without entering into any formal engagement binding the country to war if either France or Russia was attacked; indeed, as late as 1912 strategists could still seriously contemplate the possibilities of a war against the latter in certain circumstances. This view of future neutrality in a European conflict between the great powers was not taken by the War Office, which in January 1906 asked for and obtained cabinet permission to open covert discussion with the French general staff on future cooperation in the event of a war with Germany.

Front-runner in the naval race: HMS Thunderer, one of the new class of Dreadnought battleships which were the yardstick of modern naval power, 1914. (© IWM)

What turned out to be a momentous decision was taken by the new Liberal Prime Minister, Sir Henry Campbell-Bannerman, the Foreign Secretary, Sir Edward Grey, and the Minister for War, Richard Haldane. Knowledge of the Anglo-French military conversations, like that of Britain's atomic bomb programme forty years later, remained confined to an inner circle of ministers and the high-ranking officers involved. Only in 1912 was the whole cabinet informed of the by now well-advanced plan to send a 160,000-strong expeditionary force to the Franco-Belgian frontier if France was attacked by Germany.

The race to build ships continued with Britain managing to stay ahead of Germany. One of the new battlecruisers ordered in 1909, HMS *New Zealand*, was paid for by the New Zealand government, and Australia footed the bill for another, HMS *Australia*, which became the flagship of its new navy. These gestures represented a triumph for those British statesmen and diplomats who had for some years been attempting to persuade the dominion governments that it was in their interests to participate actively in the implementation of the new imperial grand strategy. It was assumed, at least by the British government, that measures undertaken to secure the defence of the homeland against the German navy were in the interests of all the dominions. Dominion politicians were not altogether convinced; Sir William Laurier, who was Prime Minister of Canada until 1911, believed that his country would remain inviolate from outside attack because of the Royal Navy and the Monroe Doctrine, by which the United States pledged itself to oppose any foreign intervention in any part of the Americas. It was therefore pointless for Canadians to reach into their pockets to subsidise defences they did not need.

Australia and New Zealand objected on other grounds. 'Germany is not a danger,' claimed Andrew Fisher, Australia's Prime Minister, on the eve of the 1909 imperial conference on defence, 'We have to look to the Pacific for a menace if there is any.' For some time, Australians and New Zealanders had been nervously glancing northwards towards Japan. What they, and Canadians looking westwards, saw was 'a thousand million Asiatics . . . looking southward with hungry eyes'. This frightening image of the restless masses of the Far East fanning out across the Pacific and eventually taking over the empty spaces of Australasia was partly the motivation behind the Defence Acts of 1903, 1904, 1911 and 1912 which introduced military training for young men. Likewise, Australia's decision to create its own navy in 1909 (which had an annual budget of over £2 million) was taken in the light of the imagined Japanese threat. New Zealand's introduction of compulsory military training in 1909 was similarly motivated.

Neither Australia nor New Zealand placed much trust in Britain's alliance with Japan, which to all intents and purposes placed the protection of British Pacific interests in the hands of the Imperial Japanese Navy. It was argued that in the event of Britain becoming embroiled in a war against Germany, Japan would snatch the opportunity to advance on Australasia and possibly British Columbia, which already had a Japanese immigrant community. It was, therefore, necessary for the British government to reassure Australia and New Zealand that by committing themselves to a grand strategy based upon the defence of Britain from the German navy, they were not leaving themselves vulnerable to Japan. At the same time, Britain could not abandon its alliance with Japan without seriously weakening its fleet in home waters.

Close and willing dominion cooperation was absolutely vital for Britain's grand strategy. If Britain found itself fighting an extended land war, it would have to rely heavily on dominion manpower since, by 1914, 20 million of the empire's 65-million-strong white population lived in Canada, South Africa, Australia and New Zealand. For this reason alone Asquith's government had to calm whatever doubts the dominions entertained about their own safety and persuade them to integrate their armed forces with those of Britain.

The 1911 conference on imperial defence witnessed the greatest breakthrough in the procuring of closer dominion participation in Britain's grand strategy. Sir Edward Grey held centre stage. In a compelling, eloquent speech, he declared that Britain would only involve itself in a European war if one of the powers adopted what he called a 'Napoleonic policy', that is establishing dominance over the entire continent by force or intimidation. In such an event, British seapower would be in jeopardy since the paramount state could confront Britain with the fleets of as many as five other countries. Grey's audience agreed that without British seapower, the dominions would be unable to survive in their present state. It was for this reason imperative that they made common cause with Britain if the circumstances described by Grey came about.

Grey assured his listeners that Britain had no hidden understandings with any other power and the dominion representatives heard nothing whatsoever about the past five years of planning for the despatch of an expeditionary force to France. Nor would they hear anything in the future, for the dominion members on the Committee of Imperial Defence were specifically excluded from discussions of military and naval matters which did not concern the dominions. Even if they were in the dark about Britain's tentative commitment to fight the Germans in north-eastern France, the dominion leaders were now convinced that they would have to support Britain if and when she believed her seapower was threatened. As Grey had made clear, not to do so would imperil each dominion.

By making seapower the issue which would decide whether or not Britain entered a European conflict, Asquith's government had brought the dominions into line. Few present at the conference could have doubted that Germany would be the power whose 'Napoleonic' pretensions would precipitate a war. Taking breakfast with David Lloyd George the morning after Grey's address, Louis Botha, the Prime Minister of South Africa, announced that immediately the conflict began he would invade German South-West Africa with 40,000 men. Australia and New Zealand had already been urged to take swift action against German colonies in the Pacific once war started, although they probably needed little encouragement. By 1912, Britain was clearly winning the naval race.

> *So long as the maintenance of Sea Power and the maintenance and control of the sea communications is the underlying motive of our policy in Europe, it is obvious how that is a common interest between us at home and all the Dominions.*
>
> SIR EDWARD GREY, 1911

THE FINAL SCORE IN 1914

	BATTLESHIPS/BATTLECRUISERS	CRUISERS	DESTROYERS
Britain:	24	91	155
Germany:	16	41	88

As expected the cost had been heavy; the annual naval budget had jumped from £29.2 million in 1900 to £47.4 million in 1914. But it had been worth the strain, for Fisher, whose optimism matched his pugnacity, boasted in June 1911 that the Royal Navy 'at this moment could take on all the Navies of the World! Let 'em all come!'

But when would they come, and why? The Balkan crisis of June–July 1914 aroused as little stir in Britain as its predecessors; even on 3 August, when Britain was on the eve of declaring war, Lady Beatty could report to her husband that, 'To see the crowds wandering round London you would not think anything is happening.' The following day was a bank holiday and visitors to Lowestoft and Yarmouth seemed as indifferent to their country's predicament as the Londoners. A party of senior officers, summoned to the Suffolk coast after a false invasion alarm, were 'driven into' by four young lady golfers, one of whose shots nearly brought down a general. Furious, he called them over and asked, 'My dear young ladies, the Germans are expected to land this afternoon. Do you know what rape is? I advise you to head for home.'

These sportswomen could be excused their ignorance of the events of the past six weeks and their climax early in August because they had not directly involved the interests of Britain or the empire. The assassination of Archduke Franz-Ferdinand and his wife in Sarajevo by Serbian terrorists had provoked a confrontation between Germany's ally, Austria-Hungary, and Serbia, which enjoyed Russian patronage.

Germany was willing to back Austria-Hungary's demands which, despite Serbia's history of sponsorship of terrorism, appeared harsh. Russia, anxious to prove itself as the champion of all Slavs, backed its protégé in what was developing into a trial of strength with Austria. Everything hung on the attitudes of Germany and Russia. The Kaiser and his high command, frightened by the scale of recent Russian rearmament, had for some time been convinced that the sooner war came with Russia the better for Germany. Czar Nicholas II and his advisers were equally belligerent, and were driven by a deep-seated urge to prove that Russia was again a power to be reckoned with. The final week of July saw a rapid escalation of the dispute with the mobilisation of the Austro-Hungarian, Russian and German armies. With Russia beset by two assailants, France fulfilled its duty and ordered mobilisation.

So far Britain was under no threat. Grey, pestered by France for help, could only promise that the fleet would prevent any German seaborne attack on the French coast. He was an interventionist but, like others within the cabinet, he knew that a declaration of war against Germany would require the backing of public opinion. There was, especially on the left, much hostility towards Russia, the most oppressive tyranny in Europe, and it could reasonably be argued that Serbia had brought its misfortunes on itself. What was needed, as in 1899, was a moral cause to unite the public. It was provided on 29 July when the German government demanded free passage through Belgium for its armies. Britain was one of the signatories to the treaty which guaranteed Belgian neutrality, and by upholding it could appear as the honourable defender of international good faith against a power which believed that might was right.

Belgium refused Germany's demand and was invaded on 2 August, giving the British cabinet the just cause it had been seeking. When, on 3 August, Grey outlined to the cabinet the reasons for intervention, one listener was surprised to hear nothing about immediate national and imperial interests. Much could have been left unsaid: Germany's occupation of the Belgian coastline; the defeat of France; and a Carthaginian peace which might involve the surrender of its fleet and colonies would all endanger Britain and the empire. So too would neutrality, for it would transform France and Russia into enemies who between them had an infinitely greater capacity than Germany to harm Britain's overseas possessions. It was safer to have that mass of men and weaponry known as the Russian steamroller trundling towards Berlin rather than the Indian frontier.

Once it was clear that Germany would trample on Belgian neutrality, Britain declared war. The order for mobilisation was given at ten to four on 4 August; army officers playing tennis or cricket that sunny afternoon were notified by the waving of white handkerchiefs. Within a fortnight, the advance guard of the British Expeditionary Force was disembarking at the ports of northern France. They were warmly welcomed.

The Balkan crisis had excited as little concern in the dominions as it had in Britain. As the situation deteriorated and Europe's armies sprang to arms, the British government initiated the precautionary procedures agreed with its dominion partners and set down in the War Book. The governments of Canada, South Africa, Australia and New Zealand recognised that the crisis had come of which Grey had spoken three years before, and that Germany was that nation whose 'Napoleonic' ambitions in Europe now imperilled British seapower. News that Canada's Prime Minister, Sir Robert Borden, had offered Britain his country's backing and 30,000 fighting men, prompted Australia to equal this number on 3 August.

The profoundly moving spirit of comradeship and carefree, jaunty patriotism which agitated the thousands of young men who rushed to recruiting stations in Britain during the late summer of 1914 was matched in the dominions. Many, perhaps the majority of young men welcomed the war as an adventure, but there was also a strong vein of patriotism running through the ranks of those who joined up. A nineteen-year-old Australian patriot wrote that he and his brothers-in-arms were preparing to uphold 'the traditions of the British race'; he was killed in action at Gallipoli. The flood of offers of men from the dominion governments which reached London within a few days of the declaration of war were a reassuring demonstration of imperial solidarity.

From Sydney to Esquimault, from the Lakes to Hudson Bay, Men who never saw you, Mother, those that left you yesterday, We have chucked the tools and ledgers, we have left the bench and mine, We are sailing east to Flanders to Join the khaki line.

We are coming, wild and woolly, Hearts and hands are with you fully, Pledged to smash the Prussian bully, Five hundred thousand strong.

CANADIAN SOLDIER-POET

Senior service:
the Anglo-German
naval race focused
public attention on
the Royal Navy and
advertisers were quick
to exploit this interest.
Images of the Royal
Navy symbolised
superior quality.
(All © Opie)

GRAND TOURS

The development of luxury liners during the last quarter of the nineteenth century encouraged cruises to hitherto remote, exotic places. For those travelling for commercial or official reasons, sea voyages were interrupted by sight-seeing excursions ashore. Egypt was a popular stopping place for those bound to India, the Far East and Australasia.

RIGHT *Promenade*:
diversion on a board a P&O liner, c.1890.
(© P&O)

BELOW *The wonders of the Orient*:
tourists pose before the Pyramids, c.1900.

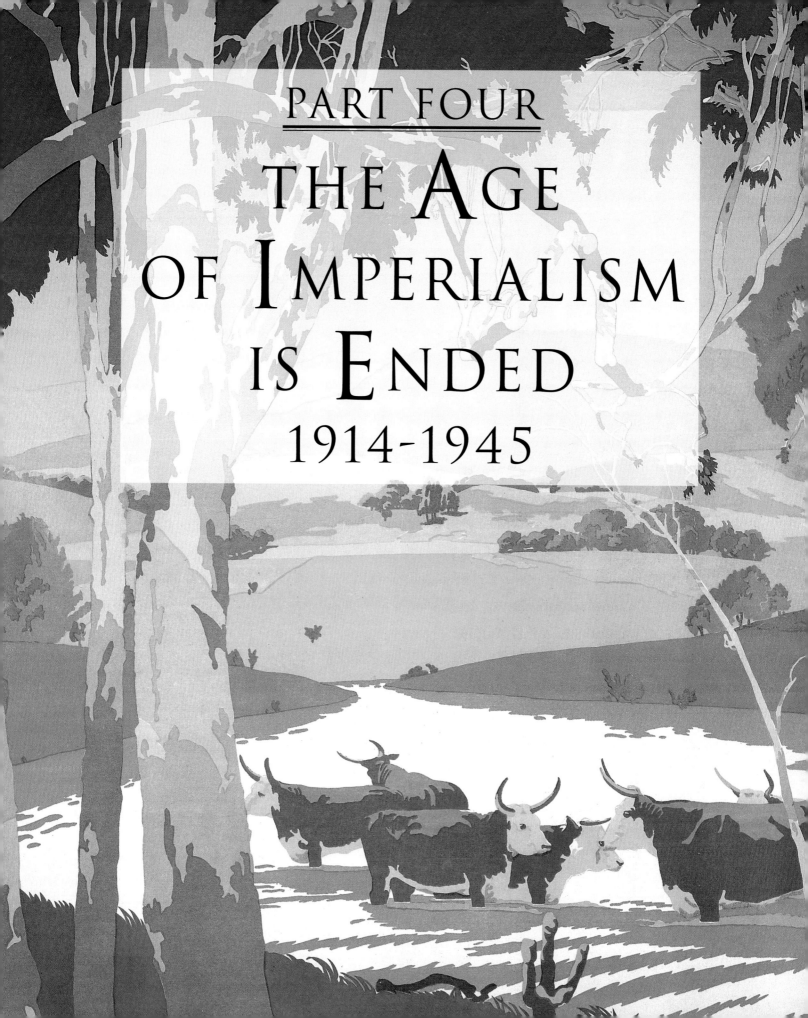

PART FOUR

THE AGE OF IMPERIALISM IS ENDED

1914-1945

I

E IS FOR EMPIRE
FOR WHICH
WE WOULD DIE:

1914–1918

The resources of the empire made Britain the most formidable power engaged in the war. The empire covered a quarter of the earth's land surface and had a population of 425 million of whom 366 million were coloured, and of these, 316 million lived in India. This manpower was ruthlessly exploited to provide both fighting men and the host of labourers and carriers which supported the imperial armies on every front. By 1918 there were nearly a third of a million Chinese, Africans and Egyptians in France alone. By undertaking the donkey work of total war, these men, like their counterparts on other fronts, released white men to replenish the firing line. The claim, based solely on a head count of servicemen, that Britain never fully utilised the empire's manpower is absurd; Nyasaland yielded 15,000 askaris and 200,000 labourers between 1914 and 1918, two-thirds of its adult male population. The proportion of black soldiers could have been higher, but the Colonial Office was nervous about black men fighting white, and senior officers wrongly imagined that the negro lacked the steadiness and fortitude of the European.

The war revealed in the starkest possible way the undercurrents of racial prejudice and tension which had long swirled and eddied just below the surface throughout the empire. Sir James Willcocks, who commanded Indian forces in France between October 1914 and September 1915, publicly praised the Indian fighting man as 'a first-class soldier and Nature's gentleman', but privately abhorred the thought of such men being tended by white nurses.

It was axiomatic among senior commanders that imperial prestige in the Middle East was best upheld by white troops. This was not entirely racial prejudice; the sudden influx of Indian and

The British Empire, 1914

‡ Naval Bases and Depôts
— Imperial cable routes
Egypt was a protectorate
Sudan was under Anglo-Egyptian rule

PREVIOUS PAGES LEFT
Australian cattle:

*an image from a 1930s
poster urging consumers
to buy empire produce.*
(© PRO)

PREVIOUS PAGES RIGHT
Holy war:

*a German cartoon of
1914 predicts a Pan-
Islamic rising which
would paralyse the empire
in the Middle East and
India. The Turkish
sultan declared a jihad,
but the results were
disappointing. British
statesmen and generals
were alarmed and
encouraged the 1916
Arab revolt in Arabia as
a counterstroke.*

black units into this region in June 1918 and the transfer to France of white soldiers fuelled rumours among the Egyptians that Britain was on the verge of defeat, and that the new arrivals were expendable men who would soon be swept aside by the Turks and Germans. That the Egyptians should have thought along these lines says much about their experience of British racial attitudes.

These were apparent elsewhere in the Middle East army, which included British, dominion, Indian and colonial troops. Men from two Royal Fusiliers battalions, recruited from London's Jewish community, protested against being brigaded with the West Indians, who themselves were angry at being placed in hospital wards alongside Asian and African invalids 'who were ignorant of the English language and western customs'. West Indians were further enraged by being ordered into foul railway carriages which Anzac soldiers had just refused to enter.

By contrast, the Indian professional soldier knew his duty and place in the scheme of things, or so his officers thought. The stress of war proved them wrong, for the fighting spirit of the two Indian divisions sent to France in the autumn of 1914 soon evaporated. Despite internal reforms of the past decade, the Indian army and its senior officers were physically and mentally unprepared to fight a modern, European war. A combination of cold, wet weather and extraordinarily heavy casualties (some units were reduced by half in a single action) suffered in battle led to a decay of morale which was reflected in a rash of self-inflicted wounds and malingering during the winter of 1914–15. In May 1915, the censors of Indian soldiers' mail revealed that a large number were infected with 'despair of survival', and Field-Marshal Lord Haig feared that a mutiny was imminent. The Indian government, which had vainly attempted to keep knowledge of its soldiers' discontent to itself, concurred, and in September the Indian contingent was pulled out of France for redeployment in Mesopotamia.

The process of finding a way to end the deadlock in the West was painfully slow and bloody. It was marked by a sequence of mass offensives between 1915 and 1918 which consumed men by the hundred thousand and yielded relatively minor tactical gains. It soon became clear that the Allies would need a continual flow of fighting men to make good the losses which were the inevitable result of a war of

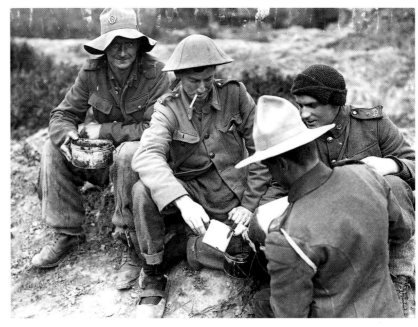

attrition. To start with, in the belief that the contest would be soon over, Britain and the dominions had relied on volunteers but by 1916 Britain followed by New Zealand were forced to introduce conscription. In Australia there was widespread resistance to compulsory service, in Canada its enforcement provoked riots in Quebec and in South Africa, where a minority of Afrikaners were pro-German, the government didn't even consider conscription. The reactions to conscription of Australian Irish, *Canadiens* and Boers were a reminder that within the white dominions were communities whose collective historic memory made it impossible for them to have any natural affinity with Britain, or any emotional attachment to the idea of empire.

By the beginning of 1915 two distinct views were emerging amongst those deciding military strategy. The 'Westerners' believed that resources should be concentrated in France on the grounds that victory could only be achieved by the defeat of the German army there. The 'Easterners' on the other hand argued that the war in France had reached a stalemate and that an attack should be made on Germany's weaker allies, whose destruction would undermine Germany.

Turkey was the first target of the Easterners. Forcing the Straits would bring down the Ottoman empire and open a passage to Russia, which was showing signs of extreme strain. Furthermore, and this made the enterprise highly attractive to imperialists such as Churchill and Kitchener, Britain could take a share of Turkish provinces. The 'scramble' for Turkey had, in fact, already started; in November 1914 an Indian expeditionary force had occupied Basra and was tentatively moving northwards, while the Russians had invaded eastern Anatolia. Diplomatic preparations for a post-war division of the spoils were in hand. By the end of the year, Russia had been allocated the Straits, and after much wrangling the Sykes-Picot agreement of May 1916 defined the boundaries of the British and French official and unofficial empires in Syria, the Lebanon, Palestine and Mesopotamia.

According to the Easterners, operations against Turkey would puncture Germany's 'soft underbelly', might lead to a Balkan front against Austria-Hungary and would provide an opportunity to extend the empire. If, as seemed likely between 1915 and 1917, it was impossible to break the deadlock in France, then a negotiated peace with Germany would follow. Britain had, therefore, to acquire some bargaining counters and look to the future. Sir Mark Sykes, a Yorkshire MP with a specialist, first-hand knowledge of the Middle East, argued in 1916 that by tightening its grip on southern Mesopotamia Britain would be better placed to resist post-war Russian

ABOVE *Rum ration*: *New Zealanders take refreshment in the trenches, June 1916.*

BELOW *Home from home*: *Newfoundland infantrymen in the snow, Hesdin, December 1917. (Both © IWM)*

encroachments in the region. He, like many others, assumed that when the war ended the great powers would restart their former global jockeying for influence and territory.

The Easterners' arguments prevailed within the war cabinet and the result was the Dardanelles expedition in the spring of 1915. Its supporters not only claimed that it would knock Turkey out of the war, but it would be a spectacular affirmation of the military might of the British empire and France. This object lesson in imperial power quickly went awry. In all, 129,000 troops were landed, a third of them Anzacs, but Turkish resistance was dogged. The campaign dragged on into the autumn, and, when it was obvious that no breakthrough could be made, the war cabinet reluctantly approved a withdrawal.

The evacuation of the Gallipoli peninsula in December 1915 was a signal humiliation for the imperial powers, particularly Britain. The conventional imperial wisdom, expressed shortly afterwards by a senior Indian army officer, held that, 'We owe our position to the fundamental and inherent superiority of the European as a fighting man over the Asiatic.' But this no longer held true: a predominantly Turkish army had beaten a predominantly white one and proved that Europeans were not invincible. Gallipoli confirmed for the peoples of Asia and the Middle East the lesson of Russia's defeat at the hands of Japan ten years before: white armies were not unbeatable. Mustapha Kamal Pasha, who had masterminded the defence of the Dardanelles and is better known by his post-war name, Kamal Atatürk, became the focus for and leader of the Turkish national movement, and an example to other Middle Eastern nationalists. A further blow to European supremacy was delivered in April 1916, when an Anglo-Indian army was forced to surrender at Kut-al-Amhara on the Tigris.

Making do:
Australian soldiers
improvised dug-outs,
Anzac Cove, Gallipoli,
1915. For Australia and
New Zealand, the killing
ground of the Gallipoli
peninsula marked a
national rite of passage;
the anniversary of the
landing was and still is
celebrated annually in
each country.
(© Australian War
Memorial)

The reverses at Gallipoli and Kut damaged British prestige. The last confirmed the unfitness for modern warfare of the Indian army, or at least its high command. The 'scramble' for Turkey was proving a far harder task than its earlier counterparts in Africa and China. In terms of winning the war, the Gallipoli and Mesopotamian campaigns were, as the Westerners had always insisted, sideshows which wasted manpower needed to fight the real war in France.

Another 'sideshow' which was to have long-term consequences for the Middle East was what became known as the Arab Revolt. At first it appeared an adroit imperial coup, devised by a handful of dedicated Foreign and War Office officials and intelligence officers based in Cairo, of whom Captain, later Colonel T. E. Lawrence (Lawrence of Arabia) became the best known. They hoped to encourage the defection of Arabs from the Turkish to the Allied cause and with this in mind they courted Hussain, sharif of Mecca. Politically, the ultra-conservative head of the Hashemite family was an ideal partner, but Hussain's cause also attracted more radical Arab nationalists, who were looking ahead to post-war Arab nations arising from the wreckage of the Ottoman empire. The trouble was, and this became increasingly clear during 1917–18 as Arab forces guided by Lawrence moved northwards from the Hejaz, Britain and France had already staked out claims to lands which the Arabs hoped to have for themselves.

Furthermore, the Indian government was laying plans for the post-war annexation of Mesopotamia, not only as a defensive measure, but as a colony which could be settled by Indian immigrants. By cultivating Arab nationalism, the London government was creating what Lord Hardinge prophetically described as 'a Frankenstein's monster'.

The United States's entry into the war in April 1917 gave comfort to the Allies, but at least a year was needed in which to recruit and equip American troops for service in France, where, it was believed, they would tip the balance. The Doughboys and the United States navy were welcomed by Britain, but not America's voice in the direction of the war. The private apprehensions of Britain's rulers were summed up by Robert Vansittart, a diplomat (*right*).

Seen from the bleak perspective of 1917 it appeared that the Allies might never beat the German army, and that the war would end with a negotiated settlement. If a treaty had to be arranged, it was assumed that it would be along the lines of the 1815 Vienna Settlement with a redistribution of territory and spheres of influence. It was therefore vital that when the fighting stopped Britain was in a position to demand and get whatever was needed to safeguard and possibly extend her existing empire.

Within a few months Lloyd George had become committed to the post-war retention of Mesopotamia and Palestine, and in June he appointed General Sir Edmund Allenby to take command of the Egyptian Expeditionary Office with orders to capture Jerusalem by Christmas. The Prime Minister hoped that this victory would simultaneously embellish the reputation of his ministry and serve as an antidote to the war-weariness that was currently infecting many sections of British society.

Jerusalem fell according to schedule, and the official newsreel of Allenby's entry was distributed to cinemas throughout the empire as a morale booster. Lloyd George, speaking in the Commons debate

For the King Emperor:
Indian lancers go
into action, Vraignies,
France, April 1917.
(© IWM)

**The United States,
still holier than we,
still mulling over
British Imperialism,
George III and the
Easter Rebellion in
Dublin, slid into the
Great War. We
wondered whether
the new belligerent's
needs would interfere
with ours.**

ROBERT VANSITTART

For King and empire:
Canadians go over
the top, 1918.
(© IWM)

before the Christmas recess, referred to the fall of Jerusalem and that of Baghdad a few months before in terms of old-style imperial conquest. The implication was clear: Britain had kept Canada and Bengal and would, therefore, retain Palestine and Mesopotamia after the war. Lloyd George's conversion to acquisitive imperialism must have pleased those high-ranking army officers who were forever worrying about safe, defensible frontiers. A swathe of Middle Eastern lands would create a vast corridor which would connect Egypt with India and serve as a shield against aggression from the north.

However, matters were complicated by the attitude of President Woodrow Wilson and his fourteen points, which he presented to Congress in January 1918 as the Allies' war aims. His list of Allied conditions was a catalogue of impeccable rectitude and included pledges of post-war self-determination for the peoples of central and southern Europe, who had hitherto been under German or Austro-Hungarian rule. Article V tentatively extended this principle beyond Europe. Decisions as to the future of ex-German colonies and Ottoman provinces would be reached after balancing 'the interests of the populations concerned' with those of the imperial power claiming the territory in question. Wilson had been extremely hesitant about this proposal for fear of giving offence to Britain, but he persevered to find a form of words which, he hoped, would not distress America's ally.

He did not succeed. Wilsonian high-mindedness had destroyed all hope of a peace along traditional European lines in which Britain would have bartered colonies for redrawn continental boundaries. This was a nuisance for Lloyd George and the government, but they had to put up with it as the price of American financial and material assistance. As Vansittart drily noted of Wilson's peace terms, 'Our ruling class did not relish the role of John Bull with a ring through his nose.' Nine months before the publication of Wilson's proposals, the former Conservative Prime Minister, Arthur Balfour, had warned the cabinet not to allow 'Central European Philanthropy' to stand in the way of the achievement of post-war imperial security. The interests of Poles, Czechs, Romanians and assorted Yugoslavs, who had done little or nothing to further the Allied cause, had to remain subordinate to those of Britain. Moreover, Australia and New Zealand, which had acquired Germany's Pacific islands, and South Africa, which had conquered South West Africa, refused to consider relinquishing them. Likewise, the British government was unwilling to surrender Togoland and the Cameroons, which had been overrun between

1914 and 1916, or German East Africa, which had been finally taken after a prolonged and arduous campaign in December 1917.

By the autumn of 1918 the German army had lost ground and the will to fight on. The end came unexpectedly for the Allies, whose high command was preparing for operations in 1919 and a possible outright victory the following year. During the first week of November the disintegration of public order in Germany, the Kaiser's abdication and a mutiny by sailors of the High Seas fleet drove the government to ask for terms. The armistice, which was tantamount to a German surrender, took effect on 11 November. On other fronts it was the same story of hammer-blows followed by a swift collapse. In the Middle East, Allenby's brilliant and fast-moving offensive shattered an outnumbered Turko-German army and Damascus was liberated by Australian cavalrymen on 30 September. Within a month, Aleppo and Antioch had fallen and the Turkish government had surrendered. Simultaneous Allied offensives in northern Italy and south-eastern Europe brought Austria-Hungary and Bulgaria to their knees. The British empire had survived and won. Curzon, in exultant mood, spoke of a future world in which the empire would be supreme.

For the dominions, the experience of war had been a rite of passage to nationhood. Anzac Day, the anniversary of the landings at Gallipoli, became a national day of remembrance in Australia and New Zealand. Its emotional meaning and the part played by those who had died in the development of national consciousness were poignantly illustrated in a small ceremony re-enacted at school morning assemblies in New Zealand during the 1920s. A boy faced a portrait of George V, saluted and then announced: 'Our King inspires loyalty and devotion to our country and its laws because he rules by consent of the people. God Save the King!' The National Anthem was sung. Afterwards, a boy recited these lines:

The Great War proved that thousands of New Zealanders thought our beautiful
country worth dying for. Like them, we pledge ourselves to live and, if necessary, die
for our country and for our comrades throughout the Empire . . .

CASUALTIES IN THE FIRST WORLD WAR		
	DEAD	WOUNDED
Great Britain:	702,000	1.67 million
India:	64,000	67,000
Australia:	59,300	152,000
Canada:	56,700	150,000
New Zealand:	16,700	41,300
South Africa:	7,000	12,000
Newfoundland:	1,200	2,200

But had men died for the empire? Recruiting slogans and posters made much of the empire; a patriotic ABC for Canadian soldiers written in 1916 included the exhortation, 'E is the Empire for which we would die', and there were plenty of illustrations which showed the British lion roaring defiance with her cubs (the dominions) adding their yelps. Keith Fallis, a missionary's son who at nineteen had enlisted in the Canadian army, believed that he, and presumably others, had been 'brainwashed' by pre-war imperial propaganda. 'I never questioned', he later recollected, 'that what we were doing was right and that the Germans were all wrong and that we were fighting to make the world safe for democracy.' The front was no place for flag-waving since soldiers' minds were wholly concentrated on staying alive or recuperating from the trauma of battle. Working-class British soldiers in France were unmoved by the word 'empire', although some were stirred by it in the mistaken belief that it referred to the Empire Music Hall!

The black soldier's motive for fighting is not always easy to discern, for he seldom left any record of his experiences. When explanations of the war were offered them, they focussed on the possibility that the Germans would come and take their land. This was what recruits in Nyasaland heard in 1914. A Nigerian who served as a porter during the 1916–18 Cameroons campaign was told 'that we were going to the great war to help keep the King's soldiers who were preventing the Germans coming to our country and burning it.'

From the beginning of the war, there had been official misgivings about the mass recruitment of black soldiers. A Colonial Office official reminded the War Office in 1915 that:

it must not be forgotten that a West African native trained to use of arms and filled
with a new degree of self-confidence by successful encounters with forces armed and
led by Europeans was not likely to be more amenable to discipline in peace time.

The point was understood on the other side of the racial barrier. In South Africa, Solomon Plaatje also recognised the danger of black fighting white. 'The empire must uphold the principle that a coloured man must not raise his hand against a white man if there is to be any law and order in either India, Africa, or any part of the Empire.' His fellow blacks were, quite deliberately, not being asked to kill white men but to do their chores, or, as George V told them when they arrived in France in July 1917: 'Without munitions of War my armies cannot fight; without food they cannot live. You are helping to send these things to them each day, and in so doing you are hurling your spears at the enemy.' What his audience made of this speech is not known. Many had been astonished by meeting educated black men, apparently equal to whites, when they briefly disembarked at Freetown, Sierra Leone. They were also amazed by the sight of white men working on the docks at Liverpool and the free and easy ways of the women of the port.

South Africa's blacks had left behind them a country where a black skin automatically relegated a man to the bottom of the social pile. West Indians came from a society where the black man enjoyed greater advantages; he was educated by missionaries and governed in a benevolent manner by a paternalist colonial administration. Despite their gallantry in the field during the Palestine campaign, West Indian volunteers, keen to serve Britain, endured racial slights which left them humiliated and angry. Their bitterness exploded in a mutiny at Taranto in December 1918. During a protest meeting one

Mind over muscle:
Canadian transport
troops supervise
indentured Chinese
labourers building
a railway, Lapugny,
France, March 1918.
(© IWM)

sergeant shouted out, 'The black man should have freedom and govern himself in the West Indies.' His views were applauded and some months after, Sir George Fiddes, the Permanent Under-Secretary at the Colonial Office, warned officials in the West Indies that the 'white class does not appreciate the altered tone of the black men'.

Indian nationalists saw their country's war effort as a step along the path towards self-government. Their leader Mohandas Gandhi, who had served with a field ambulance unit in the Boer War and during the 1906 Zulu rebellion, offered his services again, but an attack of pleurisy prevented him from going to Mesopotamia. He accepted the Wilsonian vision of the war as one being waged on behalf of the 'weaker and minor nationalities' and, in June 1918, urged his

New weapons for the imperial armoury: aircraft, used here in East Africa in 1918, were soon deployed in the Middle East and India for suppressing unrest.

followers to enlist. Nationalist volunteers, he told an audience in Bombay, would form 'a national army' of 'Home Rulers'. 'They would go to fight for the Empire; but they would so fight because they aspire to become partners in it.'

No binding ideology held together the empire's fighting men. Imperial enthusiasts, mostly in Britain, who held up wartime cooperation as a shining example of how imperial unity could work and the basis for future cohesion were out of touch with reality. An emergency had drawn together Britain and the dominions who, in 1914, were reasonably alarmed by the repercussions of German domination of Europe. British and dominion soldiers fought well, but the latter, particularly Australians and Canadians, were appalled by the rigidity of Britain's social system which had been translated in its entirety into service life. Many were glad that they or their ancestors had emigrated. Black and brown men discovered new worlds; were exposed to new ideas; became conscious of their position within the empire; and returned home questioning some of its assumptions.

Nevertheless, the late-Victorian and Edwardian dream of the various parts of empire joining together to form one solid battleline had come true. What imperialists then and after failed to appreciate was that those who had been asked to make sacrifices might expect recompense. Furthermore, in what was its final surge of empire-building, Britain had used the war to conquer territories in the Middle East in alliance with Arab nationalism. In 1918 it remained to be seen how, if at all, acquisitive imperialism could be squared with the rights of Gandhi's 'weaker and minor nationalities' in whose interests Britain had ostensibly been fighting for the last eleven months of the war.

Another novelty of world war, the armoured car, was also adapted for use in colonial conflicts. This Rolls Royce model was employed in East Africa in 1918.

2

CLEAR OUT OR GOVERN:

TROUBLES, MAINLY IRISH

1919–1939

Two viruses afflicted the post-war world. One, Spanish influenza, attacked the body and the other infected the soul; they were equally devastating. While the origins of the second sickness were the subject of conjecture and debate, its symptoms were clear enough. Treatment seemed beyond the powers of statesmen, as Arthur Balfour, then acting Foreign Secretary, remarked in a letter to Sir Reginald Wingate, the high commissioner in Egypt, at the end of March 1919 (*right*). This was a bleak diagnosis from a man who had been brought up to have faith in the eventual triumph of human progress and those civilised forces which underpinned the old world order. At the end of a distinguished political career, he looked out on a world full of mischief. Everywhere there was evidence of the disruptive energy of that protean force which appeared not only unstoppable, but threatened the existence of the empire.

In the past three months Balfour had witnessed the proclamation of an Irish republic by a band of Sinn Féin MPs, and the paralysis of Egypt by saboteurs and mobs clamouring for an end to British rule. Matters soon got worse. During April and May, Gandhi's mass protest against the sedition laws triggered disorders on such a scale as to make some officials believe that India was on the verge of a second mutiny. There were anti-white riots in Trinidad, Jamaica and British Honduras; Kurds rebelled against the new British administration in Iraq; and in May 1920, the Arabs followed suit. In the same year there were anti-Jewish riots in Palestine and the spread of a guerrilla campaign by the Irish Republican Army (IRA).

Britain was not immune from the contagion. British and dominion troops mutinied and rioted against delays in demobilisation during the winter and spring of 1919. In June, a detachment of the Staffordshire Regiment refused to leave for service in India and the summer was marked by a series of police strikes. Most alarming of all was an upsurge in trade union militancy which was reflected in a sequence of strikes throughout 1919 and 1920 that unnerved the government and stirred up fears that Britain was about to face a revolution along Russian lines.

Britain's rulers still believed that given goodwill and flexibility a solution could always be found to any problem, yet disaster had, in fact, already overtaken Ireland. Its Gaelic, Catholic majority no longer had any confidence in those essentially British ways of bringing about political accord. The failure of two Home Rule bills to be passed, and of a third to be implemented, convinced them that they could no longer rely upon the British Parliament to provide them with what they wanted. Their salvation now lay in their own hands, and after 1914 many disappointed nationalists turned towards the Sinn Féin

The Egyptian unrest is doubtless part of a world movement which takes different forms in different places, but is plainly discernible on every continent and in every country. We are only at the beginning of our troubles and it is doubtful whether, and how far, the forces of an orderly civilisation are going to deal effectively with those of social and international disintegration.

ARTHUR BALFOUR

(Ourselves Alone) party, which called upon Irishmen and women to seize freedom for themselves even at the price of their own lives. Drawing heavily on the idealism of the Italian nationalist, Mazzini, Sinn Féin encouraged the Irish to discover their own sense of national identity which would give them the fixity of purpose and inner strength necessary for the inevitable struggle against Britain.

Sinn Féin gave an inspiring example of the sort of self-sacrifice that would be needed if Ireland was to free itself on Easter Day 1916, when its members attempted an armed coup in Dublin. It failed, and the leading insurgents were court-martialled and shot at the orders of the local commander, General Sir John Maxwell, who had learned how to treat the empire's enemies in the Sudan, and who justified his actions on the grounds that traitors could expect no mercy in wartime.

The Easter Rising had been greeted with indifference by most Irishmen, but the courage of the 'martyrs', and exasperation with an alien government which showed scant interest in Irish opinion drove more and more towards Sinn Féin. British influence over southern Ireland dissolved slowly, unnoticed by a government whose attention was focussed on winning the war against Germany. Bit by bit, the administration in Dublin Castle lost its grip over the remoter parts of the country and, when conscription was introduced in April 1918, it was thought prudent not to enforce it, given the present humour of the Irish.

The test, both of public support for Sinn Féin and the authority of the British government, was the general election of December 1918. Seventy-six Sinn Féin MPs were returned (forty-seven were in gaol), together with twenty-six Unionists, and six old-style Home Rule nationalists. The Sinn Féin MPs gathered in Dublin in January 1919, formed the Dáil Eireann and proclaimed Ireland a republic. There were now two governments in Ireland, each claiming legality and denouncing its rival. One, under the Viceroy, Field-Marshal Lord French, occupied Dublin Castle, and the other, headed by President Eamon de Valera, was busy creating its own administrative apparatus and a defence force, the IRA. With the confidence provided by this force, believed to number 100,000 volunteers, the Dáil outlawed the Royal Irish Constabulary (RIC) and demanded the immediate evacuation of all British troops.

The chief objective of Sinn Féin was to prove to the British government that the authority of Dublin Castle had been superseded by that of the Dáil, which was soon running a shadow administration. The first phase of what soon came to be known as the 'Troubles' began during the early summer of 1919, when the IRA launched a systematic campaign against the RIC. The murder of policemen, lightning raids against police stations and burning of police barracks were designed to intimidate and finally destroy the principal instrument of Dublin Castle's control over Ireland. By the end of the year, the police were in disarray and, most importantly, their intelligence-gathering apparatus had fallen apart.

The British government had faced and overcome terrorist campaigns in Ireland during the 1880s, and had coped with massive civilian unrest and rebellion in 1798, the late 1820s, the 1840s and 1860s. There was, at least from the perspective of Whitehall, no reason why the methods which had worked in the past, a mixture of political concession and coercion, would not prove successful again. Ireland was part of the United Kingdom and the empire and could never be detached.

Nevertheless, the events during the first half of 1919 indicated a degree of popular dissatisfaction that had to be remedied. It was taken for granted that Sinn Féin were a small group of fanatics whose power rested on terror alone, and that most Irishmen would welcome a compromise.

The cabinet had, in fact, mistaken the temper of the great majority of southern Irishmen. A further obstacle to a settlement was the widespread contempt for the Gaelic, Catholic Irish, which was the legacy of two hundred years of religious and political propaganda. The Irish were, in English eyes, a fickle, childlike race, unable to subdue their wilder passions. For generations, *Punch* cartoons had portrayed 'Paddy' as a wide-eyed, simian-featured clown brandishing his shillelagh and looking for a fight. This stereotype and all that it implied clouded ministerial judgements. Andrew Bonar Law, the Conservative leader, considered the Irish 'an inferior race' and Lloyd George quipped, 'The Irish have no sense of humour, and that is why they make us laugh so much.'

The government thought that it could stop the violence by giving the Irish a little of what they wanted. In December 1919, the cabinet approved the draft of an Irish Home Rule bill which was laid before the Commons the following spring and passed. It was a recipe designed to satisfy Gaelic nationalism, calm Ulster Protestants and keep Ireland within the empire. First, Ireland was to be partitioned, since it was clear that the Protestant majority in Ulster, which had threatened to fight over the issue in 1886 and 1912, would never accept a government elected by all Irishmen. Ulster was still as defiant as ever. The Unionist leader Sir Edward Carson, speaking at a gathering in Belfast on 12 July 1920, claimed that Ulstermen would only join hands with their Catholic countrymen if the latter chose to stay within 'the Empire [which has] spread civilisation ... throughout vast regions'.

Irishmen would remain in the empire, at least if the British government got its way. Those in the south would have a parliament in Dublin and those in the north one in Belfast. Both assemblies would collect and spend taxes, but foreign and defence affairs would remain Westminster's responsibility. Under the terms of the new Home Rule act, elections were scheduled for May 1921, by which time, it was hoped, the British army and the reinforced RIC would have beaten the IRA.

Sinn Féin rejected all that Lloyd George had to offer. Its supporters wished to part company with Britain and its empire for ever, and the concept of a divided Ireland was anathema to nationalists with a mystical belief in the essential oneness of their land. The republicans could afford to take an unbending line, for they were gaining the upper hand in the war in which their adversaries were at a permanent disadvantage. The IRA fighting man wore no uniform and could not be identified; he slipped out of and into the crowd; and he moved among a people who, either through fear or out of sympathy, were prepared to harbour him or cover his tracks. He was also supported by another unseen army of men, women and youngsters who were his eyes and ears. They warned him of his enemy's movements and lied about his own, activities which sometimes cost them their homes, possessions and even lives.

Urban and rural guerrilla warfare was still a novelty in 1919. Its rules perplexed soldiers used to being able to recognise their opponents and led to a widespread feeling of impotent rage. It soon became obvious that the depleted and demoralised RIC could no longer withstand the IRA's guerrilla campaign without large-scale army assistance. Moreover, IRA terror tactics had reduced police recruitment so that the authorities had to look to the mainland for reinforcements and create what was, in effect, an alien *gendarmerie*. The result was the notorious Black and Tans of Irish nationalist mythology, ex-servicemen recruited in London, Glasgow and Birmingham, who appeared in Ireland in January 1920. Their improvised uniforms, a mixture of RIC dark green and army khaki, reminded somebody of a celebrated pack of Limerick foxhounds and got them their nickname. They were followed by the RIC Auxiliary Divisions

A firm grip:

Prime Minister Lloyd George had his hands full with unrest in Ireland, Egypt, the Middle East and India. In each, a hard line was followed by concessions, thanks to a lack of manpower.

('Auxis'), also recruited outside Ireland. Both bodies quickly gained a reputation for hard drinking, promiscuous brutality and savage reprisals against a population which sheltered and sympathised with their enemies. Their appearance marked the end of civilian policing over large areas of Ireland, where they were seen as a particularly undisciplined wing of an army of occupation.

By the summer of 1920, the pattern of the war had become established. IRA units, sometimes substantial flying columns, assembled, went into action, and then melted into the streets and countryside. They killed at random members of the security forces and anyone remotely associated with them, sometimes mistaking their targets. The IRA volunteer was a patriot, convinced that the moral rightness of his cause, a united republican Ireland, released him from obedience to normal codes of human behaviour. His enemies saw him as a cold-blooded murderer. Particularly horrific killings were answered by reprisals against a civilian population which was tainted with guilt by association.

As the number of reprisals increased, so did criticism of the government by the left-wing and liberal press, which compared the behaviour of British forces in Ireland with that of the Germans in occupied Belgium during the war. A gap was also opening up between politicians and army commanders, who began to argue that the imposition of martial law was the only way in which the IRA could be beaten.

During the second half of 1920 ministers agonised over how far they should go in the war against the IRA. Those in favour of a tough line argued that it would signal the determination of Britain to hold on to its empire. And yet, if the generals were given the free hand they sought, then the politicians would loose control over events. The politicians gave ground, gradually. General Sir Nevill Macready was allowed to impose martial law on four counties in December 1920 and a further four the following month. Although the internment by courts martial of 4,400 IRA suspects in six months, coordinated urban and rural sweeps and searches for arms and ammunition, were paying dividends, the British army had still not overcome many of its operational problems, not least the lack of a competent intelligence-gathering service. By early June, the two sides were facing deadlock. A truce was agreed between Sinn Féin and the government on 12 July and Irish representatives arrived in London for talks three months later.

During the height of the fighting, Colonel Lawrence warned the government that the 'ordinary Englishman' did not desire and could not afford an empire which rested solely on armed force. By June 1921, the cabinet had come to agree with him, grudgingly in some cases. Once it was clear that the IRA would do all in its considerable power to wreck the elections in the south, the only alternative was to declare the twenty-six counties a colony and administer them through a system of martial law.

What Asquith had described as the 'hellish policy' of repression and random revenge was alienating more and more Irish men and women and tarnishing Britain's moral reputation throughout the world. There was much disquiet abroad about the turn of events in Ireland. De Valera had toured the United States during 1919 and early 1920, where he was treated as a nationalist hero on a level with Gandhi and Sun Yat-Sen. He was most warmly received by Irish-American groups. These contributed $5 million in cash to help victims of the war, supplies of food and, clandestinely, arms.

Negotiations between Sinn Féin and the British government began in October and lasted for just under two months. What passed across the conference table and the treaty which was signed at the beginning of December have since been the source of considerable recrimination. Both sides regarded the truce as a breathing space and were ready to reopen hostilities. The IRA recruited 45,000 much-needed extra volunteers between July and December, and Lloyd George made it plain that he would restart and intensify the war if no agreement was forthcoming. Four days later, when the treaty was about to be signed, he warned Michael Collins, one of the Irish delegates, that the army was ready to resume operations in three days' time.

Under the terms of the Treaty, southern Ireland became a self-governing 'Free State' and a dominion. The treaty also recognised the detachment of Ulster and its Catholic minority from the Free State, and its status as a part of the United Kingdom, but with its own peculiar parliament. For those for whom

Exit:
Lord Fitzalan, the last Viceroy of Ireland, takes his leave of Dublin Castle, January 1922.

the dream of Irish nationhood encompassed a single land, a hallowed historic entity, the border between the south and the north was a wound. It was an incision made for the sake of expediency, and its existence symbolised the ancient domination of Ireland by England. The nationalist movement, like Ireland, was split by the treaty; although it was ratified in the Dáil by just seven votes, its opponents continued to fight it. The pragmatists fought and beat the idealists in a civil war that dragged on into 1923.

The final victory went to de Valera and his followers. In 1937 he reframed the Irish constitution, making Eire a republic. This was not strikingly significant, although it mattered considerably to those whose nationalism had remained unsullied by the 1921 compromise. Ever since the 1931 Statute of Westminster, Ireland, like the other dominions, had enjoyed complete freedom in the management of all its external and internal affairs. This independence was asserted in September 1939 when de Valera declared Ireland neutral in Britain's war against Germany.

The government could not indulge in tantrums: strategic considerations alone (Irish bases had been invaluable during the recent campaign against the U-boat) required that southern Ireland remained a British satellite. It was, on paper, so Curzon declared the treaty a victory for Britain, as did Lloyd George. Those on the right, like Sir

Entrance:
on the same day, Michael
Collins (in back seat) is
driven into Dublin
Castle and a place in
the administration of
the new Irish Free State.

Henry Wilson disagreed, and believed that it was 'a cowardly surrender to the pistol', that the empire was doomed, and 'We must either clear out or *govern*'. But the empire could not survive by force. It was not, and never would be, a military dictatorship.

What then would it become? In 1919 the empire had been given a new title, 'the British Empire and Commonwealth of Nations', a phrase first used by General Jan Smuts. It was a felicitous choice of words which banished from the self-governing dominions that stigma of inferiority and subservience conveyed by membership of an empire. Invented by sixteenth-century political writers, 'Commonwealth' stood for a free community of equals with shared interests who worked together for the good of all. Emotional attachment to Britain and a common ruler, the British monarch, held together a Commonwealth whose states had undergone a similar evolutionary process, passing from dependent colonies to self-governing nations. At every stage, this transformation had been made on Britain's terms, and on the assumption that Britain was legally entitled to give or withhold political rights to its subjects everywhere.

Between 1919 and 1922 the Irish had broken this pattern. They had forced an extremely reluctant British government to dance to their tune. If the empire was a monolithic, essentially authoritarian structure, then the Irish Revolution marked the beginning of its decline. If it was a living organism, continuously adapting itself to its environment, then the Irish troubles were no more than a chapter of unhappy accidents which would have little or no effect on the course of the empire's development.

3

THEIR COUNTRY'S DIGNITY:

EGYPT

1919–1942

ield-Marshal Viscount Allenby, the commander-in-chief of the army that had finally overturned the Ottoman empire and made Britain the supreme power in the Middle East, was pessimistic about the future of the empire he had enlarged. He kept his doubts to himself, for he had been made high commissioner in Egypt in March 1919, an appointment which owed much to his well-known strength of character and iron will. But he lacked the inner conviction of other warrior proconsuls, for he was a man of broad intellectual horizons with a questioning mind. This enabled him to detect the historical forces that were beginning to gather momentum and would soon be ranged against the British empire. Talking with a close friend after dinner one evening early in 1920, he remarked that the empire would inevitably fall apart once more and more of its subjects became educated. He was worried that what they learned would not provide them with the 'responsibility and integrity and leadership' which were essential for those who exercised power over others.

Events of the past eight months had made Allenby uncomfortably aware that pupils in Egypt's schools were learning to hate Britain and everything it stood for. One of them, Gamel Abdul Nasser, born in 1918, later recalled that 'when I was a little child every time I saw an aeroplane flying overhead, I used to shout: "O God Almighty, may a calamity overtake the English."' Another future Egyptian leader, Anwar el-Sadat, born in 1921, remembered the bitter anglophobia of his father, whose hero was Kamal Atatürk, the Turkish nationalist leader who had successively overcome the Italians, the Greeks and the French, and then outwitted the British. In 1932 the young Sadat was excited by what he read in the newspapers about the life of Gandhi, then passing through Egypt on his way to argue India's case before the British government.

Nasser, then a high-school student, recalled 'shouting himself hoarse' during anti-British demonstrations in 1935. Young men like Nasser and Sadat were among the thousands of Egyptians who regularly took to the streets between the wars to demand an end to British interference in the running of their country. Their protests were orchestrated by the Wafd, which was the largest political party in Egypt and, for Sadat and others like him, stood as 'a symbol of the struggle of the entire Egyptian people against the British'. For the British, the Wafd was a nuisance which might eventually go away.

The British, however, were wrong. In March 1919 there were riots in major cities and towns and a systematic attempt by strikes and sabotage to paralyse the country's rail, telephone and telegraph

Egypt erupts:
Cairo station set alight
by nationalist rioters.
British troops and
Egyptian policemen
watch as firemen
attempt to control
the fire, 1924.

networks. The local commander, General Sir Edward Bulfin, responded swiftly with condign measures. Mobs were repeatedly fired on and on occasions bombed and strafed by aircraft, and suspected agitators were flogged or executed after summary courts martial. The murder of a number of British servicemen inflamed tempers, and for a time the high command felt that its men were out of control. At least 1,500 Egyptians died during eight weeks of fighting in a campaign whose ferocity bore comparison with the suppression of the Indian Mutiny.

At this stage Allenby appeared, a commander nicknamed 'The Bull' and from whom Curzon expected a display of bullishness which would bring the Egyptians to their senses. Again, the Marquess had miscalculated. Allenby was a pragmatist with enough imagination to appreciate that he could not rule Egypt by force for ever, especially as the men available to him were becoming mutinous because of postponed demobilisation. Egypt needed a civilian cabinet filled with Egyptian ministers who would cooperate with the high commissioner in the old manner. To bring this about, Allenby offered an olive branch in the shape of an end to the banishment of the Wafd's leaders.

Allenby's concession began an elaborate political game between himself, his successors and the Wafd. For Britain, the stake was the future security of the Suez Canal, which was now sometimes called the Clapham Junction of the empire. During the early 1920s, British-registered ships accounted for between two-thirds and three-quarters of the tonnage of all the vessels that passed through the Canal. The strategic importance of the Canal became greater than ever after 1935, when Britain had to contend with the Far Eastern pretensions of Japan, and of Italy in the Mediterranean. If and when the Royal Navy had to concentrate against either power, it would have to use the Canal. The safety of the waterway rested on a British garrison and outlying detachments stationed near Cairo and Alexandria but, as Allenby realised, the Canal would be in permanent jeopardy if British forces were continually engaged in crushing Egyptian disorders. Moreover, public opinion would not have tolerated a state of unending emergency in Egypt.

Force was applied periodically to the Egyptians. It had been in 1919 and was again during the political crises in 1924–5 and 1936, when British warships appeared off Alexandria and Port Said and British regiments paraded through Cairo. On both occasions, the British government was indirectly upholding the authority of the Egyptian crown, a valuable player in the game for control of his subjects.

The Sultan Fuad (he assumed the title King in 1922) was a patriot after his own lights, and intensely anti-Wafd. This made him pro-British, insofar as he was always amenable to any manoeuvre that would hurt the Wafd. Once, in a state of rage, his words interrupted by a curious bark (the result of a throat wound he had suffered from an assassin's bullet), Fuad told Allenby that the Wafd's leaders were 'a crowd of revolutionaries and cads'.

What galled Fuad was that the Wafd represented an alternative focus for national sentiment. Its leadership was drawn exclusively from the effendiya class of landowners and professional men, including the father of Boutros Boutros-Ghali, the former Secretary-General of the United Nations. Their wealth qualified them for seats in the Egyptian parliament and provided the wherewithal to finance the Wafd's organisation. Not surprisingly, the Wafd's social and economic policies were conservative, but its uncompromising nationalism won it support from trade unionists, students, schoolchildren and the fellahin, although, as British officials rightly guessed, the peasant vote was easily gained through coercion and bribery. Throughout the 1920s and 1930s, the Wafd acted as if it possessed a monopoly of public opinion, and steadfastly refused to compromise its platform of complete independence from Britain. This intransigence was vital if the party was to hold together its various sections and resist pressure from more radical groups, such as the Muslim Brotherhood and Misr al-Fatah (Young Egypt) which emerged in the 1930s.

Trouble on the line: *Cairo trams overturned by protesters, 1925.*

The game between Britain and the Wafd drifted into stalemate. Eight formal conferences had been held between 1919 and 1935 to settle the question of ultimate sovereignty in Egypt, without success. During the same period there had been twenty different governments, but the Wafd had not gone away. In 1935 it organised a fresh wave of popular demonstrations and strikes, which had to be taken more seriously than their predecessors because Britain's position in Egypt was now under an external threat. Mussolini's brutal consolidation of Italy's hold over Libya, his dreams of the Mediterranean as 'mare nostrum', and his recent ambitions in Abyssinia made it imperative that Britain resolved the Egyptian problem. If it failed to do so, and a crisis occurred between Britain and Italy, it would be impossible to withstand an attack from Libya and at the same time hold down Egypt. The Canal mattered more than prestige and the result was the Anglo-Egyptian Treaty of 1936. It was, given the history of the past seventeen years, a diplomatic triumph: Britain retained its garrison and air bases in Egypt, continued to enjoy naval facilities at Alexandria and entered into an alliance with Egypt, which obtained full independence. The Cairo residency became the British embassy, and the high commissioner, Sir Miles Lampson, became Britain's first ambassador to Egypt since 1882.

The months which followed the outbreak of war in 1939 proved Egypt a lukewarm partner in Britain's struggle against the Axis powers. In September 1939 the Egyptian cabinet refused to declare war against Germany, but pledged that its country would stick to the terms of the treaty and 'render aid' to

Britain. During the next few months Egypt was a benevolent neutral; diplomatic relations with Germany were broken off, Germans were interned and their property confiscated. Britain went ahead with the transformation of Egypt into a formidable base for the defence of the Canal and the entire Middle East.

Lampson suspected, with good reason, that Egypt's benevolent neutrality was a façade, and that King Faruq and many close to him were hoping for an Axis victory. Faruq had become King in 1936 and there was every reason to imagine that he might follow his father and tow the British line, for he had been trained as an officer at Sandhurst, where it was hoped he had absorbed British values. But 1936 was a bad year for kings; Faruq had inherited his father's distaste for the Wafd and his ambitions to become a focus for his people's national aspirations. He, and many of his senior army officers and ministers, secretly believed that Britain was going to lose the war, an understandable view given the reverses suffered during 1940–1 in the Western Desert, Greece and Crete. Ordinary Egyptians were frightened about invasion and bombing raids (something which Cairo had suffered in 1917) and the upper classes found fascism and Naziism attractive creeds.

At the beginning of the war, Lampson had had misgivings about Egyptian loyalty and, if necessary, had been prepared to revive the protectorate. Throughout 1940 and 1941, he and the Foreign Office suppressed their suspicions about Faruq and pursued a policy of vigilant non-activity. They had an alternative government ready if Faruq began intriguing with the Germans or Italians. Ironically, Lampson believed that Britain's interests would be best served by the Wafd's leader, Mustafa al-Nahas, who, despite his party's traditional anti-British platform, was wholeheartedly pro-Allies.

By the end of 1941, the choice between the greater and the lesser evil, Faruq or the Wafd, was forced on Lampson. Faruq was swinging more and more towards the Axis and could no longer be trusted. Lampson decided the time had come either to bring him to heel or secure his abdication. During the night of 3–4 February 1942 a force of British, New Zealand and South African troops with bren-gun carriers secretly approached the Abdin Palace and surrounded it, while a number of tanks were driven to the Abdin Square. At nine in the morning Lampson entered the palace, presented the astonished Faruq with documents appointing al-Nahas Prime Minister, and demanded he signed it. Faruq complied with extreme reluctance, having, he claimed, protested strongly. He alleged that the paper he was handed was crumpled and grubby and an insult to his royal dignity. Later rumours circulated that a tank had been used to knock down the palace gates, and that two South African aides who had accompanied Lampson had brandished their revolvers at the indignant King.

Embattled proconsul: Field-Marshal Viscount Allenby, who attempted to keep the lid on Egypt by offering concessions, and fell foul of Lloyd George's government for conciliatory policies.

Lampson had preserved the security of Egypt as a base for British operations but this display of force dismayed Egyptians, reminding them that they were still an impotent people with whom the British could do as they liked. 'What is to be done now that the catastrophe has befallen us?' asked Nasser, now a junior army officer. If only Egyptians existed who were willing to fight back, he argued, then 'Imperialism . . . would withdraw and recoil like a harlot.' Nevertheless, this demonstration of his people's continued abjectness, while unavenged at the time, had made a deep impact. 'That event had a new influence on the spirit and feeling of the army and ourselves,' Nasser remembered. 'Henceforward officers spoke not of corruption and pleasure, but of sacrifice and of their willingness to give up their lives to save their country's dignity.'

4

THE HAUGHTY GOVERNESS:
THE MIDDLE EAST
1919–1942

Three years before the outbreak of the First World War, the explorer Gertrude Bell, travelling through the Middle East concluded that 'fraternity and equality' were dangerous concepts in a region where different races and religions coexisted uneasily. A complete absence of what Miss Bell called 'the Anglo-Saxon acceptance of common responsibility in the problems which beset the state' among the people of the Middle East ruled out their future participation in any form of democracy.

The next few years showed that Lloyd George's government was filled with men who were convinced that they enjoyed the right to mould the future of the Middle East and its inhabitants and they exercised this right with the utmost rigour and an astounding disregard for reality. Through a mixture of big power diplomacy and force ruthlessly applied, the government implemented a policy of aggressive and acquisitive imperialism.

In November 1918 Britain's position seemed secure. Turkey and Russia were prostrate, Mesopotamia (Iraq), Syria and Palestine were occupied; there were 10,000 men in Persia protecting oil wells and upholding British interests on the southern shores of the Caspian; a flotilla of makeshift gunboats cruised on that sea; and to the east, in Trans-Caspia, small detachments of British and Indian troops garrisoned towns, guarded railway lines, and got into scrapes with local Bolsheviks. British warships dominated the Black Sea, and Constantinople was under British control.

This unprecedented concentration of British power meant that Britain now had the wherewithal to create a secure corridor stretching from the Suez Canal to the borders of India and simultaneously form a buffer zone in central Asia, which would keep the Russians away from Persia and Afghanistan. However, the vision of the new Middle Eastern *imperium* soon turned into a nightmare. The vast army which straddled the region in November 1918 was made up of volunteers and conscripts, who had gone to war to beat Germany and Turkey and not, as they made abundantly clear, to found a new empire. During the first six months of 1919 these soldiers were sent home, their duty done, and replacements had to be found. Moreover, the British government had somehow to find extra manpower for commitments elsewhere; during 1919 and 1920 soldiers were needed to garrison the Rhineland, superintend the plebiscite in Silesia, stiffen anti-Bolshevik armies in Russia, police Ireland, defend the North-West Frontier, and pacify large areas of northern India. Soldiers also had to be retained in Britain to meet the continual threats of large-scale industrial action by miners and railway workers. India, which was providing 180,000 men for Middle Eastern units, was also feeling the strain, and complained to London about the cost and the shortage of units for internal security. The dominions were asked to lend a hand, but only New Zealand agreed, the rest arguing that they had no direct interests in the Middle East save the Suez Canal, which was not threatened.

Even if enough men could be found, the government did not have the money to pay them. The boom of 1919 burned itself out and was followed by a recession. Unemployment, which had been just under 3 per cent before the war, rocketed to 17 per cent by the end of 1921. A nation burdened with war debts faced a fall in revenue from taxation and a simultaneous increase in welfare payments. Retrenchment became an urgent necessity, and items such as the £30 million a year needed to underwrite Britain's presence in Persia were held up to close and critical scrutiny by the Treasury and taxpayers.

Troops in southern Russia were pulled out during 1920, which was just as well considering the weight of the Bolshevik offensive launched in the spring of that year. There was much grumbling about the damage inflicted on local British prestige, and there was more when the cabinet decided to evacuate units stationed in northern Persia in May 1920.

However, resistance to British ambitions came not from outside but inside the Middle East, supported by a vocal and influential lobby in Britain. Local nationalism, awakened during the last days of Ottoman rule, had become too strong a force to be pushed aside. Indeed, its present vigour and intensity were the direct result of wartime encouragement by Britain. The trouble was that fostering Arab

nationalism had been only one strand of Britain's wartime policy in the Middle East. The Sykes-Picot agreement of 1916 partitioned the area into future British and French spheres of influence, and the Balfour Declaration of November 1917 pledged a future Jewish 'homeland' in the British zone of Palestine. Matters were further confused as details of President Wilson's fourteen points began to circulate in the Middle East, making nonsense of the Sykes-Picot arrangements, which, incidentally, were well known to Arabs. It appeared that Britain and France might abandon their imperial ambitions, an impression which was confirmed in the closing days of the war when both governments announced their intention to apply Wilsonian principles to the former Ottoman empire.

It was in this knowledge that the Kurds welcomed British and Indian soldiers as liberators in the autumn of 1918. Their leader Sheik Mahmud al-Barzani kept a copy of the Anglo-

A change of masters: Jodhpur and Mysore lancers enter Haifa in the wake of fleeing Turkish troops, September 1918. (© IWM)

French pledge in an amulet as a talisman which would transform his people into a nation. Within six months he was busy setting up a Kurdish state in northern Iraq.

An independent Kurdistan, or for that matter self-government for anyone inside Iraq, was wormwood to Colonel Sir Arnold Wilson, the country's civil administrator. A former army boxing champion, who later in life seriously flirted with fascism, Wilson wanted Iraq as a dependency of India. In May 1919, Sir Arnold ordered the destruction of the embryonic Kurdish state by a column of British and Indian troops. When Kurdish guerrillas proved too hard to catch, RAF officers asked Churchill, then Secretary for War, for poison gas. He agreed, but it was not used. In less than a year, Britain had shed the mask of benevolence to reveal the snarling frown of the conqueror. The metamorphosis had begun in December 1918 during private horse-trading between the French President Clemenceau and Lloyd George. Britain took northern Iraq with its oil deposits, France got a quarter share in the company set up to exploit them, and a confirmation of its rights in Syria and the Lebanon. During the winter of 1918–19 French troops began to disembark at Beirut.

Disheartened Arab nationalists pinned their hopes on the Versailles peace conference and the conscience of President Wilson. Neither yielded much; the President prevaricated and, when confronted with Egyptian nationalists, told them that their dispute with Britain was none of his business. Syria and the Lebanon were to be given to France under a League of Nations mandate, and Palestine and Iraq to Britain. Mandate was a new word, which some thought a euphemism for old-style colonialism. The relationship between the mandatory power and its territory was the same as that of a guardian to a ward with the League of Nations Mandate Commission acting as a board of trustees. Their duty was to see that the nation which held the mandate governed in the best interests of its subjects, protected them from exploitation, and accelerated their moral, physical and political development. These arrangements were settled in May 1920 by the great powers at San Remo without heeding Middle Eastern opinion.

Arab nationalists put little faith in this brand of enlightened imperialism which reduced them to minors who could not survive without a substitute parent. The Emir Faisal, the Hashemite prince who had fought alongside the Allies in the mistaken belief that his reward would be the kingdom of Syria, returned there early in 1920 and proclaimed its independence. His gesture excited Arab nationalists in Jerusalem, some of whom were veterans of Faisal's army. There were riots in the city by Arabs who denounced the Balfour Declaration and attacked Jews and their property.

What was, so to speak, a second Arab revolt spread to Iraq, following hard on the news of what had been agreed at San Remo. Throughout Ramadan (May) Shia and Sunni religious leaders joined forces with Hashemite agents and nationalists in a sequence of public protests against the continuation of British rule. Riots turned into a revolution early in June, when a British political officer arrested a prominent nationalist sheik for alleged tax evasion. Colonel Wilson's fragile régime disintegrated swiftly, and a government strapped for cash and short of soldiers found itself dragged into a war.

By September the local commander, General Sir Aylmer Haldane, was beginning to get the upper hand, although he was still desperate enough to clamour for large supplies of poison gas. It was not needed for, as he later admitted, air power had given his forces the edge whenever the going got tough. At the end of the year order had been restored by methods which did not bear too close examination. Viscount Peel, Under-Secretary at the War Ministry, was glad that the 'sentimentalists' at home had been so distracted by the brutalities of the Black and Tans in Ireland that they failed to notice what was happening in Iraq.

The public, the press and the Commons did, however, notice that the government's policies in the Middle East were achieving nothing more than a colossal waste of money and lives. The Indian-style administration of Colonel Wilson was in ruins, and it was obvious that Iraqis did not want to be ruled by district officers who generally behaved like arrogant public-school prefects. It proved possible, largely through the employment of superior technology, for the French to crush the Arabs in Syria and the British to do likewise in Jerusalem and Iraq, but having done so, both powers faced an uphill struggle holding down their mandates. Moreover, it was impossible to square threats of using poison gas against tribesmen with the essentially humane and benevolent ideals behind the mandate system. The only answer lay in reaching an accommodation with the Arabs which would balance Britain's strategic needs with the aspirations of local nationalists.

This had been the line taken by T. E. Lawrence during 1920, when he had undertaken a press campaign in favour of Arab self-determination within the empire as an alternative to coercion. Might not the Iraqis become the first 'brown dominion'? he asked. The £40 million bill for the Iraq war convinced the government that he was right. Early in 1921 he joined the staff of Churchill, who had just taken over the Colonial Office with orders to negotiate a settlement in the mandates in which the security costs were kept to a minimum. The result was the Cairo Conference of March 1921. The wartime alliance between Britain and the Hashemite family was renewed; Faisal was given the throne of Iraq and his brother, Abdullah, that of a kingdom then known as Transjordan (Jordan) which consisted, as its name suggests, of land on the eastern bank of the River Jordan. Both kings would be advised by British officials to ensure that the terms of the mandate would be adhered to. Palestine would be the responsibility of the Colonial Office with internal security in the hands of a *gendarmerie* recruited from the now redundant Black and Tans and Auxis.

The final defeat of the Mad Mullah in 1920 had been achieved after the bombing of his strongholds in what the Colonial Office regarded as a model campaign. Its total cost was £70,000, which made it the cheapest imperial war ever, and did much to convince waverers that air control was the thriftiest way to police the empire's more unruly subjects.

The methods used to subdue the peoples of Iraq were often harsh. Within a few months of the Cairo Conference, Churchill was horrified by a report that described an air raid in which men, women and children had been machine-gunned as they fled from a village. Care was taken to ensure that the public never learned about this incident, and it was understandably excluded from a lecture given by Air-Marshal Sir John Salmon in which he explained what had been achieved by air control in Iraq between 1921 and 1925. His talk ended on an optimistic note: thanks to air control 'a heterogeneous collection of wild and inarticulate tribes has emerged in an ordered system of representative government by the vote.'

Middle Eastern reserves of oil were not yet as great a factor in international affairs as they became after 1945. During the 1920s the United States and Mexico produced over four-fifths of the world's oil, although the greater part was for American domestic consumption. The demand was rising and even before 1914 preliminary exploration work was underway in Persia and Iraq. The Persian government had granted the Anglo-Persian Oil Company a concession covering half a million square miles which expired in 1961. Drilling began in 1909 and, three years after, work started on a massive refinery on Abadan Island. Output rose from 7.5 million barrels in 1919 to 57 million in 1934. In peacetime, the safety of the wells and the uninterrupted flow of the oil depended on the Persian government's goodwill and ability to maintain internal peace. Both were guaranteed by Reza Pahlevi, a former Cossack officer, who, with British approval, had managed a coup in 1920, and made himself Shah five years later. Supported by the army, Shah Reza was the ideal 'strong man' who would cooperate with foreign business interests. Iraq's Kirkuk oilfields were opened in 1927 and run by the Turkish Oil Company, which was financed by British, French and American capital. Its security and that of the supply pipeline which stretched to the Palestinian port of Haifa depended upon the Iraqi government.

Iraq and its oil remained firmly within Britain's unofficial empire. In 1930, Britain had relinquished its mandate and Iraq received what passed for independence. In fact, it remained a British satellite under the terms of an alliance signed the same year. Britain trained and equipped the Iraqi army, was promised extensive base and transport facilities in the event of war, and retained the RAF aerodrome and garrison at Habbaniya.

The Anglo-Iraqi Treaty was, like its Egyptian equivalent signed six years later, a focus for nationalist resentment. The two agreements and the bases they guaranteed were reminders that Britain was still the paramount power in the Middle East and that, ultimately, even those states with theoretic independence would not be permitted to act in ways which might harm British interests. Britain had not had everything its own way: insurrections in Egypt in 1919 and across the Middle East a year later had forced its government to reach an accommodation with local nationalism. But the events of this period had destroyed much, if not all of the faith which enlightened and politically conscious Arabs had had in Britain.

The record of Anglo-French diplomacy during the war and immediately after it – the Sykes-Picot Agreement, the Balfour Declaration, the decisions of the San Remo Conference had shocked even the most loyal among them, and the disillusion had deepened as a result of personal contact and direct experience of mandatory rule.

Nurturing Arab goodwill became increasingly difficult after 1936. It would be hard to overestimate the effect on Arab opinion of the events in Palestine; the rebellion and Britain's efforts to overcome it became the focus of Arab nationalist passions throughout the Middle East. Palestine symbolised Arab impotence and British indifference towards Arab sentiment. The Palestinian imbroglio alternately baffled and exasperated successive British governments. As was so often the case when Britain found itself in charge of a racially and religiously divided province, the problem was how to balance the sensitivities and interests of one faction with those of the other.

Under the terms of the Balfour Declaration, Britain had pledged itself to welcome Jewish immigrants into Palestine. It had, therefore, allied itself with the international Zionist movement which had been seeking a sanctuary for Europe's Jews. Zionism was a practical response to the state- and church-sponsored anti-semitism within the Russian empire and the rising number of pogroms there. There was also the insidious, less openly violent anti-semitism which flourished in outwardly more enlightened countries such as France and Austria. Quite simply, before 1914, large numbers of European Jews faced a precarious existence, unable to rely upon the normal protection afforded by the state to its subjects and the situation became worse during and after the war, particularly in countries such as Poland and the Ukraine.

The Jewish predicament won the support of many humane and liberal-minded British statesmen such as Balfour, Churchill and Leo Amery, the latter two stalwart supporters of Zionism between the wars. But there were, from the moment that the Balfour Declaration was announced, deep misgivings among the Arabs. They naturally asked what would be the status of the Jewish refugees who entered Palestine, and how many would come.

There were many in Whitehall who shared their fears, believing that Arab rights were in danger and needed to be defended. Jewish colonists were well-financed and had the means to buy up large areas of land for their settlements, creating a class of landless labourers who were excluded from work in Jewish areas, where the owners preferred to employ men and women of their own race. Arabs began to compare Palestine to Algeria, where the French government had handed out the most fruitful land to French and Spanish colonists, and to Libya where, under Mussolini's colonisation policy, Italian settlers were edging out Arabs.

Frustration and racial tension erupted in anti-Jewish demonstrations in 1920, 1921 and 1929, when nearly 900 Jewish settlers were killed or wounded. These outbreaks were a chilling reminder that the British government would eventually have to make a definite decision as to the final racial balance within Palestine. No one was prepared to grasp this nettle, for neither side in the dispute was open to compromise, since it was bound to involve a surrender of ideals and territory. The Arabs were resisting what they considered a usurpation of lands they had inhabited and tilled for centuries, and a future in which they might conceivably be an impoverished minority within a Jewish state. The Jewish colonists believed that they were the rightful inheritors of a land long ago bequeathed them by God, which they were using to its best advantage, and which offered a safe haven for Jews everywhere. Having, in 1922, made clear that the future of Kenya would be decided in the interests of its indigenous races, rather than the white colonists, the British government thought it would be prudent to wait on events in Palestine. For a time it seemed that the problem might resolve itself naturally; between 1927 and 1932, the rate of Jewish immigration declined and, thanks to better medical treatment (a benefit of the mandate), the Arab birth rate increased. At the beginning of 1933, there were 800,000 Arabs in Palestine and under 200,000 Jews.

At this stage, events in Europe radically changed the nature and scale of the Palestinian problem. There were about half a million Jews in Germany when Hitler manoeuvred himself into power in January 1933. During the next five years the Nazi authorities encouraged 150,000 to leave the country, even making arrangements with the Jewish Agency in Palestine to facilitate emigration there. At the same time, the numbers of Jews under Nazi rule increased with the annexation of Austria (1938) and Czechoslovakia (1938–9). Furthermore, the example of the Nazis encouraged anti-semitism in countries where the disease was already rife, and Jews found themselves persecuted in Poland, Hungary, Romania and the Baltic states. There were, therefore, two mass exoduses of Jews from Europe. The first involved the flight of refugees from territory under Nazi government, of whom 57,000 went to the United States, 53,000 to Palestine and 50,000 to Britain. The second was undertaken by the Jews of Eastern Europe, including 74,000 who fled from Poland to Palestine. In all, 215,000 Jews reached Palestine in these six years, raising its total Jewish population to 475,000.

Islam, in stark contrast to the Catholic and Orthodox churches, had traditionally shown toleration to Jews, but the prospect of a flood of Jewish immigration, and with it further transfers of land, provoked the Arab higher committee to seek restrictions on both and a timetable for Palestinian self-government. An equivocal response, together with economic distress, led to the Arab Revolt which began in April 1936. The uprising exposed the fragility of internal security within a region where, despite eighteen years of British rule, brigandage was still common and firearms were easily obtainable. As in southern

Counter-insurgency operations, Palestine, 1936–9: an Arab is searched for arms by a British patrol. (© IWM)

Ireland in 1919, the local police force was unable to withstand a campaign of systematic ambushes, murders, sabotage of communications and a general strike. Efforts to restore the government's authority were feeble and fumbling. Nine thousand troops were drafted to Palestine in September 1936, but when they arrived their orders were hopelessly confused. On one hand, they were warned that 'All Arabs are your enemies', and on the other they were told to ensure that, 'Every effort was made to conciliate, to heal instead of wound afresh, and to restore order by pacific measures.' This conundrum reflected irresolution at the top. In September the cabinet had sanctioned the bombing of villages used as bases by partisans, and early the next month sanctioned martial law. General Sir Arthur Wauchope, the High Commissioner, refused to implement the first and thought the second unnecessary as it would impede progress towards a negotiated settlement, decisions for which he and the cabinet were later censured by the Mandates Commission.

For the next three years, the army, navy and RAF waged an anti-guerrilla war during which large areas of the country, including Jerusalem and Nablus, passed temporarily into their enemies' control. At first it was hoped that a compromise might be achieved through a royal commission, that standard procedure by which British governments simultaneously avoided the necessity for an immediate political decision and allowed tensions to subside. The high-minded and well-meaning members of the Peel Commission collected evidence, sifted through it and, in September 1937, proposed partition and a reduced quota of Jewish immigrants. After some wavering, both sides rejected this solution.

By now the local difficulties in Palestine were becoming an international embarrassment for Britain. Haj Amin al-Hussaini, Grand Mufti of Jerusalem and the most trenchant Arab spokesman, fled into exile and began to persuade the independent rulers of neighbouring Arab states to exert pressure on Britain. His peregrinations and the flow of anti-British propaganda which poured from Palestinian Arabs and their supporters disturbed the Foreign Secretary, Sir Anthony Eden, and many of his officials who feared, with good reason, that continued equivocation and repression in Palestine might undermine British influence throughout the Arab world.

Growing Arab antipathy towards Britain was a bonus for Italy and Germany, and both began fishing in the troubled waters of Palestine. During 1938 and 1939, the propaganda agencies of these powers cynically broadcast allegations of British atrocities against Arabs. These stories, some of which were true, came from Arab sources outside Palestine, but at the beginning of 1939 British intelligence there was on the trail of two Nazi agents who had been collecting material which discredited British troops and, it was suspected, dispensing cash to Arab guerrillas. There was evidence that Russia was recruiting agents from among the Arabs and had sent a handful to Moscow for training. Despite counter-propaganda by the BBC's Foreign Service, British repre-

Taking on the mandate:
Arab guerrillas, c.1936.

sentatives in Arab states were obliged to ask the government to adopt milder measures in Palestine.

The war of words would have been no more than an irritant had it not been for the international situation. Relations with Italy had deteriorated after its invasion of Abyssinia in 1935, the Sino-Japanese War had broken out in July 1937, and during 1938 Britain had discovered that it could only maintain a balance of power in Europe by making concessions to Germany, which served only to increase its strength and appetite for land. Whatever the circumstances or timing of a future collision with Japan or the Axis powers, Britain could no longer allow itself to be weakened by the Palestinian ulcer. In the event of war with Japan or Germany or Italy, Arab alienation and continued turbulence in a region which bordered on the Suez Canal would have been extremely dangerous.

After years of dithering, the government took swift and decisive action to pacify Palestine. In the months after the Munich agreement, reinforcements were hurried to Palestine, and operations there were intensified. By the early summer of 1939 a semblance of public order had been restored. In May, a white paper was published outlining the province's political future: Britain would keep the mandate for the next five years, cut Jewish immigration to 25,000 a year and prepare the ground for an independent state in which the Arabs would be a permanent majority. An attempt was made to divert Jewish refugees to other colonies, but with small success. The governor of Kenya thought a Jewish enclave would prove 'an undesirable feature', although he had no objections to the 'right type' of Jew (i.e. Austrian or German); the white settlers of Northern Rhodesia were very cool; and only British Guiana was encouraging.

Strategic necessity had ended nearly twenty years of procrastination. Whatever its rights and wrongs, and nearly all Jews saw only wrongs, the 1938–9 military–political settlement revealed that in an emergency Britain could act with determination and ruthlessness. The same qualities were apparent in the early war years when it was clear that a considerable body of Arab opinion was hoping for an Axis victory as the Middle East's only means of escape from Britain's domination. In Iraq, where the repercussions of events in Palestine had been strongly felt, anti-British sentiment was strongest among the officer class. Britain's supervision of the Iraqi army had not prevented those who passed through its military college from being taught to see themselves as an élite destined to be the liberators of their nation. Political circumstances encouraged their daydreams; there had been no stability since Faisal's death in 1932 and for the next eight years transitory civilian governments were more or less the instruments of a cabal of colonels.

Although Iraq was technically allied to Britain, its government was grudging in the assistance it rendered to the British war effort, and, like Egypt's, hardly bothered to hide its sympathy for the Axis powers. In March 1940, the situation was such that the high command in Cairo prepared plans to occupy the Mosul oilfields as a precautionary measure, although no one had any idea where to find the necessary men. Eight months later, deciphered German signals revealed that an overland attack on Iraq was being considered in Berlin. The German thrust through the Balkans and into Greece in the spring of 1941, and the likelihood that the Vichy authorities in Damascus would connive at German bases in Syria forced Britain to intervene in Iraq. Two brigades of Indian troops were landed at Basra with orders to proceed to positions from where they could protect the northern oilfields.

This manoeuvre was completely within the terms of the Anglo-Iraqi treaty, but nationalists believed it was a prelude to an attack on Baghdad. Rashid Ali, the Prime Minister who had seized power with army backing on 3 April, appealed directly for Axis help a fortnight later. The British were forewarned of his intrigues through intercepted German and Italian wireless messages, and forces in Palestine were ordered to enter Iraq. An Iraqi attack on Habbaniya aerodrome was beaten off, and British motorised columns reached Baghdad by the middle of May. German and Italian aircraft, flown from Greece to Syria, arrived too late to influence the outcome of the six-week campaign in which 3,000 Iraqi troops were killed. Three thousand nationalist officers were subsequently purged from the army by a new, pro-British government under Nuri es-Said, who had fought alongside T. E. Lawrence twenty-five years earlier. Rashid Ali escaped and made his way to Berlin.

The *coup de main* against Iraq and the palace coup in Cairo nine months later were proof that, despite over twenty years of nationalist ferment, British power in the Middle East was still firm. Both were, however, exceptional measures, undertaken in the face of dire emergencies by a country fighting for its life. This was not how it looked to Egyptians and Arabs. Each display of force left a deep sense of bitterness and frustration because it had amply demonstrated the victims' powerlessness. Britain was still the dominant power in the region and would go to any lengths to get its way there.

5

A NEW FORCE
AND
NEW POWER:
INDIA
1919–1942

The Indian empire had always been a heterogeneous organism. Its political map was a mosaic of princely states (there were over 500 in 1919) and provinces directly governed by British officials. These states covered two-fifths of the subcontinent and contained a quarter of its population. It would have been impossible to have drawn an exact racial or religious chart of India, although, as a general rule, Muslims were concentrated in the north-western regions and Bengal. They were a minority comprising a seventh of a population which stood at 280 million in 1940.

Racial and religious tolerance was scarce in India. The Ghurka soldiers who shot down demonstrators in Amritsar in 1919 later admitted that they had enjoyed killing people of the plains. In 1923 intelligence sources revealed that Hindus had been secretly pleased by recent air raids on Pathan villages on the North-West Frontier. An army inquiry of 1943 as to which soldiers were best suited for policing duties revealed that, 'The Sikh would at heart enjoy nothing more than hammering Muslims.' There is no reason to disbelieve these statements, nor dismiss out of hand nationalist assertions that the British cynically exploited racial and religious antipathies in order to 'divide and rule'.

On the other hand, those diehards who wanted the raj to continue come what may, claimed that Britain alone could keep the peace and act as a dispassionate umpire, balancing the rights of one faith against the other. This argument was strengthened during the 1920s when sectarian disorders increased alarmingly. The most trivial incident could spark off massacre and looting: a street squabble between two schoolboys, one Hindu, the other Muslim, led to ten days of rioting and pillage in Dacca in 1929. The leaders of the dominant Indian National Congress were horrified by such events, and sectarian malevolence in general. It was the greatest obstacle to national unity for it prevented Indians from thinking of themselves as Indians first and Muslims or Hindus second, and acting accordingly. Jawaharlal Nehru saw religion as India's greatest bane, believing that it fostered dogmatism and narrow-mindedness.

Most Indians, whatever their creed, were desperately poor, lived in villages, and made their living from the land. Gandhi who, from 1919, was the conscience of Congress, wished all Indians to remain a simple folk, and he encouraged them to cultivate the agrarian virtues which he believed would regenerate India. For this reason he spun cotton and spent much time persuading others to do so. He mistrusted the centralisation and industrialisation of the modern world, which he feared would erode all that was good in the traditional India. Gandhi also wanted to replace English as the language of education with Gujarati, and yet he and the upper echelons of his party had been taught in English (he was a Middle Temple barrister), and their political principles were essentially British.

In a sense the British-educated Congress élite were the product of the labours of those nineteenth-century idealists who had believed that education would emancipate India. A knowledge of Western philosophy and science would unlock the Indian mind and create a class of enlightened men fit to run their own country. Education along British lines had spread throughout India, but unevenly. In Travancore (a princely state), 68 per cent of the population were literate, but there were other areas where the proportion was less than 20 per cent. A systematic attempt had been made to indoctrinate the sons of princes and business and professional men with the ideals of the British ruling classes through Indian public schools. These were reproductions of their British originals, and like them dedicated to the cultivation of 'character'.

'Grinding grit into the Kashmiri' was how Cecil Tyndale-Briscoe, headmaster of the Church Missionary School at Srinigar between 1890 and 1947 summed up his life's work. An energetic, singleminded, muscular Christian and Cambridge rowing blue, he was abundantly qualified for the task. Cricket, rugger, soccer and boxing (which he imagined was an antidote to the sodomy he feared was too common among Kashmiri adolescents) were the backbone of his curriculum. Tyndale-Briscoe also encouraged, with equal vigour, a sense of public duty. His boys formed a fire brigade, learned to stand up for the weak and poor, were taught to treat animals with kindness, and did their bit in helping relief work during a cholera epidemic. There were others like him scattered across India, not only in schools, and on the whole what they did had a lasting value.

At university, Indian secondary-school pupils found themselves in surroundings where they were free to explore and discuss political ideas and apply what they learned to contemporary India. Generations of young Indians were absorbing a tradition of political thought which emphasised the rights of the individual and the limitations of the legal power of the state. Those who had learned to reason in the British way imagined themselves the intellectual equals of their rulers, and naturally wished to be treated accordingly by the British. This was not easy for men and women who had been conditioned to believe themselves the representatives of a superior culture, and besides the educated élite of India was a tiny segment of Indian society. Seen from above, the advancement of Indians was an inexorable but very slow process.

After 1919 the pace of India's march towards self-rule quickened, gathering a momentum which simultaneously increased the impatience of nationalists and frightened conservatives in India and Britain. The engine for change had been the war. India had shown extraordinary steadfastness between 1914 and 1918, its people had resisted German-inspired subversion, provided 500,000 extra fighting men and donated £100 million to the imperial war chest. Effort on this scale deserved a generous response from Britain and, in August 1917, a grateful British government publicly committed itself to policies designed to set India along the road to 'responsible government' within the empire. Originally the promise had been for 'self government', but Curzon had objected.

On one level this gesture, like the pledges given to the Arabs the following year, reflected the government's willingness to accept that the principles of self-determination were, in theory, not racially exclusive. On another, less obvious level, the declaration was an admission that the government of India needed a thorough overhaul. Edwin Montagu, whom Lloyd George appointed Secretary of State for India in 1917, had previously observed that, 'The government of India is too wooden, too iron, too inelastic, too antediluvian for the modern purposes we have.' Montagu visited India in 1918, making him the first Secretary of State who bothered to find out about the country at first hand. He combined with the new Viceroy, Lord Chelmsford, to produce a series of reforms which became law in March 1919. They intended to give the Indians their first taste of responsible government through the creation of eleven autonomous provinces in which such 'national building' activities as public health, education and

New power:
Gandhi leaves Downing Street, 1931.

agriculture would be managed by elected Indian ministers. Finance and public order were placed in the hands of ministers, British or Indian, chosen by the Viceroy.

Congress had wanted India to stride rather than inch cautiously towards self-government, and its members were therefore disappointed by the measure and detected a niggardly spirit behind it. Moreover, the announcement of the Montagu–Chelmsford reforms coincided with the introduction of the Rowlatt Acts, a sequence of laws devised to facilitate a clamp-down on subversion. This legislation symbolised all that was autocratic about the raj and so became a convenient focus for Congress agitation.

The struggle against the Rowlatt Acts was the first major contest between the raj and Congress. It also provided the testing ground for the principles of popular resistance which had been developed by Gandhi in his campaign for Indian rights in Natal twenty years before. Gandhi's weapon was satyagraha, which he variously translated as 'soul force' or 'love force'. As he explained to his followers during March 1919, they would harness metaphysics to political protest. Satyagraha was a spiritual state achieved by a man or woman which gave them the inner fortitude, patience and faith in God that were needed for passive resistance against an immoral authority. The degrees of physical suffering which the satyagraha acolyte endured would serve as a measure of his own integrity and that of his cause. On the surface, satyagraha was a perfect instrument with which to challenge the raj. His target was the conscience of Britain. For generations the British people had assured themselves that they ruled India with the consent of its people, an assumption which meant that they could accept the idea of empire with a good conscience. If, as Gandhi intended, thousands, perhaps millions of Indians signified, in the gentlest possible way, that this was no longer so, then the ethical basis of the raj vanished.

Gandhi proposed a nationwide hartal on 6 April as a protest against the Rowlatt Acts. This was a traditional public demonstration of mourning or disapproval during which all shops, businesses and schools were closed and public transport halted, leaving large numbers free to take to the streets and form processions. There was a body of sophisticated, middle-class Congress members who could grasp the essence of satyagraha and submit to the self-discipline it demanded. Most who joined the hartal appreciated neither. Marches became riots in which demonstrators fought with the police, attacked and murdered Europeans, and plundered and set fire to property. Even Gandhi was appalled by the depth and passion of anti-British feeling which had been released and seemed beyond his control.

The upheavals were most aggravated in the Punjab, where Sir Michael O'Dwyer was governor. He was a forthright, pugnacious Irishman who had a strong sense of justice and ruled with an iron hand. O'Dwyer had faced sedition during the war and got the better of it, and in April 1919 he was determined to do so again. The most destructive riots were in Amritsar, where Europeans had been slaughtered and where, for a time, the government had lost all control. Here arrived Brigadier-General Reginald Dyer with instructions to impose martial law and restore civil peace. He was not the ideal man for the job; over twenty years before, when at staff college, a brother officer had described him as a soldier 'happiest when crawling over a Burmese stockade with a revolver in his mouth' and, in 1919, a painful illness sharpened his natural belligerence.

When local Congress leaders defied his ban on public meetings, and after he had received an inflammatory leaflet predicting a mutiny by Indian soldiers, Dyer decided on a show of force. He led a small detachment into Amritsar where a demonstration was underway at the Jalianwala Bagh, and ordered his men to fire into the crowd. The carefully directed volleys lasted for ten minutes, killed 379 Indians and wounded hundreds more. Afterwards, Dyer regretted that he had been unable to use the machine-guns mounted on two armoured cars which he had brought into the city. In the next few days, he had real and suspect miscreants flogged, and ordered Indians to crawl on their bellies along a street where a woman missionary had been assaulted by rioters, and, incidentally, rescued by other Indians.

1919 was a turning point in the history of India and Amritsar was the pivot. On 18 April, five days after the shooting there, Gandhi called off the hartal. He had clearly lost control over his followers, although he blamed the turbulence on the police, claiming, with astonishing naïveté, that Indian crowds were 'the easiest in the world to disperse'. His faith in satyagraha was still firm, and in June he declared that the hartal had revealed 'a new force and new power – a force that could prove irresistible under every conceivable circumstance provided that the truth was on our side.' And so it seemed to be, for the Amritsar massacre proved that British rule in India ultimately rested upon force. This was confirmed in the minds of Gandhi and the Congress by the events which followed the pacification of the Punjab.

News of what exactly had happened in Amritsar spread slowly, and once its enormity had been recognised the government set up an inquiry under a Scottish jurist, Lord Hunter. Dyer's judgement was found wanting and he was effectively dismissed from the army, while O'Dwyer, who had ordered the bombing of rioters elsewhere in the Punjab, was exonerated. This verdict angered the British community in India, officers everywhere, and Conservatives in Britain who believed that the brigadier and the governor were heroes who had saved India from anarchy.

Dyer's British champions raised his case in Parliament. His motives and actions were the subject of a vinegary debate in July 1920, in which right-wing Conservatives bayed for Montagu's blood. Unperturbed, Montagu castigated Dyer for the 'racial humiliation' he had inflicted in Amritsar which violated the 'principles upon which our Indian empire had been built'. He proceeded, amid catcalls, to denounce the racialism of Dyer's allies.

The government won in the division, but there was still plenty of fight left in the Dyer camp. The *Morning Post* opened a fund for him, and within a few weeks over £26,000 had been collected from donors, who included Kipling. Army officers were particularly sour about the treatment of a man who had done his duty as he saw fit, and then had been deserted by a government which should have loyally supported its servant.

The repercussions of the Amritsar debate, as much as what had happened in the city, had a profound effect on Indian opinion. Gandhi and the Congress had hitherto proceeded in the belief that they could sway the collective moral conscience of Britain, but the debate over Dyer showed that no such thing existed. There was, as Montagu's speech proved, a body of liberal-minded opinion which held that educated Indians deserved to be treated as rational creatures and were fit to exercise the freedoms cherished in Britain, but there was another section of British public opinion which claimed that Indians were intrinsically incapable of responsibility. Consider a *Spectator* editorial of December 1919, which argued that British rule in India was an 'absolute necessity' since the raj protected Hindus and Muslims from themselves. If the British departed, India would fall into the hands of 'the Brahminical caste' and slide into anarchy. 'We Anglo-Saxons like to rule ourselves,' the piece concluded. 'Why assume that our desire is not shared by men of darker complexion? The answer is to be found in the Oriental temperament and Oriental History.' Both disqualified Indians from self-government then and for many years to come, if ever.

For most people in Britain and India, Congress meant Gandhi. It would be as hard to overestimate his influence over events in India after 1919 as it is to strip away the layers of sentimental adulation that have been applied to him by his various hagiographers. He was an international figure who captured headlines and the imaginations of his countrymen, as well as those of nationalists engaged in struggles against Western imperialism outside India. His charisma was remarkable, although there were times when his humility seemed close to inverted arrogance. Gandhi's most impressive achievement was to stamp his ideals of non-violence on the Congress party, even though, as he admitted to an Australian journalist in April 1942, the mass of Indians seemed unable to appreciate what satyagraha required.

From 1920, Gandhi's aim had been swaraj, complete self-government and independence, which were one part of a vast programme for the moral regeneration of the Indian people. During the 1920s, he spent much time and energy in trying to convert the Indian middle-class Congress members to cotton-spinning and with it the discovery of their true roots in the countryside. His insistence on a

An Indian is a person who is tolerable so long as he obeys your orders, but if he thinks for himself, if once he takes advantage of the educational facilities which you have provided for him, if once he imbibes the ideas of individual liberty which are dear to the British people, why then you class him as an educated Indian and an agitator.

EDWIN MONTAGU, 1920

revolution within the individual soul rather than one within society as a whole did not satisfy many Congress members. Nehru, for one, could not subscribe to his master's reverence for poverty, which the younger man hoped to eliminate. Nor was it practical to disregard what had occurred within India during the past two hundred years and embrace the Gandhian ideal of small, self-sufficient rural communities. And yet the force of Gandhi's spirituality was so great that the radical wing of Congress acquiesced to his authority and guidance. While Gandhi's obstinacy exasperated the British, his leadership of the Indian national movement gave them many advantages. He restrained the firebrands and turned the party away from the paths of Communism and armed revolution. His influence, as much as police surveillance, ensured that in 1942 the Indian Communist party had only 5,000 members.

The struggle for swaraj was slow and convoluted. Congress sought to extract concessions, through a sequence of peaceful acts of defiance and non-cooperation, which invariably ended in bloodshed. The

British government attempted to keep the initiative through offering compromises, but dodged the issue of when and how full independence might be achieved. From 1929 everything hinged on the phrase 'dominion status' which had been hesitantly offered to India. As understood by all involved, dominion status would give India the same political freedom and detachment from Britain as was enjoyed by, say, Canada. But what if India took the path of another dominion whose people's ties with Britain were, to say the least, extremely tenuous – Ireland? For India to follow such a course was unthinkable for it would have knocked away the chief prop of British power in Asia and the Middle East.

Whatever settlement was reached, Britain could never permit India the right to neutrality implicit in dominion status. To have done so in

Yesterday's assassin, tomorrow's hero: Bhagat Singh, executed for terrorism in 1931, is celebrated on a postage stamp of an independent India.

the international situation of the mid-1930s would have been suicidal. It was, however, possible to extend the participation of Indians in government without engaging head-on the knotty question of dominion status. The 1935 Government of India Act created a federation embracing the British-ruled provinces and the princely states in which provision was made for the representation of the non-Hindu minorities. Elections for the provincial governments were held in 1937, and Congress secured a dominant position.

Congress's electoral success was to have been expected. It had about a million members across India, and a country-wide organisation which gave it its muscle and an advantage over all other parties. For this reason, it had always asserted that it was the voice of India. And yet, even in the periods of intensive public protests in 1919 and 1930–4, it had never come close to toppling the raj or even proving beyond doubt that India was ungovernable. There were no more Amritsars, but the authorities somehow managed to keep the upper hand through mass arrests of leading party activists, including Gandhi, and disorders were held in check by the police with army help. When matters appeared on the verge of getting out of control, as they did during the 1930 disturbances in Peshawar, armoured cars and aircraft were deployed. Such astringent measures were exceptional; there were 200,000 police in India in the 1930s, and they were well paid and their morale remained high. With a loyal police force, the backing of an army which numbered 194,000 in 1939, and a considerable degree of determination among its officials, the raj was able to hang on without too much strain on its resources.

And yet, while the raj still appeared formidable, especially from the perspective of the streets of Peshawar or anywhere else in India during the 1930s, its future was no longer certain. All three British political parties had acquiesced to the gradual introduction of self-government since 1919, despite the outcry on the right of the Conservatives. There was a general understanding that, in principle, a limit now existed to the life of the raj, although no one had yet drawn up the timetable for its extinction. Congress accepted, grudgingly, the 1935 Act but only as a milestone on a road which led to unconditional swaraj in the near future.

It had been assumed during the early stages of the campaign for Indian independence that the state which would emerge would encompass all the territory then under British rule. This seemed reasonable during the early 1920s, when an accord existed between the overwhelmingly Hindu Congress and Muslim organisations but there was a steady growth of Muslim apprehension about the power of

Sectarian fault lines: Muslims and Sikhs clash in Lahore, 1935.

Congress, and the position of Islam within an Indian state in which Hindus were paramount. Clashes between Muslims and Hindus increased in scale and ferocity; the refusal of Muslim shop-keepers to join a hartal in Calcutta in February 1930 lead to a riot in which between four and five hundred died. This resurgence of Muslim consciousness directly threatened Congress, since hitherto its political strength had rested upon its claim to be the authentic voice of the entire population, and its programme for complete inde-pendence had emphasised the ability of all Indians to live in harmony.

The historic memory of India's Muslims, who had been the country's masters during the Mughal period, gave an added edge to existing reli-gious antipathies. When Dr Muhammad Jinnah, President of the Muslim League, proceeded through Karachi in October 1938, he was followed by a three-mile-long procession of supporters, a parade which had marked similarities to the public shows held by the Mughal emperors.

By this date, the Muslim League had become the focus for Muslim aspirations and the guardian of their political interests. It may have exaggerated its grass-roots support, but by the end of 1943 the League was claiming to speak for all of India's Muslims. The British, following that well-established imperial rule of doing business with those who appeared to possess power, accepted the League's credentials. These had been considerably enhanced by the results of the 1937 elections, which revealed that Muslims were fast losing confidence in Congress. More and more Muslims were alienated by Congress's attempts to secure a monopoly of power within the provincial governments and its agrarian reforms, which hurt Muslim landowners. Conscious of its value to the British as a counter-weight to Congress, the Muslim League began to nudge its way towards a final settlement of India that would involve partition and the establishment of a Muslim state, Pakistan.

The idea of Pakistan had begun to circulate in Muslim intellectual circles in the mid-1930s. There was much subsequent debate as to how and when a division of India became unavoidable, and even more as to whether it was desirable. What mattered was that in August 1940 the Muslim League publicly committed itself to the formation of Pakistan, and during the next three years it transformed itself into a mass political organisation dedicated to that end.

On 3 September 1939 the Viceroy, Lord Linlithgow, announced on the wireless that India was at war with Germany. He was perfectly entitled to do so under an amendment to the Government of India Act which had been rushed through Parliament the previous April. Congress was stunned, and protested that a Scottish aristocrat had no right of any kind to drag the Indian people into a war on Britain's behalf. Yet while the Viceroy's action symbolised India's continued subservience to Britain's will, Congress members were also acutely aware that Britain was fighting against political systems which most found repugnant. During the past four years, Congress had taken a left-wing stance on foreign policy, opposing the appeasement of Hitler and Mussolini and British neutrality during the Spanish Civil War.

India and Burma have no natural association with the Empire, from which they are alien by race, history and religion, and for which as such neither of them have any natural affection, and both are in the Empire because they are conquered countries which had been brought there by force, kept there by our controls, and which hitherto it has suited to remain under our protection.

LORD LINLITHGLOW

Divisions over what, if any, part it ought to play in India's struggle against Naziism and fascism contrasted with Congress's determination to use the war as a chance to squeeze concessions from Britain. The years between 1939 and 1941 were relatively calm. Gandhi neither said nor did anything that might have disrupted the war effort, but continued to press for complete independence.

The Japanese entry into the war in December 1941, their capture of Singapore in February 1942, and the subsequent swift advance through Burma the following month brought the war to India's borders by April. Burma, which had been officially separated from India in 1935, had its own nationalist movement, which was quick to throw in its lot with the Japanese. Military intelligence reported droves of Burmese peasants, policemen and students coming forward to assist the invaders.

Even before the Japanese army had exposed the fragility of Britain's power in Asia, Linlithgow was full of pessimism (*left*). The army's intelligence department kept a close surveillance over Indian troops and examined their letters for traces of dissatisfaction, restlessness and political agitation. Sixty per cent of the Indian officers serving in Malaya during 1941–2 had strong nationalist sympathies and looked forward to an independent India at the end of the war.

Somehow brown men had to be persuaded to die for a white man's empire. One way in which this could be done was by breaking the deadlock over India's future, and in March 1942 Sir Stafford Cripps, a left-wing Labour minister with lofty principles, was sent to India to reach an accord with Congress. He failed, despite United States intervention, largely because neither he nor the war cabinet could accept Congress's demands for immediate participation in all areas of government, particularly defence.

It was Gandhi's turn to seize the initiative. At the end of April he wrote that if Britain immediately withdrew from India, the Japanese would not attack. India's enemy was British, not Japanese imperialism, and United States military assistance then pouring into India would mean 'American rule added to

British'. He had never seen the Japanese as liberators, but he imagined that if their army invaded
India they could be overcome by satyagraha! The
British certainly could, he believed, and in July he
called upon his followers to mobilise.

Even though Congress was disunited over the
new 'Quit India' campaign, it could not have come
at a worse time for the British. Preparations were in
hand for the defence of the North-West Frontier
against a possible German advance from the
Caspian, and there was a revival of unrest in this
area, led by Mirza Ali Khan (the Faqir of Ipi), an
old-style messianic Muslim holy man who had
been directing Pathan resistance for the past seven
years. On the North-East Frontier a Japanese attack
was expected, which might be combined with a
seaborne invasion of south-eastern India or Ceylon.

The 'Quit India' campaign was launched
during the second week of August and took the
form of a mass effort to paralyse the country, with
systematic attempts to sever rail and telegraph
communications. The areas worst affected were
Madras, Bihar and the United Provinces, where
rail links between Calcutta, Delhi and Bombay
were imperilled, and British servicemen were
attacked and murdered by rioters. The Muslim
League, which had been solid in its support for the
war, stood aloof. The government was ready for
the emergency and acted with the utmost rigour:
Gandhi and hundreds of Congress leaders were
arrested and interned; the press was censored;

*Waiting for trouble:
watchful British army
and police officers
during the Lahore
religious disturbances.
As independence
approached, clashes
between Hindus,
Muslims and Sikhs
became more common,
despite Gandhi's pleas
for tolerance, 1935.*

fifty-seven brigades of Indian and British troops were diverted from training camps to support the police;
urban mobs were fired upon and, at Lithlingow's orders, aircraft were permitted to strafe rioters tearing
up railway lines.

Order was restored within six weeks. At the beginning of September, the official, and lowest,
estimate of deaths was 300. Despite fears that the unrest was a cover for pro-Japanese fifth columnists,
there was no evidence of collusion between Congress and Japan. Once again, the raj had emerged from
a prolonged period of civil disturbance as strong as ever, although those within and outside India could
be excused for believing that its underlying authority rested on armed force. Gandhi and Congress had
been temporarily discredited by the upheavals, particularly in the United States which, during the first
six months of 1942, had been applying pressure to Britain to come to a solid agreement with Congress.

The raj had survived the strains of three years of war, and for the next two, India would remain a
safe base for Allied forces in south-east Asia. No constitutional settlement had yet been reached which
satisfied Indian nationalists and their rulers. By the end of 1942 it was clear that when such an arrangement was thrashed out, the final word would rest with the Indians and not their masters. Indian politics
no longer revolved around the question of how long the raj would last, but how it was to be dismantled
and what would replace it.

NORTH-WEST FRONTIER

The old problems of tribal feuding persisted until the end of the raj and required a strong military presence in the frontier. Small-scale wars of pacification and reprisal were common.

RIGHT *Ticket to adventure*:
men from the Royal West Kents arrive at Malakal station at the start of the 1917 Mahsud campaign. India's rail network had in part been designed to concentrate men and material on the frontier in the advent of a Russian invasion.

BELOW *Up the Khyber*:
an Anglo-Indian column proceeds along a valley road.
(© IWM)

RIGHT *River crossing*:
*men and mules head
into Mahsud territory,
1917.*
(© IWM)

LEFT *Refreshmen*t:
*like his fictional
counterpart,
Gunga Din, an
Indian servant
stands by as clean
water is distributed,
in this case for
thirsty mules.*
(© IWM)

RIGHT *New technology*:
*by the early twenties,
armoured cars and
aircraft were widely
used in frontier wars.
Together with tanks,
which appeared in
1935, these weapons
were condemned as
unsportsmanlike by
the Pathans.*
(© IWM)

6

FOR THE BENEFIT OF EVERYONE:
CONCEPTS OF EMPIRE
1919–1939

The First World War had dealt a mortal blow to jingoism, although its death throes continued for a further forty or so years. The belligerent patriotism of pre-1914 Britain, which had been stirred to fever pitch during the war, had a hollow ring after 1918, when a stunned nation contemplated the mass slaughter, and asked whether it had been really worthwhile. The experience of the Western Front and the new public mood made it impossible to resuscitate the late-Victorian and Edwardian jingoistic imperialism, which had shouted defiance at the world and urged men and women to sacrifice themselves for the empire.

Not only was the old imperialism discredited and out of fashion, but its champions were revealed to have had feet of clay. The wartime strategic and tactical decisions taken by those imperial warriors who held high command came under critical scrutiny, and were found wanting. Haig, who had sincerely imagined himself destined by God to save the British empire in its time of extreme peril, was toppled from his pedestal. Yesterday's heroes and prophets became today's figures of ridicule. In his *Eminent Victorians* (1918), Lytton Strachey poked fun at, among others, Gordon of Khartoum. Collectively and in unflattering form, the living old guard of empire were embodied in the stout figure of Colonel Blimp, a walrus-moustached retired officer with diehard Tory views, created in 1934 by the Australian cartoonist David Low.

Conservatives no longer chose to beat the imperial drum, preferring instead to court the electorate through policies of low taxation, the extension of earlier welfare legislation, and home-ownership. The mixture worked; the Conservatives were in power throughout most of this period, and dominated the Lloyd George coalition and the 1931–5 national government. Imperial issues were pushed into the background by more pressing matters such as the economy and the quest for international security.

The empire was no longer of central importance and public perceptions towards it had also changed. Addressing the Commons during a debate on the colonies in 1938, Ernest Evans, a Liberal MP, contrasted the popular view of the empire in his youth with that of the present day. Born in 1885, his boyhood had been a time 'when the idea of Empire in the minds of the people was associated with the spirit and practice of flag-waving'. Now, the temper of the country was very different: there was a deeper knowledge of the empire, regret for some of the exploits of the past and a sincere desire to develop the colonies for the benefit of everyone.

This selfless view of Britain's duty towards its subjects was not new. It owed much to those late eighteenth- and nineteenth-century evangelical and liberal idealists who had believed that it was

Britain's mission to uplift, morally and physically, ignorant and backward races. To some extent, this vision of an essentially benevolent empire had been lost sight of during the aggressive expansion of the 1880s and 1890s, when empire-building had been a competitive activity in which economic and strategic advantages were the prizes. And yet, even when the jingoes roared the loudest, imperialism had not shed its moral principles. They continued to flourish, although their application was confined to the white dominions which enjoyed the freedoms of the mother country and, ultimately, achieved home rule.

The post-war world was more receptive to this traditional concept of empire as an agency for regeneration and progress. Unselfish, paternalist imperialism had been revived by the League of Nations when it introduced the mandate system in 1920. Britain received former German East Africa, renamed Tanganyika, the Cameroons, Iraq and Palestine, while New Zealand and Australia shared Germany's Pacific colonies. Each nation solemnly promised to devote itself to 'the well being and development of colonial races' that had been placed under its charge. How these aims were being fulfilled throughout the empire was explained by William Ormsby-Gore, the Colonial Secretary, in a BBC broadcast in May 1937. His department was responsible for forty Crown colonies and mandated territories with a combined population of 55 million. Their future depended upon their people mastering what he called 'the art and practice of civilised administration' through instruction and example. In time, 'a native Civil Service completely and finally responsible for administration' would emerge and step into the shoes of its British predecessor. This was both inevitable and welcome for, as Orsmby-Gore concluded, 'even the best and most enlightened external rule is in the long run no satisfactory substitute for self-government in accordance with the traditions and local characteristics of one's own people.'

The quality of British colonial administration was the source of justifiable pride. 'The peoples of the colonies are not merely content to be His Majesty's subjects,' boasted Malcolm MacDonald, Colonial Secretary from 1938 to 1940, 'they are positively happy to be his Majesty's subjects.' This was how they appeared in the popular press. In April 1939, readers of *Picture Post* saw photographs of keen Indian schoolboys clustered round a blackboard in an open-air school. A month later the magazine showed chiefs from the Cameroons being taught how to govern justly, with text that contrasted the humane enlightenment of the present British administration with that of Germany, which had ruled the colony before 1916.

The chiefs' lessons were part of what MacDonald had called 'an evolutionary process' that was underway throughout the colonial empire. Official policy towards Africans was: '"to teach them and to encourage them always to be able to stand on their own feet". That love of ours of freedom not only for ourselves but for others, inspires policy right through the Colonial Empire.' Turning this principle into action would take time, and he added pointedly that Nigeria, then one of the most advanced colonies, was 'not ripe for self-government'. In the words of one contemporary commentator on imperial affairs, 'In relation to the European the African is still a schoolboy.' This was, at least, a marginal improvement on the childlike ignorance and wilfulness which had characterised him fifty years before.

When the black and brown races of the empire moved forwards, it was tacitly assumed they were also moving upwards. Mankind's progress towards civilisation was still seen as the steady ascent of a

Exotic and erotic: an advertisement of 1919 offers the allure of the Orient.

mountain. Europeans had climbed most rapidly and were now close to the summit, if not astride it, while other races had not passed the foothills. This perception of the nature of human progress, together with the recent theories of Social-Darwinism, gave Europeans a powerful sense of racial superiority. While they may have adapted well to their environments, the peoples of Asia, Africa and Australasia manifestly lacked the scientific and technical skills which had propelled Europeans forward and, during the nineteenth century, made them masters of most of the world. By contrast, so-called backward or primitive peoples had been held back by an irrational attachment to absurd, even dangerous shibboleths. Hence the references, still common in the inter-war years, to Hindu practices as a brake on India's advancement.

The taboos and observances of African animists were commonly represented, particularly by missionaries, as obstacles to moral and physical improvement. For those at its centre, the heart of darkness often appeared impossible to illuminate. In 1921, a Kenyan missionary lamented the power which pagan beliefs still exercised over the minds of young natives. 'A girl', he wrote, 'is a chattel under the care of her heathen mother whose ideas of sex and relaxation appear unspeakably vile in the light of Christian teaching.' Just what he had in mind was described by a Kenyan magistrate who witnessed a female circumcision ceremony in 1944. Afterwards he wrote, 'The whole business was fanatical and diabolical and left me wondering whether we were getting anywhere with the Africans.' Such experiences convinced even the most liberal-minded that the redemption of Africa was a sisyphean undertaking which would require many decades to accomplish.

Popular travel literature emphasised either the backwardness of Britain's colonial subjects or the quaintness of their customs and dress. An account of a journey through Nigeria in 1925, dedicated to shooting its wildlife, contained this revealing aside: 'Here is manhood fully attained in respect to physical development, but possessing a mind still in the process of evolution, cognition being present to a limited degree.' The author considered this state of affairs as the consequence either of 'laziness' or 'incomplete brain development'. More usually, writers about Africa and Australasia concentrated on the exotic and, through a combination of condescending prose and glamorous photographs, portrayed the tropical empire as a sort of human menagerie inhabited by creatures who wore picturesque clothes or sometimes none at all.

Another familiar stereotype of the period was the comic black man of the stage and humorous magazines. He appeared frequently during the late 1930s in the *Punch* cartoons of Charles Grave, which were usually set against a West African background. These burlesques relied upon the appearance of the characters, who often wore travesties of European dress, and their pidgin dialect. In one, a stevedore working on a dockside encounters a rather swell-looking African in an ill-fitting white suit, battered homburg and wing collar, who is wearing sunglasses. The caption reads: 'Why you wear dem dark glasses? Is der somethin' wrong wid yo' eyes?' 'No; but dey go wed me face.'

Images like this and the portrayals of native peoples in more serious books and magazines were indirect reminders that there was still a racial hierarchy within the empire. Those at the bottom of the pile were there because of a variety of shortcomings, mainly moral. They were, however, free to elevate themselves if they dropped values and customs abhorrent to their rulers and accepted their guidance. And yet when they took this course they were liable to ridicule and could not expect automatically to achieve equality with the white man and enter his society.

New bonds:
wireless masts appear on an Ascension Island stamp of 1936: they would have relayed the annual royal Christmas Day broadcasts.

Rites of passage: Basuto girls perform a dance which represents the wooing song of birds and was part of an initiation ceremony. Less innocuous African customs presented the colonial authorities with a dilemma: were they to be tolerated or uprooted in the name of civilisation? (© Church of Scotland World Missions)

Was the effort worth it? Thomas Birley, the Bishop of Zanzibar, whose diocese extended across Tanganyika, wondered in 1920 whether a black man was ultimately the loser when he attempted to transform himself into a 'base imitation' of the white. 'Becoming conscious of what Europeans despise in them', negroes 'seek to "camouflage" themselves by feeble imitations of the "higher race"'. Those whose outlook was being changed through a Western education were also perplexed by what was happening to them, particularly their alienation from their roots. In 1916, the *Lagos Daily Record* suggested that educated Nigerians might learn something from the recent history of Japan, a nation that had absorbed much from Europe, but which had not jettisoned its indigenous religion, ethical codes and styles of dress. Such an appeal was understandable once black men began to find themselves frozen out of the company of whites who, in terms of accomplishment, might be considered their equals.

The West Indian writer C.L.R. James thought they should, and explained why in a talk broadcast by the BBC in May 1933. It was the centenary of the abolition of slavery, and James, the descendant of slaves, described how his family had advanced itself through education. Listeners were reminded that the West Indian cricket XI that had toured Britain in 1931 contained teachers, businessmen, a cashier and a sanitary inspector, who represented the growing middle class of the islands. And yet the whites still argued that blacks were unready for self-government. West Indian loyalty to the empire was very strong, as had been proved in the First World War and would be again in the Second, but, James argued, 'People who are governed from abroad often feel that they are considered in some way inferior, backward or immature, and that many of us resent.'

According to James, the West Indies's future lay in the hands of its young men, who were then going to Britain to study. Some would have experienced a frosty welcome. None, whatever their qualifications, would have been allowed to study at St Mary's Hospital, London, since its dean, Churchill's doctor Lord Moran, had an aversion against all blacks. Black men were also debarred from enrolment at the Royal

Academy of Dramatic Art. These were outstanding examples of what was then called the 'colour bar', a lattice fence of individual prejudices which excluded black and brown people from lodgings, hotels and places of public entertainment, notably dance halls, across Britain.

The depth and violence of British racism had been revealed in the Liverpool and Cardiff race riots of June 1919. Both cities possessed unusually large black populations made up of seafarers and recent arrivals who had come seeking wartime work on the docks and in factories. The experience of Irish and Jewish immigrants during the previous century had shown that tension was always worst in areas where they had congregated in great numbers, and where the struggle to find work was always intense. These circumstances applied in Liverpool and Cardiff as discharged servicemen entered the labour market, and they added to racial antipathy.

In Liverpool, where the black population was estimated at about 5,000, a coloured men's boarding house was attacked by a 2,000-strong mob. In Cardiff, where there was a community of negroes, Arabs and Somalis, the trouble started with a brawl between groups of black and white men close by the Labour Exchange. This led to a large-scale riot during which gangs rampaged through what the locals called the Nigger Town district, close to the docks. Mobs stormed black people's homes, and some owners defended themselves with revolvers. An Irishman and a negro were killed. Reports of these disorders mentioned that very considerable animus was shown against black men who had married white women.

This revelation aroused Ralph Williams, a former administrator in Bechuanaland, to a pitch of fury. He wrote to *The Times* and asserted that 'intimate association between black or coloured men and white women is a thing of horror' to every white man in the tropics. Sexual anxieties and jealousies were close to the heart of British, and for that matter American, racism. For centuries, negroes were believed to possess a peculiar sexual energy, part animal and part on account of that legend which endowed them with larger penises than white men. No such sexual envy or accompanying animosity was directed towards the men of the Far East or the Maoris, who were thought not to measure up to Europeans, which may explain New Zealand's fine record of racial harmony. Unease about the black man's alleged sexual powers lay behind the laws in those parts of southern Africa that had been colonised by Europeans, such as South Africa's 1927 Immorality Act, which forbade casual sex between the races. British actors who travelled to South Africa for the making of the film *Zulu* in 1962 were lectured on the country's sexual interdictions, which prompted Sir Stanley Baker to remark that several hundred Zulu women extras represented at least a thousand years in prison. Mixed marriages were allowed in South Africa until 1949, but those who contracted them faced ostracism and, for white women, the contempt of their own race. In 1915, when the Rajah of Pudukota married Miss Molly Fink, an Australian girl, he faced the combined disapproval of Austen Chamberlain, the Secretary of State for India, George V and Queen Mary, and forfeited any chance of ever being presented at court. Interestingly, at this time thirty out of forty-eight American states banned mixed marriages.

It was axiomatic that the life and virtue of a white woman were sacrosanct throughout the empire, at least as far as the natives were concerned. The murder of a British woman and the abduction of her daughter by Pathans on the North-West Frontier in 1923 convinced one senior officer that Indians no longer respected British power. Convention did not extend the same protection to black and brown women. 'Europe embraces the African woman, and calls the African man "a damned nigger",' was how Bishop Birley of Zanzibar described the distinction. It was also evident in that contemporary practice by which it was permissible for respectable publishers to illustrate books with photographs of bare-bosomed, scantily clad African and Australasian women, but not near-naked white women. Needless to say, unclad black men were always coyly posed.

To a large extent, the colour bar was a barrier against sexual contact and was welcomed as such. 'What a packet of trouble there would be if susceptible English youths went dancing every night with

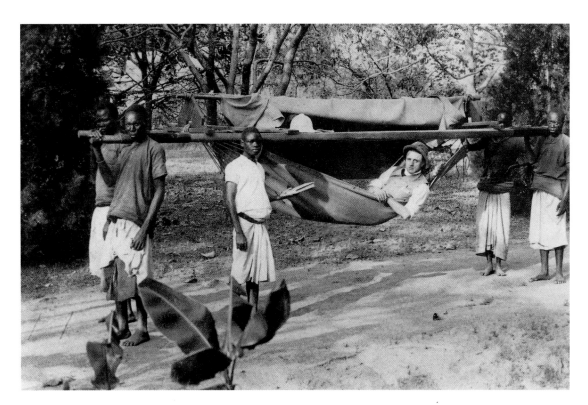

Mission fulfilled:
Church of Scotland
missionaries, Nyasaland
(Malawi) c.1910 and
c.1930. Christian
missions, supported by
churches in Britain,
produced both converts
and a body of educated
Africans, many of whom
proceeded to universities.
Some would emerge as
political leaders after
the war.
(© Church of Scotland
World Missions)

pretty and lady-like Malay, Chinese and Indian girls, and there are plenty of them about,' an anxious mother informed a London local newspaper in 1943. Such prejudice was not confined to uneducated whites or the Blimpish right; it transcended all class boundaries and political affinities.

The colour bar was a canker within the empire. It had been experienced, in varying degrees, by black and brown soldiers during the First World War, and had shaken their faith in the empire as a community of equals. The colour of a man's skin determined whether or not he could settle in Australia, vote in British Columbia, and circumscribed his every activity in South Africa. The British too were tainted. When Sir Hugh Knatchbull-Hugessen became ambassador to Persia in 1934, he discovered that, 'There

was a feeling that we had not yet divested ourselves of the "nineteenth-century complex" and were not disposed to treat the Persians as equals.' Egyptians, Arabs and Indians shared this sentiment, and detected that behind successive British governments' stonewalling over increased self-determination for their countries lay a fundamental belief that the non-white races suffered from some inbred incapacity to manage their own affairs. By contrast, political maturity was more easily and quickly attained by white men. For the impatient and the disappointed, the Commonwealth was a white man's club as racially exclusive as those of Singapore, Nairobi or, for that matter, the Hammersmith Palais de Dance.

7

THE BOND OF
ONE SPIRIT:

THE PUBLIC FACE
OF EMPIRE

1919–1939

The colour bar was making itself felt during a period when tremendous efforts were being made to promote Commonwealth and imperial unity. The revolution in communications, which gathered pace after 1919, enhanced the prospects for a more closely bonded empire. Long-distance air travel and wireless had the potential to liberate the empire from the fetters of its geography. Aviation was immediately recognised as a cord which could bind together territories scattered at random across the globe. After his epic twenty-day flight from London to Australia at the end of 1919, Sir Ross Smith believed that he had helped 'bind closer the outposts of the Empire through the trails of the skies'. Another pathfinder, Mrs J. A. Mollinson [Amy Johnson], told a BBC audience in 1932 that the purpose of her latest flight from London to the Cape by way of West Africa had been to 'keep together in friendship and good fellowship all the scattered parts of our Empire'.

The wireless also drew people together. It enkindled a sense of community among the disparate races of the empire; strengthened the ties of kinship between Britain and the dominions; and, most important of all, focussed the loyalty of all the empire's subjects on the figure who symbolised imperial unity, the monarch. It was appropriate that on Christmas Day 1933 members of the extended imperial family heard the gruff, fatherly voice of George V speaking from Sandringham. In the first royal Christmas message, the King thanked his subjects for their loyalty, pledged his continued service, and sent them the season's good wishes. This brief, simple and warm address had been preceded by an hour-long programme made up of short pieces contrived to convey a sense of familial closeness among the peoples of the empire. There were short live broadcasts from Canadian, Australian and New Zealand towns and cities, Gibraltar and a ship lying off Port Said.

RIGHT AND BELOW
RIGHT *Imperial tourism*:
*Travel posters offer the
romance and glamour
of the Middle East
and India.*
(© P&O)

OPPOSITE ABOVE
AND LEFT *Fly the
Empire way*:
*QANTAS posters adver-
tise imperial air travel.*
(© QANTAS)

LEFT *Screen empire*:
*Balliol-educated
Ghul Khan listens
to Roger Livesey in
The Drum (1938).*

BELOW *Great
white father*:
*District Commissioner
Sanders lends an ear to
the natives in* Sanders
of the River *(1935) and*
Bosambo *(Paul Robeson,
centre, with chief's
medal inscribed GRI)
learns the art of fair
government. Among
the extras was a Kenyan
student, Jomo Kenyatta.
(Both © Kobal)*

RIGHT: *Imperial swashbuckler*: Errol Flynn takes a Russian battery in splendid style in The Charge of the Light Brigade *(1936).* *(© Kobal)*

BELOW: *Hollywood's raj:* a fanatic Muslim leader who bears a resemblance to Gandhi is held prisoner in Gunga Din *(1939). In a few moments he will leap into a pit of snakes and be praised by his captors as a brave man fighting for his country.* *(© Kobal)*

*On the warpath
a second time*:
Sudanese extras from
The Four Feathers
(1939) set off for
Omdurman; some
had taken part in the
actual battle forty-one
years before.
(© Kobal)

George V's 1933 broadcast was an imperial *coup de théâtre*. The airwaves had united the empire in a wonderful and moving manner, and a technically more ambitious programme was prepared for Christmas Day 1934. Again, the themes were kinship and harmony, but the rich diversity of the empire's people was also explored. A handful were invited to speak about themselves and their daily lives. So, during the prelude to the King's address, listeners heard, among other things, songs sung by native 'boys' on a Cape vineyard, an officer speaking from an outpost on the Khyber Pass, and a few words from a life-saver on Bondi Beach, Sydney. There was an endearing candour about some of the performances. A Tasmanian fisherman drily announced, 'There ain't much difference being a fisherman here and a fisherman anywhere else. It's mostly pretty cold and pretty wet.' An old Cotswold shepherd remarked, impromptu, that he had a brother in New Zealand who, if he was listening, might take the trouble to write home. At three in the afternoon, the King spoke and praised that 'bond of one spirit' which held all his scattered subjects together.

The wireless was also helping the people of the empire to find out about each other. The BBC, then guided by the high-minded principles of Sir John Reith, its director-general, gave time to fifteen-minute talks by experts on different aspects of the empire, past, present and future. Controversial issues were not side-stepped or glossed over; in 1930, the archaeologist Louis Leakey drew on his Kenyan experience to warn that if officials continued to govern Africa 'in ignorance of native custom' they ran the risk of accumulated resentment breaking into unrest. These broadcasts were reminders of the continual need to inform the public about the empire, what it stood for, and how its existence benefited them.

The empire was 'sold' to the public in an unprecedented and unashamed manner by the British Empire Exhibition held at Wembley during 1924 and 1925. It was a splendid show in which the exotic and progressive aspects of the empire were carefully interwoven. The exhibition's vari-

No laughing matter:
a Punch *cartoon of 1933*
mocks the bodyline
bowling controversy, but
few Australians would
have seen the joke.

ous pavilions and 'palaces' were spread across a two-hundred-acre site and were connected by streets with such names as Dominion Way and Atlantic Slope, which had been chosen by Kipling. The total cost of the show was £2.2 million, half of which was provided by a government keen to foster imperial trade. At the official opening of the exhibition in April 1924, the Prince of Wales promised his father, George V, 'a complete and vivid representation of your Empire' and an advertisement to the world 'that the most powerful agency of civilisation had its heart set upon peaceful actions and the good of mankind'. In reply, the King extolled 'the spirit of free and tolerant cooperation which had inspired peoples of different races, creeds, institutions and ways of thought to unite in a single Commonwealth.'

Twenty-seven million people visited the exhibition. They came away with an impression of a thriving, forward-looking and diverse empire, and memories of glimpses of how some of its more picturesque inhabitants lived. 'Dusky figures flit about the spot for all the world as if one was actually in Africa, instead of a few miles from Charing Cross,' enthused one journalist.

George V and his eldest son were closely identified with the exhibition and its objectives. The monarch had always been a symbol of imperial unity, a totemic figure who commanded affection and loyalty. Abstract bonds had to be strengthened, and so the monarch, or more usually his or her immediate kin, had periodically to reveal themselves to the distant peoples of the empire. In 1877 the Prince of Wales traversed India in what was the first official royal tour of the empire and his son, George V, made a magnificent tour in 1912, receiving the homage of the Indian princes at a huge durbah in Delhi.

There was less accent on pseudo-Mughal pageantry and pomp during the post-war royal tours undertaken by the Prince of Wales. The future Edward VIII was sent off on his travels by Lloyd George, who saw the royal peregrinations as an exercise in political showmanship that would entrance the dominions and make their rulers more tractable. 'The appearance of the popular Prince of Wales might do more to calm the discord than half a dozen solemn Imperial Conferences.' Up to a point the Prime Minister was right. The young prince was a decent, affable fellow whose good looks, youthfulness and unstuffy manner made a favourable impression throughout the empire. He had been well prepared for his duties; Churchill coached him in the art of public oratory, and Lord Stamfordham, the King's secretary, lectured him on the seriousness of his new responsibilities. 'The Throne is the pivot upon which the Empire will more than hinge,' he intoned. 'Its strength and stability will depend entirely on its occupant.'

With this admonition hanging over him, the Prince embarked for Canada in August 1919. During the next nine years, he successively visited the West Indies, New Zealand, Australia, India, Canada again (in 1923 and 1927), the Gambia, the Gold Coast, Nigeria, South Africa, Kenya and Uganda. He was fêted everywhere, and received local worthies, inspected guards of honour, opened public buildings and made the appropriate speeches with a cheerful enthusiasm that must at times have been hard to sustain. When he

Great White Chief: the Prince of Wales in Indian dress during the royal tour of Canada, 1920.

Collecting the empire:
from the thirties onwards,
colonial postage stamps
were contrived to appeal
to collectors. Their
images reflected the
diversity of the colonies,
their products, people,
and flora and fauna.
Royal occasions were
marked by special issues
with uniform designs.

ascended the throne in January 1936, Edward VIII knew more about the empire and its people than any of his predecessors. As Lloyd George had predicted, he had won hearts and had done what he could to ease ethnic and political tensions in Canada and South Africa. Given to occasional radical outbursts at home, the prince revealed himself a reactionary abroad, observing that Indians were unfit to govern themselves and openly sympathising with the white settlers in Kenya.

It would be impossible to calculate what contribution these and other royal tours made to imperial cohesion. Documentaries like *50,000 Miles with the Prince of Wales* (1925) and newsreels of his and other imperial progresses showed images of diverse peoples cheering and waving flags, united in loyalty to the Crown and, by inference, the empire. It was all very reassuring, as were newspaper reports of facile and emollient speeches of welcome and thanks, which emphasised allegiance and affection on one side and paternal devotion on the other. No chance was missed to reiterate the common values upon which the Commonwealth and empire were based.

On the whole, the British public was more familiar with the empire than it had been in any previous period. This is not to say that whenever people gathered in pubs, railway carriages or on the football terraces they fell to talking about the empire. At a time when the ordinary people of Britain were more concerned with knife-and-fork issues such as jobs, the means test and the prospects for industrial revival, such recondite matters as Indian constitutional reform or native policy in Kenya could hardly have been expected to stimulate much public interest. Nonetheless, through the wireless, cinema and lessons in school, more and more people were aware of the empire's existence. They were also, and this was most important, conscious of the empire as a valuable asset of which the British people could feel proud. Its public face was always a benevolent one, and its subjects appeared to be contented and glad to be British. The collective imperial image projected on the cinema screen or brought into people's homes by the annual royal broadcast was reassuring and, so to speak, exorcised any feelings of guilt about oppression and exploitation.

At the time, the public knew that the empire was changing for it was, after all, a force for human progress. No one knew how long the present era of transition would last or in what form the empire would emerge. Neville Chamberlain, who became Prime Minister in 1937, imagined that India would only achieve full independence by 1980 at the earliest. Churchill thought in similar terms and, in 1937, wrote to the Viceroy, 'I want to see the British Empire preserved for a few more generations in its strength and splendour. Only the most prodigious exertions of British genius will achieve this result.' The strength and splendour of the empire were there for all to see as they watched newsreels of battleships steaming into Cape Town or Sydney harbours, conveying royal princes to their adoring subjects. But was the empire permanent? Probably not, but its possession was very comforting in a world which had suddenly become mutable and dangerous.

8

FINEST HOUR:
THE EMPIRE AT WAR
1939–1941

Until the mid 1930s Britain's rulers did not expect to have to repeat the Herculean effort of the Great War. They had done everything in their power to construct and operate a system for international stability and peace based upon the League of Nations and a sheaf of non-aggression pacts signed during the 1920s. What became known as collective security was not only a guarantee of a new international order in which war was outlawed, it created a world in which the empire would be protected and allowed to flourish. The rise of Hitler in Germany and Mussolini in Italy put an end to these hopes.

Initially the British government, anxious to avoid war, followed a policy of appeasement towards the two dictators. In September 1938, following Germany's occupation of the Sudetenland, the region of Czechoslovakia whose inhabitants were predominantly German, the Prime Minister, Neville Chamberlain flew to Munich where he received assurances from Hitler that all remaining Anglo-German differences would be reconciled. Chamberlain was therefore stunned when in March 1939 the Führer occupied the rump of Czechoslovakia. Reluctantly, after much agonising and under intense parliamentary and public pressure, Chamberlain reversed the course of British foreign policy and pledged Poland every support if Germany threatened its independence. On 1 September the German army marched into Poland and two days later Britain was at war with Germany.

Chamberlain announced the declaration of war to the British people with a BBC broadcast in which he harped on about the personal slights he had suffered from the man he had trusted. More inspiring, perhaps, was the legendary cable which arrived in London from the West Indies: 'Don't worry; Barbados is with you.' So too were the rest of the colonies which, of course, had no choice, and India, where, as has been seen, the Viceroy's declaration of war upset the Congress party.

Australia had followed events in Europe closely, despite having had some difficulty in extracting secret documents from the British government. On 25 August, the Prime Minister, Robert Menzies, had broadcast to the

275

Competition:
American-made Ford
'Tin Lizzies' in the Gold
Coast (c.1930). Here
and elsewhere in the
empire, American and
Japanese manufacturers
were pushing out
British imports.
(© Unilever)

people, reminding them that, 'We in Australia are involved, because the destruction or defeat of Great Britain would be the destruction and defeat of the British Empire, and leave us with a precarious tenure of our own independence.' The same arguments had prevailed in 1914 and again swung Australia and New Zealand behind Britain.

In South Africa the ruling United party (formed in 1934 to reconcile Boers and British) favoured benevolent neutrality. When this was put to the parliament, eighty members voted against and sixty-seven for, forcing the Prime Minister, General Hertzog, to resign on 5 September. His deputy, Smuts, took power after the governor-general had rejected a call for a general election, and South Africa entered the war. Boer extremists were bitter; many openly sympathised with Naziism and one, the future architect of apartheid, Dr Malan, proclaimed that, 'The Union of South Africa has sunk to the level of a vassal state of Europe.'

Fears that French Canadians would strenuously oppose the war quickly evaporated. Mackenzie King gave notice of his emotional support for Britain in a broadcast on 3 September, and seven days later sought parliamentary approval for a declaration of war, which was accepted without a division. Maurice Duplessis, the Quebec Nationalist leader, dissolved his province's assembly and called a general election in October. It proved a damp squib; pro-war candidates took sixty-eight of the eighty-six seats.

The Commonwealth and empire went to war in the first week of September, but its unity had by no means been unquestioning or instantaneous. There was none of the emotional, patriotic shenanigans of August 1914; rather the mood of the public was sober and businesslike. A hard task lay ahead, and those about to get down to it rolled up their sleeves rather than unrolling and waving flags. They were about to fight the 'People's War', and, when it was over the people, not only in Britain but throughout the empire, would expect a reward for their toil.

Buy empire!:
during the thirties,
British consumers were
urged to buy the products
of the empire.
Colonial economies
were stimulated and,
as they prospered, the
colonies became markets
for British goods.
(© PRO)

Marching in step: a volunteer for the Australian Royal Women's Army Corps stands in front of a recruiting poster that emphasises wartime unity throughout the empire. (© Australian War Memorial)

The first few months of the war saw little military activity and became known as the 'phoney war'. All this changed when in May and June 1940 the *Wehrmacht* and *Luftwaffe* swept through Belgium, Holland, Denmark and Norway. Seeing which way the wind was blowing, Mussolini declared war on 11 June. Four days later, the French government opened negotiations which ended with its unconditional surrender on the 18th. Britain's position was now extremely perilous. For the first time since 1806 it lacked allies and faced a Europe whose manpower and industry were at the disposal of a tyrant intent on the destruction of Britain and the eventual dispersal of its empire. During the earlier crisis the imperial base had been relatively safe, thanks to an unbeaten and superior battlefleet, but in the summer of 1940 Britain was vulnerable to aerial attack and a cross-Channel invasion. The situation seemed hopeless, and in Washington General George C. Marshall, the US Chief of Staff, and many others predicted that Britain would be knocked out of the war within six weeks.

What followed was the British people's 'finest hour'. The phrase was Churchill's and part of a stirring call to arms delivered on 18 June, just over a month after he had become Prime Minister: 'Let us therefore be braced to our duties, and so bear ourselves that, if the British Empire and its Commonwealth last for a thousand years, men will say: "This was their finest hour."'

Churchill guided the country through the twelve months between the surrender of France and Hitler's invasion of the Soviet Union on 22 June 1941, during which time Britain and its empire alone defied the Axis powers. Throughout this year and for the next four, Churchill spoke and acted as if the empire would outlast the war and continue unchanged. There was, therefore, an extraordinary paradox in the fact that his greatest stroke of genius was the recognition that Britain's survival depended ultimately on America, a nation whose rulers and citizens were instinctively hostile towards the British empire.

Cooperation:
the Canadian cruiser
Uganda *takes on fuel*
while an Australian
destroyer comes
alongside with mail,
the Pacific, 1945.
(© IWM)

America took time to swing behind Britain. During June and July 1940 senior officials and commanders favoured conserving America's resources rather than delivering them to a nation which appeared to be on the verge of defeat. Only when the chances of a successful German invasion of Britain diminished in the late autumn of 1940 was Roosevelt at last certain that Britain was now America's first line of defence. The result was that America became what Britain had been during the Revolutionary and Napoleonic wars, part banker and part armourer, providing the wherewithal for others to make war. The Lend Lease Act was passed by Congress in February 1941 and gave Britain sufficient credit to purchase whatever it required in return for a pledge to repay the debt when the war was over.

Churchill also pinned his hopes on Roosevelt being able to handle what he called the 'Japanese dog' in the Pacific. At the end of November 1940, Churchill was assured by an intelligence assessment of the Far Eastern situation that the Japanese would stay out of the war until the spring, and then their first target would be a soft one, Siam (Thailand).

The Japanese government did not behave as predicted. By early autumn, the new Prime Minister, General Hideki Tojo, and his cabinet had decided to attack British, Dutch and American colonies in the Far East if, as was likely, the three nations refused to lift an oil embargo imposed on Japan after the occupation of Indo-China. The oil blockade hurt, but what really swayed the Japanese ministers was the possibility that Germany would beat Russia and Britain during the following year, thereby making it easier for Japan to retain the former British, French and Dutch colonies which could fall into its hands. Tojo and his colleagues also naïvely imagined that, in time, America would accept the new imperial *status quo* in Asia.

Japan's war plans were audacious and ambitious. On 7 December, carrier-borne aircraft attacked the United States navy's anchorage at Pearl Harbor, knocking out several battleships and temporarily swinging the Pacific balance of naval power in Japan's favour. Between 8 and 17 December, seaborne forces landed on the coasts of Siam (which immediately surrendered), Malaya, Borneo, Sarawak, the Philippines, Guam and Wake Island. Conventional naval wisdom had hitherto ruled out the possibility of Japan undertaking so many operations simultaneously, and surprise was all but total. After the war, mischievous allegations were made that Churchill had been informed by signals intelligence of the movement and destination of the Pearl Harbor force, but refused to alert Roosevelt so as to make certain America's entry into the war. This is a *canard*; signals picked up by the Hong Kong listening post were believed, probably rightly, to be from a Japanese flotilla heading through the South China Sea for Malaya, not from the Pearl Harbor armada.

Britain's Far Eastern empire fell with a swiftness which both astonished and dismayed everyone. Singapore's uselessness as a base was demonstrated by air raids by bombers based in Indo-China on 8 December. Two days later, bombers flying from Saigon sank the *Repulse* and *Prince of Wales*, while RAF, RAAF and RNZAF aircraft were busy trying to stem the Japanese advance from the three bridge-heads they had established on the eastern shores of Malaya. On land, the Japanese advanced through the jungle with a deadly efficiency, and their aircraft systematically destroyed British airfields, nearly all of which were sited in the north of the colony. After three days of an unequal aerial contest, the local RAF commander warned that his forces could only last for a fortnight. By the end of the month, British, dominion and Indian ground troops were in full retreat towards Singapore, having fought gallantly against an enemy their commanders had so grossly underrated.

Hong Kong capitulated on Christmas Day. Its position had been precarious since the outbreak of the Sino-Japanese war four years before. At the end of 1940 there had been a serious mutiny by Sikh artillerymen in the garrison, who, it appeared, had been subverted by Japanese propaganda. White troops were needed to defend a white man's empire so, during 1941, Canadian infantry were sent to the colony at Britain's request.

While imperial troops were being forced back through the jungles of Malaya, and Singapore, the keystone of the empire's defences in the Far East, stood in increasing jeopardy, Churchill's mood swung between despair and exhilaration. The latter predominated; on 11 December 1941 Germany and Italy declared war on America and spared Roosevelt the awkward necessity of having to seek Congress's approval for entering the European conflict. With the United States now a full combatant, Churchill felt sure that the Allies would eventually win the war on all fronts, although there was no way of knowing how long this would take.

The Prime Minister and his chiefs of staff were unwavering in their belief that, despite the recent setbacks in the Far East and the Pacific, Britain's primary objective was still the defeat of Germany. Japan would have to wait and British prestige and territories in Asia would have to be sacrificed, although for a short time hope was placed on the Allies being able to hold a defensive line stretching from Burma southwards through Singapore and the Dutch East Indies to the northern coast of Australia.

If this route was fractured, the defence of India and the Far East, as well as that of the Middle East and Mediterranean would be gravely

Imperial paladin: *Winston Churchill, who would lead the empire through its 'finest hour', as a Hussar subaltern in 1898.*
(© Popperfoto)

imperilled. Faced with what might turn out to be a double-pronged German assault on the Middle East during 1942, Churchill sailed to America on 15 December prepared to convince Roosevelt that the only viable Allied strategy had to be one in which Germany was overcome first. In reaching this conclusion, he and his advisers had to face the bitter fact that, for the time being, imperial interests in Asia would have to be abandoned, although Churchill hoped that those defending them would fight stubbornly. Their efforts would, however, turn out to be futile if Germany was allowed to establish itself in the Middle East, and thereby secure the means to cooperate direct-ly with Japanese forces which, by the turn of the year, were beginning to advance westwards through Burma to the borders of India. By sacri-ficing one part of the empire, Churchill hoped that he might ultimately secure all of it.

Allied grand strategy for 1942 was ham-mered out by Churchill, Roosevelt and their

Too little, too late:
the battleship Prince
of Wales at Singapore,
December 1941. Its
arrival, together with
the battlecruiser Repulse,
did not deter the Japanese
and both ships were
sunk within a few days.
(© IWM)

advisers during the last two weeks of December. They agreed to the principle of Germany first, then Japan. First would come the expulsion of German and Italian forces from North Africa, and then USAAF and RAF bombers would begin the systematic pounding of Germany, using British airfields. No longer able to defend itself, the British empire in the Far East would pass under American protection; GIs were to be rushed to Australia and, if the Philippines fell, the remnants of its garrison would be shipped to Singapore, if it was still tenable.

Asia for the Asiatics!:
Burmese welcome
Japanese troops, 1942.
Cheers would turn to
tears as they and other
peoples in South East
Asia discovered the
cruelty and ruthless-
ness of their liberators,
Nonetheless, in 1945
there was little desire
to restore the pre-war
imperial status quo.
(© IWM)

9
STEADFAST COMRADES:
THE STRESSES
OF WAR

The year 1942 was a bleak one for the British empire. On 15 February, the 130,000-strong garrison of Singapore yielded to a smaller Japanese army. Four days later, the war reached Australia; Darwin suffered a devastating air raid while a panic-stricken government in Canberra prepared for invasion. Burma was overrun, with Rangoon falling on 1 March and Mandalay on 1 May. The Andaman Islands were captured on 23 March, and during the first fortnight of April a Japanese armada cruised at will in the Bay of Bengal. Calcutta and Colombo suffered air attacks and two British cruisers were sunk. A weak Allied squadron was overwhelmed in the Battle of the Java Sea at the end of February, and within two months Japanese forces had conquered the Dutch East Indies, the Philippines, much of New Guinea and a string of British island colonies in the south-western Pacific. In the meantime, Japanese strategists were planning the seizure of Fiji and long-range operations in the Indian Ocean.

Britain's lost colonies, if not its prestige, were eventually restored through the efforts of the United States which, at the beginning of 1942, had taken over the main burden of imperial defence. It was American warships which defeated the Japanese navy in engagements at the Coral Sea and Midway in May and June. The latter victory swung the balance of seapower in the Pacific in the Allies' favour and halted Japanese expansion. By August, American and Australian forces had counter-attacked and begun the long, grinding process of ejecting the Japanese from the south-western Pacific. The defence of India and the reconquest of Burma in 1942–5 was conducted by imperial forces, but here, as on all other fronts, American-made aircraft and armaments were vital.

These events caused consternation in Britain. The country was already in the middle of a period of intensely critical self-examination as plans were being framed for post-war reconstruction. There was an overwhelming sense that there could never be a return to the pre-war world with its inefficiencies, social inequality and economic drifting. The new Britain would be a nation which cultivated social harmony and devoted a substantial portion of its wealth and energies to the regeneration of industry, full employment and providing a fair and generous system of education and welfare for all. How this last might be achieved was set out in the famous Beveridge report, which was issued in December 1942, and widely welcomed as a goal worth fighting for. The country was going to change for the better; but what of its empire?

The empire's past, present and future came suddenly under public scrutiny during the weeks after the fall of Singapore. The shock of a capitulation which effectively shattered Britain's admittedly fragile pretensions as a global, imperial power was followed by a series of disconcerting revelations about the character of the empire. A frank and devastating analysis of the background to the surrender written by *The Times*'s Far Eastern correspondent was published on 18 February. It argued that the 'easy-going routine of colonial administration' had sapped the will of officials who had shown themselves devoid of the 'dynamism' and 'aggression' now evident in other areas of public life. 'The government had no roots in the life of the people,' the writer concluded. An editorial condemned the Malayan administration for the 'lack of touch between the local Government and the vast Asiatic population, whose attitude, with the honourable exception of the Chinese, was passive, timorous and apathetic.'

Official censorship prevented the publication of details of defections to the Japanese by Malays, disheartened Indian troops and Burmese. Nonetheless, parliamentary critics of the government contrasted the indifference of the natives of Malaya with the fierceness with which the Filipinos were fighting for their American masters, who had promised the Philippines self-government after the war.

In broad terms, the débâcle in Malaya was yet another example of the failure of the old order and its servants. The figure of Colonel Blimp soon entered the debate. He had come to symbolise the ossified thinking, complacency and obscurantism which were now seen as the outstanding features of the 'Old Gang', that band of men who, according to left-wing mythology, had guided the country so maladroitly between the wars. The routine analysis of servicemen's mail undertaken to measure morale revealed that in the wake of the disasters in the Far East there had been an increase in complaints about Blimps in high places. A. L. Rowse, a distinguished Oxford historian, used the columns of *The Times* to speculate on how far the empire's recent misfortunes stemmed from that dogma fostered in public schools, which elevated character over cleverness. It was the latter quality which had marked the men who had built the empire in the time of Elizabeth I, Anne and the two Pitts. On the same day, the government announced rigorous testing of all army lieutenant-colonels over the age of forty-five, presumably to weed out Blimps.

There were some in America and Britain who were wondering whether the class which still largely had the governance of the empire deserved to retain its power. 'There must be no place after the war for special privileges, either for individuals or nations,' Roosevelt had proclaimed in November 1941. His countrymen tended to agree, as did a substantial body of opinion in Britain, mostly on the left and centre. So too, but to a lesser degree, did the government, whose propaganda continually exhorted everyone to work together and share the burdens of war equally.

Within the empire the social hierarchy was unshaken by the war. Servicemen attached to the units which reoccupied Malaya in the summer of 1945 were hurt by the snobbery of those they had liberated, the planters and their wives, who, like the Bourbons, appeared to have remembered everything and learnt nothing. This was not surprising; throughout most of the empire's existence the élite which managed the colonies had been drawn almost exclusively from the upper and upper-middle classes. Men in senior positions during the war had been recruited from public-school alumni, who had passed through Oxford or Cambridge and shown themselves more adept on the playing field than in the examination hall. Character counted for much; when interviewing potential district officers, Sir Ralph Furse made a point of looking for such telltale signs of an interior weakness as 'a languid handshake'. Before 1914, and probably after, a 'social test' was applied, and the candidate who offered his interrogator a Virginia rather than a Turkish cigarette was automatically scratched for what was then a social solecism.

The war in the Far East, which in the spring of 1942 showed every sign that it would soon extend to the Indian Ocean, was a racial conflict. Japanese propaganda hailed the fall of Singapore, Hong Kong and Manila as triumphs for the peoples of Asia and milestones on the road to their liberation from white rule. Australian POWs were forced to sweep the streets of Singapore as a token that the old racial order had been overturned; white civilian and military prisoners were systematically humiliated and maltreated in what the victims interpreted as a form of racial revenge; and some were wantonly murdered, like the twenty-two administrators, missionaries and wireless operators killed in the Gilbert Islands in October.

*Let the women of
Britain's Empire
Sing praises and their
warriors inspire
Steadfast comrades
who stand ready to
die for liberty.
Sons of the
Dominions and India
And far-flung islands
of the seven seas,
Sons of the
Motherland,
England the
Motherland,
Sing out, women of
the Empire.*

GOLD COAST LYRICIST

Japan's call for a race war reached many ears. 'I have heard Natives saying, "Why fight against Japan? We are oppressed by the whites and we shall not fare worse under the Japanese,"' Smuts wrote after inspecting a newly raised contingent of black troops. 'But', he consoled himself, 'I am sure the great majority are still loyal in their conservative way.' Many Indians, Malays and Burmese were not. In what still remains a shadowy episode in the war (thanks to the furtiveness of Britain's official secrecy regulations) large bodies of Indian, Ghurka and Tamil troops defected to the Japanese and formed the Indian National Army (INA), a nationalist force dedicated to the overthrow of the raj. The full numbers are not known; in 1944, military intelligence believed the INA contained 35,000, and a year later it was estimated that 20,000 Indian troops had gone over to the Japanese, two out of every seven captured.

In the summer of 1945, when the Indian army had the wretched task of sifting through the survivors of the INA, its intelligence staff identified a hard core of 7,600 who had actively assisted the Japanese, and in some cases committed horrendous war crimes which deserved punishment. The

rest were for the main part decent soldiers disorientated by the chaotic retreats in Malaya and Burma during the winter and spring of 1941–2, or prisoners who collaborated to get better rations and treatment. In this category were many who had been genuinely shocked by the defeats inflicted on Britain and had lost confidence in their old rulers.

The INA was part of a wider, Japanese-supervised organisation for nationalist subversion in India and anti-European propaganda throughout Asia. It included the Swaraj Young Men's Training School in Rangoon, which specialised in sabotage and guerrilla warfare, and an academy in Penang which trained Malay, Chinese and Siamese propagandists. INA soldiers were told that once they and the Japanese penetrated Bengal, there would be a mass anti-British uprising. In the meantime, trained saboteurs and

Imperial mobilisation:
Bombay women
textile workers help
the war effort, 1941.
(© IWM)

partisans were landed from submarines, but nearly all were intercepted. By the end of October, forty-two Japanese Inspired Fifth Columnists (JIFs) had been rounded up. On the battlefield, the INA proved a disappointment to its masters and desertions back to the British were frequent. The government in India took the INA very seriously, fearing that its propaganda might entice front-line troops to surrender, and that its agents might foment sedition in areas already convulsed by Congress agitation. There was, therefore, close surveillance of Indian units and the inspection of troops' mail for signs of discontent.

Among the troops fighting in Burma during 1944 were 30,000 askaris from East and West Africa, and, like their Indian comrades, they had their correspondence and conversations monitored for signs of political restlessness. Although the War Office had allowed the issuing of commissions to men of mixed race in October 1939, black troops continued to be commanded by white officers. In the case of the Gold Coast askaris, white officers were imported from the settlers of Southern Rhodesia.

While the war loosened the social hierarchy in Britain, its racial counterpart in Africa and the West Indies remained as rigid as ever. The Colonial Office went to considerable lengths to ensure that its black subjects were cocooned from any outside influences that might upset them or make them unhappy with their lot. Contact between British blacks and negro American servicemen was officially seen as a potent source of discontent and disruption. Well-dressed and well-paid black American GIs turned the heads of poorer Bermudan blacks and so, under Colonial Office pressure, the former were withdrawn. Black servicemen stationed in Liberia were banned from taking leave in nearby British African colonies, again for fear that their self-confidence and prosperity might cause unrest.

As in the First World War, all the resources of the dominions and colonies were mobilised for war. Raising and training fighting men and women was still immensely important.

FULL TOTALS OF FIGHTING MEN AND WOMEN TRAINED FOR THE SECOND WORLD WAR

Great Britain:	4,650,000
Australia:	570,000
Canada:	770,000
India:	1,789,000
New Zealand:	97,000
East African colonies:	225,000 (plus 30,000 pioneers)
West African colonies:	150,000 (plus 16,000 pioneers)

These figures represent the sum of all men and women in the services and ignore the fact that, at various stages of the war, there were partial demobilisations. The South African 1st Division returned home after the liberation of Abyssinia, and, the Japanese having been evicted from New Guinea, Australian and New Zealand servicemen were released for industry during 1943 and 1944. Nonetheless, Australia had 365,000 men and women under arms in 1945, four-fifths of them volunteers. Canada faced the same manpower problems it had in the First World War; by 1943 the number of volunteers for overseas service was dwindling and conscription was introduced the following year, although the pressed men were sent for garrison duties in the West Indies rather than to the fronts in France and Italy.

The African record was particularly impressive. At the beginning of 1943, Nyasaland had contributed 20,000 men to the King's African Rifles, and a further 103,000 were undertaking war work, most in the Northern Rhodesian copper mines. This represented over a third of the adult male population.

Those who had served in the war acquired higher aspirations and expected a brighter future. In October 1945, a survey of Indian soldiers revealed that after the war they wanted, in order of preference: a comfortable home, a pension, a loving wife, children, an understanding of how to take precautions against malaria, one or two cows, schools, a maternity and general hospital, a gun for shooting game and a horse.

For many Indian soldiers the experience of service on the Italian front in 1944–5 had been a revelation of the extent of their country's backwardness, and had left them with a strong urge to return home and put matters right. Knowledge appeared to be the key to national salvation, and some demanded a national education system that promoted the teaching of technical subjects.

The war had also encouraged African soldiers to examine themselves and the world outside their villages and to acquire new tastes, such as smoking, tinned foods and newspapers. One casualty of this revolution was the old African culture.

Ploughshares
into swords:
Indian workers making
shellcases in a converted
factory owned by the
American Metal Box
Company, 1941. In India
the demands of both
world wars accelerated
industrialisation.
(© IWM)

10

THE DEFENCE OF ARCHAIC PRIVILEGE:

THE EMPIRE RESTORED

1942–1945

Just over a year after the end of the war, Willie Gallacher, the Communist MP for West Fife, declared to the Commons that, 'The British Empire [is] handed over to the American pawnbroker – our only hope.' To prove his point and taunt the Conservatives, he quoted a remark Churchill had made to Roosevelt in August 1941, 'Without America, the Empire cannot stand.' Like all maverick MPs, Gallacher had a knack of bluntly expressing home truths which other politicians preferred to ignore or evade.

Since 1941, Britain had been mortgaged to the United States. As the war had progressed, it became clear that the loss of financial independence had reduced the government's freedom of choice when it came to making decisions about the empire's future. American opinion could not be disregarded because American fighting men were bearing the brunt of the war against Japan. Victories in the Pacific between 1942 and 1945 were making it possible for Britain to regain its Far Eastern colonies. For large numbers of Americans this was not a worthy cause; many asked why American manhood should be sacrificed in order that Britain could continue to lord it over Malays and Burmese.

Emotional anti-imperialism was endemic in America. The general line was that all empires, including the British, were parasitic tyrannies which were fast becoming obsolete. Dynamic historical forces were gathering momentum which would create a new world order in which no country could expect the right to rule others without their consent. The man on the sidewalk concurred; opinion polls taken in 1942 and 1945 suggested that 56 per cent of Americans believed that the British empire was in some way 'oppressive'.

American anti-imperialists set the greatest store by the Atlantic Charter, an idealistic statement of Anglo-American war objectives, which had been agreed between Churchill and Roosevelt in August 1941. For many, perhaps the majority, of those who read it, the Atlantic Charter was a blueprint for a new and just world order. Taken literally, it appeared to undermine the moral base for all empires. The President and the Prime Minister had pledged themselves to uphold 'the rights of all peoples to choose the form of government under which they live; and they wish to see sovereign rights and self-government restored to those who have been forcibly deprived of them.'

Churchill disliked this phraseology which, taken at face value, challenged Britain's right to rule her colonies. On reflection, he satisfied himself that in the case of those colonies in Japanese hands the 'sovereign rights' concerned were those of Britain and not the indigenous inhabitants. Churchill also

THE RISE & FALL OF THE BRITISH EMPIRE

OPPOSITE

Call to arms:
Sir Osei Agyeman,
Asantehene of the Asante,
inspecting the Kumasi
Home Guard in 1942.
He reminded his subjects
of their warrior traditions
and called for recruits:
he gave generously to
the Spitfire fund.
(© Church of Scotland
World Missions)

conveniently assumed that the rest of the colonial empire was exempt from the Atlantic Charter. His deputy, the Labour leader Clement Attlee, thought otherwise and, like many within Britain and the empire, believed the Charter had universal application. The Colonial Office adopted a grudging, middle-of-the-road position, indicating that in the 'far distant future' some colonies might achieve dominion status. Others never would; strategic considerations demanded that Britain held on perpetually to Gibraltar, Malta, Cyprus and Aden, and for various other reasons could not relinquish control over the Gambia, Borneo, Malaya, Hong Kong, Bermuda, Fiji, the Falkland Islands and British Honduras (Belize). Those responsible for war propaganda in the colonies were instructed to stay as mute as possible about the Charter and its implications.

One way to sidestep the moral dilemma created by the Atlantic Charter was to persuade the Americans that the empire's subjects were not downtrodden and exploited. From 1941 onwards, the government went to considerable lengths to educate American politicians and opinion-makers, a process which continued for the next twenty years. The message was always the same: British colonial government was unselfish, humane, just and always conducted in the best interests of people who would be lost without it.

During the war percipient Americans detected two Britains, strangely at odds with each other. In April 1942, the columnist Walter Lippmann told John Maynard Keynes that there existed in America 'a strong feeling that Britain east of Suez is quite different from Britain at home, that the war in Europe is a war of liberation and the war in Asia is the defence of archaic privilege.' Up to a point, Lippmann was right, although when he was writing the 'archaic privilege' of the old colonial order was withering. It had been physically overturned in shameful circumstances when Singapore fell, and its ethical foundations were being eroded by public criticism in Britain and the United States. British public opinion, as much as American anti-imperialism, made it impossible for the British government to put the clock back. Henceforward, the empire's rulers knew that for the colonies to survive in the post-war world they would have to jettison the maxim 'Nanny knows best', and instead listen and respond to the aspirations of their subjects. A new age was imminent and it would be Britain's duty to extend to the colonies those fundamental freedoms for which the war was being fought.

By 1945, there was a consensus as to the direction the empire should take: the colonies would slowly be transformed into self-governing dominions, wherever such a change was viable. The Labour party had already pledged itself to Indian home rule, and promised the same to the colonies, with the caveat that they needed to remain under British control 'for a long time to come'. The Labour minister Herbert Morrison put it more bluntly; premature independence for the colonies would be a folly equivalent to delivering 'a latch key, a bank account and a shot-gun' to a ten-year-old child.

Imperial propaganda was adjusted to the new mood in Britain, taking on a defensive, sometimes apologetic air. 'To many people nowadays the word "Empire" has a nasty sound. It reminds them of Nazi ideas of a master-race ruling others,' ran an advisory pamphlet issued by the Directorate of Army Education in April 1944. Teaching soldiers about the empire and the vital part it would play in the post-war world had been one of the tasks of army instructors since the end of 1941. Classes were to be reminded that to be a part of the empire was to be 'a member of a great powerful world-wide family instead of the citizen of a small, weak country'. Colonial peoples were now partners with Britain, which safeguarded them against exploitation by 'ruthless private enterprise', and helped them towards prosperity and independence. Benevolent imperialism had come of age. Like Britain, the empire was moving into a new and better era in which the well-being of its subjects was of paramount importance.

Not only did Britain have to convince the United States that its empire was a force for good, it had to secure American assistance for the defence of India and the recovery of its colonies in the Far East. Both were secondary war aims and far beyond Britain's capabilities. Allied resources and strategy in the region were in the hands of South-East Asia Command (SEAC), set up in the summer of 1943, and

quickly nicknamed 'Save England's Asiatic Colonies' by cynical Americans. SEAC also had the task of reviving Britain's almost moribund prestige in the area, and Churchill was anxious that it should have a British commander-in-chief.

His choice was Vice-Admiral Louis Mountbatten, the younger son of a German princeling who was a member of Queen Victoria's distended family, and had made himself an impressive career in the Royal Navy. For Churchill, Mountbatten was the ideal figurehead for what was essentially an imperial campaign. All SEAC's offensive operations required American sanction. The situation was candidly summed up by General Sir Henry Pownall, Mountbatten's chief of staff, in April 1944: 'The Americans have got us by the short hairs . . . We can't do anything in this theatre, amphibious or otherwise, without material assistance from them . . . So if they don't approve they don't provide.' It was the same in the Mediterranean in 1943–4, when the American high command was extremely reluctant to send landing craft and warplanes to the Italian front, which was considered of secondary importance to the Pacific.

In SEAC's area, the United States set its highest hopes on Chiang Kai-Shek's nationalist army, followers of a loftier cause than the restoration of British, French and Dutch colonies. Moreover, American post-war plans envisaged China as the major regional power in the Far East, and assumed that it would take on major peacekeeping responsibilities. Until his replacement in October 1944, Chiang's chief of staff was the anglophobe, anti-imperialist General 'Vinegar' Joe Stilwell, who, while civil in public, was contemptuous of the British in private. Mountbatten was at various times reviled as 'the Glamour Boy', 'an amateur', 'a fatuous ass', 'childish Louis, publicity crazy' and a 'pisspot'. His countrymen were 'bastardly hypocrites [who] do their best to cut our throats on all occasions. The pig fuckers.'

Stilwell's expletives were a vivid reminder of American misgivings about Britain's wartime goals. In the Far East these were contrary to Allied ideals; by no stretch of the imagination, and in spite of the brutality of Japanese rule, could the retaking of Burma and Malaya be depicted as liberation. Both were repossessed by their former owner, Britain.

In December 1943 Roosevelt announced that he intended to have Indo-China administered by an international commission rather than let it remain in French hands. It was harder to extend such an arrangement to Britain's former colonies, since Churchill was adamantine whenever the subject of the post-war empire was raised. With strong, all-party backing he and his successor, Clement Attlee, stonewalled at the Yalta and Potsdam conferences when discussions moved towards some form of international control for Europe's colonies. Americans were also disturbed by Britain's policy in Greece where, during 1944–5, British troops supported the anti-Communist faction, in what resembled a Palmerstonian bid to secure total control over the eastern Mediterranean. As the tide of war turned during 1944, it seemed that Britain, so lately the champion of democracy and freedom, had metamorphosed into the hungry imperial lion of a past age, wanting the biggest share of whatever was available.

Shortages of the wherewithal to wage war slowed down the lion in the Far East. India had finally been made secure by the battles of Kohima and Imphal in March and June 1944. Eight months before, Churchill had pressed for Operation Culverin, a landing on Sumatra, which would provide a base for an attack on Singapore. It was abandoned because Churchill's attention had been taken up by another chimerical scheme, the expulsion of the Germans from the Dodecanese Islands, which, he imagined, would propel Turkey into the war as an ally. This was overruled by the Americans, who rightly wanted all spare forces concentrated on the imminent invasion of France. European fronts continued to enjoy precedence over the Far East; in October 1944 Mountbatten was told that no forces could be spared for a seaborne assault on Rangoon.

It was only in February 1945 that permission was given for an advance on Rangoon. This was to be followed by large-scale seaborne landings on the Siamese and Malaya coasts between June 1945 and March 1946, codenamed Roger, Zipper and Mailfist. (There is a peculiar poetry about the titles given to Second World War operations; their origins and originators deserve a close study.)

As it was, Zipper and Mailfist turned out to be bloodless enterprises. Overstretched everywhere since the middle of 1942, Japan had been fighting and losing a defensive war. The Imperial Japanese Navy had lost both its preponderance and initiative at Midway and, despite considerable effort, failed to recover either in the next two years. By the winter of 1944–5, American forces had secured the Ryukyu Islands, Iwo Jima and Okinawa, and by the spring mass raids against Japanese cities by the USAAF's B-29 bombers were underway. In June 1945, less than a month after Germany's defeat, a detailed plan for invasion of Japan had been prepared. Hitherto, Britain had played virtually no part in the Pacific war, but once the defeat of Germany was imminent, Churchill fulfilled his pledge to Australia and began to move ships to join the USN. Neither the ships nor the elaborate plans for landings on the Japanese mainland and Malaya were needed. On 6 August an atomic bomb was exploded over Hiroshima, followed by another over Nagasaki three days later. These blows, combined with Russia's declaration of war, forced the Japanese government to surrender unconditionally on 15 August. The way was now open for Britain to take back its colonies, and incidentally assist the French and the Dutch to regain theirs. Rangoon had fallen in the spring, and on 9 September British and Indian forces went ashore in Malaya. Three days later Singapore was recaptured without a fight.

The British empire had survived the war without loss of territory, although damage to prestige, sustained since Munich, was impossible to calculate. The human cost of victory had been far less than in 1918.

CASUALTIES IN THE SECOND WORLD WAR			
	DEAD	MISSING	WOUNDED
Great Britain:	233,042	57,472	275,975
Canada:	36,018	2,866	53,073
Australia:	21,415	6,519	37,477
New Zealand:	9,844	2,201	19,253
South Africa:	6,417	1,980	13,773
India:	23,295	12,264	62,064
Colonies:	6,741	14,811	6,773

Britain had emerged from war with a huge debt to the United States but still possessing the largest empire in the world and clinging to old pretensions of global power. Russia and America had become, through their industrial and armed strength, 'superpowers', leaving Britain to occupy a humbler position. The United States was for the moment the mightier of the two superpowers; she held two-thirds of the world's gold reserves, aerial and naval supremacy and, most importantly, the technology to produce atomic bombs. Her industrial and banking systems were undamaged by war, and she was to all intents and purposes enjoying the same international pre-eminence as Britain had in 1815.

The empire alone qualified Britain to project itself as a global power. Its future in a world dominated by two states which, for various economic and political reasons, were inimical to territorial as opposed to ideological or economic empires, was far from certain. Furthermore the new Labour government had, since 1938, promised to give India self-government, and was determined to honour this pledge. Independence was also the destination of the larger colonies, although no one was prepared to say how long the journey would take. In terms of political logic, if such an abstraction exists, Britain had now committed itself to the eventual dissolution of its overseas empire and therefore its world power. Of course, the new pattern of thinking about the empire was not seen as a suicide note; it was assumed that old colonies would become new dominions whose association with Britain would somehow preserve her as a force to be reckoned with in the world.

PART FIVE
THE
SETTING SUN
1945-1993

I

THE COLONIALISTS ARE ON THE RAMPAGE:

THE EMPIRE IN THE POST-WAR WORLD

The history of what turned out to be the final decades of the British empire was largely determined by the course of the Cold War. It began in the winter of 1944–5, when British and American strategists began to get the jitters about the extent and purpose of the formidable build-up of Soviet military strength in eastern and central Europe. It ended in December 1988, when Mikhail Gorbachev announced the imminent dismantling of Russia's European war machine. In some respects the Cold War was like its predecessor, known less menacingly as the Great Game, which had been played between Britain and Russia in central Asia throughout the nineteenth century. It was a contest of nerve, diplomatic manoeuvre, arms races, intelligence gathering and subversion in which each side was continually nervous about the other's intentions and capability for making mischief. Here the similarities end, for more was at stake in the Cold War. Antagonists in both camps regularly predicted that their goal was a world dominated by either Communism or capitalism. Furthermore, from August 1949, when the Soviet Union tested its first atomic bomb, there was always a chance that a severe crisis might lead to a nuclear war.

The Cold War was not started deliberately nor, in its early stages, was anyone clear as to how long it might last or what course it would take. What was clear to those in Washington and London with responsibility for forward planning was that by the end of the war Russia would possess a vast unofficial empire in eastern Europe. Fears that it might extend it by proxy, using the expanding European Communist parties, were confirmed with the outbreak of the Greek Civil War in December 1944. Four months later, Macmillan described Stalin as 'a sort of Napoleon', a conclusion already reached by American strategists who, from May 1944, felt that Britain could not resist post-war Russian encroachments in western Europe without the United States' assistance.

During the first half of 1946, Russia demanded bases in Libya and the Dardanelles, and refused to evacuate northern Persia. Soviet attacks on British policy in the Mediterranean, India, Persia and the Dutch East Indies during the first United Nations meeting in February 1946 convinced the Foreign Secretary, Ernest Bevin, that Russia 'is intent on the destruction of the British Empire'. The same view was taken by American military planners, who were now regarding the empire as a valuable asset in what might develop into a protracted global confrontation.

Anglo-American solidarity was now as vital as ever it had been during the war. The point was vividly emphasised by Churchill in his celebrated 'Iron Curtain' speech, delivered with President Harry Truman's warm endorsement at Fulton, Missouri, in February 1946. America's need of Britain as an ally against a malevolent Russia helped soften Washington's attitude towards the empire. There had been signs of a change of heart during the winter of 1944–5, after Roosevelt had relaxed his objections towards France's repossession of Indo-China. There were substantial Communist, anti-Japanese resistance movements there (Ho Chi-Minh's Viet Minh) and in Malaya. Both had a vast potential for subversion, and it was, therefore, politically prudent to allow the re-occupation of both colonies by their former rulers. Decolonisation would follow, but the process was best left to Britain and France, who would deal with the local Communists before handing over power to more tractable groups. The first skirmishes of the Cold War were fought around Saigon during the winter and spring of 1945–6, when Anglo-Indian forces secured the city in readiness for the disembarkation of an army from France. Japanese POWs were re-armed and took part enthusiastically in the operations against the Viet Minh partisans. General Douglas MacArthur was incensed by the cynical employment of old enemies against old friends; obviously he had still to grasp the new pattern of loyalties and alignments which was emerging throughout the world.

Once in power, Labour's colonial policy in practice differed little from old-style benevolent imperialism. Social justice and economic regeneration took precedence over schemes for self-government, although the two were ultimately complementary. The problem was that Britain's tropical colonies were impoverished and backward. A commission of enquiry which had toured the West Indies shortly before the war uncovered a stagnant backwater: illegitimacy rates were between 60 and 70 per cent, venereal diseases were spreading and malaria was endemic. The remedy for such economic and physical debilitation was the Colonial Development Acts of 1940 and 1945, which offered grants and loans for road and bridge building, clinics, schools and hospitals, and waterworks. An efficient infrastructure would, it was argued, prepare the way for economic self-sufficiency. It was axiomatic that the colonies could only govern themselves if they had the means to support themselves. Between 1946 and 1951, £40.5 million was distributed for improvements, but during the same period the Treasury insisted that £250 million earned by the colonies from their export trade was deposited in London to bolster Britain's sterling reserves. It was a crazy situation; the colonies made do on a shoestring of government hand-outs while their real wealth remained idle in London.

Treasury intransigence was compounded by Colonial Office folly. Grandiose, state-funded plans for the mass production of eggs in the Gambia and groundnuts in Tanganyika came to expensive grief through slipshod preparation and mismanagement. The latter consumed £40 million, for which the Tanganyikans gained 11,000 acres of tillable land, three cattle ranches and a tobacco plantation. Another government-financed venture, the Colonial Development Board, also foundered with no advantage to the colonies and great loss to the taxpayer. Two strands in Labour's thinking contributed to these disasters. The first was the dogma that private investment in the colonies equalled exploitation, whilst enterprises underwritten by the state did not. Secondly, there was a feeling that carefully planned development of colonial production, particularly of foodstuffs, would save much needed dollars. Britain could import comestibles without using up precious dollar reserves, and colonial exports would augment them. In the end nobody benefited, and in the colonies there was a feeling that their economies were being manipulated solely to enrich Britain. This was true up to a point, but defenders of the government's colonial enterprises argued that they would in time enrich the colonies involved.

Business misadventures in Africa coincided with a sequence of domestic and international crises. In 1948 the Cold War entered a new and dangerous phase with the Russian annexation of Czechoslovakia, the blockade of Berlin and the start of the Communist guerrilla campaign in Malaya. Britain and the empire were already committed to supporting the United States, which, by the Truman Doctrine of March 1947, was now pledged to resist further Soviet expansion, whether in the form of direct aggression or conspiracy. A year later, Marshall Aid began to flow into western Europe to succour economies and populations which, if unassisted, could fall to Communism.

PREVIOUS PAGES

Attachment to the Crown and British traditions was one of the cements of the emerging Commonwealth:

HM the Queen opens the Ghanaian parliament in March 1957: the throne and bewigged officers indicate British traditions. Within a few years, Ghana became a one-party dictatorship under Kwame Nkrumah who siphoned much of the state's wealth into his own pocket.

(© Popperfoto)

Communists against the empire: women guerrillas captured in Selangor in 1953.

(© Popperfoto)

The iron economic and military realities of the post-1945 world relegated Britain to the position of America's junior partner. Filling a supporting role did not come easily to the servants of a nation which had grown accustomed to being at the centre of the stage. They continued to think and act as if they were the policy-makers and agents of a great power. The most striking evidence of their attitude was the decision to proceed with the manufacture of an atomic bomb. The Prime Minister, Clement Attlee, was worried whether at some future date the United States might revert to its customary isolationism, leaving Britain alone to face the Red Army. The atom bomb had become the mid-twentieth century equivalent of a fleet of Dreadnoughts; the symbol of a global power's determination to hold on to its status. Britain needed to cooperate with the United States in the fabrication of a barrier of mutually dependent states in Europe, the Middle East and Asia, strong enough to withstand Russia. The first link, the North Atlantic Treaty Organisation (NATO) was in place by 1949, guaranteeing the security of western Europe.

American and British strategists identified the Middle East as a region ripe for Soviet subversion and penetration. Its Cold War significance was twofold. From the end of 1947, America's war plans depended on Middle Eastern bases for an atomic strike against the industrial heartlands of the Don basin. Secondly, their oilfields were taking up the spiralling demand for oil; by 1950–1, and after a period of rapid development, they were producing 70 per cent of the West's requirements. Britain had traditionally been the dominant power in this region, and during the late 1940s America was prepared to underpin this arrangement for no other reason than necessity. In 1949–50, the Pentagon's gurus estimated that, in the event of a global war, no American forces could be spared for the Middle East for at least two years, and so British and Commonwealth troops, ships and aircraft would have to hold the line.

Whether they could undertake such a responsibility was open to question. During 1946 Attlee had been disturbed by the costs of Britain's presence in the Mediterranean and the Middle East, and he had contemplated a large-scale withdrawal. He was dissuaded by Bevin, the Foreign Secretary, who argued that the Russians would take over once Britain had departed. The chiefs of staff threw their weight behind Bevin, threatening resignation in the event of any evacuation. Early in January 1947 Attlee caved in. Within a year, his government was forced to cut off aid to Greece and Turkey, and pull its forces out of Palestine. The trouble was that Britain could no longer afford a champagne-style foreign policy on a beer income, which was what the country had been reduced to by 1947.

Both Labour and then the Conservatives made a substantial political and emotional investment in the new, multi-racial Commonwealth. The dividends then and after were scanty. Two non-white dominions, India and Ceylon, refused to become Britain's allies in the Cold War; Burma left the Commonwealth in 1948, having become a republic, and was followed by Ireland, also now a republic, in 1949. India adopted a republican constitution in the same year but, after some legal acrobatics, remained a member of a Commonwealth whose nominal head was King George VI. The reason for permitting this anomaly was the fear that India, once outside the Commonwealth, might easily slide into the Communist block. Pakistan joined the anti-Soviet Baghdad Pact in 1955, not as a favour to Britain, but as a result of having been seduced by America, which had come courting with a gift of military aid worth $25 million dollars. The white dominions had been indifferent to calls to defend the old imperial lifeline through the Mediterranean and across the Middle East. It now mattered less than ever; the safety of Australia and New Zealand was in American hands, as it had been effectively since 1942, and Canada was solely concerned with the Atlantic and western Europe.

In a sense the Commonwealth was becoming a surrogate empire. Indeed, when plans for colonial self-government finally matured, it was assumed in London that the former colonies would automatically join the Commonwealth. Whether this body would endow Britain with the same authority, armed strength and prestige it had enjoyed when it ruled a territorial empire and the dominions did whatever London decreed was open to question. And yet, few in mid-twentieth-century Britain chose to examine the nature and function of the Commonwealth too critically. A BBC talk, delivered after the end of the Commonwealth foreign ministers' conference at Colombo in January 1950, suggested that the Commonwealth might be dismissed as a 'sentimental, disintegrating club for Blimps'. Then, having said that the Commonwealth lacked both a unified voice on foreign affairs and material strength, the speaker turned a somersault and announced that it 'has brought us close to the One World idea'. If this was the case, the sceptical listener might have wondered why two members, India and Pakistan, were at daggers drawn over Kashmir, and a third, South Africa, in the midst of constructing apartheid, a social order based upon the supremacy of the white race.

As Britain entered the second half of the twentieth century it began to fall victim to the politics of illusion. In 1950 the Labour and Conservative parties had convinced themselves that the Commonwealth was something that should be cherished and was beyond criticism. It was simultaneously advertised to the world as a shining example of international cooperation and evidence of Britain's continuing status as a world power. This was make-believe on the part of politicians who had failed to come to terms with Britain's relative decline, and still hoped that the country might somehow manage to stand apart from its overmighty patron, the United States, and a Europe which, by the early 1950s, was taking its first steps towards economic unity. The illusion of power was better than none at all, and Commonwealth leaders were willing accessories in the charade. It offered them the chance to attend high-level conferences and be treated with a reverence their standing and calibre might otherwise not have commanded.

The increasing use of the word 'Commonwealth' to encompass the colonies as well as the dominions coincided with a sustained Communist propaganda campaign in which 'colonialism' was equated with the 'slavery' and 'exploitation' of coloured races by the capitalist powers. Whatever their political complexion, colonial protest movements were grouped together as part of a world-wide struggle against rapacious imperialism. External Communist propaganda produced by Russia, its satellites, and later China, presented colonial unrest everywhere as part of a single, global struggle between the haves and have-nots, and pledged Communist support to the latter. The fear of Russian and Chinese-sponsored mass revolution in what today is called the Third World scared Washington and London. Whether or not the alarm was in proportion to the actual threat is irrelevant. What mattered was that from 1948 onwards both the British and American governments were extremely jumpy about subversion, not least because they were aware that in many colonies the social and economic conditions were perfect for Communist agitation. Whatever their actual root cause, strikes and political demonstrations were regularly diagnosed as symptoms of underground Communist activity.

The prospect of the colonies becoming a Cold War ideological battlefield had a profound effect on policy towards self-government. During 1947, senior Colonial Office officials had been compiling detailed plans for the slow, systematic and piecemeal transfer of power within the colonies. It would be an evolutionary process, beginning with elected local councils, and proceeding as it were upwards, towards a national parliamentary government with powers over the colony's internal affairs. With a fully fledged parliamentary democracy, the colony would be ready for independence. Nothing was to be rushed; it was calculated that it would take at least twenty, probably thirty years for native populations to learn the ways of democracy and, most importantly, to create a body of responsible and trustworthy native politicians.

This tidy, pragmatic and above all realistic programme was suddenly jettisoned in 1948. The immediate cause was the panic which beset the Colonial Office after the Accra riots in February, whose roots were economic distress rather than impatience with the pace of political change. Nonetheless, an official investigation recommended a swift constitutional change, promoting Africans to the Gold Coast's Executive Council. The further opening of government at all levels was proposed by a second report, compiled in 1949 by a commission of Africans under an African judge. The British government accepted

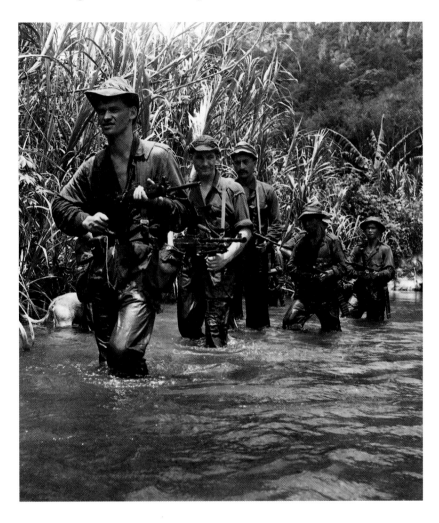

Cold war in the jungle: New Zealand troops on patrol in Malaya during operations against the Communist insurgents. Under the pressure of the Cold War, Britain needed Commonwealth forces. (© Popperfoto)

both reports, and the process of evolution was effectively compressed into a few years, for elections were held in 1950. In February 1952, Kwame Nkrumah, leader of the majority Convention People's party, became Leader of Government Business and, a year later, Prime Minister.

Why did the government take fright in 1948? The Gold Coast administration had been taken unawares by the disturbances, and its reaction was ham-fisted. There was no guidance from above as to how to handle riots, and it was only in 1955 that the Colonial Office attempted to devise a common policy on riot control. The preliminary enquiry yielded a fascinating variety of techniques; under the 1948 regulations for the St Vincent police, the issue of blank cartridges was forbidden, as was firing over the heads of rioters since 'this may give confidence to the daring and guilty'. Whatever the circumstances, shooting rioters, as occurred in Accra, looked bad in the press, and from 1945 the government had found it impossible to keep details of colonial unrest from the newspapers.

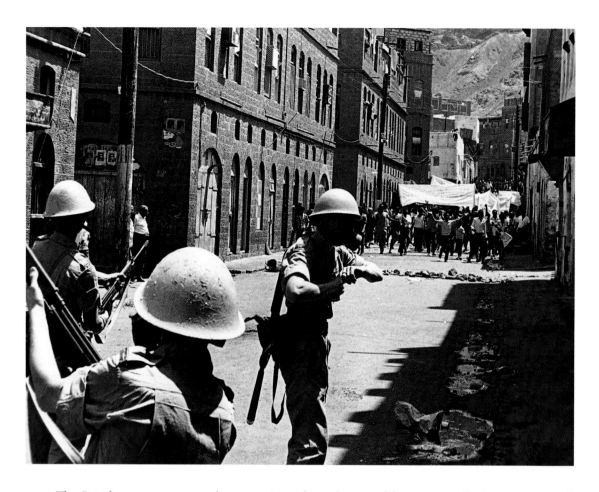

Nationalism at bay: soldiers from the Lancashire regiment prepare to fire tear gas against Arab nationalist demonstrators, Aden, 1967. (© Popperfoto)

The British government was always sensitive about the use of force, especially firearms, to quell colonial tumults because it was a denial of what the empire stood for. In theory and popular imagination, British rule had always rested on the goodwill and collaboration of the governed, not coercion. The latter had to be applied in certain situations, but as a final resort and sparingly. Rather than ruthlessly crush dissent, the British government chose to embrace and, so to speak, smother it. By accelerating the Gold Coast's passage to self-government, Britain imagined it had rescued the colony from possible Communist subversion. The conditions of the Cold War had wiped out the chances of a leisurely, measured progress from colonial tutelage to responsible government. Henceforward, British policy would concentrate on the cultivation of the most influential native politicians, who could be trusted to take over the reins of government in the empire's successor states. It was an answer to the problems of decolonisation which dismayed many, who foretold that it would create as many problems as it solved.

It is worth remembering that at the moment when Britain was making arrangements which would lead to the liquidation of the empire, there were still areas which had been under effective colonial rule for less than a man's lifetime, and there were others where imperial authority was precarious and shallow-rooted. Even under Labour, old hierarchies stayed the same; there were, in 1949, ten lavatories on the railway station at el Qantara in the Suez Canal Zone, labelled as follows:

Officers European
Officers Asiatic
Officers Coloured
Warrant Officers and Sergeants European
Warrant Officers and Sergeants Asiatic

Warrant Officers and Sergeants Coloured
Other Ranks European
Other Ranks Asiatic
Other Ranks Coloured
ATS [Auxiliary Territorial Service – i.e. women]

2

FRIENDLY RELATIONS:

INDIA AND THE LIQUIDATION OF EMPIRE

1945–1947

I n 1945, the gravediggers of empire commenced work. No government before or after 1945 ever took a conscious decision to dissolve the empire, but equally none was prepared to embark on an alternative course, its preservation come what may. The ministers, diplomats, soldiers and civil servants who found themselves responsible for devising and carrying out the policies of imperial disengagement did not imagine that they were parties to a funeral. Rather, they saw themselves as midwives, facilitating the births of new nations which were emerging from the imperial womb. The conventional, bipartisan wisdom which held sway for the next twenty-five years insisted the infant states would grow up within the extended family of the new, multi-racial Commonwealth, whose members shared a maternal affection for Britain, its democratic system and traditional respect for individual freedom. Never was an empire dismantled with such a sense of hope for the future.

There were circumstances in which Britain was willing to forgo an orderly retreat from empire and dig its heels in, but they were exceptional. Britain was engaged in the Cold War, and so no colony could be allowed to pass under Communist control after independence. So, while committed to future Malayan self-determination, Britain was prepared in 1948 to fight an extended campaign (euphemistically called an 'emergency' to avoid charges of colonial oppression) against local Communist guerrillas. Nor could the government allow a colony to dissolve into chaos, and for this reason operations were undertaken against the Mau Mau in Kenya between 1952 and 1954; another 'emergency'.

None of Britain's rearguard colonial wars matched the ferocity and length of those waged by the French in Indo-China and Algeria, and the Portuguese in Angola and Mozambique. British politicians needed to look no further than events in North America in the 1770s or, more pertinently, in southern Ireland after 1918 to identify the pitfalls that lay in wait for those who wanted to cling to empire at any cost. The Irish campaign also illustrated the fact there was a point beyond which the public was unwilling to tolerate armed coercion.

Furthermore, for the first time in its history, the entire British people was directly involved in the defence of the empire. Between 1947 and 1960, its outposts and trouble spots were manned and policed by peacetime conscripts, national servicemen. Professional fighting men played their part, but the casualty rolls of imperial conflicts now included sons and sweethearts who were not under arms by choice.

'Emergencies' were relatively rare. The British empire did not dissolve like the French, Portuguese, and for that matter the Russian, in tears and blood. In India and the colonies an alternative way was devised, which involved an orderly and cordial withdrawal, and the assumption of power by a government which had been elected. At its best, from Britain's standpoint, this arrangement was accomplished with a minimum of fuss, and wherever possible the retention of strategic bases, behind-the-scenes political influence and commercial advantages. What had to be avoided at all costs was a helter-skelter retreat which left behind a political vacuum or, worse, chaos.

Mastering the arcane diplomatic art of colonial disengagement took time, and to begin with its practitioners were moving in the dark and learning as they went. With little else to guide them, they turned, in British fashion, to the past and adopted the old empire-builders' rule, which was to find someone with legal authority, such as a chief or rajah, and do business with him. Now, the empire's demolition men had to cultivate and work in harness with the new power-brokers, local politicians. The leaders of various parties and national movements were assumed to speak for the majority of the people. Whether or not they did, these tribunes found themselves treated as spokesmen for nations and the eventual successors to the imperial administration. There were certain rituals; at some stage local political leaders would find themselves in collision with the colonial authorities and were consequently locked up in prison. In time, and with their nationalist credentials enhanced by their detention, they were discharged to take their places at their gaolers' conference tables. This pattern had been established during the 1930s and 1940s when Indian Congress leaders, including Gandhi, were incarcerated: Nkrumah, Jomo Kenyatta and Dr Hastings Banda followed, in the Gold Coast, Kenya and Nyasaland respectively.

On the one hand, those responsible for surrendering power wanted above all to deliver it to someone who could exercise it effectively and preserve order. On the other, Britain was publicly pledged to confer on its colonies parliamentary government and a legal system designed to protect individual freedoms. This transfer of institutions had been easily undertaken in the white dominions, for their inhabitants were already steeped in British political tradition, but in India and the colonies there was a very different political culture. Organised political activity in the Western manner had begun very recently (the Indian National Congress had been founded in 1885, the African in 1912) and, from its beginnings, had revolved around a single issue: the termination of foreign rule. This overriding objective determined the evolution of political life and its domination by tightly organised parties, which had to be big enough to engage a powerful and equally monolithic government. Circumstances had, therefore, discouraged a diversity of parties or the growth of two or three of more or less equal popular appeal as had occurred in Britain and the dominions. The one-party state had its genesis in the history of Indian and colonial struggles for independence.

Another legacy of the British empire was imperial demography, which hindered decolonisation. No one concerned with drawing the empire's frontiers had ever imagined that he was setting the boundaries for a future self-governing independent state. Antipathetic racial, tribal and religious groups had often been corralled together willy-nilly. When the depth of ethnic, tribal and sectarian antagonism became apparent, it was argued that they could be contained by a firm, even-handed imperial administration backed by police and soldiers. So it was that in India, Ceylon, Burma and elsewhere Britain became the protector of various minorities who were shielded from the ill-will of their neighbours. Old prejudices were not, however, eliminated by the fear of imperial punishment; they remained, as it were, frozen. The makers of new governments had to find ways to provide for the continued safety of vulnerable minorities even if this meant the dilution of the democratic ideal.

India's progress to self-government was a compelling drama with a convoluted plot that unfolded at two levels. On the upper, British and Indian statesmen, politicians, lawyers and administrators sat in rooms in Delhi and, when it became too stifling, Simla, and endeavoured to construct an apparatus of government that would satisfy the whole of India. They were participants in a race against time for, on the lower level, and in the cities, towns and countryside, hundreds of thousands of Indians were beginning to turn against and kill each other. As the violence spread and the casualties multiplied, onlookers feared the onset of a civil war which the principal actors were powerless to stop.

The chief British actor was Attlee, who towards the end of his life believed that he would be best remembered for what he had done to facilitate the transfer of power in India. He saw it as a moral duty, to which he and his party had long been pledged, and, since he was a pragmatist, an advantage to Britain. The Treasury would no longer have to dispense money to maintain a British garrison in the subcontinent and, if Britain got the terms it desired, commerce with India would continue to flourish. Attlee also appreciated that a peaceful exchange of power and a stable India would add to British prestige and serve as a bulwark against Communism in Asia. He and his chiefs of staff also wanted India within the Commonwealth, and if possible as an ally which would continue to host British bases. Attlee's mandate to Mountbatten, delivered in February 1947, was to 'secure the closest and most friendly relations between India and the UK. A feature of this relationship should be a military treaty.' By this time, Attlee had conceded that the subcontinent would be split between India and Pakistan, which he had not wanted, for it was not in Britain's interests. A divided India was a weakened India, and the western

Smiling through: Mountbatten and Dr Jinnah pose after the transfer of power to the new Muslim state of Pakistan, August 1947. Over the past months of negotiations, the Viceroy had done little to hide his personal dislike of Jinnah.

segment of its most vulnerable portion, Pakistan, faced Afghanistan and beyond it Russia. In terms of the Cold War, the partition of India was a setback.

Mountbatten was the last in a sequence of officials and ministers sent to negotiate with the Indian leadership, which consisted of Nehru, Gandhi and Dr Jinnah of the Muslim League, who spoke for the subcontinent's 92 million Muslims. His predecessor as Viceroy had been Field-Marshal Wavell, who was removed by Attlee for his pessimism. While the architects of India's future deliberated, the people became increasingly restless. During the winter of 1945–6, the government's decision to prosecute a handful of prominent former INA men for treason, and in some instances war crimes, was bitterly opposed by Congress. In September 1945 Congress had resolved that the thousands of INA soldiers could be 'of the greatest service in the heavy work of building up a new and free India'. In the next few months they were lionised as heroes by Congress and those imprisoned or awaiting trial received the aura of martyrdom. In January 1946, an outraged *Hindustan Times* alleged that twenty-five INA prisoners had been bayoneted for singing the Congress anthem 'Jai Hind' (Long Live India), but an official investigation revealed that they had been 'prodded' in the buttocks. These men's case had been taken up by Gandhi, whose attitude towards the ex-INA men was characteristically ambivalent. 'Though I can have nothing in common with any defence by force of arms,' he wrote, 'I am never blind to the valour of patriotism often displayed by persons in arms, as seems to be the case here.' He did not say whether his definition of patriotism embraced the two million Indians who had fought for rather than against Britain.

Death in the Punjab: a Sikh stands by the body of his father, a victim of a Muslim murder gang, August 1947.

In midsummer 1946 the cabinet mission recommended an elaborate constitution with a federal government for the whole country and, below it, two layers of local and provincial assemblies, which were designed both to satisfy and safeguard minorities. At first both Congress and the Muslim League acquiesced to this formula, but mutual suspicion proved too deep-rooted, and the two sides were soon squabbling over minutiae and the balance of communal representation. The upshot was Jinnah's determination to go it alone and demand an independent Pakistan.

Jinnah called a Muslim hartal in Calcutta on 16 August. Four days of religious riots followed in which 4,000 were killed and 10,000 wounded. The British general whose Anglo-Indian forces restored order thought the slaughter many times worse than the Somme. News of what was happening in Calcutta sparked off massacres in Bombay where 1,000 died and over 13,000 were wounded. In Bihar, where the allegiance of the local police was wobbling, Hindus murdered 150 Muslim refugees in November. Here and elsewhere, the victims of religious frenzy were poor and humble; some months later a British journalist observed that few of their bodies were ever claimed from the police morgues.

As the religious massacres proliferated, India appeared to be moving inexorably towards a civil war. After visiting Calcutta, Wavell concluded that the game was up, and drew up exigency plans for the evacuation of all British civilians and servicemen. Their safety was paramount, and if necessary they would depart before any political settlement, and certainly before the onset of the bloodbath which Wavell expected.

Wavell's scheme was political disaster for India, Britain and the Labour party. Attlee was determined to prevent it, and in December Wavell was removed. He was succeeded as Viceroy by Mountbatten, Attlee's choice and a brilliant one in terms of *Realpolitik*. At a time when the royal family was held in almost pious awe, Mountbatten as a member of that family was more immune to public criticism than other comparable figures in public life. Most importantly, he saw eye-to-eye with Attlee on what had to be done in India and the speed with which it had to be accomplished.

Mountbatten arrived in India at the end of March 1947. He threw himself into his tasks with immense zeal and energy, using every ounce of his charm to persuade and cajole India's tribunes, although he was brusque with Jinnah to the point of rudeness. He was assisted by his wife, Edwina, who had an engaging manner and a cocktail-party vivacity which captivated Nehru, now Prime Minister in an interim government and the voice of Congress. The Mountbattens at Viceregal House were a refreshing change from the staid Wavells; the Field-Marshal was a scholarly, contemplative and shy figure, and Lady Mountbatten once remarked that Viscountess Wavell dressed like her maid. Whatever else they did, the Mountbattens ensured that, at the top level at least, the final act in the drama of India's independence was played out with panache.

The new Viceroy's most important duty was to stick as closely as possible to the revised timetable for self-government that had been set by Attlee. Previously, power was to have been handed over in June 1948, but in the light of the gradual disintegration of public order the date was brought forward to 15 August 1947. The new schedule was revealed by Mountbatten at a press conference on 4 June and was received with a mixture of delight, amazement and, in some quarters, foreboding. Soon after, he issued his officials with a 'tear-off calendar indicating the days left for the partition' as if the event was the last day of a public-school term. The divorce of Hindu and Muslim India had been a political reality since the December 1945 and March 1946 local and provincial elections, in which Hindu Congress candidates had secured 90 per cent of the votes in the predominantly non-Muslim regions, and Muslims had come out on top in their areas. No number of intricate political checks and balances could have prevented the polarisation of India and preserved it as a single polity. This was reluctantly recognised by Congress, and during May a plan for partition was agreed by Mountbatten and the Indian leadership, and subsequently rubber-stamped by the cabinet in London.

During the parade to mark Pakistan's independence, an Indian remarked to a British officer, 'Ah, Sahib, the British have been very cunning. We Muslims have our Pakistan; the Hindus have their Hindustan; and the British soldiers will be able to go home.' Sadly, it was not that simple. It would have been beyond the wit of any man to have created boundaries which would have satisfied everyone; there were bound to be communities who found themselves on the 'wrong' side of the frontier and felt isolated, outnumbered and frightened.

Fear was greatest in the Punjab, home to a substantial portion of India's five-and-a-half million Sikhs (one in six of the province's population), which was to be split between India and Pakistan. The Sikhs rejected Muslim domination and answered Jinnah's newly-coined slogan *Pakistan Zindabad!* (Long Live Pakistan) with *Pakistan Murdabad!* (Death to Pakistan). By late spring, the Punjab was wracked by massacres, counter-massacres, looting and arson. Their heritage of Muslim persecution and their historic reaction to it gave the Sikhs a peculiar resilience, and a powerful urge to seek revenge. An indication of their sufferings and present temper may be found in a leaflet circulating at the beginning of April 1947 (*right*).

Thousands of Sikh and Hindu women have been murdered; Keshas *[long tresses] and beards of hundreds have been chopped off and an effort has been made to convert them to Islam; hundreds of women have been abducted. Whole villages have been burnt up . . . Rest assured, as it is only a small specimen of Pakistan and more terrible incidents are yet to come. But* Khalsaji *[warriors], we are Sikhs of that Guru who having had his four children slaughtered said, 'What if four have fallen? Thousands will survive.' We have to fight this tyrannical Pakistan . . .*

SIKH LEAFLET, 1947

Fear and loathing in the Punjab:

for many weeks before independence, there had been communal massacres in the Punjab. When the province was divided between India and Pakistan, the violence increased and millions fled: Hindus and Sikhs to India and Muslims to Pakistan. Mountbatten's security arrangements were inadequate to prevent a catastrophe.

A British civil servant, Sir Cyril Radcliffe, drew the line which bisected the Punjab. It was a thankless task whose consequences haunted him until his death. The massive bloodletting which occurred across northern India after partition is well known. Perhaps half a million died, although no one has ever calculated the exact numbers killed. The details were reported by news-papermen, most notably Louis Heren of *The Times*. He and others heard the grisly catalogue of past outrages which were the murder gangs' justification for their crimes. In August, Sikhs and Hindus were killing Punjabi Muslims in revenge for the massacre of their co-religionists in Rawalpindi the previous March. This holocaust was vengeance for the slaughter of Muslims by Hindus in Bihar five months before, and, in turn, this was retaliation for the bloodbath in Calcutta in August 1946. One eyewitness description of events in Lahore (Pakistan) in mid-August, a soldier's, may stand for many others:

> *Corpses lay in the gutter. Nearby a posse of Muslim police chatted unconcerned.*
> *A British Major (a sapper) had also arrived. He and his driver were collecting the*
> *bodies. Some were dead. Some were dying. All were horribly mutilated. They were*
> *Sikhs. Their long hair and beards were matted with blood. An old man, not so bad*
> *as the rest, asked me where we were taking them. 'To hospital,' I replied; adding to*
> *hearten him, 'You're not going to die.'*
>
> > *'I shall,' he said, 'if there is a Muslim doctor.'*

There is no simple answer to the question whether all this could have been avoided. Mountbatten's reactions showed him at his most shallow; back in England in November he tried to minimise the scale of the disaster, and claimed that it had surprised him. But there had been a steady build-up of violence since August 1946 and military intelligence knew that it would worsen. Aware of this, Field-Marshal Auchinleck had wanted to keep British troops behind after independence, but had been overridden by Mountbatten. And yet, if such a course had been followed, British servicemen would have become embroiled in a struggle from which it might have been very hard to extricate them.

Senior military men in India were critical of Mountbatten, whose Toad-of-Toad-Hall exhibition-ism irritated a caste which traditionally prized reticence and self-effacement. Lieutenant-General Sir Reginald Savory, Adjutant-General of the Indian army, accused him of having 'tried to make it appear to India and the world and to ourselves that we were committing a noble deed'. This charge confuses Mountbatten's self-publicity with government policy; he was always Attlee's agent, carrying out the will of the cabinet and Parliament. He thought he had done the job rather well, and said so so often that it was easy to forget this fact.

What he had accomplished was essentially a pragmatic measure which was, as Attlee appreci-ated, a sensible reaction to historic forces which had been gathering momentum for thirty years. The raj could not be maintained by force, for its end was wished by the great mass of the Indian people, and there is no reason to believe that the British would have been willing to see it prolonged at the cost of an interminable war of repression. There were some on the right who muttered about a failure of 'nerve' in India and elsewhere in the empire, but nerve without muscle could not have saved the raj or the colonies.

The loss of India was felt most keenly by the men and women who had served there and devoted their lives to its people's welfare. Many old servants of the raj were bitterly dismayed by the unseemly haste of the transfer of power and its baleful consequences. The rearguard of 1947 and previous exiles found it extremely hard to accept the emotional break with a country and a people which they had come to love and to which they had given so much of their lives. Forty-five years later, newspaper announce-ments of various Indian reunion dinners, usually regimental, in London clubs are a testament to their sense of comradeship and nostalgia for the raj.

TOUR OF DUTY

While the world outside changed, the everyday routines of the empire continued as they had before the war and its officials went about their business, upholding the law and attending to the welfare of their charges. Their lives were full of incident.

RIGHT *The cattle-market at Elgeyo in the Maraqwet district of Kenya's Rift Valley province. This market had been established so that local tribesman could sell their cattle at a railhead. Some, having taken cash for their beasts, stole them from the pound and returned wih them to their villages, well satisfied with their first encounter with the market economy.*

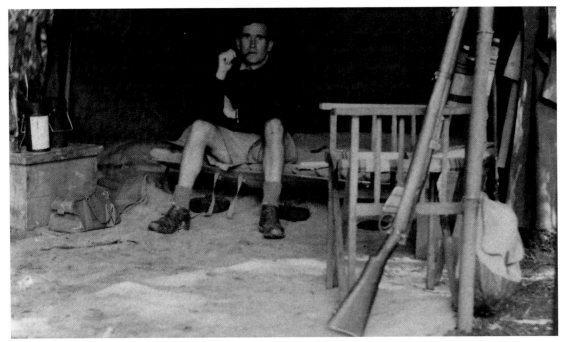

ABOVE AND OPPOSITE *A detachment of police, led by Gordon Hector, the local commissioner, was sent to bring back the cattle. Noticing in his diary an imminent eclipse of the moon, Hector warned the miscreants that not only the King, but their gods were angered by the fraud, and that the latter would show their displeasure. After the eclipse most of the cattle were returned.*

3

THE WORLD
AS IT IS:
MIDDLE EASTERN
MISADVENTURES
1945–1956

The Labour MP Richard Crossman, defending his party from charges of irresolution during a debate on the Middle East in July 1951, argued, 'We have to make a policy on the assumption that there is not an Indian army to send to Basra.' According to the Conservatives, the past six years had witnessed the sacrifice of British interests in an area where previously they had been upheld with the utmost vigour. And yet, during the same period, Attlee's government had been channelling large sums into the development of a British atomic bomb, possession of which would uphold Britain's claim that it still was a world power.

It was easier for Labour to acquire the sinews of power than it was to exercise it. In 1945, Attlee inherited all the pre-war problems of the Middle East: the worsening Arab-Jewish conflict; the simmering resentment of the Egyptians against alien domination; and the widespread feeling that Britain was the greatest hindrance to Arab national aspirations and unity. Labour was instinctively sympathetic to liberation movements; it was an internationalist, progressive party which thought itself in harmony with the trends of the modern world.

High principles and ideals of international brotherhood were not always compatible with the pursuit of British interests, particularly in the Middle East and under the conditions imposed by the Cold War. The government had constantly to heed the demands made by its partner, the United States. During 1946, Pentagon and Whitehall strategists began to plot the course of a hypothetical war against Russia and both concluded that control of the Middle East was vital for victory. If the Soviet Union was to be beaten, a substantial part of its war machine would have to be destroyed by atomic bombs. Nuclear attacks on Russia's industrial heartlands required bases relatively close to its borders. So, in the summer of 1946, Britain secretly agreed to allow B-29 bombers to fly nuclear sorties from airfields in East Anglia and Egypt. The latter were crucial, for they made possible a concentrated nuclear assault on the oilfields, refineries and industrial centres of the Caucasus and Don basin. With these levelled, Russia's capacity to wage a war in Western Europe would be severely curtailed. Atomic weapons alone would redress the imbalance between Russia's massive ground forces and the West's. Local defence, indeed that of the entire Middle East, was entrusted to British and Commonwealth forces.

The British chiefs of staff, particularly Air-Marshal Lord Tedder and Field-Marshal Montgomery, believed that it was imperative for Britain to maintain its old predominance in the Mediterranean and

Middle East. Their argument was simple: Britain would remain a first-rate, global power and enjoy a measure of independence from the United States if it acquired atomic bombs and the means to deliver them against the Soviet Union. In the event of war, a substantial part of Britain's nuclear strike force would fly from the Canal Zone towards southern Russia. During the next six years, Britain implemented an ambitious nuclear programme. Work went ahead on the development of the long-range, jet-powered V-bombers and the first, the Valiant, was operational by 1955. Three years before, Britain's first atomic bomb was tested off Monte Bello island on the north-west coast of Australia.

It was not assumed that a nuclear exchange would bring outright victory to either side and although crippled, the antagonists would, it was believed, still retain the will and some of the wherewithal to fight on with conventional weaponry. In this situation, Britain would have to defend the world's sealanes which provided it with access to food and oil.

The Canal Zone therefore became a vital integer in the sombre arithmetic of nuclear war. If such a conflict was winnable, and the strategists who drew up the various warplans believed it was, then Anglo-American control of the Middle East had to be maintained. Even without schemes for launching potentially war-winning nuclear attacks against southern Russia, the region would have had to be kept within the western camp and defended for the sake of its oil. The Second World War had seen the transformation of the world pattern of oil consumption. By 1951, the Middle East was providing 70 per cent of the West's oil, and all its reserves for the future were thought to be concentrated in Saudi Arabia and the Persian Gulf.

Oil and airfields had replaced the defence of India as Britain's reason for paramountcy in the Middle East. In a sense, the old strategic and geo-political catchwords of Disraeli and Curzon still held true. They were heard frequently during the late 1940s and early 1950s, largely from the Conservative benches and in the committee rooms of the War Office, Admiralty and Air Ministry. But had Britain kept its old nerve and was it, when faced with difficulties, prepared to act boldly? On paper Britain was as formidable a power in the region in 1945 as it had been twenty or so years before. In 1945, Jordan, Iraq, Iran and the sheik-doms of the Persian Gulf were still in Britain's thrall. So too was Egypt, the sullen host to the vast Suez Canal Zone complex of barracks, storehouses and airfields which straddled the Canal. This strip, 120 miles long by 30 wide, was the largest military base in the world, and the pivot of British power in the Middle East and Africa. Radiating from it was a web of satellite garrisons,

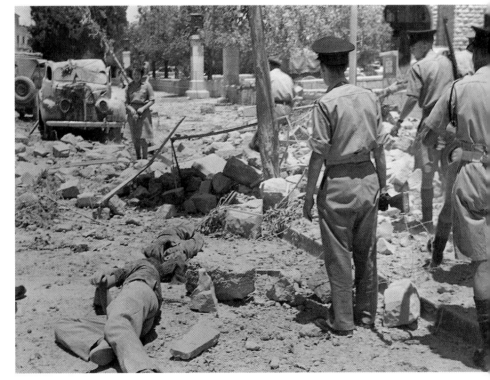

Death in Jerusalem: victims of the blowing up of the King David Hotel by Jewish terrorists, 1946. (© IWM)

aerodromes and naval bases in Malta, Cyprus, Haifa, the ex-Italian colony of Libya (which Russia had briefly coveted), Jordan, Iraq, Aden and the Persian Gulf.

These scarlet specks on the War Office's map offered little comfort to Bevin, who was aware of a new, uncompromising and anti-British mood abroad in the Middle East. Nowhere was this more true than in Palestine where, since the end of 1944, British forces had been vainly attempting to contain a Jewish revolt. It was a guerrilla campaign of assassination and sabotage waged by partisans as elusive, intrepid and ruthless as the IRA. Like the Irish campaign, the Palestinian one earned Britain opprobrium

Sailing to the
Promised Land:
Jewish refugees from
Europe on board the
Josiah Wedgwood, *July*
1946. Post-war mass
immigration made
impossible any settlement
of the Arab-Jewish
question in Palestine.
(© IWM)

abroad, particularly in America, and used up scarce treasure. The lack of funds dictated policy. At the end of September 1947, the cabinet washed its hands of the embarrassing and costly Palestinian imbroglio. One hundred thousand servicemen had not broken the cycle of terror and counter-terror, and the province was clearly ungovernable. Britain surrendered its mandate to the United Nations with a promise of evacuation by May 1948.

This announcement was tantamount to a victory for the Jewish partisans, who were quickly embroiled in a civil war with the Palestinians. During the next eight months, the United Nations tried unsuccessfully to arrange a partition of the country between two races who were each set on the other's extinction. It was bad enough that Britain had had to scurry out of a protectorate which it had ruled for barely thirty years, but worse followed. The last days of the mandate witnessed the massacre of 240 Arabs, including women and children, by a Jewish unit at Deir Yassim. This incident helped trigger a mass exodus of Palestinians and, by 1949, 720,000 refugees had fled either to Gaza or Jordan. Their legal statelessness and bleak camps were a reproach to Britain, and a reminder to the Arab world of her impotence and perfidy. After 1948, Britain and the infant state of Israel became symbols of alien domination and Arab powerlessness. It was left to the United States to offer the refugees financial assistance and, where possible, attempt their resettlement.

Whatever post-war official spokesmen said to the contrary about Britain's future good intentions in the Middle East, it had not shaken off its pre-war reputation for high-handedness and Machiavellian intrigue. Lawrence of Arabia may have been a hero in his own country, but for the Arabs he was just the first in a line of imperialist tricksters who had coveted their resources and land. 'The British position in the whole area is hopeless. They are hated and distrusted almost everywhere,' concluded a *Time* survey which appeared at the beginning of 1952. A fortnight later, the magazine noted the 'old game of baiting the British' was being played with relish in Egypt and Persia; it could have added that the players were feeling more confident than ever of eventual victory.

In April 1951, Dr Mohammed Mussadiq's Nationalist party had won the general election in Persia, or Iran as it now called itself, having plucked a name of antique glory from the history books. The frail, elderly Mussadiq had come to power on a programme of anglophobia and national regeneration. He captivated the masses by the power of his eloquence, sometimes fainting in mid-flow, physically overcome by the emotion of his rhetoric. He saw himself as his country's saviour, once telling an audience in New York that Iran in 1951 was doing what America had done in 1776: freeing itself from an arbitrary and rapacious overlord.

Iranians, like other peoples of the Middle East, had had their destinies decided for them; now, Mussadiq believed, they were about to make their own history. It was futile to explain to him and those who cheered his speeches that Britain had changed, and that it was now ready to help them in the development of their country as friendly partner, or that British companies were progressive and philanthropic employers. They may have been, but they were also the beneficiaries of past injustices, and this was how they appeared to Mussadiq and millions of other Iranians.

In May 1951, Mussadiq kept faith with those who had voted for him by nationalising the Anglo-Iranian Oil Company's assets. This firm was a symbol of Iranian subservience and British power, a leech which had been sucking Iran's life blood, leaving its people poor and hungry. The riches generated by the oil company had been unevenly distributed; in the year before nationalisation, Iran received £9 million in royalties, a million more than the Inland Revenue took from the company's profits. As the crisis unfolded and details of Anglo-Iranian's record became known, there was much muted criticism of its past selfishness in the corridors of Whitehall. But in public, ministers and the press presented the company as a model of commercial generosity.

More than Anglo-Iranian's contractual rights were at stake. Iranian oil provided 31 per cent of Europe's imports, and 85 per cent of the fuel used by the Royal Navy. Moreover, and this animated everyone on the right and quite a few on the left, Musaddiq had snapped his fingers at Britain, setting an example which, given the present temper of the whole area, might be followed elsewhere. 'Once upon a time Asiatics would be cowed by a show of force,' announced the *Economist*, echoing Conservatives who thought that this still ought to be the case. The trouble was that nowadays Iran would protest to the general assembly of the United Nations about British aggression, and win support from Middle Eastern, Asian and Latin American countries, and, of course, the Communist bloc. Nonetheless, Bevin's successor and fellow devotee of Palmerston, Herbert Morrison, ordered the cruiser *Mauritius* to heave to off Abadan Island. In the meantime, staff officers gathered and produced two aptly named exigency plans, 'Buccaneer' and 'Midget', one for armed intervention, the other for the evacuation of the 4,500 British technicians who ran the refinery. If they left, the installations would quickly fall into desuetude, for the Iranians lacked the expertise to operate them. Like silly children who meddled with what they could not understand, the Iranians would learn a lesson. This might prove harder than first imagined, for the Admiralty was having trouble finding the ships required for 'Buccaneer' since the navy was heavily committed to the Korean War.

The American Secretary of State, Dean Acheson, feared that the Russians would snatch at any chance to slip back into northern Persia, their old stamping ground, and Attlee had no wish to turn Iran into a Cold War cockpit. Moreover he had, in December 1950, flown to Washington to persuade Truman to disavow General MacArthur's proposal to use an atomic bomb against Chinese forces in Korea. A soft line on Iran was a diplomatic *quid quo pro*.

On 27 September, Mussadiq took control over the Abadan refinery and its staff departed. A few weeks later Acheson stung Evelyn Shuckburgh with the remark, 'You must live in the world as it is.' The events in Iran during the past few months had provided a glimpse into the future. Britain could no longer expect to do business either with deferential sheiks, grateful for a sackful of sovereigns, or conservative and compliant politicians in frock coats and tarbooshes, who could be scared by threats of battleships if they stepped out of line. Now Britain faced populists who ranted about imperialism. Mussadiq was a man in the new mould; he wore green pyjamas when he received Sir Francis Shepherd, the ambassador in

Tehran. This insult, together with his habit of swooning in public, convinced Shepherd that the Iranian was mad, a diagnosis which was accepted in Whitehall and by the British press.

The government put its faith in a novel form of gunboat diplomacy. In 1952 MI6 fomented a plot to overthrow Mussadiq with the help of Iranian dissidents. This exercise in subversion was known as Operation Boot, and among those drawn in was Kermit Roosevelt, the grandson of President Theodore Roosevelt and a Central Intelligence Agency (CIA) employee with Middle East responsibilities.

Early in 1953, the new Eisenhower administration took over 'Boot' which was renamed 'Ajax'. American Cold War warriors were haunted by the 'loss' of Czechoslovakia to a Russian *coup d'état* in March 1948 and that of China a year after. Iran was seen as vulnerable to Soviet-inspired sedition and Mussadiq had revealed himself as too volatile to make a steadfast ally. The upshot was the implementation of 'Ajax' under Kermit Roosevelt's vigorous direction. In August 1953, an uprising in Tehran was financed and stage-managed by CIA agents with some British help. Mussadiq was toppled and replaced by the exiled Shah Mohammed Reza Pahlevi, the son of the former Cossack officer whom Britain had assisted to the Peacock Throne thirty years before. Iran had been snatched for the West, and Shah Mohammed Reza served his American patrons faithfully until 1979. He was, in turn, overthrown by the Ayatollah Khomeini, who had written of the events of 1953 that Iran had been 'the slave of Britain one day, of America the next'. This was just the invidious comparison which the American policy-makers were striving to avoid. Sir Anthony Eden, the new Foreign Secretary, while satisfied with the result of 'Ajax', was 'jealous' of what had been an American triumph.

While on his way to lay Iran's case before the United Nations in November 1951, Mussadiq had briefly stopped over in Cairo. His welcome was ecstatic, there were anti-British riots, and he joined with the Egyptian Prime Minister, Mustafa al-Nahas, to declare that 'a united Iran and Egypt will together demolish British imperialism'.

Al-Nahas had been chipping away at the foundations of British power since January 1950, when the Wafd had come to power with over half the popular vote. Its platform was the same as it had been during the 1920s and 1930s: an end to the British military presence in Egypt and the restoration of Egyptian sovereignty over the Sudan. The disastrous 1948–9 war against Israel had given Egypt a further grievance against Britain, which was accused of having prevented the Egyptian armed forces from acquiring modern weapons. As far as Britain was concerned, Egypt counted for a bagatelle, and had been equipped with what Bevin once called 'junk'.

It was the Canal Zone base which remained the chief source of contention. Its barbed wire, concrete and tarmac symbolised Egypt's subservience to a foreign power, which believed it had the inalienable right to interfere in Egyptian affairs whenever it chose, and had done so as recently as 1942. Furthermore, for those who shaped his destiny, the Egyptian remained a lower form of life. During conversations with senior British diplomats and commanders in 1950, George McGhee, an American emissary, detected the 'traditional condescension' towards the Egyptians, who were commonly spoken of as 'Gippies'. Contempt was matched by malevolence; another American emissary reported at the end of 1951 that 'The hatred against them [the British] is general and intense. It is shared by everyone in the country.'

McGhee and his colleagues came and went from Egypt as part of an intensive diplomatic effort contrived to prevent it from sliding towards Russia. But attempts to persuade al-Nahas and the rest of the Egyptian cabinet foundered because they insisted that British imperialism, not Communism, was Egypt's real enemy. Americans tended to sympathise, but they could not ignore the strategic importance of the Canal Zone and its airfields, still earmarked for the nuclear offensive against Russia. The 1936 Anglo-Egyptian treaty had permitted a garrison of 10,000, but by 1950 the base was home to 38,000 British servicemen, including 8,000 infantry from Mauritius who acted as guards, and contained stores worth £270 million. Ideally, from the American standpoint, the British should have withdrawn, leaving the facilities intact and ready to be put on a war footing at the first hint of an international crisis, a solution which

**New tricks for
an old lion**:
*Persian Prime Minister
Mussadiq suggests that
his Egyptian counter-
part, Mustafa al-Nahas,
follows his example
and makes an infirm
Britain do as it is told
(Punch 1951).*

the chiefs-of-staff would have tolerated. Anglo-Egyptian discord might then cease, and Egypt could be invited to join America in an anti-Soviet regional defence pact. Negotiations over these points dragged on from the middle of 1950 until the autumn of 1951 in an atmosphere of increasing frustration and acrimony.

On 8 October 1951, al-Nahas unilaterally revoked the 1936 Treaty, theoretically terminating British occupation of the Canal Zone. His sense of timing was acute and provocative; the last British technician had left Abadan Island four days before, and the British general election campaign had been underway for three days. Within a few weeks, the 70,000-strong Egyptian labour force had left the Canal Zone, and a campaign of terrorism began with covert government backing.

Churchill, then Prime Minister, was furious and put into action a plan to restore the old order in Egypt. By the end of December, Whitehall's strategists had concocted Operation Rodeo, a repeat performance of the 1882 occupation of Egypt. Forces from the Canal Zone, reinforced by units from Malta, Libya and Cyprus, were to occupy Cairo, the Nile delta and Alexandria, the last being taken by an assault from the sea.

In the meantime, the Canal Zone had been placed under military government, which involved disarming all the Egyptian police within its perimeter. On 25 January 1952, an auxiliary detachment at Ismailia refused to give up their guns, barricaded themselves inside their station and were evicted only after a siege in which fifty were killed and a hundred wounded. At last the 'splutter of musketry' had been heard, and the 'about-time-they-were-taught-a-lesson' Conservatives were cock-a-hoop. Their oracle, the *Daily Express*, proclaimed that Britain was now 'making a mighty affirmation of its Imperial Destiny'. In revenge, Cairene mobs stormed the citadels of their overlords and burned down the Turf Club, Shepheard's Hotel and various British commercial premises, murdering those of their occupants whom they caught.

The Canal Zone was now embattled and could no longer be counted upon in an emergency. Like the British garrison, Egypt's old ruling class also had their backs to the wall. King Faruq sacked al-Nahas and his ministry immediately after the riots, and was himself deposed in July 1952 by a knot of army officers led by General Mohammed Naguib. The stout monarch shuffled off to continue his sybaritic existence in various Mediterranean resorts. Egypt's new governors were soldiers who, following the tradition of Urabi Pasha, regarded themselves as the nation's saviours, ordained to lead it, advance its honour and defend its integrity. They were idealists who wanted a social revolution, and their creed was a blend of Islamic ethics, pan-Arabism and socialism.

British reaction to the July revolution was fumbling. The embassy had no forewarning of trouble, and the ambassador was on holiday. Five days after the coup, the chargé d'affaires suggested that Britain could reverse the course of events 'by a clear show of determination and by an immediate show of force at the appropriate moment'. The ghosts of Cromer, Milner and Allenby would have applauded.

The CIA was better informed. It had got wind of the plot against Faruq, but it was unperturbed, having long recognised the need for radical social change inside Egypt. Moreover, the Americans had good reason to believe that the revolutionaries, of whom Colonel Nasser was the most dynamic, might align with the West if carefully handled. Britain remained the chief obstacle to such an understanding. Soon after he had taken over the State Department, John Foster Dulles described Britain's presence on Egyptian soil as the 'psychological block' which prevented Egypt from joining an anti-Soviet pact. Furthermore, the Canal Zone had now become a strategic white elephant. Incidents during the past two years had revealed how vulnerable it was to sabotage by disaffected Egyptians, and recent advances in thermonuclear weapons (America exploded its first hydrogen bomb in March 1954) dictated that in future bases would have to be smaller and dispersed. As it was, the USAAF's airfields in Turkey were now operational, making their British-run, Egyptian counterparts redundant.

There was, therefore, no purpose in Britain's continuing to dig its heels in. The 1936 Anglo-Egyptian treaty expired in 1956, and in July 1954 arrangements were agreed for a piecemeal evacuation of the base over the next two years. There was a settlement too of the old dispute over the Sudan, where Britain had made an astute alliance with local nationalists who were averse to any restoration of Egyptian sovereignty. On 1 January 1956 the Sudan became independent.

Some years ago I was told by one who had been among the last British servicemen to leave the Canal Zone that as his boat drew away from the Port Said quayside, an Egyptian youth raised his robe and passed water onto the soldiers below. One looked up, and took a shot at him. Whether or not this story is true, it was in a way oddly symbolic of the past thirty or so years of Britain's presence in Egypt.

4

KICK
THEIR BACKSIDES:
THE SUEZ WAR
AND BEYOND

Between March and October 1955, Turkey, Iraq, Iran and Pakistan were induced to join the anti-Soviet Baghdad Pact. Britain kept its Iraqi airfields and promised aid in the event of a conventional Russian offensive.

The Baghdad Pact was wormwood to Nasser, Egypt's Prime Minister and from 1956 its President. He reviled the agreement as a thinly disguised attempt by Britain to reassert its old supremacy and split the Arab world. He responded with a campaign of virulent radio propaganda beamed across the Middle East and North Africa, addressed to the masses and designed to discredit Britain and its stooges. Nasser's message was simple and compelling: Egypt was the spearhead of revolutionary nationalism and he, a modern Saladin, was ordained to unite all Arab peoples and destroy their enemies. For millions of Arabs who read or listened to his words he became an almost messianic figure, a liberator who would free them from a past in which they had been divided and subservient.

The British government was determined to engineer a showdown with Nasser. Just how this might have been achieved will remain obscure until all the official papers are released. What is known strongly suggests that British intelligence had been ordered to contrive a situation akin to that of 1882, when the Egyptian government had lost control and internal disorder was getting out of hand. Such circumstances were, of course, an excellent pretext for armed intervention and the installation of a puppet administration, which was what Sir Anthony Eden, the Prime Minister, wanted.

The showdown with Nasser was not long in coming. Nasser was determined to set Egypt on a collision course with Britain which, he believed, would result in a new balance of power in the Middle East favourable to Egypt. At the beginning of 1956 he undertook an extended tour of non-aligned states in Asia to establish his credentials as a leader of the anti-imperialist, neutral block. He also showed that he was his own man by recognising Communist China and receiving Russian emissaries in Cairo.

Inside Egypt, his attentions were occupied by the projected Aswan high dam and the future of the Suez Canal Company, in which foreign investors still had a 49 per cent holding. On the surface, the question of which powers would underwrite the building of the dam and the nationalisation of the Canal have always appeared connected. On 19 July, the Americans bluntly informed Egypt that no American loan would be forthcoming for the dam, and as a tit-for-tat Nasser took over the Canal seven

Target:
Port Said: amphibious forces supported by helicopters head for Port Said, November 1956.
(© IWM)

days later. In fact he had been contemplating sequestering the Canal Company and its assets for some time. From the start he had known that such a gesture would be a gamble, but he estimated that the odds were in his favour. America would be distracted by the campaign for the presidential election at the beginning of November, France had its hands tied by the Algerian war and only Britain might take action.

Egyptian intelligence was therefore instructed to assess Britain's readiness. Nasser discovered that no immediate response was possible, and that at least eight weeks were needed for Britain to mobilise for an invasion of Egypt. Everything would therefore depend on Eden's grit, and Nasser, on the strength of a single meeting two years before, took him to be a man who would mask interior weakness by public bravado. He would plump for a war. Even so, the chances of a fight would progressively diminish as time went by; Nasser calculated that they were 90 per cent before 10 August and would then plummet to 20 per cent by the second half of October. Israel was not included in his reckonings.

Two plans of action were adopted by the British government. On one hand, Britain rallied international support for a diplomatic offensive which might force Nasser to disgorge the Canal. On the other, it prepared for war, summoning up reservists on 2 August. Anglo-French forces would deliver an aerial bombardment of Egyptian strategic targets (including Radio Cairo), undertake a landing at Port Said and seize the Canal. Having defeated Egypt and presumably overthrown Nasser, three or four divisions would garrison the country until a suitable government could be found. The cabinet expected that there might be a brief interim period in which British administrators would assist in the governance of Egypt.

Such a far-reaching and, given the climate of British and world opinion in 1956, daring reassertion of unofficial empire needed substantial backing at home and abroad. From the start, Britain had the wholehearted support of France, whose animus towards Nasser stemmed from his help to the Algerian nationalists.

To judge by the tenor of the Commons debates during the early days of the crisis, Eden might have got away with a swift retaliatory grabbing back of the Canal. But it was beyond the capacity of the army,

Politicians don't know Orientals like we do, they don't know that the only way to deal with them is to kick their backsides.

BRIGADIER M. F. FARQUHARSON-ROBERTS

navy and air force to mount such a surgical operation. The result was a policy which thrust in two opposite directions; Britain and France were openly and ponderously preparing for war at the same time as actively encouraging an international settlement by negotiation.

Time seemed to be running in Nasser's favour and against Eden. Unable to gain a favourable solution through diplomacy, Eden faced either a decision to attack or a climb-down. A gallup poll in August showed that 59 per cent of the country backed his mixture of firmness and apparent diplomatic flexibility but, by the middle of September, this total fell to 49 per cent. There were fresh difficulties at the beginning of October, when there were indications that after the recent upsurge in cross-border raids, an exasperated Israel might attack Jordan, forcing Britain to come to the rescue of its ally. On 11 October, the Israeli government was officially warned that Britain would defend Jordan. Three days later United Nations discussions of the Canal question reached an *impasse*, when Russia employed its Security Council veto.

For some weeks the French had been courting the Israelis, who they believed could help find a way out of the diplomatic deadlock. It was a simple stratagem, so much so that it convinced no one at the time, although the exact details of the hugger-mugger deal were not known until twenty years after. Israel attacked Egypt and its forces advanced through Sinai, thereby providing Britain and France with a pretext to seize the Canal on the grounds that they were protecting it, as well as separating the combatants. Eden jumped at what was a last-moment chance to avoid a humiliating climb-down, and on 17 October Canberra heavy bombers were on their way to airfields in Cyprus. Six days later, the British, French and Israelis signed the secret Treaty of Sèvres, of which no copy seems to have survived, but whose outlines were made abundantly clear by the events of 29–30 October.

There were two Suez wars in November 1956. The first was fought by British, French, Israeli and Egyptian forces in the Sinai peninsula, Port Said and along the banks of the Suez Canal. The second was

Streetfighter: Lieutenant-Colonel 'Mad' Mike Mitchell (right) asks directions in an Aden street. A dashing, no-nonsense officer, Mitchell was perhaps the last of an old breed of imperial warriors. (© Popperfoto)

fought in the Commons chamber, newspaper columns and everywhere where people gathered in Britain, and concerned whether or not the British government had acted wisely and honestly.

The first war ran according to the Sèvres schedule and took Nasser by surprise, for he had never expected Israel to intrude itself into the Canal dispute. Indeed, after September had passed, he had picked up from American sources information which led him to think Egypt would not be attacked.

The Suez War started on time, with the Israeli irruption into Sinai on 29 October. The following day, as Israeli troops and armour sliced through the dazed Egyptian army, Britain and France issued an ultimatum, giving both sides twelve hours in which to stop fighting. This was ignored, and on 1 November Canberra bombers began high-level attacks on Egyptian strategic targets and cities, while airborne and amphibious units prepared for the landings at Port Said. The next day, the United States (backed by Australia among others) supported a United Nations motion for an immediate ceasefire by all the belligerents. Britain and France were thrown into a panic. They bargained for time, insisting that they would only agree to an armistice if United Nations forces took control of the Canal, and at the same time hurried forward the deadline for the invasion.

The barren rocks of Aden: British troops patrol the hinterland of the last imperial toehold in the Middle East, Aden, 1967. (© Popperfoto)

Following a new schedule, the first para-troopers landed on 5 November and the amphibious forces were ashore on the 6th. In the meantime, there had been two further United Nations calls for a truce and, with their forces in possession of Port Said and a twenty-three-mile-long section of the Canal, the British and French governments complied on the evening of 6 November. In purely military terms, the operation was a shining success; Egyptian losses had been over a thousand and Anglo-French under a hundred. 'It was all like a bloody good exercise,' a colonel told one journalist, 'a lot of fun and very interesting.'

The other Suez War also had its moments. Eden's moves between 30 October and 6 November were a catalyst for a political rumpus which convulsed the entire nation. Inside the Commons, government statements on Egypt were a signal for uproar; fists were shaken and catcalls exchanged. The Conservatives were 'fascists' and 'murderers' (this from the sturdy Mrs Bessie Braddock) and Labour were 'cowards', who had stabbed their country in the back. The press took up the cudgels, mostly for the government, and there were two mass demonstrations, one outside the Commons, the other in Trafalgar Square.

Having agreed to an armistice, the government insisted that Anglo-French units in Egypt should remain, and form part of the United Nations force which would eventually take over the Canal. America stuck out for unconditional evacuation and a brief, one-sided test of wills followed.

Between August and November 1956 there were a series of runs on the pound, triggered by fears that Britain would overreach itself and become entangled in a Middle Eastern war which it could not afford. By the end of November the country's reserves had dropped to £1,965 million and Macmillan was forced to appeal to the International Monetary Fund for a loan. The American government refused his request, relenting only when Britain agreed to pull all its forces out of Egypt. On 10 December, Macmillan heard that $1,300 million had been placed at Britain's disposal to help shore up sterling.

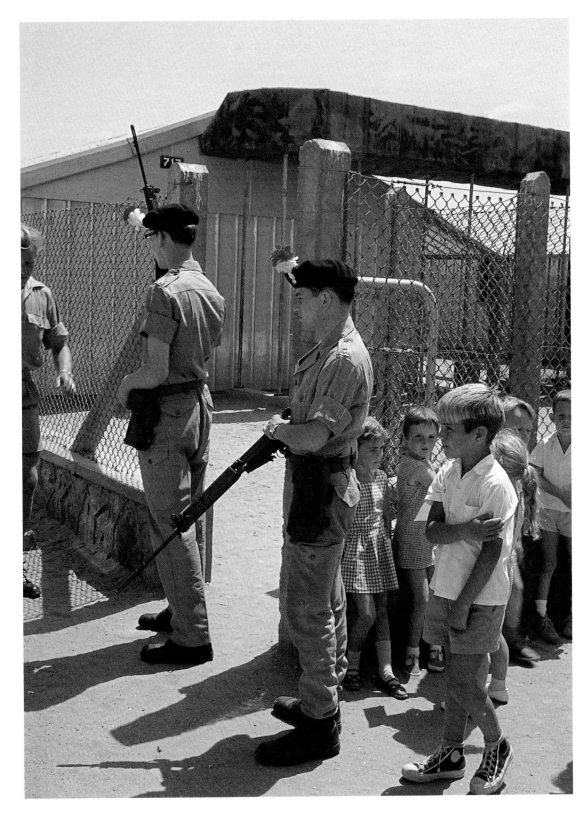

The school run:
*British soldiers guard
the children of service
personnel against Arab
nationalist terrorists,
Aden, 1967.
(© Popperfoto)*

According to Angus Maude MP, the outcome of the Suez War left Britain with no choice but 'to admit to the world that we are now an American satellite'. Subservience to the United States was, in some ways, harder to swallow than the knowledge that the days of ruling the roost in the Middle East were finally over.

5

THE OLD RED, WHITE AND BLUE:
REACTIONS TO A DYING EMPIRE

As well as coming to terms with the reduction of their country's international power and standing, the British people had to face the disappearance of its territorial empire. In the thirteen years following Suez, nearly all the African, Far Eastern and West Indian colonies received their independence and became part of an enlarged Commonwealth. The trauma, both in Britain and the colonies, was remarkably mild. Outsiders were astonished, the more so since the Algerian war brought about the downfall of the Fourth Republic in 1958, a large-scale mutiny by the French army in 1961, tumults in Paris, and a spate of terrorist outrages undertaken by the Algerian settlers movement, the OAS (Organisation Armée Secrète) during 1961–2. Portugal's farewell to empire was equally turbulent and bloody: between 1960 and 1976 135,000 Portuguese troops were deployed against nationalist partisans in Mozambique and Angola. There were also repercussions at home with a revolution which overthrew the right-wing régime of President Caetano in April 1974. Within a month of Belgium granting independence to the Congo (Zaïre) in June 1960, the new state had disintegrated into anarchy and civil war with massacres of white settlers.

Britain was spared such upheavals; it carefully avoided being dragged into futile wars; its soldiers did not mutiny in protest against decolonisation; and the white settlers of Kenya and Southern Rhodesia did not explode plastic bombs in London streets. In February 1963, an anglophile American sociologist attributed the comparative orderliness of the dissolution of empire to the evolution of enlightened national spirit:

> [The] progressive moral transformation which was expressed in the willingness to
> renounce the empire has been manifested in the unwillingness to continue with
> the ancien régime. Respect for the rights of Indians and Africans is of a piece with
> the aspirations to improve the quality of life, the level of taste, to cultivate the
> whole capacities of the whole population, to make society more just, more efficient
> and more humane.

This was very satisfying, but not altogether surprising. For at least thirty years, politicians of both parties had repeatedly promised that the colonies were on course for independence, although they were evasive about precisely how and when it would be obtained. The officially inspired public perception of the empire made it virtually impossible for any government to justify extended wars of repression fought to maintain British rule perpetually. When they proved unavoidable, as in Malaya, elaborate efforts were made to present the conflict in such a way as to reassure the public that Britain had the best interests of its subjects at heart.

The Cold War ruled out handing over power to Communists, although even Conservative ministries were content to make terms with nationalists of a pinkish complexion, as most were. Decolonisation policies were, by and large, bipartisan with Labour tending to favour speeding up the process. The Conservatives had to be more cautious because of right-wing elements in the party which mistrusted nationalists, or were sympathetic towards the white settler communities in East and Central Africa. This group found natural allies among former colonial civil servants who were unhappy about policies which paid too much heed to nationalists and too little to tribal rulers.

The behaviour of some colonial politicians aroused anger among those on the outer fringes of the right. In 1950, the veteran Tory spokesman on colonial policy, Captain Gammans, was outraged by the substitution of Nkrumah's name for God's in the Lord's Prayer, and for Christ's in *Hymns Ancient and Modern*, as they were read and sung in the Gold Coast. Those who felt strongly could join the League of Empire Loyalists, founded in 1954 to defend the empire. Its upper echelons included a bevy of retired high-ranking officers of Blimpish frame of mind, who were apoplectic about the

Honour bestowed: the British honours system had been extended throughout the empire: here the Reverend Edward Mpatose, a clergymen and Second World War veteran receives the MBE, Basutoland, 1964.

decay of everything they had held dear. The nostalgic fantasies of upper- and upper-middle-class men and women who had talked about and thought on England as they sipped gin on colonial verandahs must have been often rudely and swiftly dispelled when they returned home. High blood pressure and enlarged spleens were not, therefore, surprising, and the League catered for both.

Its programme looked back to a golden age when Britannia had ruled the waves and the world, and was largely negative. It was against Asian and African nationalism, coloured immigration, the United Nations, the present-day Conservative party, Harold Macmillan, Jews and the United States, but favoured apartheid and getting back the empire. The League saw its tasks as shaking the country out of its liberal complacency, and most of its energies were spent on a series of stunts designed to publicise its causes and embarrass its adversaries. Like other fringe right- and left-wing groups, the League was extremely friable, and in time its few hundred members drifted off to embrace other outlandish and hopeless causes. Its farcical exploits achieved no more than a few headlines.

Harold Macmillan was a constant target for the League, as he is for its mental offspring, the young fogeys of 1990s journalism. Prime Minister from January 1957 until October 1963, he considered himself patrician, a believer in 'one-nation' paternalist Conservatism, and, on matters relating to the empire and his country's place in the world, a pragmatic realist. During his term of office the following colonies and protectorates received independence: Gold Coast (Ghana), Malaya (joining with North Borneo [Sabah] and Sarawak to make Malaysia in 1963), Cyprus, Nigeria, Somaliland (with Italian Somaliland as Somalia), Sierra Leone, Jamaica, Tanganyika, Uganda, Kenya and the Gambia. Plans were also in hand for the independence of Northern Rhodesia (Zambia) and Nyasaland (Malawi) and the creation of the West Indian federation. Attlee apart, no other prime minister was responsible for such a sweeping programme of decolonisation.

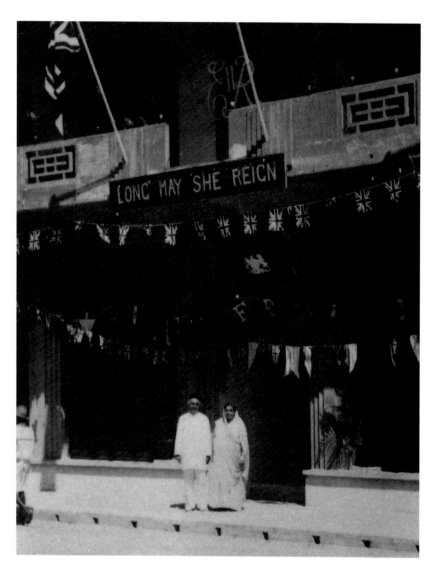

Although it would be hard to quantify exactly, it appears that the mass of British voters were largely indifferent to the loss of colonies whose names were probably best known by stamp collectors. No party had consciously adopted imperialism as part of its ideology. National self-respect had not been diminished by the slow disengagement from empire; rather it had been enhanced, since the process had been undertaken in the name of a higher morality and was being accomplished without excessive bloodshed or recriminations. Sidelong glances at how France and Portugal were managing served as a salutary reminder of the results of a policy of clinging on at all costs.

There were small groups who regretted the passing of empire but, while sometimes clamorous, they carried little political clout. Few outside some London clubs and service messes were agitated by the knowledge that Britain could no longer lay down the law throughout the Middle East, or that white settlers in East and Central Africa were about to face a future ruled by black men. The settler lobby did, however, have tentacles which stretched into right-wing Conservative circles, and so Macmillan had to tread carefully over African policy if only to secure his base inside the party.

Loyal celebrations:
an Indian storekeeper
and his wife pose outside
their decorated premises
in the Seychelles,
Coronation Day, 1953.

No jobs were lost, factories closed or investment opportunities frustrated as a result of the loss of the colonies. Britain's exports to Commonwealth countries grew fitfully: in 1958 they totalled £1,240 million, in 1962 £1,193 million and in 1969, £1,419 million. By contrast, exports to the countries of the European Economic Community (EEC) were increasing, standing at £2,634 million in 1969, although Britain had to wait a further four years for full membership. Patterns of trade were changing rapidly with Commonwealth members seeking new markets and sources of raw materials outside the group. Canada's exports to the United States rose from £329 million in 1958 to £534 million in 1962. The new states which had replaced the old colonies did not automatically give Britain special trading advantages. In Africa only the Gambia and Malawi (ex-Nyasaland) were offering British importers preferential terms in 1967, together with South Africa which had left the Commonwealth six years before.

The Britain of the post-war era was undergoing profound social changes. What amounted to a revolution in the ways in which the British people behaved, thought and regarded themselves had begun in the early 1950s. At first, its pace was slow and uneven, and no one could then have foretold either its future tempo or what its end might be. That this transformation coincided with the break-up of empire is important for two reasons. First, it encompassed a radical assault on traditional values and attitudes, many of which were closely associated with the empire and those who had made and ruled it. If their ideals were bogus, then perhaps the institution itself was rotten throughout. Second, as the pace of change quickened and the public, particularly the young, found themselves with more money to spend on diversions, it mattered little that Britain was a declining power.

As the British empire disappeared, one of its most cherished assumptions came under attack. The so-called superior civilisation which it had offered its subjects was nothing of the sort, and certainly not a justification for the wholesale destruction of other systems. Britain should feel guilt rather than pride for its imperial past. In November 1967, Dennis Potter, the left-wing, iconoclastic television playwright summed up the new orthodoxy: 'Perhaps the noblest task of the popular historian should be to make us ashamed of our forefathers ... now that the hilarious residue of the White Man's Burden has been chased out of the reading books of schoolboys.'

It was relatively easy for the post-imperial guilt complex to penetrate the public consciousness during the late 1960s. The image of empire, as daily projected in the television news, was one of iron-fisted coercion in Viet Nam, Mozambique, Angola, South Africa and, from 1972 onwards, Southern Rhodesia. The news from those countries where the Union Jack had been recently hauled down was also bleak and bloody. In 1966, the year of a Commonwealth conference in Lagos, there was a military coup in Nigeria and another in Ghana. 1967 saw the beginning of a three-year civil war in Nigeria and a new wave of military take-overs in Ghana and Sierra Leone. There were military coups in the Sudan in 1969, and two years later the preposterous General Idi Amin seized power in Uganda and began a reign of terror. For its former subjects, the inheritance of empire appeared to be political corruption, a succession of praetorian governments and internecine warfare. Not surprisingly, touring companies of British actors found African audiences very responsive to *Macbeth*, *Julius Caesar* and *Richard III*, all of which mirrored political life in their countries. It was natural in the successor states, and in some quarters in Britain, to blame these woes on the empire.

Faced with what appeared to be the failure of its imperial mission, Britain was also undergoing a re-evaluation of the principles which had formerly guided its rulers and empire. From the mid-1950s, social anthropologists had been busy analysing what was called 'the establishment'. They uncovered and closely examined the world and values of an exclusive network which extended through London's club-land, politics, the higher civil service, the colleges of Oxford and Cambridge, the boardrooms of banks and large companies, the bench of bishops, the judiciary and the commanders of the armed services. Public school and Oxbridge education formed a common bond and had helped to mould a common humane, cautious, conservative outlook. Britain's rulers were also the empire's rulers. The establishment saw the exercise of power as a right, and its members had relished governing India and the empire since they had been able to do so without being unduly trammelled by expressions of the popular will.

Those who scrutinised the establishment were also its critics. The general argument ran that those who had discreetly but firmly pulled the strings for so long were to a great extent responsible for national decline and stagnation. They were also capable of colossal blunders. 'After Suez we can no longer have ... confidence in this government's sanity,' observed one establishment analyst, himself a former Tory MP. The same could have been said, and was, somewhat less harshly, after the fall of Singapore. The difference was that in the mid-1950s everything seemed to be going wrong for Britain abroad. All that the establishment seemed able to do was either reach for old remedies, like Eden, or stand back in bewilderment. From the military wing of the establishment, Glubb Pasha complained: 'While British

The Army, the Navy and the Air Force, Are all we need to make the blighters see It still belongs to you, the old red, white and blue.

Those bits of red still on the map We won't give up without a scrap.

THE ENTERTAINER, 1957

Royal favour:
HM The Queen and
Prince Philip visiting
Fiji: these visits were
an excuse for festivities
and strengthened the
emotional bond within
the Commonwealth.

citizens discuss ... noble plans for the betterment of the human race a great part of the world is convinced that Britain is greedy, reactionary and intent only on exploiting other nations.'

Misunderstood abroad, Britain's establishment was coming under fire at home, and seemed unable to find the confidence to defend itself. The television programme 'That Was the Week that Was' and the satirical magazine *Private Eye*, both of which appeared in 1961, lampooned public figures with a contemptuous abandon that had not been seen since the eighteenth century. In 1963, the Profumo scandal inflicted a further blow on the establishment by revealing that some of its members enjoyed eighteenth-century-style sexual lives. Ridicule of the establishment, hints of its moral bankruptcy, together with a pervasive feeling that it had somehow failed the country, contributed to Harold Wilson's general election victory in October 1964. On the hustings, Labour alternately berated the stuffy old guard and promised a dazzling era of social and economic regeneration.

As the empire passed away, late nineteenth-century anti-imperialism, padded out with currently fashionable Marxism, became campus and classroom orthodoxy. All overseas empires were extensions of capitalism, which oppressed and exploited their subjects pitilessly. The children and grandchildren of those who had been taught to feel pride in the empire, now learned to be ashamed of it. Britain had been demeaned and corrupted by its empire, and whether true or not, this knowledge may have made its loss more bearable.

6

UHURU:
TYING UP
LOOSE ENDS

1959–1980

I t is hard nowadays to comprehend the optimism which attended the gradual granting of independence to Britain's African colonies during the early 1960s. Independence day ceremonies were conducted with a remarkable degree of goodwill in a carnival atmosphere. Royalty stood by as flags went down and up, and speeches were made in which Britain wished the infant nation every good fortune. The paraphernalia of the post-colonial order was reassuring: there were secret ballots, and elected assemblies with maces, and wigged and gowned speakers. African judges, who had learned their law at London's Inns of Court and wore robes of scarlet and ermine, presided over replicas of English assize courts. Democracy and the rule of law seemed firmly in place. Britain could feel satisfied that it had guided its subjects wisely and that they were setting off along the right road.

This euphoria was premature and probably naïve. For the Sudan, Ghana, Sierra Leone, Nigeria and Uganda the post-independence path led to the overthrow of democracy, a sequence of praetorian coups, military dictatorships, corruption and chronic economic instability. This was all grist to the mill of those, like the Marquess of Salisbury, who had doubted the African's ability to manage his own affairs unaided, and naturally were quick to say 'we told you so'. Others, disappointed by what seemed the failure of a noble experiment, argued that Africa's woes were a direct result of the imperial era. State boundaries drawn for the convenience of bureaucrats or at the whim of representatives of the great powers created tribal mixtures that were bound to fail. Moreover, the colonial era had witnessed the dislocation of old local social and economic orders, and it was foolish to imagine that colonial government, which had seldom lasted for more than a man's lifetime, could have created a powerful sense of national coherence and identity. In any case, this had never been its primary purpose.

It was certainly true that at least until 1948 the British government imagined that the time would not be ripe for independence until the last quarter of the century. In any event, the timetable would have to be staggered according to the political sophistication of the natives and the experience of

The prevailing order: a native constable and, to judge by his medal ribbons, ex-askari, presents his morning report to the District Commissioner, while a member of the TP (Tribal Police) stands by, Kenya, 1947.

The King's peace:
Fort Wajir, northern
Kenya (above) and a
Somali Tribal Police
detachment being
reviewed by the governor,
Sir Philip Mitchell, 1948
(right). Here and in other
remote districts of Africa,
small forces were deployed
to check cattle rustling
and feuding, habits which
died hard.

those who would take over the reins of government. But expediency had intervened when events in the Gold Coast made it clear that if the brake was applied violence might follow. Even so, this colony had had longer experience than others in democracy. Since 1894, ratepayers had been able to vote for half the membership of village and town councils, but it was a right which few chose to exercise. In 1922 only 46 of the 1,117 registered electors in Accra turned out on polling day and none of the 717 in Sekondi bothered to appear at all.

In tone and behaviour, African politics closely resembled those of pre-independence India, and Egypt during its struggle against Britain. African political movements tended to focus on a single charismatic figure, the leader of a monolithic, well-disciplined party which claimed to speak for the entire nation. The chants and responses of the mission churches were adapted to create a nationalist liturgy, which would be recited at mass political rallies.

These forms of mass persuasion were needed to give Africans a sense of power and confidence in themselves. Tom Mboya recalled how in 1952 his father and tribal elders had advised him to steer clear of politics: 'We can never compete with the European. After all, he has aeroplanes, he flies about while we walk on foot. He has cars and guns.' And yet within five years Ghana had gained independence, and for a time became the powerhouse for African nationalism. In 1958 Accra was host to the first All-African Peoples Conference which called for the liberation of the whole continent from imperial rule.

For the British government it was not a question of whether the African empire would be dissolved, but when and how. The process had been relatively easy in Ghana, and afterwards with the other West African colonies for they had wholly black populations. In East and Central Africa the situation was complicated by the presence of white settlers, largely of British stock, who looked upon themselves as the economic backbone of their colonies and had grown accustomed to lording it over the blacks. In Southern Rhodesia the whites had had a measure of self-government since 1923, but in Kenya the Colonial Office had deliberately blocked any attempt by the colonists to acquire political paramountcy.

Any residual belief that the white settlers in Kenya might go it alone was shattered by the Mau Mau uprising which started in 1952. It was a peasant *jacquerie*, confined to the Kikuyu, and randomly directed against all things European. Mau Mau was a cabalistic union whose members were bound together by oaths, sworn to the accompaniment of horrific sexual rituals. Most of Mau Mau's victims were Kikuyu who were suspected of collaboration with the colonial authorities. These reacted by declaring a state of emergency, and by December 1953 over 150,000 Mau Mau suspects were in detention centres, 12,000 had been convicted of membership and 150 hanged. The war was savage and one-sided; between November 1952 and April 1953, 430 prisoners had been shot dead while attempting to escape, and there were cases of others being tortured.

Mau Mau had brought about a civil war among the Kikuyu, the majority of whom sided with the British, who held all the trump cards. Their enemies possessed few firearms and were nowhere near strong enough to engage the colonial forces on equal terms. Very few settlers were killed by the Mau Mau, but its psychological effect was

'Uhuru!' [Freedom]
'Uhuru!'
'Uhuru na umoga!'
[Freedom and unity]
'Uhuru na KANU!'
[Freedom and the
Kenyan African
National Union]
'Uhuru na KANU!'
'Uhuru na Kenyatta!'
[Freedom and
Kenyatta]
'Uhuru na Kenyatta!'

KANU CHANT

Suspects:
Masai auxiliary police
keep watch over Kikuyu
suspected of having taken
the Mau Mau oath,
Kenya 1953.
(© IWM)

enormous, reminding them of their smallness in numbers and isolation. Mau Mau was the ultimate white man's nightmare whose ingredients were images of a dark, impenetrable Africa of witchcraft and fear of sudden attack by crazed tribesmen armed with pangas and spears. But Kenya's whites, after some nail-biting moments, were able to sleep in peace thanks to British-trained askaris (who did the brunt of the police work), regular soldiers, national servicemen and aircraft. By 1956, all but a handful of guerrillas had been tracked down, and the rest were either dead or incarcerated in camps, where they underwent a form of brainwashing designed to release them from the magic of their oaths.

For all its nihilism, Mau Mau briefly caught the imagination of other Africans. 'We want Mau Mau here; we want to kill Europeans because we are tired of them,' shouted one African at a political meeting at Lusaka, Northern Rhodesia, in April 1953. The police intelligence officer who took down his words also noted that Harry Nkumbula, the President of the Northern Rhodesia African National Congress, urged his listeners to wage war with words.

The struggle in Northern Rhodesia was against the Central African Federation. This hybrid had been foisted on the Labour government in 1951 by tidy-minded Colonial Office officials, who believed that it would solve the future economic and political problems of Southern Rhodesia, Northern Rhodesia and Nyasaland. It was a shotgun marriage which forced cohabitation between two Crown colonies, with tiny white minorities, and white-dominated Southern Rhodesia. At its birth in 1953, the proportion of white to black in the Central African Federation was 1 to 66. Most whites lived in Southern Rhodesia, where there were 220,000 to 3.5 million Africans. Blacks had no faith whatsoever in the new state, which they believed would extinguish their political rights and drag them into the orbit of Southern Rhodesia.

Just what this might entail was spelled out in the 1950 version of Southern Rhodesia's handbook for British immigrants. Only skilled men were wanted, 'Because of our African population, and the fact that Africans do the unskilled and bulk of the semi-skilled work.' A good life was promised, especially for women: 'On the whole, the lot of the Rhodesian housewife is much more pleasant than that of her sisters in England.' Black servants were plentiful, but the newcomer had to bear in mind 'that the average Native servant is of childlike simplicity' and prone to pilfering, so firmness was vital.

Segregation was enforced rigorously everywhere. Visiting the country in 1955 to advise on its broadcasting system, Sir Hugh Greene encountered Sir Godfrey Huggins, then the Federation's Prime Minister, who told him that white and black MPs were forbidden to dine together in Parliament House. Nothing had changed since the time of Rhodes and Jameson. That year, a white man who had flogged to death one of his servants was given a year in gaol and ordered to pay his victim's family £100 compensation. An African found guilty of stealing sixteen shirts also got a year's imprisonment. It was, therefore, not really surprising that the Colonial Office found it hard to whip up enthusiasm for the Federation among blacks in Northern Rhodesia and Nyasaland.

Opposition to federation was most vehement in Nyasaland where, from July 1958, the newly returned Dr Banda had taken over as President-General of the African National Congress. The governor, Sir Robert Armitage, toed the official line over the Federation, and was scared by Banda's trenchancy and the support he was gathering. In what turned out to be a ham-fisted attempt to force a show-down, Armitage declared a state of emergency in Nyasaland on 18 February 1959, using the discovery of an alleged Mau Mau-style conspiracy to massacre the colony's 8,000 whites as an excuse. Plot or no plot, and the evidence is far from certain, Armitage had secured a chance to uncover the real strength of the anti-Federation movement and silence it. The suspension of normal legal rights and judicial processes allowed for dawn raids, arrests and internment. Banda was seized and bundled off to Gwelo gaol in Northern Rhodesia and troops were rushed in from Northern Rhodesia and Tanganyika to handle the inevitable protest demonstrations. Within four weeks the death toll had risen to fifty-two.

Armitage's action had embarrassed the government at a time when it was facing criticism for the deaths of Mau Mau detainees in Hola Camp in Kenya. The Colonial Secretary, Alan Lennox-Boyd, was anxious to forestall television criticism of the state of emergency, and there were charges in the Commons that the Nyasaland authorities had tried to censor journalists reporting on conditions there. Resisting pressure from Southern Rhodesia, where the Nyasaland clamp-down had been welcomed, Macmillan ordered a senior judge and sometime Tory candidate, Lord Devlin, to chair a commission of inquiry into the causes of the emergency.

Devlin's report appeared at midsummer and made disturbing reading. Armitage had blundered, Banda was exonerated, and Nyasaland was described as 'a police state'. Macmillan was furious and claimed that the judge had acted out of ancestral and personal spite. He was Irish ('no doubt with that Fenian blood that makes Irishmen anti-Government on principle'), a lapsed Catholic with a Jesuit brother (in fact a missionary in Northern Rhodesia), and was getting his own back for not

Africa transformed: Prince Philip visits a Nigerian car factory. Industrialisation came slowly and unevenly to British Africa but its impact was enormous, leading to growing urbanisation and the fracturing of traditional tribal and village life. (© Unilever)

having been appointed Lord Chief Justice. The cabinet rejected Devlin and hurriedly drew up a counterblast, allegedly penned by Armitage, which was published on the same day as the judge's report.

Together, the reports on the killings at Hola Camp and the blunders in Nyasaland were an indictment of a colonial policy which had lost direction and moral basis. Enoch Powell, a former government minister, took his colleagues to task on the last score in a speech which repeated the classic argument that imperial authority could never exist in an ethical vacuum, or in defiance of its subjects' wishes. It was indefensible to say: 'We will have African standards in Africa, Asian standards in Asia and perhaps British standards here.' He continued:

> *All Government, all influence of man upon man, rests on opinion. What we do in Africa, where we still govern and we no longer govern, depends upon the opinion which is entertained of the way in which Englishmen act. We cannot, we dare not, in Africa of all places, fall below our own highest standards in the acceptance of responsibility.*

To this invocation of traditional benevolent imperialism was added a warning from the Opposition front bench, delivered by Aneurin Bevan, to the effect that Britain could not allow its national life to be poisoned in the way that France's had been by African conflict. Central Africa might yet prove Britain's Algeria.

Macmillan was determined that this should not happen. In the wake of the Nyasaland débâcle, he had decided to send a commission under Sir Walter Monckton, a silver-tongued lawyer and skilled arbitrator, to investigate opinion throughout Central Africa. This was wormwood to the Federation's new Prime Minister, Sir Roy Welensky, a former railwayman and prize-fighter, who had never pulled his punches. In 1957 he had ominously remarked that he had never believed 'that the Rhodesians have less guts than the American Colonists had'.

In August, Macmillan had counselled Monckton to do all in his power to create a multi-racial state in Central Africa. Failure would turn the region, and Kenya as well, into 'a maelstrom of trouble into which all of us will be sucked'. He added that white supremacy was foredoomed, but hoped that something might be accomplished to accommodate the white settlers, who were vital for the continent. The alternative was another extended and unwinnable conflict of the sort which was then being fought in

Algeria. British treasure and British blood would never be expended to defend white supremacy in East and Central Africa.

His standing within the Conservative party enhanced by his sweeping victory in October, Macmillan was free to embark on a radical African policy. His chosen instrument was the forty-six-year-old Iain Macleod, a talented, sharp-witted and sometimes acerbic liberal Conservative who was temperamentally suited to carry out what were at heart paternalist colonial policies. He had what the Prime Minister called 'the worst job of all' with the prospect of bloodshed if he failed. After a year in office, Macleod justified his actions to his party conference on the grounds that they were an extension to Africa of the 'one nation' principles of Disraeli. Black and white would have to be drawn together in the same way as the rich and the poor of Victorian Britain.

Procuring compromise and cooperation were not easy, but Macleod had a flair for chairing conferences and considerable patience. He was also willing to stick his neck out: one of his first acts was to end the state of emergency in Kenya; in April 1960 he restored normal government to Nyasaland and, two months later, had Banda released in spite of howls of anger from Armitage and Welensky. Macleod was publicly announcing that he was the friend of African nationalism, although common sense demanded an end to the Nyasaland emergency which had become a heavy burden on the colony's limited resources. In 1939 the total bill for policing had been £22,000; in 1960, it was £1 million, a sixth of the entire colonial budget.

Macleod's greatest achievement lay in the revision of the schedules for independence and overseeing the peaceful dismemberment of the Central African Federation. His work was acknowledged, at least by Africans, for 'Iain' became a popular Christian name in Uganda and Nyasaland, where, after independence a thoroughfare in Blantyre was named 'Macleod Street'. This was some reward for labours which ended with Tanganyikan independence in 1961, Ugandan in 1962 and Kenyan in 1963, and in the same year the dissolution of the Central African Federation. The next year Nyasaland became independent as Malawi, and Northern Rhodesia as Zambia.

Macmillan had been the guiding force behind these changes. He had always judged the empire in empirical rather than emotional terms, asking what economic or strategic value colonies possessed for Britain. It was as a pragmatist that he made his celebrated tour of sub-Saharan Africa at the beginning of 1960. He was rowed ashore at Accra like Sanders of the River, and in Nigeria he found a successor to that fictional district officer in the sagacious figure of Sir James Robertson, the colony's governor-general. Robertson told Macmillan that, while Nigerians might need twenty-five years in which to prepare themselves for self-government, it was wiser to let them have it immediately. Delay would turn those intelligent men who were now being trained for leadership into rebels and 'violence, bitterness and hatred' would follow. The choice was between instant Uhuru and twenty years of repression.

In South Africa, it was Macmillan's turn to deliver a homily, designed to be heeded by whites throughout the continent. It was delivered to the South African parliament in Cape Town and opened with a history lesson: 'Ever since the break-up of the Roman Empire one of the constant facts of political life in Europe has been the emergence of independent nations.' This process was now underway throughout Africa, and, during his passage through the continent, Macmillan had been struck by its inexorability. The South African MPs politely applauded, but it took thirty years for the import of Macmillan's words to sink in.

For white settlers in Britain's African colonies Macmillan and Macleod were a pair of Judases whose words and actions added up to a form of treason. 'We've been thoroughly betrayed by a lousy British government,' complained one Kenyan farmer in 1962. 'We'll throw in our allegiance with somebody who's not always prepared to pull the bloody flag down.' He had first come to the country in 1938, secured a 999-year lease on his Crown land farm, and had been officially encouraged to see himself as part-squire part-schoolmaster when dealing with the blacks: 'I'm not a missionary, I hate the sight of the bastards.

The wind of change is blowing through this continent, and, whether we like it or not, this growth of national conscious-ness is a political fact. We must all accept it is a fact, and our national policies must take account of it.

HAROLD MACMILLAN

A small investment: funds for development in Africa were always limited. Here in the Nadi Kapsabet District in Kenya, government officials pay the wages of Africans who are clearing bushland that will be used as grazing land. Men slash and uproot while women carry away branches.

But I came here to farm, and look after these fellows. They look up to you as their mother and father; they come to you with their trials and tribulations.' Now, Kenya's future Prime Minister and President, Kenyatta, was saying that any white Kenyan who still wanted 'to be called "Bwana" should pack up and go'. This form of address, and the deference it implied, mattered greatly to some; Kenya's white population fell from 60,000 in 1959 to 41,000 in 1965.

The evidence heard by the Monckton Commission sealed the fate of the Central African Federation. It was universally detested by blacks throughout Nyasaland and Northern Rhodesia and was, therefore, unenforceable. Its obsequies were conducted by Macleod's successor, R. A. Butler, at a conference at the Victoria Falls in the summer of 1963. Northern Rhodesia and Nyasaland proceeded on separate paths to independence, while Southern Rhodesia sulkily prepared to go it alone. A new party, the Rhodesia Front, made the running on a white supremacy ticket.

Between 1963 and 1980 successive British governments were tormented by the Rhodesian ulcer. It was a source of international embarrassment, the cause of interminable rows inside the Commonwealth, and a distraction from more pressing domestic and European matters. It was the last and least welcome legacy of empire and, as the Commonwealth and United Nations made repeatedly clear, it could only be cured by Britain.

With the disintegration of the Central African Federation, the Rhodesian whites were overwhelmed by a feeling that Britain had deserted them, and that henceforward they would have to shape their own destiny. This was independence under the 1961 Constitution which perpetuated white paramountcy. As Ian Smith, the Rhodesian Front leader, was fond of saying, there would be no black majority rule in his or his childrens' lifetimes. Smith, who became Prime Minister in 1964, was an unlikely man to take on the empire, for he saw himself and his countrymen as embodiments of all those old, manly imperial virtues which would have been applauded by G. A. Henty. As a negotiator, Smith was stubborn and cunning by starts. As a politician he was plain-spoken and, according to his lights, intensely patriotic. His following among the white community was enormous; in the May 1965 elections his Rhodesia Front won all the fifty seats reserved for whites.

This election provided the popular imprimatur for UDI (Unilateral Declaration of Independence) which was announced on 11 November. It had been preceded by desperate last-minute negotiations between Smith and Harold Wilson, who had flown to Salisbury. The British Prime Minister insisted, as did his successors, that the British Parliament alone had the legal right to grant Rhodesia its independence, and then only when blacks as well as whites had the vote. The talks broke down and Wilson returned after what had been a highly disagreeable mission.

On his homecoming, Wilson publicly announced that in the event of UDI Britain would not employ force to bring Rhodesia back to its obedience. It was an immensely controversial statement which gave heart to Smith who, with good reason, was worried that his own army and air force would shrink from fighting the British. Wilson was unaware of his anxieties; what he did know was that the Rhodesian forces were well-equipped and trained, and that Britain's service chiefs were nervous about engaging them with extended lines of communication. Moreover, it would take time to establish a secure base in Zambia. Even if logistical problems were overcome, there was no popular enthusiasm for the war, although the Archbishop of Canterbury and Jo Grimond, the Liberal leader, were making loud belligerent noises. Opinion polls suggested that they were out of touch with public opinion, which was against a Rhodesian war. This was comforting for Wilson, who was not a warrior by nature and feared that precipitate action might lead to a second Suez, or worse, a British Viet Nam. Rhodesia, he announced, would be overcome by economic sanctions.

Britain lost the war of attrition against Rhodesia. The rebel state flourished and confidence soared. Between 1967 and 1973, 39,000 immigrants arrived to share its prosperity. According to the BBC's local correspondent, 'most of them ... are in Rhodesia for the good life, and there's no doubt that they are getting it.' Negotiations continued fitfully. Wilson and Smith met twice, first in December 1966 on board the cruiser *Tiger*, and again in October 1968 on board its sister ship *Fearless*. Both meetings ended in deadlock over majority rule. During the first encounter, the naval officers' feelings had been 'Good Old Smithy, bloody old Wilson'. They changed their tune after intimate contact with the Rhodesians who revealed themselves 'rude, racist and even nigger-bashing in their conversations in the mess'.

Those Rhodesian qualities which some found repellent, attracted others, especially on the outer right wing of the Conservative party. One such, Harold Soref MP, claimed that: 'Rhodesia represents Britain in its halcyon days: patriotic, self-reliant, self-supporting, with law and order and a healthy society. Rhodesia is as Britain was at its best.' This other Eden was sometimes known as 'Basingstoke-in-the-Bush', a parody of a pre-war middle-class suburb transported across the Equator, complete with its tennis and golf clubs, and populated by aggressively hearty men in shorts, blazers and cravats, who talked of nothing but sport, and women who knew their place. So too did the black man. Soon after UDI, a former recruit to the Rhodesian police told a journalist that he had been taught that the African 'is muck to be kicked down and kept there'.

Inevitably Africans fought back. Black nationalist movements had been banned and their leaders were either under arrest or in exile. The armed struggle began slowly after UDI and only began to gather momentum by 1972. The pattern of the war was familiar: raids and assassinations by guerrillas, called the 'boys in the bush', designed to wear down the enemy's will. There were two main partisan armies: Joshua Nkomo's Zimbabwe People's Revolutionary Army (ZIPRA) and Robert Mugabe's Zimbabwe African National Union (ZANU). The guerrillas knew their trade, they were armed with modern Soviet weaponry, including rockets, and were trained in extensive base camps in Zambia and, from 1975, in Mozambique.

The anti-guerrilla war was a corrosive, inconclusive struggle which ate up Rhodesia's manpower and treasure. By 1979, 47 per cent of Rhodesia's revenues were consumed by the war effort, and the government was being forced to mobilise more and more black men to fill the gaps in its army. At the same time, its adversaries seemed to be getting stronger; in September 1978 the guerrillas used a Sam 7 heat-seeking missile to shoot down a Viscount airliner on an internal flight, and another was similarly

Black man's burden: a young black recruit crawls through the mud as part of his basic training in the Rhodesian army for anti-guerrilla operations. (© *Camera Press*)

Rebels and their cause:
Ian Smith as seen by
Gerald Scarfe.
(© Gerald Scarfe/Centre
for the Study of Cartoons
and Caricature)

destroyed in February 1979. Rhodesians began to feel that victory was beyond their grasp and voted with their feet. Between 1977 and 1980, 48,000 whites, a fifth of the European community, emigrated.

The truth was, as it had been in Kenya and the Portuguese colonies, that the settlers could not sustain their position without the military power of the mother country. Moreover, by the late-1970s the technical gap between the equipment of the Rhodesian forces and their opponents was narrowing. The destruction of the two airliners had been dramatic proof of this. A similar lesson would be learned more painfully by the Soviet Union during the early 1980s, when it embarked on an imperial war of coercion in that former graveyard of British armies, Afghanistan.

Hunting the terrorists: a Rhodesian patrol scours a native village. In the end, Rhodesia could no longer sustain the effort in an unwinnable war. (© *Camera Press*)

By the beginning of 1978, Smith and the Rhodesia Front had to choose between fighting on and possibly losing a war of attrition, or a salvage operation which would involve considerable concessions to the blacks. They decided on the latter and entered into an alliance with three relatively moderate African parties, Bishop Abel Muzorewa's United African National Council, Ndabaningi Sithole's African National Council, and Chief Chirau's Zimbabwe United People's Organisation. The upshot was the 'internal settlement', which created a constitution that increased black representation. In April 1979, Bishop Muzorewa became Prime Minister of the cumbersomely named Zimbabwe-Rhodesia. A month later, the Conservatives under Mrs Margaret Thatcher won a general election, raising hopes in Rhodesia that a settlement with Britain was imminent.

The Rhodesian imbroglio was one of many intractable problems bequeathed Mrs Thatcher by her predecessors. She was determined to act decisively and swiftly and, at the same time, demonstrate how fumbling past governments had been. At the Lusaka Commonwealth conference in the summer she insisted that Britain alone would unravel the Rhodesian knot. The answer lay in bringing the country back under a British government, which would supervise an election in which all political parties, including those of Mugabe and Nkomo (who had boycotted the April poll) would compete. The Commonwealth ministers, who had no alternatives, acquiesced. Zimbabwe-Rhodesia, war-weary and still without the international recognition it craved, also agreed.

Representatives of all factions, including Ian Smith (who had been allowed immunity from a prosecution for treason), assembled in London in the autumn. The Lancaster Gate conference chaired by the Foreign Secretary, Lord Carrington, finally lanced the Rhodesian ulcer. The country passed back to Britain's jurisdiction and its new governor, Lord Soames, with a small contingent of troops and advisers, oversaw the surrender and disarming of the guerrillas and a general election. It was won by Mugabe who became Prime Minister in a coalition government in which his Zimbabwe African National Union shared power with Nkomo's Zimbabwe African People's Union. Mr Smith held one of the twenty seats reserved for whites in the new Zimbabwe assembly. One of its first acts was to pull down a statue of Cecil Rhodes.

7

UNFINISHED
BUSINESS

While Zimbabweans were plucking down Rhodes from his plinth, the British were trying to forget about him and the rest of their imperial past. All that now remained of it were a few scarlet pinpricks on the globe: Gibraltar, Ascension, St Helena, Tristan da Cunha, the Falklands and their scattered, snowbound dependencies, Pitcairn Island (home to the descendants of the *Bounty* mutineers and their Tahitian brides), Hong Kong, Bermuda, the Cayman Islands and Montserrat. Few people knew where they were, let alone how and why they had been first obtained. They were an imperial legacy and their inhabitants' welfare was and is Britain's responsibility.

The possession of these outposts was largely irrelevant to a nation which entered the 1980s in search of a new, post-imperial identity. It proved hard to find. For the past fourteen years Britain has been a wavering and lukewarm European power, forever wary of its partners' motives, and, at the same time, a zealous client of America.

The Commonwealth remained and today has forty-nine members, representing a quarter of the world's population. Its size is a reflection of the empire at its height and a reminder of Britain's impact on the world. The history of North America, most of Africa, India, the Middle and Far East has been shaped by Britain and in many of these regions English is still the language of the law, commerce, government and education. And yet, inexplicably, Britain's part in the transformation of the world is gradually being excluded from the history syllabuses of its schools. A generation will grow up whose knowledge of the empire, how it grew and what it did for its subjects and for Britain will be drawn from fiction and films.

The empire strikes back:
a Harrier lifts off somewhere off the Falklands.
(© MOD)

As a political force in the world, the Commonwealth's achievements have been severely limited. Throughout the 1970s and 1980s its regular heads of government meetings have been stormy with Britain's prime ministers having to endure hypocritical harangues about its handling of the Rhodesian crisis, and, more recently, its alleged half-heartedness in backing economic sanctions against South Africa. Mrs Thatcher found these occasions bothersome and did not always hide her feelings. Once, during the 1985 Nassau conference, she rounded on a Ugandan delegate after he had lectured her on racial discrimination, and reminded him of his country's shameful expulsion of its Asian population. Afro-Asian states are always touchy whenever attention is drawn to their racism. Moreover, sermons on human rights from leaders of those Commonwealth states which lock up dissidents or smother political debate sounded like humbug.

By contrast, the Commonwealth functions more smoothly and effectively at the middle and lower levels. Exchanges of ideas and cooperation in such practical areas as education, medicine, agriculture and technology provide an invaluable bridge between its rich and poor members. The sundry good works sponsored by its agencies provide vital assistance for developing nations and, in a way, are a fulfilment of the old ideals of benevolent imperialism. One feels that Joseph Chamberlain would have warmly approved of Canadian vets working to improve Kenyan cattle stocks or young men and women from Britain teaching English in Indian schools. He, and all those of similar mind, would have enjoyed seeing African, Asian and Chinese names among the lists of graduates from British universities and those attaining British professional qualifications in law and accountancy. What Edmund Burke once called the 'small platoons' of individuals with common interests and working together are strong and active throughout the Commonwealth. What they are achieving explains why two former Portuguese colonies, Angola and Mozambique, have recently applied to join it.

Royal tours of Commonwealth countries continue. These progresses generate much goodwill and provide plenty of excitement and fun for all involved, as well as occasional entertaining ruckuses over protocol. Queen Elizabeth II is known to have a strong affection for the Commonwealth and she undertakes her duties towards its members with charm and dignity. Her and her family's peregrinations have a deeper significance: they provide a sense of historic continuity for the former subjects of the empire and their descendants. They may, at times, regret their imperial past, but feel unable to turn their back on it and their former mentor. The Queen represents that shared past, and that she can return to her father's colonies as a welcomed and fêted guest may say something about the nature of imperial rule and how it was ended.

The Conservative governments which have ruled Britain since 1979 have not been noted for their strong sense of history. Indeed, Mrs Thatcher and those ideologically close to her have an instinctive dislike of arguments which appeal to past traditions, particularly of their own party. There is no room in the universal free market for sentimentality about days gone by, or public institutions whose survival has, in part, depended on a reverence for the ways things have always been done. Three of the latter, the Commonwealth Office, the British Council and the BBC World Service have suffered cuts in their budgets. These lacerations have been made in the name of economy and despite arguments that each of these public services has helped to win hearts, minds and friends throughout the world. Britain's international reputation as a moral and cultural force cannot be easily measured in terms of profit and loss.

The prevailing philosophy among Mrs Thatcher's and John Major's supporters has been that the empire, the Commonwealth and all that went with them in the way of obligations belong to the past. And yet unlooked for events in the Falkland Islands in 1982 and the termination of the ninety-nine-year lease of Hong Kong have made it impossible for either prime minister to escape from history. The Argentinian invasion of the Falkland Islands on 1–2 April 1982 was a bolt from the blue. Critics of the war which followed have claimed that the withdrawal of a British warship from the South Atlantic encouraged the Argentinian junta, and that intelligence assessments of its intentions were hopelessly mistaken. Be that

The Falkland Islands and their dependencies must remain British territory. No aggression and no invasion can alter that simple fact. It is the Government's objective to see that the Islands are freed from occupation and returned to British administration at the earliest moment . . . The people of the Falkland Islands, like the people of the United Kingdom are an island race . . . they are few in number, but they have the right to live in peace, to choose their own way of life and to determine their own allegiance. This way of life is British: their allegiance is to the crown.

MARGARET THATCHER

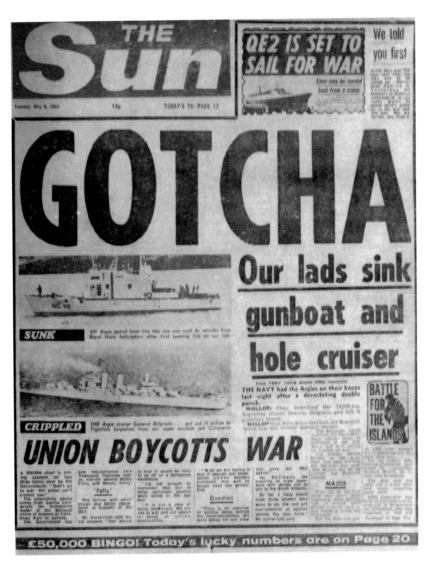

Jingoism revived:

The Sun *announces the*

sinking of the Belgrano.

as it may, there is also evidence to suggest that the clique of senior officers who ran the Argentine acted precipitately, and that the assault on the islands was mounted at less than twenty-four hours' notice. Britain reacted with a mixture of astonishment and fury.

The Falklands, although a colony, were an extension of Britain. Michael Foot, the Labour leader, reminded the Commons that the Argentinian junta was a collection of military thugs whose hands were stained with the blood of their countrymen. The Falkland Islanders should be delivered from their tyranny for they had a right to live in association with Britain and 'we have a moral duty, and a political duty, and every other kind of duty to ensure that that is sustained.' The mood of the Commons was angry and in favour of war; Julian Amery spoke for many on both sides when he referred to 'a stain on Britain's honour'.

So Britain embarked on its last imperial war to redeem its honour and recapture what had always been seen as one of the least of its colonies. It was ironic that many of the warships which steamed to the South Atlantic had been earmarked for the scrapyard by defence cuts proposed the year before by the Defence Secretary, John Nott. Alternately petulant and lugubrious, Nott appeared regularly on television with one of his civil servants, chosen it seemed for his funereal voice, to explain the daily course of the war. At the same time, a squad of military experts offered their interpretations of war as well as unsolicited advice. These armchair strategists were a substitute for first-hand footage of the fighting, which could not be transmitted directly.

The outcome of the war depended upon the cooperation of the United States, which was confronted with a war between a major and a minor Cold War ally. President Ronald Reagan plumped for Britain, despite pleas that such a choice would jeopardise relations with other South American states. During the campaign, United States weaponry and intelligence was placed at Britain's disposal.

American newscasters called this war 'the Empire strikes back'. Inside Britain, there was a strong, and at times unpleasantly strident feeling that a country that had for so long patiently endured knocks throughout the world was at last hitting back. A spirit of jingoism of Boer War vintage pervaded the popular press and reached its highest peak with the *Sun* headline 'Gotcha', which appeared over a photograph of the waterlogged Argentinian cruiser *General Belgrano*. The sinking of this formidable warship was one of the most controversial episodes in the war. Orders to intercept and destroy it had been given after signals intelligence revealed that it was about to engage the British task force.

Those who were, in principle, opposed to the war claimed that the torpedoes which holed the *Belgrano* ended all chances of a negotiated peace, although there was very little evidence to suggest that the Argentinian junta was on the verge of a *volte face*. What upset the left more than the fate of the

Belgrano was the way in which the war revealed the depth and intensity of residual, aggressive John-Bullish patriotism. It seemed strongest among sections of the working class; a few days after the invasion of the Falkland Islands, a body of skinheads gathered outside a recruiting office in the Midlands, demanded rifles, and were angry when told that they would need to be trained. Old, belligerent, imperial emotions had not been dispelled by the disappearance of empire, and they surfaced again during the 1991 war against Iraq. It might also be said that they are frequently heard, seen and felt whenever English soccer teams play abroad. A sizeable body of young working-class men now regard an away match in Europe as a chance to create mayhem, and they seem unstoppable. There is much official hand-wringing, in which Dr Johnson's observation about what is called insolence in the masses in time of peace being called courage in time of war, is conveniently forgotten. Whatever else it may have done to the national character, the loss of empire and world power has not made the British less aggressive.

The reconquest of the Falklands at the end of May was a triumph for the stamina and courage of Britain's fighting men, and a tribute to the resolution of Mrs Thatcher. It also gave a fresh lustre to national pride which had become tarnished after years of retreat from empire, economic debility and internal industrial strife. Overnight, Britain had been transformed from a passive nation, an international has-been to which things happened, into a power to be reckoned with. What was, in effect, Britain's last imperial war, fought in unforeseen and extraordinary circumstances, reversed a string of humiliations going back to Suez. It also enhanced the reputation of Mrs Thatcher, now the 'Iron Lady', and helped her win a second term of office in 1983.

Disengagement from Hong Kong has occasioned no flag-waving. Most of the mainland colony had been leased from China in 1898 and Hong Kong island had been acquired as a result of the 1839–42 Opium War. The colony's existence since 1949 has depended on the tolerance of the People's Republic of China which, as heir-general of the Manchus, acquired the right to reoccupy what its predecessor had granted away. For these reasons, successive British governments had not treated Hong Kong like other parts of the empire and its people were not prepared for self-government in the 1950s and 1960s. The official line with the Hong Kong Chinese was Louis Phillippe's dictum '*enrichissez-vous*', and the colony prospered, becoming, by the 1980s, one of the leading commercial and banking centres of the Far East. As the rest of China began to share in the boom and, tentatively, to embrace capitalism, it appeared that when the time came for it to resume control over Hong Kong, it would treat it gently as a valuable asset.

Sunset postponed:
British troops on
the Falklands.
(© IWM)

Ending in tears:
Chris Patten sheds a tear
at the ceremony which
hands over power to Hong
Kong: Prince Charles
(left) looks concerned.
(© Popperfoto)

This may have been wishful thinking, designed to assuage the fears of the people of Hong Kong and make the task of the British government easier. From 1984 onwards it had been willing to allow limited representative government in Hong Kong, and had pledged that democratic institutions would survive the transfer of power. The terms of this had been agreed by 1989, but the mass shootings of pro-democracy dissidents in Tiananmen Square, Peking were a brutal reminder that China was an authoritarian state. The British government faced a quandary: on one hand it knew that China possessed a *force majeure* which it could not match, and, on the other, it was under pressure from Hong Kong to speed up the process of democratisation. But to follow this course would provoke China and so the future of Hong Kong became a struggle between expediency and principle.

The new governor, a former Conservative minister, Chris Patten, appointed in 1992, adopted a traditional paternalist line, insisting that 'Our responsibilities to Hong Kong's citizens come first.' He pressed ahead with the introduction of reforms for elections in 1994 in the teeth of opposition from China, which, in December 1993, withdrew from discussions of the issue. The solution is presently far from clear, nor can it be certain that China's ageing ruling élite will be in place for much longer.

The issue of Hong Kong's future is about more than the last act of imperial disengagement. Governor Patten and his supporters have put forward classic imperial arguments involving a duty towards Britain's subjects. Their adversaries claim that such moral responsibilities are a luxury which modern Britain cannot afford. Career diplomats believe that muted sycophancy is the best approach to Peking, which, if offended, might harm British trade or worse.

In the past fourteen years, variations on the view that commercial considerations are always paramount have carried great weight within Thatcherite circles in the Conservative party. While making much of herself as a global champion of democracy, Mrs Thatcher has not shrunk from currying favour with autocrats, most notably King Fahd of Saudi Arabia and the sheiks of the Persian Gulf, all of whom are customers for British-made weaponry. What might be called the policy of guns before principles led her government to grovel to the Saudis in 1982 after they made a fuss about a television film, *Death of a Princess*. By contrast, Mrs Thatcher dealt sharply with a loyal ally, the gallant and humane King Hussain of Jordan, when he chose to tread cautiously after his powerful neighbour, Iraq, invaded Kuwait in 1990. The moral imperative which lay behind the Falklands War did not extend into other areas of foreign policy.

Another moral issue emerged during the debates over the future of Hong Kong. This was the question of whether large numbers of Hong Kong Chinese should be admitted to Britain. The 1948 British Nationality Act had extended British citizenship to subjects in all the colonies. As it passed through the Commons, the steamer *Empire Windrush* docked at Tilbury and four hundred West Indian immigrants came ashore. Like the English, Scots and Irish who had crossed the Atlantic in the seventeenth and eighteenth centuries, they had left poverty behind them and come in search of prosperity.

The years which saw the dissolution of the empire witnessed the last of the great migrations it had made possible. From 1948 onwards large numbers of West Indians, Indians and Pakistanis and smaller numbers of West Africans, Maltese and Cypriots settled in Britain. The flow of immigrants gathered pace in the late 1950s and early 1960s and continued after two acts of 1962 and 1968 which were designed to restrict it. This is not the place to discuss the consequences of this shift of populations for Britain, which, by the 1970s had become a multi-racial society, even though the bulk of the new arrivals had settled in London, the Midlands and the decayed industrial towns of northern England. Reactions to this demographic change have been mixed and often, as they had been towards the Irish in the nineteenth century, violent. Old imperial attitudes played their part in determining how the immigrants were received. Imperial ideas of racial superiority led to condescension or even contempt, but at the same time benevolent imperial paternalism dictated that blacks and Asians should be treated decently and fairly. How the immigrants, their children and grandchildren fare will depend ultimately on the moral sense and flexibility of the British people.

The story of the rise and yet-to-be-completed fall of the British empire suggests that they once had both qualities in abundance, as well as ruthlessness and rapacity. A superficial glance at Britain's imperial past can lead to the conclusion that the last two were always in the forefront, but this is misleading. Britain's empire was a moral force and one for the good. The last word should lie with Nelson Mandela, recalling his schooldays in Natal in the 1920s:

> *You must remember I was brought up in a British school, and at the time Britain was the home of everything that was best in the world. I have not discarded the influence which Britain and British history and culture exercised on us. We regarded it as the capital of the world and visiting the place therefore had this excitement because I was visiting the country that was my pride . . . You must also remember that Britain is the home of parliamentary democracy and, as people fighting against a form of tyranny in this country, we look upon Britain to take an active interest to support us in our fight against apartheid.*

Few empires have equipped their subjects with the intellectual wherewithal to overthrow their rulers. None has been survived by so much affection and moral respect.

PICTURE CREDITS

Australian War Memorial 197 (negative number A05215), 226 (negative number P1732.001), 279 (negative number VIC1410A); Blair Athol Estate 65, 132–3; Boston Picture Library 10, 59; British Library 34, 63, 119, 122 (top right & bottom), 130; British Museum 51, 57; Camera Press 333, 335; Christie's Images 114; Church of Scotland World Missions 86, 263, 265, 288; Conway Library, Courtauld Institute of Art 113; Country Life Picture Library 25, 89, 137; Crown Copyright/Royal Commission on the Historical Monuments of England 69; e.t. archive 92, 105; Foreign and Commonwealth Office 115 (top), 178; The Fotomas Index (UK) 21; Hulton Getty Picture Library 202; Imperial War Museum 88 (both), 117, 140, 158 (bottom), 160, 161 (top), 200 (top), 215, 225 (both), 227, 228, 229 (both), 231 (both), 243, 247, 256, 258 (bottom), 259 (all), 280, 282 (both), 285, 286, 309, 310, 316, 327, 339; The Kobal Collection 173, 268 (both), 269 (both), 270–1; Mary Evans Picture Library 17, 27, 29, 55, 83; Ministry of Defense 336; National Army Museum 30, 66, 68 (top), 84, 93, 97, 98, 102 (bottom),103 (top), 107 (both), 121 (both), 122 (top left), 123, 124, 125, 127, 128, 134 (both), 135 (both), 139, 141, 142, 151, 152, 153, 154 (both), 155, 157, 167, 168, 171, 172, 174, 175, 176, 188, 191 (both), 201 (middle & bottom), 212 (middle); National Library of Scotland 95, 99, 112; National Maritime Museum 35, 36, 80; By courtesy of the National Portrait Gallery 71, 75, 79, 211; Robert Opie Collection 94, 101, 106, 110 (both), 111 (both), 163 (both), 203 (right), 205, 206, 207 (both), 219 (all); Peter Newark's American Pictures 22; P&O 90, 212 (top), 221, 267 (top, bottom right); Popperfoto 281, 292, 295, 297, 298, 317, 318, 319, 340; PRO (Public Record Office) 15, 183, 222, 278 (all); Qantas 266, 267 (left); The Royal Collection © Her Majesty The Queen 47; Gerald Scarfe from Scarfe's People/Centre for the Study of Cartoons and Caricature, University of Kent, Canterbury 334; Scottish Record Office 195 (both); Collection of Michael Staniforth 81; By kind permission of Unilever Historical Archives 180 (both), 181, 182, 276, 329; Warburg Institute/Royal Commission on the Historical Monuments of England 41; Wilberforce House Museum, Hull/Bridgeman Art Library 91; Collection of A.V. Williams 3, 78, 87, 158 (top), 177; The Provost and Fellows of Worcester College, Oxford 44, 46; Yale Center for British Art, Paul Mellon Collection 39. All remaining illustrations are from the author's own collection or other private collections.

Every effort has been made to trace the copyright holders but if any have been inadvertently overlooked the publishers will be pleased to make the necessary arrangements at the first opportunity.

INDEX

Countries have been indexed under the name by which they were known at the time, with references to alternative names. Numbers in *italics* refer to the pages containing illustrations.

Abbas II, Khedive, 167–8, *175*
ABC for Baby Patriots, An, 113
Abdullah, King of Transjordan, 245
Abdullah bin Muhammad Khalifah, 114, 171, *175*, 176
Abercromby, General Lord, 45–6
aborigines, 72, 194
Abu Klea, battle of (1885), 170
Abukir Bay, battle of (1798), 79
Abyssinia (Ethiopia): 19th-century campaigns, 96, 98; Italian ambitions, 172, 174, 240; Mussolini invades, 248
Accra, 297
D'Achée, comte, 40
Acheson, Dean, 311
Adams, John, 56
Addison, Richard, 29
Aden, 288, 298, 309, *317, 318, 319*
Admiralty, 40, 41, 71, 216, 309, 311
advertising, 114–15
Afghanistan, 80, 96, 101, 116–17, 123–4, *200*, 334
Africa: slave trade, 21–2; 'new imperialism', 104; 'scrambles' for, 177; missionaries, 179, 182; British methods of control, 181–2; newspaper accounts of, 181–2; First World War, 223; 'backwardness', 262; Second World War, 286; post-war expectations, 286; independence, 335; *see also* East Africa; North Africa; West Africa *and individual countries*
African National Congress, 328
African National Council, 334
Afrikaners, 225
Agra, 126, 128–9
Agyeman, Sir Osei, 289
Air Ministry, 294–5, 309
air travel, 266
Aix-la-Chapelle, Peace of (1748), 36, 37
Ajax, Operation, 312
Albemarle, Lord, 39–40

Alcock and Brown, 266
Alexandria, 165–6, 240, 311, 314
Algeria, 97–8, 246, 320–1, 329–30
Ali, Rashid, 249
Ali Dinar, Sultan of Darfur, 176–7
All-African Peoples Conference, 327
Allenby, Field-Marshal Viscount, 227–8, 229, 238–9, 240, *241*
Amboina Island, 22–3
American Intercourse Bill (1781), 58
American Union Pacific Railroad, 185–6
American War of Independence, 31, 40–1, *51*, 53–9
Amery, Julian, 338
Amery, Leo, *211*; supporter of Milner, 203–4, 211; support for Zionism, 246
Amherst, Lord, 136–7
Amherst, Major-General Jeffrey, 45–7, 53
Amin, General Idi, 323, 634
Amoy, 136–8
Amritsar, 250, 252–3, 279
Andaman Islands, 283
Anglo-American War (1812), 74
Anglo-Egyptian Treaty (1936), 240, 312–13, 314
Anglo-Egyptian War (1882), 166–8
Anglo-Iranian (Persian) Oil Company, 245, 310–11
Anglo-Iraqi Treaty (1930), 245–6, 249
Anglo-Irish Treaty (1921), 236–7
Anglo-Japanese alliance (1902), 141–4, 214–15, 216–17
Anglo-Russian Convention (1907), 215
Anglo-Saxon character, 109–12, 117
Angola, 85, 320–1, 338
Anne, Queen, 284
Anson, Admiral Sir George, 38
Antarctica, 72
Anti-Jacobin, 77
anti-semitism, 246, 247
Anti-Smoking League, 210
Antigua, 19, 28–9, 93–4
Anzac Day, 229–30
Anzacs, 195–6, 224, 225–6
apartheid, 195–6, 296
Arab Revolts, 226–7, 246, 247–9
Arabs: nationalism, 226–7, 243–9; independence movements, 233;

and Zionism, 246; and Jewish immigration to Palestine, 247; Second World War, 286; and the creation of Israel, 309–10
Argentina, 280, 338–41
Armitage, Sir Robert, 327–9, 330
Arnold, Benedict, 54
Arnold, Dr Thomas, 109–12
Arrow, 139
Asante, 95–6, 185–6, 190
Ascension Island, *262*, 281–2, 336
Asquith, Herbert, 206, 216–17, 236
Atatürk, Kamal, 226, 238
Atlantic Charter, 287–8
atomic bombs, 290–1, 293, 294–5, 308–9, 311
Attlee, Clement, 9; and the Atlantic Charter, 287–8; Yalta and Potsdam conferences, 290; and the atomic bomb, 294–5, 308; wants to withdraw from Mediterranean and Middle East, 295–6; Cold War, 296; and Indian independence, 301–3, 305; Iranian crisis, 311
Auchinleck, Field-Marshal, 305
Australia, 70–5; Cook claims for Britain, 71–2; aborigines, 72, 194; convicts transported to, 74; trade with Britain, 86; independence movement, 96–7; and imperial unity, 109; self-government, 113, 194–5; expansionists, 146–8; emigration to, 192–5; distinctive identity, 195–6; defences, 196–7, 216; and the Boer War, 198–9; emotional kinship with Britain, 199; First World War, 218, 223–5, 228, 229–30; cricket, 272; war declared, 275–7; Second World War, 283–3, 286, 291
Austria, 78–9, 80–1, 82–3
Austria-Hungary, 217–18, 225–6, 228, 229
Aztecs, 16

Bacchus, Charles, 23
Bacon, Sir Francis, 16–17
Bacon, Nathaniel, 25
Badahur Shah, 125–6
Baden-Powell, Major-General Sir Robert, *202*, 210
Baggal, 190–1
Baghdad Pact, 296, 315, 316

Bahamas, 25
Baker, Sir Stanley, 264
Baldwin, Stanley, 240, 260
Balfour, Arthur, 228, *233*
Balfour Declaration (1917), 243, 244, 245–6
Balkans, 217–18, 225–6
Baltimore, Lord, 14
Baluchi tribesmen, 123–4
Banda, Dr Hastings, 300, 327–30
Bangalore, 124
Banks, Sir Joseph, 72, 74
Barbados, 18–19, *20–2*, 24, 26, 28–9
Barbados Company, 18–19
Barcelona, 34
Baring, Sir Evelyn, *see* Cromer, Lord
Barker, Lieutenant George, 126–8
Bart, Jean, 32
al-Barzani, Sheik Mahmud, 243
Basutoland, 154–5, *263, 321*
Batavia, 22–3
Baylen, 83
BBC, 248–9, 260–1, *262–3*, 266–72, 296
BBC World Service, 337
'Beaconsfieldism', 101
Beale, Anthony, 29
Beatty, Lady, 217
beaver pelts, 24, 42
Bechuanaland, 108–9, 156
Bedford, Duke of, 39–40
Bee Hive, 97
Belgium, *186–7*, 218, 279, 320–1
Belize, 233, 287–8
Bell, Gertrude, 242
Benbow, Vice-Admiral John, 34
Bengal, 60, 62–3, 126, 210, 250, 285
Bengal Horse Artillery, *122*
Bentinck, Captain John, 35
Bentinck, Lord William, 120–2
Berkeley, Sir William, 24–5
Bermuda, 285–6, 287–8, 336
Bevan, Aneurin, 328–9
Beveridge, Senator A. J., 104–5
Beveridge report, 283–4
Bevin, Ernest, 293, 295–6, 302, 309–10
Bhagat Singh, *254*
Bharatpur, 64, 69, *119*
Bida, 189
Birley, Thomas, Bishop of Zanzibar, *262–3*, 264

Birmingham, 31–2
Bismarck, Prince Otto von, 146–8
Bismarck Archipelago, 148
Black and Tans, 235–6, 244–5
'blackbirds', *147*
blacks: slavery, 20–2, 28–9, 56–7, 72–3, 146–8; 'noble savage', 72–4, 95, 96–7; in First World War, 230–2; 'backwardness', 262; desire for self-government, 262–4; stereotypes, 262–3; colour bar, 263–5, 266; race riots, 263–4; in Second World War, 285–6; *see also* racism
Blackstone, Chief Justice, 72
Blair, Tony, *340*
Blatchford, Robert, 208–9
Blathwayt, William, *25*
Bligh, William, *71*, 72–3
'Blimp, Colonel', 184–5, 260
Blücher, Marshal, 82–3
Blunt, Wilfred Scawen, 166–8
bodyline controversy, 272
Boer War, 8–9, 113, 114–15, 116–17, *158–61*, 162–4, 184, 197, 198, 202, 205
Boers, 108–9, 149–51, 152–3, 154–6, 160–2, 183–4, 225
Bombay, 60, *114*
Bonaparte, Joseph, 82
Bonny, *181*, *182*
Boot, Operation, 312
Borden, Sir Robert, 218
Borgu, 189–90
Borneo, 142–5, 287–8; *see also* North Borneo
Boscawen, Edward, 38, 39, 45–6
Boston, 24, 27, 53, 54–5
'Boston Massacre' (1770), 50–1
Botany Bay, 74
Botha, Louis, 217
Bougainville, Louis-Antoine de, 71–3
Boulton, Matthew, 73–4
Bourne, Colonel, 153–4
Boutros-Ghali, Boutros, 240
Bowring, John, 138–9
Boxer Rebellion, 141–2
Boy Scouts, *202*, 210, 214
Boys Brigade, 210
Boys' Own Paper, 112
Braddock, Bessie, 318
Braddock, General Edward, 14–15, 44–6
Bradford Exchange, 89
Braide, Chief Will, *180*
Brazza, Savorgnan de, 186–7
Brereton, Captain F. S., 113
Bright, John, 96–7

Bristol, 8
British Columbia, 216
British Council, 337–8
British East Africa, 182–3; *see also* Kenya
British Empire Exhibition (1924–5), 272–3
British Expeditionary Force, 218
British Guiana, 86, 188, 248–9
British Honduras (Belize), 233, 287–8
British Imperial East Africa Company, 156–8, 171–2, 173–4, 180–4
British Nationality Act (1948), 341
British South Africa Company, *158*
Brooke, Sir James, 142–5, 156, 186–7
Brown, George, 95
Brown, William, 160–1
Brunei, 144–5
Buchan, John, 211
Buenos Aires, 82
Bulfin, General Sir Edward, 238–9
Buller, General Sir Redvers, 163–4
Bülow, Prince von, 148
Burgoyne, General, 40–1, 56
Burke, Edmund, 51–2, 63–4, 66–8, 205–6, 251, 338
Burma, 95–6, *130*, 256–7, 283, 285–6, 296
Burma War (1824), 122–3, 124
Burnaby, Colonel Frederick, 170
Burnet, Gilbert, Bishop of Salisbury, 20–1
Burton, Sir Richard, 122–3
Bute, Marquess of, 39–40
Butler, R. A., 332
Byng, Admiral John, 38

Cabot, John, 17
Caetano, President, 320–1
Cairo, 239, *240*
Cairo Conference (1921), 244–5
Calcutta, 60, 62–3, 68, 123–4, 126–8, 302
Caledon, Lord, 149
Cambridge Union, 96
Cameroons, 228–9, 260–2
Campbell, General Sir Colin, *127*, 128–9
Campbell-Bannerman, Sir Henry, 215–16
Canada, 95–6; conflicts between Britain and France in, 36, 39–40, 45–7; Catholicism, 52; and American War of Independence, 54–5, 59; North-West Passage, 72; trade with Britain, 86;

independence movement, 96–7; self-government, 113, 194–6; emigration to, 192–5; French population, 196–8; and the Boer War, 198–9; defences, 216; First World War, 218, 223, 225, 229–30; Second World War, 276–7, 283, 286, 291; trade with America, 322
Canal Zone, *see* Suez Canal
Canary Islands, 24
Canton, 136–9
Cape Breton Island, 36
Cape Colony, 83, 96, 149–55, 194–6
Cape Finisterre, 36
Cape Florida, 27–8
Cape of Good Hope, 22–3
Cape Horn, 70
Cape Town, 77–9, 81–2, 149
capital, overseas investment, 86
Caribbean, *see* West Indies
Carleton, General Guy, 54–5
Carnarvon, Lord, 152–3
Carnatic, 60–2, 63–4
Carolina, 21
Caroline Islands, 148
Carrington, Lord, 335
Carson, Sir Edward, 235
Cartagena, 36
Carter, Sir Gilbert, *178*
Castlereagh, Viscount, 87–8
Catherine of Weymouth, 12
Catholic Church, 14, 51–2, 235
Cavendish College, Cambridge, 113
Cawnpore, 126, 128–9
Cayman Islands, 336
Central Africa, 170–7, 327
Central African Federation, 327–30, 332
Central Intelligence Agency (CIA), 312, 314
Cetshwayo, *153*, *154*
Ceylon, 41, 77–8
Chamberlain, Austen, 264
Chamberlain, Joseph, 105–8, 182–3, 338; background, 109–12; imperialism, 109–12; Royal Navy loses control of Mediterranean, 116–17; and the Matabele Wars, 158–60; and the Jameson Raid, 162; East African railway, 183–4; and West Africa, 188, 189–90; Irish Home Rule, 197–9; tariff reform campaign, 203–5, 206–7
Chamberlain, Neville, 275, 315; and Indian independence, 274; declares war, 275

Chandra Sahib, 60–1
Chapman, George, 11–12, 15
Charge of the Light Brigade, The (film), 269
charities, emigration help, 192
Charles I, King, 14, 18–19, 24–5
Charles II, King, 21–2
Charles Edward, Prince (the 'Young Pretender'), 36
Charles, Prince of Wales, *202*, *340*
Charleston, 29
Chartists, 194–5
Chatham, Lord, *see* Pitt, William
Chelmsford, 2nd Baron, 153–5
Chelmsford, 1st Viscount, 251–2, 260
Chesapeake Bay, 12–13, 26–7
Chesney, Sir George, 116
Chiang Kai-Shek, General, 290
Childers, Erskine, 113, 116
China, 95–6, 136–44; trade, 26, 105–8; Opium Wars, 136–9; suppression of piracy, 137–9; Britain dominates commerce, 140–1; 'new imperialism', 140; Sino–Japanese War, 140–1, 248–9, 280–1; Boxer Rebellion, 141–2; American post-war plans for, 290; Communism, 312; and Hong Kong, 339–40
Chinese: emigration, 193–4; indentured labourers in South Africa, 204–5
Chinese Eastern Railway, 140–1
Chinese Labour Corps, 223
Ching dynasty, 136–7
Chinkiang, 137–8
Chirau, Chief, 333–5
Chitral, *200*, *201*
Choiseul, Étienne-François, duc de, 39, 40
Christianity, 85; missionaries, 179, 182
Chums, 112
Church of England, 14, 50, 210–11
Churchill, Winston, 210, 273–4, *281*, 314, 315, 332; *Malakand Field Force*, 131; in the Sudan, 174–5; and tariff reform, 204–5; Gallipoli campaign, 225–6; and Ireland, 236–7; and the Kurds, 243; air control of Iraq and Jordan, 245; support for Zionism, 246; and Indian independence, 274; Second World War, 279–82, 283; Atlantic Charter, 287–8; and SEAC, 288; Operation Culverin, 290–1; Cold War, 293–4; Iranian crisis, 311
cinema, 272–4, 323, 324

Civil War, 24

Clarkson, Thomas, 91–3

class, 27–8, 284–5

Claydon House, Buckinghamshire, 137

Clemenceau, Georges, 244

Clinton, Sir Henry, 54, 56–8

Clive, Robert, 9, 38–9, 61–4, 66, 142–4, 208–9

Clunies-Ross, John, 142–4

Clydeside, xiii, 192–3

Cobden, Richard, 89

Cochin China, 97–8

Cochrane, Lieutenant Charles, 54–5

Cockerell, Sir Charles, 8, 89

Cocos-Keeling islands, 142–4

Colbert, Jean-Baptiste, 32

Cold War, 293–8, 299, 300–2, 308–9, 311–12, 321

Collins, Michael, 236, 237

Colonial Development Acts, 294

Colonial Development Board, 294

Colonial Office: suppresses slave uprising in British Guiana, 93–4; and Australian expansionism, 146–8; political development of South Africa, 151–2; and Northern Rhodesia, 160–1; and East Africa, 182–3; Kenya policy, 184–5; and West Africa, 190–1; First World War, 223–4, 230; racial prejudice, 223–4; Arab Revolt, 226–7; and the Middle East, 244–5; in Second World War, 285–6; Atlantic Charter, 287–8; post-war plans, 294; and press freedom, 296–7; and colonial self-government, 297; and the Central African Federation, 327–8

colour bar, 263–5, 266

Commerson, Philibert, 72–3

Committee of Imperial Defence, 166–8, 216–17

Commonwealth of Nations, 296, 299; transformation of empire to, 237; racism, 265; as surrogate empire, 296; and the Suez war, 316; trade with, 322; present situation, 337–9

Commonwealth Office, 338–9

Communism: subversion, 233–4, 296–7; in India, 254; Cold War, 293–5; Malayan guerrilla campaign, 294–5, 299–300; anti-colonial propaganda, 296; and decolonisation, 321

Compagnie des Indes, 60–2

Compagnie van Verre, 22–3

Company of Royal Adventurers, 21–2

Congo, 320–1; see also Zaïre

Congo Free State, 105–8, 170–2

Congreve, General Walter, 238–9

conscription, 214, 224–5

Conservative party: foreign policy, 97–8; Joseph Chamberlain splits, 109–12; and tariff reform, 204–5, 206–7; and Irish Home Rule, 206; attitudes to imperialism, 260; and the Commonwealth, 296; and the Middle East, 308; Cold War, 309; Iranian crisis, 311; British occupation of Canal Zone ended, 314; and the Suez war, 318; decolonisation policies, 321–2; African policies, 332

Continental Congress, 49, 52, 53, 56

convicts: North American colonies, 14; West Indies, 20; transportation to Australia, 74; in West Africa, 184–5

Cook, Captain James, 46, 70–4, 75

Cooke, Joseph, 218

Coote, Sir Eyre, 69

Cornwallis, General Sir Charles, 41, 56–9, 64, 66, 68–9

Cortés, Hernán, 16

cotton, 58, 60, 86, 140–1

Cowper, William, 53, 71

Cranworth, Lord and Lady, 184

cricket, 272

Crimean War (1854–6), 89, 96, 100–1, 151–2

Cripps, Sir Stafford, 256

Cromer, Lord, 166, 168–9, 177

Cromwell, Oliver, 20

Cronjé, Piet, 163

Crossman, Richard, 308

Cruisers and Convoys Act (1708), 34

Cuba, 86

Cuddadur, 69

Culverin, Operation, 290–1

Curaçao, 77–8

Curragh Incident, 206–7

Curtis, Lionel, 211

Curzon, Marquess, 228, 309; Viceroy of India, 108–9, 118–19, 130; First World War, 229; and Ireland, 237; and Indian independence, 251

Cyprus, 100–1, 287–8, 296–7, 299–300, 309, 321–2

Czechoslovakia, 294, 312

Daily Express, The, 314

Daily Graphic, The, 114

Daily Mail, The, 108, 211

Dalhousie, Lord, 125–6

Dalrymple, Stair, 60–1

Dardanelles, 225–7, 245, 293–4

Dartmouth, Lord, 47–8, 53–4

Darwin, Charles, 85, 109

De Valera, Eamon, 234, 236–7

Death of a Princess (film), 341

Declaration of Independence, 56

decolonisation, 299–300, 320, 323

Decouer, Captain, 188

Defoe, Daniel, 15, 20

Delagoa Railway, 161–2

Delcassé, Théophile, 170–1, 176–7

Delhi, 126, 128, 129, 273

Demerara, 77–8

Deng Xiaoping, 630, 632

Denmark, 279

Derby, Lord, 97–8

Dervishes, 168–9, 170, 176–7

Deutsche-See-Handels-Gesellschaft, 148

Devastation, HMS, 100

Devlin, Lord, 328–9

Diamond Jubilee (1897), 113, 115, 198–9

Dickens, Charles, 89, 95

Dieskau, Johann Herman von, 45

Dilke, Sir Charles, 108–9, 165–6

Dillon, Michael, 175–6

Diqna, Uthman, 168–9

Directorate of Army Education, 288

Discovery, 70

Disraeli, Benjamin, 98–101, 309, 329–30

Dobbie, James, 193

Dr Barnado's, 192

documentary films, 274

Dodecanese Islands, 290–1

Dolphin, 24

Dominica, 39–40, 294

dominions: self-government, 194–6; and idea of imperial federation, 211; defences, 216–17; First World War, 218; conscription, 224–5; and Irish 'Troubles', 236–7; India offered dominion status, 254; and the Cold War, 296; see also individual countries

Donne, John, 15

Dost Muhammad, 129

Drake, Sir Francis, 12, 16, 18, 29

Dreadnought-class battleships, 215–16, 294–5

Driberg, Tom, 288

Drum, The (film), 268

Dufferin, Lord, 130

Dulles, John Foster, 314, 315–16

Duncan, Admiral Lord, 78–9, 82–3

Dundas, Henry, 77–8, 79–80

Dundonald, Lord, 170

Dunedin, 198

Dunmore, Lord, 56–7

Dupleix, Joseph-François, Marquis, 60–2

Duplessis, Maurice, 276–7

Duquesne, Marquis, 43–4

D'Urban, Sir Benjamin, 150

Durham, Lord, 194–5

Dutch East India Company, 149

Dutch East Indies, 283, 293–4; see also Indonesia

Dutt, Palme, 284

Dutton, Sir Richard, 20–1

Dyer, Brigadier-General Reginald, 252–3, 279

Dyrham Park, 25

East Africa, 108–9, 178–91, 286, 327

East India Company: textile trade, 21–3; expansion of, 23; directors as MPs, 31–2; Tea Act (1773), 50–1; power in India, 69; Bengal War, 62–4; conflicts with French, 62; trade with China, 72; autocratic paternalism, 119–23; opium trade, 136; tea trade, 136; and James Brooke, 142–4; dissolution, 129

East India House, 34

East Indies, 77–8, 142–4

Easter Rising (1916), 174–5, 225, 233–4

Economist, The, 140, 166

Eden, Sir Anthony, 279; and the Arab Revolt, 247–8; Suez war, 315–17, 318; and Iranian crisis, 312; wants overthrow of Nasser, 312, 315

Edinburgh, 8–9

Edinburgh, Philip, Duke of, 302–3, 324, 329

Edmondson, Judge George, 129

education: public schools, 109–12, 210, 250–1, 284, 323, 324; in India, 119–22, 129–30, 250–1

Edward VII, King, 202

Edward VIII, King, 273, 274

Edwardes, Herbert, 118–19

Egypt, 165–77, 220, 238–41, 308–14, 315–19; Napoleon invades, 64, 79–81; British occupation of, 108–9; nationalism, 165–8, 205–6, 238–41; Anglo-Egyptian War (1882), 166–8; British occupation, 166–8, 215; importance of Nile to, 170–2;

France tries to regain interest in, 173–4, 175–7; independence movement, 233; Anglo-Egyptian Treaty, 240, 312–13, 314; Second World War, 240–1; Suez war, 296, 315–19, 320; importance in Cold War, 308–9; British occupation of Canal Zone ended, 312–14; July Revolution, 314; Eden wants Nasser's overthrow, 315, 316; Soviet influence, 315

Eisenhower, Dwight D., 312
El Dorado, 11–12
Elgin, Lord, 138–9
Elizabeth I, Queen, 15–16, 284
Elizabeth II, Queen, 324, 338–9
Ellenborough, Lord, 119–20, 123–4
Elliot, Captain Charles, 136–7
emigration: to North America, 14–15, 26–9, 48–9; to dominions, 192–5, 199; to Britain, 341
Empire Day, 208–10
Empire Day League, 208–9
Empire of India Exhibition (1895), 118
Empire Windrush, 341
Endeavour, 72
English Channel, 41, 80–1
entente cordiale, 215
EOKA, 315–16
Equatoria, 171–2
Española, 18
es-Said, Nuri, 249, 315–16
Essequibo, 77–8
Essex, USS, 74
'establishment', 323
d'Estaing, comte, 41
Ethiopia, *see* Abyssinia
Evangelicals, 68–9, 91–3, 188–95
Evans, Ernest, 260

Fabians, 202–3, 204–5
Faisal I, King of Iraq, 244–5, 248–9
Falkland Islands, 78, 280, 287–8, 339–41
Falklands war (1982), 336–41
Fallis, Keith, 230
Farquharson-Roberts, Brigadier M. F., 316
Faruq, King of Egypt, 240–1, 314
fascism, 286
Fashoda, 174, 175–7
Fiddes, Sir George, 231–2
Fiji, 145–8, 193–4, 283, 287–8, 324
films, 268–71, 274
Fink, Molly, 264
First World War, 223–32; patriotism, 211, 214, 218, 230; origins of, 214–15; German naval

rearmament, 214–18; war-mongering, 214; Royal Navy modernisation, 214–18; defence of dominions, 216–17; war declared, 218; soldiers from the dominions, 223–5; India in, 224–32, 251; conscription, 224–5; post-war settlements, 227–9; armistice, 229; casualties, 229–30; jingoism, 260
Fisher, Admiral Lord, 149, *168*, 214–16, 217–18
Fisher, Andrew, 216
Fitzalan, Lord, *236*
Fleetwood, Bishop, 20–1
Fleming, Lieutenant, 150–2
Florida, 41
Foochow, 137–8
Foot, Michael, 338
Forbes, Brigadier John, 45–6
Foreign Office, 87–8, 160–1, 226–7, 240–1, 285–6
Formosa (Taiwan), 140–1
Fort Duquesne, 67
Fort Wafir, 326
Four Feathers, The (film), *173*, 270–1
Foxe, John, 18
France: North American interests, 24–5; wars with Britain in eighteenth century, 31–4, 36, 38–40; conflicts with Britain in North America, 36, 37, 42–7; naval rearmament, 40–1, 116–17; and American War of Independence, 40–1; North American fur trade, 42–4; Indian interests, 60–2; Napoleonic Wars, 76–83; 19th-century relations with Britain, 87–8; Franco-Prussian War, 89, 185–6; empire-building, 97–8; Opium Wars, 138–9; interest in Indo-China, 140–1; 'new imperialism', 146; and Egypt, 165–6; contest for Central Africa, 171–2; interest in West Africa, 185–90; *entente cordiale*, 215; First World War, 218, 224–5; Middle Eastern interests, 244; Second World War, 279; and Indo-China, 293–4; Suez war, 316–19; Algerian War, 320–1
Franco, General, 179
Franco-Prussian War (1870–1), 185–6
Franklin, Benjamin, 47–8, 50
Franz-Ferdinand, Archduke, 217–18
Frederick II, King of Prussia, 38–9
free trade, 86, 104–8, 202–3

French, Field-Marshal Lord, 234
French Congo, 171–2
French Revolution, 76
Frere, Sir Bartle, 153–5
Freycinet, Charles de, 186
Frobisher, Sir Martin, 16
Fuad, King of Egypt, 239–40
Fulani tribe, 190–1
fur trade, 42–4
Furse, Sir Ralph, 284, 298

Gallacher, Willie, 287
Gallieni, Joseph Simon, 177
Gallipoli, 226, 229–30
Gama, Vasco da, 22–3
Gambia, 21–2, 74, 184–5, 186–7, 287–8, 294, 321–2
Gammans, Captain Leonard, 321–2
Gandhi, Mohandas, 236, 238, *251*, 253, 254–5; First World War, 231–2; passive resistance, 233, 251–4; background, 250–1; importance of, 253–4; in Second World War, 256; 'Quit India' campaign, 256–7; imprisonment, 300; Indian independence, 302
Garrick, David, 40
Gaspée, 51
Gates, General Horatio, 56
General Belgrano, 338, 341
General Post Office, 272–3
George II, King, 35–6, 46
George III, King, 39, 227; and the Seven Years War, 39–40; North American colonies, 48, 49–50; and American independence, 51–2, 53; American War of Independence, 53–4, 58, 287; and exploration of Pacific, 73
George V, King, 229–30, 264; Indian tour, 210; First World War, 231–2; and Ireland, 236; Christmas broadcasts, 266–72; and British Empire Exhibition, 272–3; Delhi durbar, 273; Silver Jubilee, 274
George VI, King, 286, 296
Germain, Lord George, 46, 54, 56
German East Africa, 171–2, 173–4, 179–80, 229, 260–1; *see also* Tanganyika
Germany: 'new imperialism', 104–5, 146–8; naval rearmament, 116, 214–16, 217–18; interest in China, 140–1; African colonies, 156, 161–2; contest for Central Africa, 170–4; British war-mongering, 214; origins of First World War, 214–18; First

War, 217–18, 224–5, 226–7, 229; expulsion of Jews, 247; Second World War, 279, 281–2; *see also* Prussia
Ghana, 21–2, *109*, 323, 325–7; *see also* Gold Coast
Ghurkas, *109*, 126–8, 250
Gibraltar, 281–2, 287–8, 336; occupation of, 33, 34
Gilbert and Ellice Islands, 148
Gilbert Islands, 284–5
gin trade, 185–6
Girl Guides, 210
Girls' Friendly Society, 210
Gladstone, W. E., 145–6; wins 1868 general election, 98–100; denounces Turkey, 100–1; wins 1880 general election, 101, 154–5; and Egypt, 108–9, 166; indifference to social reform, 109–12; Sudanese campaign, 170–1; and Irish Home Rule, 197–8
Glorious Revolution (1688–9), 31
Glubb Pasha, 323–4
Goddeffroy & Son, 147
Gold Coast, 186–7, 189–90; Asante wars, 95–6, 190; inhospitable conditions, 184–5; Second World War, 285–6; Communist influences, 296–7; Accra riots, 297; self-government, 298; Nkrumah imprisoned, 300; independence, 321–2, 325–7; *see also* Ghana
gold mines, Transvaal, 155–6
Golden Jubilee (1887), *105*
Goldie, George Taubman, 186–7, 188, 189, 190
Gorbachov, Mikhail, 293
Gordon, General Charles, *107*, 168, *173*; hero, 9, 114, 168–9, 170–1, 208–9, 210–11; in Khartoum, 168–71; background, 168–9; death, 170–1, 174–5; in *Eminent Victorians*, 260
Government of India Act (1935), 254–5, 256, 260
Grand Alliance, 33, 34
Grasse, Admiral de, 41, 57–8
Grave, Charles, 262–3
Greece, 290
Greek Civil War, 293–4
Greene, Sir Hugh, 327–8
Grenada, 39–40
Grenadier Guards, 113–14
Grenville, Lord, 49
Grey, Sir Edward, 215–17, 218
Grimond, Jo, 332

Grose, Lieutenant-Governor Francis, 75
Guadeloupe, 38–40, 46–7, 77–8, 82–3
Guiana, 15–16
Gujars, 126
gunboat diplomacy, 88, 312
Gunga Din (film), 269
Guyana, 83

Haifa, *243*, 309
Haig, Field Marshal Lord, 176–7, 224–5, 260
Hakluyt, Richard, 12, 18
Haldane, General Sir Aylmer, 244–5
Haldane, Richard, 215–16
Hankow-Peking railway, 141
Hanotaux, Gabriel, 188–9
Hanover, 37, 38, 39–40
Hardie, James Keir, 205–6
Hardinge, Lord, 226–7
Hare, Alexander, 142–4
Harmsworth, Lord, 108
Harrow School, 210
Hart, Sir Robert, 140–1
Hashemite family, 244–5
Hasim Jeal, regent of Brunei, 144–5
Hassan, Muhammad Abdille ('Mad Mullah'), 177, 210–11, 245
Hastings, Warren, 66, 300
Havana, 36, 39
Havelock, General Sir Henry, *113*, 126–9
Hawaii, 71, 72, 73–4
Hawke, Rear-Admiral Sir Edward, 39
Hawkins, Sir John, 18
Hazara, 131
Heber, Reginald, Bishop of Calcutta, 120–3
Hector, Gordon, *306*
Henderson, Arthur, 205–6
Henrietta Maria, Queen, 14
Henry VII, King, 17
Henty, G. A., 112–13, 117, *332*
Heren, Louis, 305
Hermes, HMS, 138
Hertzog, General, 276–7
Hicks, Colonel William, 168–70
Highlands and Islands Emigration Society, 192–3
Hindus, 66–8, 120–2, 125–6, 250–1, 254–5, 261–2, 302–3, 305
Hindustan Times, The, 302
Hiroshima, 290–1
Hispaniola, 18
Hitler, Adolf, 288; expulsion of Jews, 247; rise to power, 274
Ho Chi-Minh, 293–4
Home, William, 80

Home Guard, 77, 279
Hong Kong, *139*, 140–1, 287–8, 336, *340*; trade with Britain, 86; Opium Wars, 137–8, 341; Second World War, 280–1, 284–5; expiry of lease, 339; Joint Declaration, 632, 635; handover, 635–7
House of Commons, 31–2, 284, 317–18, 339–41
House of Lords, 206, 330–1
Howe, Sir William, 54–7
Hsien-feng, Emperor of China, 139
Hudson's Bay Company, 42–3
Huggins, Sir Godfrey (Lord Malvern), 327–8
Hume, David, 20–1
Hundred Years War, 12
Hungary, 247
Hunter, Lord, 253
Hurd, Douglas, 634
Hussain, King of Jordan, 341
Hussain, sharif of Mecca, 205–6
al-Hussaini, Haj Amin, 247–8
Hyder Ali Khan, Sultan of Mysore, 65–6
Hyderabad, 62–3, 64

Illustrated London News, The, 96
immigration, *see* emigration
Immigration Restriction Act (1901), 193–4
Imperial Airways, 272–3
Imperial Conferences, 202, 216–17
imperial federation, 196–7, 199, 211
Imperial General Staff, 216
Increase, 26
India, 60–9, 118–35, 250–9, 299–307; under British rule, 69; conflicts with French in, 60–2; Bengal War, 62–3; acquisition of wealth in, 63–4; administrators, 64; Napoleon's threat to, 79–81; trade with Britain, 86; Russian threat to, 116–17; Mutiny, 96, 125, 238–9; Cawnpore massacre, 96; Victoria declared Empress of, 101; importance to empire, 104, 108–9; self-government, 113; North-West Frontier, 114, 131; Britain's economic dependence on, 118–19; government by autocratic paternalism, 118–23; importance of British soldiers to, 123–5, 128–9; investment in, 124–6; tax collection, 124–5; civil service, 129, 129–30; education, 129–30, 250–1; move towards self-government, 130; nationalism, 130, 205, 210, 231–2; emigration,

183–5, 193–4; German threat to, 217; First World War, 223, 224–5, 229–30, 231–2, 251; Muslim jihad, 226; moves towards independence, 233, 251–6; sectarian disorders, 250–1; Amritsar massacre, 252–3; partition of, 255–6; Second World War, 255–7, 283, 285, 290–1; 'Quit India' campaign, 256–7; radio, 272; Prince of Wales tours, 273; independence, 274, 288, 291, 300–2; Churchill opposes self-government, 279; post-war expectations, 286; and the Commonwealth, 296; Muslim-Hindu fighting, 255, 257, *302*, *304*; creation of Pakistan, 303–5
India Acts, 66–9
Indian army, 69, 224, 284–6, 296, 302, 303, 308
Indian National Army (INA), 284–6, 302
Indian National Congress, 129–30, 250–6, 257, 300, 302
Indian Ocean, 83, 246
Indians, North American, *see* Native Americans
Indo-China, 140–1, 290, 293–4, 296
Indomitable, HMS, 215
Indonesia, 22–3, 296
Industrial Revolution, 41, 85–7, 105–8
industry, manufacturing, 85–6, 112
Inflexible, HMS, 215
Inland Revenue, 310–11
Inquisition, 18
International Monetary Fund, 318–19
Inuit, 16
investment, 86
Ionian Islands, 83
Iran, 309, 310–12; *see also* Persia
Iraq, 205–6; Kurds, 243; under British mandate, 244–5, 260–1; Anglo-Iraqi Treaty, 245–6, 249; oil, 245; Second World War, 248–9; British bases in, 309; Gulf War, 338–9, 341; *see also* Mesopotamia
Ireland, 233–7; British settlement of, 16–17; French campaigns in, 32; emigration, 48, 193; Home Rule, 109–12, 130, 197–9, 206–7, 225, 233–5; Easter Rising, 174–5, 225, 233–4; Curragh Incident, 206–7; republic declared, 233, 234, 237; 'Troubles', 234–7, 299–300, 337–8; creation of Free

State, 236–7; civil war, 237; leaves Commonwealth, 296
Irish Republican Army (IRA), 233, 234, 235–7, 309–10, 337–8
Iroquois Confederation, 42, 43–4, 49
Islam, *see* Muslims
Ismail, Khedive, 165
Ismailia, 314
Israel, 309–10, 312, 317–18
Italy: 'new imperialism', 104–5; interest in Ethiopia, 171–2, 173–4; occupation of Libya, 246; Second World War, 240–1; Abyssinian crisis, 248–9
Ivory Coast, 189–90

Jacobins, 76–7, 79–80
Jacobites, 20, 36
Jamaica, 19, 20, 21, 28–9, 96–7, 233, 321–2
James, C. L. R., 263
James I, King, 11, 12–13, 14, 16–17, 24–5
James II, King, 31, 32
Jameson, Dr Leander Starr, *158*
Jameson Raid, 161–2, 174
Japan: 'new imperialism', 104–5; opens to Western trade, 137–8; Sino-Japanese War, 140–1, 248–9, 280–1; Anglo-Japanese alliance (1902), 141–4, 214–15, 216–17; Russo-Japanese War, 142–4; Australia mistrusts, 216; Second World War, 256–7, 280–1, 283, 284–5, 290–1
Jauréguiberry, Admiral Jean de, 186
Java, 22–3, 83
Jenkins, Captain, 35–6
Jerusalem, 227–8, *309*
Jervis, Admiral Sir John, 78–9
Jewish Agency, 247
Jews: Zionism, 246–7; migration to Palestine, 247, 248–9; revolt in Palestine, 309–10; creation of Israel, 309–10
Jhansi, Rani of, 285
jingoism, 95, 100, 205, 211, 260, 341
Jinnah, Dr Muhammad, 255–6, *301*, 303–5
Joffre, Joseph Jacques, 177
Johnson, Samuel, 52, 54, 339
Johnston, Sir Harry, 160–1
Jonson, Ben, 11–12, 15
Jordan, 309, 317
Josiah Wedgwood, 310
journalism, 96
Jung-lu, General, 141–2
Jutland, battle of (1916), 226–7

Kaffirs, 95–6

Karachi, 172

Keating, Paul, 283

Kendall, Thomas, 188

Kenya, 116, 247, 248–9, 279, *306*, *325*, *326*; under British control, 173–4, 182–3; development of, 183–5; settlers plan *coup d'état*, 184–5; female circumcision, 262; Mau Mau 'emergency', 299–300, 327–9; independence, 300, 321–2, 327, *331*

Kenyatta, Jomo, 300, 330–1

Kerr, Philip, 211

Keynes, John Maynard, 288

Khalsa, 123–4

Khartoum, 104–5, 166–71, 174–6

Khoikhois (Hottentots), 149, 151–2

Khomeini, Ayatollah, 312

Khyber Pass, 123, 258

Kiachow, 140–1

Kidd, Captain, 32–3

Kikuyu tribe, 279, 327–8

Kimberley, Lord, 145–6

King, William Mackenzie, 276–7

King's African Rifles, 286

Kipling, Rudyard, 131, 170, 181–2, 253, 272–3

Kitchener, Lord, 163, 164, 174–6, 177, 225–6

Knatchbull-Hugessen, Sir Hugh, 264–5

Kofi, Asantehene of the Asante, 185–6

Korea, 141

Korean War, 296, 311

Kowloon peninsula, 140–1

Kruger, Paul, 156, 161–3

Krupps, 216

Kuala Kangsor, 145–6

Kurdistan, 243

Kurds, 233, 243, 279

Kut-al-Amhara, 226

Labouchere, Henry, 158–60

Labour party: attitude to empire, 204–6; class politics, 206–7; and Indian independence, 253–4, 291; opposition to racism, 264–5; 1945 general election, 284; colonial policies, 288, 294, 296; Cold War, 296; and the Commonwealth, 296; and the Middle East, 308; and the Suez war, 318; decolonisation policies, 321; 1964 general election, 324

Lads Drill Association, 208–9

Lagos Daily Record, 263

Lahore, 255, 257

Lake, General Sir Gerard, 64–5

Lakes Company, 179–80

Lampson, Sir Miles (Lord Killearn), 240–1

Lancashire, 8, 58, 60, 86

Lapugny, *231*

Laurier, Sir William, 216

Law, Andrew Bonar, 234–5

Lawrence, T. E., 156, 249; as a hero, xv; Arab Revolt, 226–7; on Ireland, 236; suggests 'brown dominions', 244–5; Arab view of, 309–10

League of Empire Loyalists, 321–2

League of Nations, 244, 260–1

League of St George, 210

Leakey, Louis, 272

Lebanon, 244

Leeds Mercury, The, 182

Leicester, Earl of, 12

Lend Lease, 280, 291

Lennox-Boyd, Alan, 328–9

Leopold II, King of the Belgians, 171, 172, 173

Levant Company, 22–3

Lévis, chevalier de, 47

Lhasa, *201*

Liaotung Peninsula, 140–1

Liberal party: foreign policy, 98–100, 101; belief in free trade, 105–8; and tariff reform, 204–5; and Home Rule, 206

Liberia, 285–6

Libya, 240, 246, 293–4, 309

Light, Sir James, 188

Lin Tse-hsü, 136–7

Linlithgow, Lord, 256

Liotard, Victor, 173–4

Lippman, Walter, 288

Liverpool, 8, 24, 263–4, 309

Livingstone, David, 8–9, 85, 86, 95, 158–60

Lloyd George, David, 203, 217, 235, 242, 260; First World War, 225; Middle East policy, 227–8, 244; and Egypt, 240; encourages royal tours, 273–4

Lobengula, 156–8

Loch, Lord, 196–7

Locke, John, 21

London, 8, 31–2, 86–7, 341

Loraine, Commander Sir Lambton, 87–8

Loudoun, John Campbell, Earl of, 45

Louis XIV, King of France, 33

Louis XV, King of France, 37, 39

Louis Phillippe, 339

Low, David, 184–5, 260

Low Countries, 78–9

Loyalism, in North America, 56–7

Lucknow, 126, *128*

Luftwaffe, 279

Lugard, Lord, 177–82, 186–7, 188, 189–91, 223–4

Lyautey, Louis Hubert, 177

MacArthur, General Douglas, 293–4, 311

Macartney, Lord, 136–7

Macaulay, Thomas, 119–20

McCosh, Captain, *134*–5

Macdonald, Major J. R. L., 174–5

MacDonald, Malcolm, 261–2

MacDonald, Ramsay, 205–6, 260

Mackinnon, Sir William, 171–2

Macleod, Iain, 9, 330

Macmillan, Harold, 9; Cold War, 293–4; Suez war, 318; decolonisation policy, 321, 322; and Central Africa, 330; in South Africa, 330; African policy, 332

Macready, General Sir Nevill, 236

Madagascar, 21–2

Madoc, 17

Madras, 60

Mafeking, relief of (1900), 114–15

magazines, 112–13

Mahdi, 168–71, 175–6

Mahdist movements, 190–1

Mahmud, *176*

Mahratha Confederacy, 62–3, 64–5, 122–3

Mahratha War (1817–19), 64–5

Major, John, 337

Makins, Mrs Robert, 315–16

Malacca, 22–3, 144–5

Malan, Dr, 276–7

Malaya, *145*, 287–8, 297; spice trade, 22–3; informal empire in, 142–6; Second World War, 256–7, 283–4, 290; class snobbery, 284; Communist guerrillas, 294–5; 96–78 'emergency', 299–300, 320–1; independence, 321–2

Malaysia, 321–2

Malcolm, John, 68–9

Malta, 77–8, 83, 96–7, 287–8, 309

Malthus, Robert, 192

Manchuria, 141, 142

Manchus, 136–7

Mandela, Nelson, 341

Manila, 39–40, 284–5

manufacturing industry, 85–6, 112

Maoris, 91–3, 95–6, 193–5, 264, 273

Marchand, Captain Jean-Baptiste, 173–6, 189

Marianna Islands, 148

Marlborough, John Churchill, Duke of, 33, 34

Marshall, General George C., 279

Marshall Aid, 294–5

Marston, John, 11–12, 15

Martin, Captain Sir Henry Byam, 70

Martinique, 39–40, 41, 77–8

Marvel, 210

Mary, Queen, consort of George V, 264, 273

Mary II, Queen, 31

Maryland, 13, 14–15, 21–2, 24, 26

Mashonaland, 156–8

Massachusetts, 52, 53–4

Massachusetts Bay Company, 13, 16–17, 26–8

Matabele Wars, 156–60

Mau Mau, 296, 299–300, *327*

Maude, Angus, 319

Mauritius, 83

Mause, Captain William, 82–3

Maxwell, C. V., 148

Maxwell, General Sir John, 174–5, 234

Mazzini, Giuseppe, 233–4

Meath, Reginald Brabazon, Earl of, 208–9, 210

Mediterranean: Royal Navy forced to withdraw from, 32; War of the Spanish Succession, 33–4; Napoleonic Wars, 78–80; strategic importance, 80–1; naval bases, 83; naval weakness in, 116–17; Second World War, 281–2

Meerut, 125–6

Meinertzhagen, Colonel Richard, 180, 183

memsahibs, *134*–5

Menelik II, Emperor of Ethiopia, 174

Menon, Krishna, 253–4

Menzies, Robert, 276–7

mercantilism, 24–5, 58

Mesopotamia, 215, 225–8; *see also* Iraq

Metal Box Company, 286

MI6, 312, 315

Michael, Lewis, 162

Middle East: nationalism, 226–7, 242–9; First World War, 223–4, 229; British policy, 227–8; British mandate, 244; oil, 245, 295–6, 309; Second World War, 281–2; post-war defences, 295–6; post-war policies, 308–9, 315; *see also* individual countries

Mill, James, 119–20

Mill, John Stuart, 124–5

Milner, Viscount: on Rhodes, 155–6; Boer War, 162–3; imperialism, 202–3; and tariff reform, 203–5; and Chinese indentured labourers, 204–5; kindergarten, 211

Milton, John, 15–16

Minorca, 33, 34, 38, 41, 77–8

Mir Jafir, 62–4

Mirza Ali Khan, Faqir of Ipi, 257

Misr al-Fatah (Young Egypt), 240

missionaries, 94–6, 265; West Indies, 20–1; Pacific Islands, 73–4; in Africa, 179–80, 181–3

Mississippi River, 37

Mitchell, Lieutenant-Colonel 'Mad' Mike, 317

Mitchell, Sir Philip, 326

Miwok Indians, 16

Moctezuma, Emperor, 16

Mohammed Reza Pahlevi, Shah of Iran, 312

Mollinson, Mrs J. A., 266

Molucca Islands, 22–3

Monckton, Sir Walter, 329

Monckton Commission, 329, 332

Monroe Doctrine, 216

Montagu, Edwin, 251–3

Montauban, General de, 139

Montcalm, Louis-Joseph, marquis de, 46–7

Montgomery, Field-Marshal, 308–9

Montgomery, General Richard, 54–5

Montreal, 46–7

Montserrat, 19, 336

Moran, Lord, 263–4, 279

Morant Bay insurrection (1865), 96–7

Morgan, Edward, 29

Morning Post, The, 253

Morocco, 215

Morrison, Herbert, 288, 311–12

Mosul, 249

Mountbatten, Lady, 302–3

Mountbatten, Lord Louis, 9; in charge of SEAC, 288–91; in India, 301; and Burmese independence, 302–3; and Indian independence, 301–5

Mozambique, 320–1, 333–5, 338

Mpatose, Rev. Edward, 321

Mugabe, Robert, 332–3, 335

Muhammad Ali, Khedive of Egypt, 165

Muhammad Ali Khan, 61–2

Mulraj, 124

Mun, Thomas, 29

Munich agreement (1938), 248–9

Musketeer, Operation, 316

Muslim Brotherhood, 240

Muslim League, 255–6, 257, 302

Muslims: in India, 124–6, 250–1; in West Africa, 190–1; jihad against Britain, France and Russia, 226–7; clashes with Hindus, 254–6, 302–3, 305; creation of Pakistan, 255–6, 303–5; and Indian independence, 302

Mussadiq, Dr Mohammed, 309–12, 313

Mussolini, Benito: occupation of Libya, 240, 246; appeasement of, 256

Muzorewa, Bishop Abel, 333–5

Mysore, 63, 64

Nagasaki, 290–1

Nagpur, 64

Naguib, General Mohammed, 314

al-Nahas, Mustafa, 240–1, 313, 314

Namibia, see South West Africa

Nana Sahib, 125–6, 128–9

Naking, Treaty of (1842), 137–8

Napier, General Sir Charles James, 121, 123–4

Napier, Lord, 300

Napoleon I, Emperor, 64, 76, 79–81, 82–3

Napoleon III, Emperor, 139

Napoleonic Wars, 76–83, 100–1

Nasser, Gamel Abdul: Egyptian nationalism, 238, 241, 309; July Revolution, 314; opposes Baghdad Pact, 315; Suez war, 315–18

Natal, 151–2, 153–5, 162–4, 195–6

national debt, 65–6, 77

National Review, The, 96

National Service League, 208–9, 214

nationalism: Indian, 130, 205, 210, 231–2; Irish, 130; Egyptian, 165–8, 205–6, 238–41; Middle East, 226–7, 242–9

Native Americans, 16–17, 25, 42–3, 48

Nautical Almanac, The, 70

Naval Defence Act (1889), 116

Naziism, 247, 276–7, 286, 288

Ndebele tribe, 156–60

Negri Sembilan, 145–6

negroes, see blacks

Nehru, Jawaharlal, 250–1, 253–4, 302–3

Nelson, Lord, 9, 19, 79, 80–1, 208–9

Nepal, 65–6

Netherlands: spice trade, 22–3; Napoleonic Wars, 78–9; Second World War, 279

Neufeld, Karl, 170

Nevis, 19

New Britain, 95

New England, 14, 16–17, 24, 25, 26–7, 28

New France, 42, 43–4, 45–7

New Guinea, 146–8, 148, 283

New Guinea Colonial Company, 146–8

'new imperialism', 104–17, 141, 146–8

New South Wales, 71–2, 74, 75, 109, 196–7

New York, 38, 43–4, 55–6, 57–8

New Zealand, 70–5, 91–3; trade with Britain, 86; Maori wars, 95–6, 194–5; independence movement, 96–8; emigration to, 192, 193–4, 195; and the Boer War, 198–9; emotional kinship with Britain, 199; defences, 216–17; First World War, 218, 223, 224–5, 228, 229–30; race relations, 264; Second World War, 276–7, 286, 291

New Zealand Company, 193–4

Newcastle, Duke of, 38, 46

Newfoundland, 12, 13–14, 17, 34, 39–40, 195–6, 229–30

News of the World, 96

newspapers, 95–6, 108, 114, 296–7

newsreels, 114

Nicaragua, 19

Nicholas II, Czar, 217–18

Nigeria, 116, 181–2, 189–90, 191, 329; Royal African Company trading station, 21–2; Royal Niger Company, 113, 186–7; inhospitable conditions, 184–5; palm oil trade, 185–6; indirect rule of, 190–1; First World War, 226–7, 230; 'backwardness', 262; independence, 321–2, 325–7, 330; civil war, 323

Nile, HMS, 117

Nile, River, 108–9, 170–1, 173–4

Nine Years War, 31

Ningpo, 137–8

Nkomo, Joshua, 332–3, 335

Nkrumah, Kwame, 294, 300, 321, 323

Nkumbula, Harry, 327–8

'noble savage', 72–4, 95, 96–7

Nonconformism, 50, 205

Norfolk Island, 75

North, Lord, 51, 52, 53, 55–6, 58

North Africa, 282

North America: establishment of colonies in, 11–17; transatlantic trade, 24–5; immigration, 26–9, 47–8, 49; wars with French in, 36, 37; conflicts between Britain and France in, 42–7; expansion of settlements, 42–3; independence movement, 49–52; and the Stamp Act, 49–50; War of Independence, 31–6, 40–1, 287; see also Canada; United States of America

North Atlantic Treaty Organisation (NATO), 295–6

North Borneo, 321–2; see also Borneo

North Borneo Company, 156–8

North Sea, 214–16

North-West Frontier, 95–6, 112, 114, 129, 131, 177, 250, 257, 258–9

North-West Passage, 72

Northern Rhodesia, 160–1, 248–9, 286, 321–2, 327–8, 330, 332; see also Zambia

Norway, 279

Nott, John, 338

Nova Scotia, 17, 34, 35–6

Nuba Mountains, 177

nuclear weapons, 290–1, 293, 294–5, 308–9, 311, 314

Nyasa, Lake, 158–60, 179–80

Nyasaland, 116, 265; First World War, 223–4, 230; Second World War, 286; Central African Federation, 327–9, 332; state of emergency, 327–9; Hastings Banda imprisoned, 300, 329–30; independence, 321–2; see also Malawi

Observer, The, 318

Ochterlony, Major-General Sir David, 123

O'Dwyer, Sir Michael, 130–1

Official Secrets Act (1912), 214

Ohio Company, 43–4

Ohio valley, 37, 44–5

oil: Middle East, 245, 295–6, 309; Iran, 310–11

Omdurman, battle of (1898), 174–7

opium, 60, 136, 136–7, 138–9, 140–1

Opium Wars, 136–9

Orange Free State, 108–9, 114–15, 116, 149–50, 162–3, 164, 194–6

Orangemen, 235

Orme, Robert, 61

Ormsby-Gore, William, 260–1

Osborne, John, 323

Ottoman empire, 80–1, 225–7, 228, 238

Oude, 125–9

Outram, General Sir James, 128–9

Oxenham, John, 18

Pacific Ocean, 70–4, 104–5, 146–8

Pahang, 145–6

Paisley, 47–8

Pakistan, 255–6, 296, 300–2, 303–5

Palestine: British claim to, 227–8; under British mandate, 244–5, 260–1; Arab Revolt, 246, *247*, *248*; Zionism, 246–7; Jewish immigration, 247, 248–9; Jewish revolt, 309–10

Palestinians, 309–10

palm oil, 185–6

Palmerston, Lord, 89, 98–100, 136–7

Pan American airlines, 281–2

Papua, 146–8

Paramatta, 194–5

Paris, Treaty of (1763), 39–40

Parliamentary Reform Act (1832), 90–1

Pathans, 129, 131, 250, 257, 264, 279

patriotism, 54; Napoleonic Wars, 83; Disraeli and, 98–100; jingoism, 100–1, 205, 211, 260–1, 341; boys' stories, 112–13; in advertising, 114–15; Boer War, 114–15, 199; 'Cockney patriotism', 117; Primrose League, 208–9; Empire Day, 208–10; First World War, 211, 214, 218, 230; Falklands war, 339–41

Patten, Chris, *340*

Patteson, Bishop, 112

Pearl Harbor, 280–1

Peel, Viscount, 244–5

Peel Commission, 247–8

Peking, 139, *142*

Penang, 284

Pennsylvania, 83, 85, 87, 90, 56

Pequot wars (c.1636–7), *17*

Perak, 144–6

Perry, Admiral, 137–8

Persia, 80–1, 95–6, 215, 242–3, 245, 287, 293–4; *see also* Iran

Persian Gulf, 309

Peshawar, 254–5

Peterborough, Lord, 34

Peters, Carl, 171–2

Philadelphia, 56

philanthropists, 96

Philip, Prince, *324*, *329*

Philippines, 104–5, 282, 283–4

Phillip, Captain Arthur, 74–5

Picture Post, 261

Pine, Edward, 85, 193–4

Pinney, John, 20–1

pirates, 137–9, *144*

Pitcairn, Major John, 53–4

Pitcairn Island, 336

Pitt, William, Earl of Chatham, 9, 35–6, *41*, 50, 77–8, 284; and defence of Hanover, 37; Seven Years War, 38–9; resignation, 39–40; conquest of Canada, 45–6; American War of Independence, 51–2

Pitt, William the Younger, 78–9, 81–2, 284

Plaatje, Solomon, 230–2

Plassey, battle of (1757), 62–4

plays, 11–12, 323, *323*

Pluck, 112

Pocock, Admiral Sir George, 39–40

Poland, 247, 275

Pollock, General Sir George, 123–4

Polynesia, 73–4

Pondicherry, 63–4

Poor Law, 85–6, 192

Pope-Hennessey, Lieutenant Ladislaus, 190

Popham, Admiral Sir Home, 81–2

Port Arthur, 141–4

Port Chalmers, *199*

Port Said, 239–40, 309, 314, *316*, 317–18

Porto Bello, 36

Portugal, 17, 22–3, 81–2, 320–1

postage stamps, 273–4

Potsdam conference (1945), 290

Potter, Dennis, 323

Pownall, General Sir Henry, 290

press gangs, 38

Pretoria, *157*

Primrose League, 208–9

Prince Edward Island, 49

Prince of Wales, 282

privateers, 32–3

Profumo, John, 324

Prompt, Victor, 170–1

propaganda: Second World War, 286; after Second World War, 288; Communist, 296

protectionism, 104–8

Prussia, 37, 78–9, 80–1, 82–3, 89; *see also* Germany

public opinion: 19th-century, 90–3, 96–7; First World War, 215–16; changes after First World War, 260–1; after Second World War, 288; *see also* patriotism

public schools, 109–12, 210, 250–1, 284, 323, 324

Pudukota, Rajah of, 264

Punch, 234, 262

Punjab, 62–3, 95–6, 122–4, 125–6, 126, 252–3, 303–5

Purchas, Simon, 15–16

Puritans, 14, 24–5, 26–7

QANTAS, 267

Quakers, 44, 45

Quebec, 34, 36, 38–9, 42–3, 45–8, 54–5, 225, 276–7

Quebec Act (1774), 48, 51–2, 52, 58

Queensland, 196

'Quit India' campaign, 256–7

race riots, 263–4, 288

racism: Indian Mutiny and, 96; during First World War, 223–4, 231–2; against Irish, 234–5; towards Arabs, 245–6; anti-semitism, 246, *246*, 247; in India, 250–1; stereotypes, 262–3; colour bar, 263–5; sexual envy, 264–5; in Second World War, 285–6; in America, 288; African, 337

Radcliffe, Sir Cyril, 303–5

Radicalism, 205

radio, 266, 272, 297

Radio Cairo, 315, 316

Radio Tunis, 286

Raffles, Sir Stamford, 142–4

railways: Chinese Eastern Railway, 140–1; Trans-Siberian Railway, 140–1; Hankow-Peking Railway, 141; Cape Colony, 152–3; East Africa, *183*; plans for Cape to Cairo line, 185–6; West Africa, 185–6; Berlin-Constantinople-Baghdad railway, 217

Raleigh, Sir Walter, 11–12, 15–16, 89

Rangoon, 290–1

Reagan, Ronald, 338

Red Sea, 185–6, 226–7

Reform and Redistribution Acts, 90–1

Reformatory and Industrial Schools Act (1891), 192

Reith, Sir John, 272

Réunion, 83

Reza Pahlevi, Shah of Iran, 245

Rhode Island, 14, 50–1

Rhodes, Cecil, 9, 160–1, 335; background, 155–6; ambitions, 155–6; annexation of Bechuanaland, 156; incursion into Zambesia, 156–8; Jameson Raid, 161–2; and South African federation, 161–2; plans Cape to Cairo railway, 185–6

Rhodes Trust, 211

Rhodesia, 114, 116, 156–60, 160–1, 184–5, 333, 335; *see also* Southern Rhodesia

Rhodesia Front, 332, 333–5

Ripon, Lord, 129–30

Roanoke Island, 12

Roberts, Field Marshal Lord, 114–15, *116*, 122–3, *163*, 208–9

Robertson, General James, 56–7

Robertson, Sir James, 330

Rockingham, Marquess of, 49, 51–2, 58

Rodeo, Operation, 314

Rodney, Admiral Sir George, 9, 39, 41

Roma, Spiridone, *34*

Romantic Movement, 91–3

Roosevelt, Franklin D., 274, 284; Second World War, 280–1, 282; Atlantic Charter, 287–8; and Indo-China, 290

Roosevelt, Kermit, 312

Rorke's Drift, battle of (1879), 153–4

Rosario, HMS, 148

Rose, John, 158–60

Rosebery, Lord, 161–2, 173–4

Round Table, 211

Rowlatt Acts, 251–3

Rowntree, Seebohm, 210

Rowse, A. L., 284

Royal African Company, 21–2

Royal Air Force (RAF): 'air control' in Iraq and Jordan, 245; Arab Revolt, 247–8; Second World War, 281–2, 282; nuclear programme, 308–9

Royal Indian Air Force (RIAF), 302

Royal Indian Navy (RIN), 302

Royal Irish Constabulary (RIC), 234, 235–6

Royal Navy: withdraws from Mediterranean, 32; blockades French navy, 36; living conditions, 38; press gangs, 38; Seven Years War, 38–9; Napoleonic Wars, 78–9, 81–3; overseas bases, 83; two-power standard, 116–17; campaign against 'blackbirding', 147; modernisation (1904), 214–15, 217–18; battle of Jutland, 226–7; importance of Suez Canal, 239–40

Royal Niger Company, 113, 156–8, *180*, *181*, 186–7, 188, 189–90

Rumania, 247

Russia: Napoleonic Wars, 76–83; threat to India, 116–17; Crimean War, 89; empire-building, 97–8; naval rearmament, 116–17; interest in China, 140–2; war with Japan, *143*; Anglo-Russian Convention, 215; expansionism,

215; origins of First World War, 217–18; and Turkey, 225–6; Revolution, 233; *see also* Soviet Union

el-Sadat, Anwar, 238
Saigon, 293–4
St Eustatius, 41
St Helena, 41–2, 82–3, 336
St Kitts, 19
St Lawrence River, 36, 46
St Lucia, 18–19, 39–40, 41, 77–8, 83
St Pierre and Miquelon islands, 197–8
St Vincent, 39–40
Les Saintes, 77–8
Les Saintes, Battle of (1782), 41
Salisbury, 3rd Marquess of, 141, 171–2, 174–5, 188
Salisbury, 5th Marquess of, 325
Salmon, Air-Marshal Sir John, 245
Salvation Army, 192
Samoa, 148
Sanders of the River (film), 268
Sandwich, Lord, 53–4
Santiago de Cuba, 36
Sarawak, 144–5, 321–2
Saturday Review, The, 158
satyagraha, 252
Saudi Arabia, 309, 310–11
Saunders, Admiral Sir Charles, 46
Savory, Lieutenant-General Sir Reginald, 305
Saxony, 37
Schnitzer, Eduard, 171–2
Scotland, 36, 192–3
Scottish Martyrs, 75
Scottish Presbyterian African Lakes Company, 158–60
scurvy, 38
Second World War, 275–82, 283–6, 287–92; Egypt in, 240–1; India in, 255–7, 284–7; 'phoney war', 279; American involvement, 279–80, 281–2, 283; Churchill's importance, 279–80; in far East, 281–2, 283; Australia in, 283, 283, 286, 291; fall of Singapore, 280–1, 283–4; class factors, 284–5; black soldiers, 285–6; racism, 285–6; propaganda, 286; atomic bombs, 290–1; casualties, 291
Seeley, Sir John, 109
Sekhukhuni, 152–3, 154–5
Selangor, 144–6, 295
Selbourne, Lord, 162
Selous, Sir Frederick, 158–60
Senegal, 21–2, 38–41

Seng-ko-lin-chin, Prince, 139
Serbia, 217–18
Seringapatam, 78
Seven Years War, 31, 39, 58–9
Sèvres, Treaty of (1956), 317–18
sexuality: in India, 122–3; and racism, 264
Seychelles, 322
Seymour, Admiral Sir Beauchamp, 166
Sezincote, Gloucestershire, 8, 89
Shanghai, 137–8, 140–1
Shantung, 140–1
Shaw, Bernard, 205
Shepherd, Sir Francis, 311–12
Shepstone, Sir Theophilus, 153–4
Shovell, Admiral Sir Clowdisley, 34
Shuckburgh, Evelyn, 311
Siam (Thailand), 290–1
Sierra Leone, 93, 185, 186–7, 189–90, 321–2, 323, 325–7
Sikhs, 123, 126–8, 250, 280–1, 303–5
Silver Jubilee (1935), *274*
Simple, Peter, 321–2
Sind, 95–6, 123–4, 125–6
Singapore, 144–5; Raffles establishes, 142–4; trade with Britain, 86; Second World War, 280–1, 284–5, 290–1
Sinn Fein, 233–5, 236–7, 337–8
Sino-Japanese War (1894–5), 140–1
Sino-Japanese War (1937), 248–9, 280–1
Siraj-ud-Daula, nawab of Bengal, 62–3
Sithole, Ndabaningi, 333–5
slavery: West Indies, *21, 22, 23,* 28–9; American War of Independence, 56–7; abolition of, 72–3, *91, 92*; 'blackbirding', 147
Smith, Adam, 60
Smith, General Sir Harry, 124, 149–50
Smith, Ian, 332, 332–5
Smuts, Jan, 276–7, 284–5
Soames, Lord, 335
social Darwinism, 109, 202–3, 261–2
socialism, 311
Society for the Propagation of the Christian Gospel, 21
Solomon Islands, 148, 287, 298
Somalia, 321–2
Somaliland, 210–11, 321–2
'Sons of Liberty', 52
Soref, Harold, 333
South Africa, 149–64; Boer War, 113, 114–15, 116–17, 162–4,

184, 197–9, 202, 205; Boers, 149–51, 154–6, 161–2; strategic importance, 149; Xhosa wars, 150–2; diamonds, 151–3; proposed federation, 152–5, 160–2; Zulu War, 153–5; Jameson Raid, 161–2; self-government, 194–6; apartheid, 195–6, 296; Chinese indentured labourers, 204–5; race relations, 205–6; First World War, 218, 223, 225, 228, 229–32; sexual laws, 264; Second World War, 276–7, 291; Macmillan visits, 330–1
South America, 86
South-East Asia Commmand (SEAC), 288–90
South West Africa, 108–9, 156, 217, 228
Southern Rhodesia, 327, 328–9; *see also* Rhodesia; Zimbabwe
Southey, Robert, 192
Soviet Union: and Middle East, 243; Second World War, 281–2, 290–1; as superpower, 291; Cold War, 293, 294, 296, 308–9; anti-colonial propaganda, 296; influence in Egypt, 315; Afghan war, 333–5; *see also* Russia
Spain: competition with England in the Americas, 12; Treaty of Tordesillas, 17, 73–4; fights British in Caribbean, 18–19; War of the Spanish Succession, 33–4; War of Jenkins' Ear, 35–6; Seven Years War, 39–40; and American War of Independence, 41; Napoleonic Wars, 81–2
Spanish Civil War, 256
Spanish Main, 18
Spectator, The, 171, 253, 274
Sphere, The, 262
spice trade, 22–3
sports, *212–13*, 274
Stalin, Joseph, 291, 293–4
Stamfordham, Lord, 273
Stamp Act (1765), 49–50
stamps, *274*
Stanley, Sir Henry, 87, 171–2
State Department (US), 314
sterling crises, 318–19
Stewart, James, 188
Stilwell, General 'Vinegar' Joe, 290
Strachey, Lytton, 260
Straits Settlements, 144–6
Stuart, Major-General James, 65–6
Sudan, 109, 116, 196–7; Mahdism, 168–71; Gordon in, 114, 168–71; British occupation of, 174–6, 177;

independence, 314, 325–7; military coup, 323
Suez Canal, 149, *166–7*, 248–9; Disraeli takes controlling interest in, 98–100, 165; strategic importance, 108–9, 116–17, *166–8*, 239–40; security of, 242; Suez war, 296, 315–19, 320; importance in Cold War, 308–9; British occupation of Canal Zone ended, 312–14
Suez Canal Company, 315–16
sugar, 18–20, 86
Sultan, HMS, 88
Sumatra, 290–1, 302
Sun, The, 338
Sun Yat-Sen, 236
Surinam, 20, 83
Swinhoe, Robert, 139
Sydney, 74–5, 85
Sydney *Bulletin*, 196
Sykes, Sir Mark, 225
Sykes-Picot agreement (1916), 225–6, 243, 245–6
Syria, 244, 315

Tahiti, 71–2, 73
Tanganyika, 171–2, 173–4, 260–1, 294, 321–2, 330; *see also* German East Africa
tariff reform, 203–5, 206–7
Tawfiq, Khedive, 165
Tea Act (1773), 50–1
tea trade, 23, 136
Tedder, Air-Marshal Lord, 308–9
telegraph, 96, 114
television, 299–300, 321, 323
textiles: Indian, 21–3; cotton, 58, 60, 86, 140–1; wool, 75
Thailand *see* Siam
Thakombau, King of Fiji, 145–6
Thant, U, 321–2
'That Was the Week That Was', 324
Thatcher, Margaret, 333–5, 337–9, 339–41
theatre, 11–12, 323
Theodore, Emperor of Abyssinia, 95–6, 98–100
Thugs, 120–2
Thunderer, HMS, *215*
Tiananmen Square massacre, 340
Tibet, *201*, 279
Tientsin, Treaty of (1858), 138–9
Time, 310
Times, The, 97, 189, 204, 264, 284, 305, 636
Tipu Sultan, 63, 78
Tissot, James, 170
tobacco, Virginia, 13

Tobago, 39–40, 41, 77–8, 83
Togoland, 228–9
Tojo, General Hideki, 280
Tordesillas, Treaty of (1494), 17, 73–4
Tories, and American independence, 50–2; *see also* Conservative party
Toulon, 32, 34, 80
Touré, Samory, 189–90
trade: East India Company, 21–3, 60; slaves, 21–2; textiles, 21–3, 24; spices, 22–3; tea, 23, 136; transatlantic, 24; fur, 42–4; cotton, 58, 60; mercantilism, 58; free trade, 58–9, 86, 104–8, 202–3; wool, 75; protectionism, 104–8; with India, 118–19; opium, 136, 138–9; with China, 140–1; West Africa, 185–6; tariff reform, 203–5, 206–7
trade unions, 233
Trafalgar, battle of (1805), 80, 82–3
Trans-Siberian Railway, 140–1, 141
Transvaal, 101, 108–9, 116; Boer occupation, 149–50; proposed South African federation, 152–3, 154–5; railways, 152–3, 155–6; war of independence, 154–6; Jameson Raid, 162; Boer War, 162–3, 164; self-government, 194–6
Treasury, 272–3; and colonial profits, 294; and Indian independence, 300–2
Trincomalee, 77–8
Trinidad, 77–8, 83, 188, 233
Tristan da Cunha, 336
Trollope, Anthony, 166–8
Truman, Harry, 293–4, 311
Truman Doctrine, 294–5
Trumbull, Jonathan, 50
Turkey, 100–1, 225–6, 245, 314
Turkish Oil Company, 245
Tyndale-Briscoe, Cecil, 251
Tyne, river, 8
Tzu-hsi, Dowager Empress of China, 142

U-boats, 237
Uganda, 109–12, 116, 171–2, 173–4, 180–1, 182–3, 321–2, 323, 325–7, 330
Uitlanders, 162
Ulster, 235, 236–7
Ulster Unionists, 332, 337
Ulster Volunteers, 206–7
Umm Diwaykarat, battle of (1899), 176
Union Jack, 337

Union Jack, 112, 210
Unionists, 109–12
United African National Council, 333–5
United Nations, 311, 321–2; and Cold War, 293–4; creation of Israel, 309–10; and the Suez war, 318
United States of America: 'new imperialism', 104–5; industries, 105–8; emigration to, 193–4, 195; Monroe Doctrine, 216; First World War, 227, 228; and Irish 'Troubles', 236–7; isolationism, 275; poor relations with Britain, 275; Second World War, 280, 281, 283, 290–1; anti-imperialism, 287; British financial dependence, 287, 291; Atlantic Charter, 287–8; British hostility towards, 288; racism, 15; and SEAC, 288–90; Lend Lease, 291; as superpower, 291; Cold War, 293–4, 308–9, 311–12; Truman Doctrine, 294–5; and NATO, 295–6; and the Iranian crisis, 311–12; Korean War, 311; deteriorating relations with Britain, 311–12; and the Suez war, 315, 318, 319; Vietnam War, 321; and the Falklands war, 341
Upper Niger, 186–7, 189, 190
Urabi Pasha, 165–8, 314, 318–19
Uruguay, 280
USAAF, 282, 287, 290–1, 308–9, 314
Utrecht, Treaty of (1714), 34

Vancouver, Captain George, 71–2, 73–4
Vansittart, Lord, 227
Vereeniging, Treaty of (1902), 164
Vernon, Admiral Edward, 36
Versailles, Peace of (1783), 41
Versailles Treaty (1919), 244
Vibart, Cadet, 122
Victoria (Australia), 196
Victoria, Lake, 170–2
Victoria, Queen, 94, 105, 106, 118, 139; Empress of India, 100–1; Diamond Jubilee, 113–14, 198–9; head of state of self-governing colonies, 195–6
Viet Minh, 293–4
Viet Nam, 97–8
Virginia, 11–13, 14, 21–2, 24–5, 26
Virginia Company, 12–13, 14–17
Vladivostok, 141–2
Voltaire, 38
Voltigeur, 186
Vraignies, 227

Wafd, 238, 239–41
Wakefield, Colonel Edward Gibbon, 193–4
Walsingham, Sir Francis, 12
War of the Austrian Succession, 31, 60–1
War Office, 116–17, 150, 152, 215–16, 285–6, 309
War of the Spanish Succession, 31, 33–4
Ward, Sir Joseph, 216
Warwick, Earl of, 18–19
Washington, George, 44, 55, 56, 58
Waterloo, battle of (1815), 82–3
Wauchope, General Sir Arthur, 247–8
Wavell, General Sir Archibald, 281
Webb, Beatrice, 205
Webb, Sydney, 202–4, 205
Wehrmacht, 279
Welensky, Sir Roy, 329–30, 330
welfare state, 203–4
Welldon, J. E. C., 112
Wellesley, Richard, Marquess, 64, 64–6, 68–9, 79–80
Wellington, Arthur Wellesley, Duke of, 65–6, 81; in India, 64, 66–8; Napoleonic Wars, 82–3
West, Benjamin, 47
West Africa, 97–8, 108–9, 178–91; Lugard and, 177, 180–1, 188–91; inhospitable conditions, 184–5; wars with French in, 185–90; Second World War, 286; Communist propaganda, 296–7; independence movements, 325–7
West Africa Frontier Force, 189
West Indies: settlement of, 18–22; slaves, 20–2, 28–9; defences, 25; War of Jenkins' Ear, 35–6; Seven Years War, 38–40; and American War of Independence, 40–1; Napoleonic Wars, 77–8; sugar, 86; abolition of slavery, 93–4; emigration to, 193–4; First World War, 231–2; desire for self-government, 262–4; Second World War, 285–6; impoverishment, 294; emigration to Britain, 637, 638
Western Front, 176–7, 211, 224–5, 260
whaling, 36
Wheatley, Brigadier-General Philip, 184–5
Whigs, 37, 195–6
White, George, 12
Wilberforce, William, 91–3, 120–2
Wilhelm II, Kaiser, 155–6, 162, 214, 217–18, 229

Willcocks, Colonel James, 189–90, 223–4
William III, King, 31, 32
Williams, Ralph, 263–4
Williams, Roger, 14
Wilson, Colonel Sir Arnold, 243, 244–5
Wilson, Sir David, 635
Wilson, Harold, 324, 332–3, 336
Wilson, Field-Marshal Sir Henry, 237
Wilson, Woodrow, 228, 233, 238–9, 243, 244
Wingate, Sir Reginald, 170–1, 176, 177, 233
Winthrop, John, 14
wireless, 41
Wolfe, James, 9, 47
Wolseley, Sir Garnet, 122–3, 318–19; in India, 128–9; in South Africa, 154–5; in Egypt, 166; Sudanese campaign, 170, 196–7
Wolters, Richard, 40
wool trade, 75
working classes, 206–9
Wright, Sir James, 50

Xhosa tribe, 149, 150–2

Yalta conference (1945), 290
Yangtze River, 137
Yeh Ming-chin, 139, 140
York, Duke of, 65–6
Yorktown, battle of (1781), 57–8
Young Egypt party, 205–6
Young England, 112
Younghusband, Major-General Sir George, 131
Yü-hsien, 142

Zaghlul, Said, 238–9, 240
Zaïre, 320–1; *see also* Congo
Zambesia, 156–8
Zambia, 160–1, 321–2, 330, 332, 333–5; *see also* Northern Rhodesia
Zanzibar, 158–61, 173–4
Zimbabwe, *see* Rhodesia; Southern Rhodesia
Zimbabwe African National Union (ZANU), 332–5
Zimbabwe African People's Union, 335
Zimbabwe People's Revolutionary Army (ZIPRA), 332–5
Zimbabwe United People's Organisation, 333–5
Zionism, 246–7, 279
Zulu wars, 96, 101, 153–5
Zulus, 96, 149–50, 152–3